Spanish Society, 1400–1600

A Social History of Europe

General Editor: Raymond Pearson

Spanish Society 1400–1600 is the second volume to be
published in a major new Longman series. Wide-ranging both
geographically and chronologically, it will explore the history
of the peoples of Europe in an ambitious programme of
analytical surveys, each examining a nation, state or region
in a key phase of its development. The books will be written
by leading experts; and each, while synthesizing the latest
scholarship in the field, will be invigorated by the findings
and preoccupations of the author's original research.

The series is designed for a wide audience: the volumes will be
necessary reading for serious students and fellow scholars, but
they are also written to engage and interest the non-specialist
coming to the subject for the first time.

Inaugurated by the late Harry Hearder, the series is under the
General Editorship of Professor Raymond Pearson, Professor of
European History at the University of Ulster at Coleraine.

Titles available in the series:

A Social History of the Russian Empire 1650–1825
Janet Hartley

French Society 1589–1715
Sharon Kettering

Spanish Society 1400–1600
Teofilo Ruiz

Forthcoming titles in this series:

A Social History of Italy in the Twentieth Century
Jonathan Dunnage

French Society 1700–1810
Gwynne Lewis

French Society 1815–1914
Roger Magraw

Modern Spanish Society 1939–2000
Michael Richards

A Social History of the Russian Empire 1810–1917
David Saunders

A Social History of Europe

Spanish Society, 1400–1600

Teofilo F. Ruiz

University of California at Los Angeles

An imprint of **Pearson Education**

Harlow, England · London · New York · Reading, Massachusetts · San Francisco · Toronto · Don Mills, Ontario · Sydney
Tokyo · Singapore · Hong Kong · Seoul · Taipei · Cape Town · Madrid · Mexico City · Amsterdam · Munich · Paris · Milan

Pearson Education Limited

Edinburgh Gate
Harlow
Essex CM20 2JE

and Associated Companies throughout the world.

Visit us on the World Wide Web at:
www.pearsoneduc.com

———————————

First published 2001

© Pearson Education Limited 2001

ISBN 0582 28692 1

British Library Cataloguing-in-Publication Data
A catalogue record for this book is available from the British Library

Library of Congress Cataloging-in-Publication Data
Ruiz, Teofilo F., 1943–
   Spanish society, 1400–1600 / Teofilo F. Ruiz.
      p.   cm. – (Social history of Europe)
   Includes bibliographical references and index.
   ISBN 0-582-28692-1 (pbk.)
   1. Spain – Social conditions – to 1800.   2. Spain – Social life and
customs.   3. Spain – History – 711–1516.   4. Spain – History – 16th
century.   5. Social classes – Spain.   I. Title.   II. Series.
   HN583 .R85   2001
   306′.0946–dc21   00-046139

10 9 8 7 6 5 4 3 2
06 05 04 03

Typeset in $9\frac{1}{2}$/$12\frac{1}{2}$pt Stone Serif by 35
Produced by Pearson Education Asia Pte Ltd.
Printed in Malaysia, LSP

To
Sir John H. Elliott

¡Qué amigo de sus amigos!
¡Qué señor para criados
y parientes!
¡Qué enemigo de enemigos!
¡Qué maestro de esforçados
y valientes!
¡Qué seso para discretos!
¡Qué gracia para donosos!
¡Qué razón!
¡Qué benigno a los sujetos
y a los bravos y dañosos,
un león!

Jorge Manrique

Contents

General editor's preface

For far too long 'social history' was regularly, even routinely defined dismissively and negatively along the lines of 'history with the high politics, economics and diplomacy left out'. Over the latter decades of the twentieth century, however, a virtual revolution in the sub-discipline of 'social history' gathered momentum, fuelled not only by historians but also by specialists from such established academic disciplines as anthropology, economics, politics and especially sociology, and enriched by contributors from burgeoning cultural, demographic, media and women's studies. At the cusp of the twenty-first century, the prime rationale of the recently launched 'Social History of Europe' series is to reflect the cumulative achievement and reinforce the ripening respectability of what may be positively yet succinctly defined as nothing less than the 'history of society'.

Initiated by the late Professor Harry Hearder of the University of Wales, the 'Social History of Europe' series is conceived as an ambitious and open-ended collection of wide-ranging general surveys charting the history of the peoples of the major European nations, states and regions through key phases in their societal development from the late Middle Ages to the present. The series is not designed to become necessarily either chronologically or geographically all-embracing, although certain pre-eminent areas and periods will demand a systematic sequence of coverage. Typically, a volume covers a period of about one century, but longer (and occasionally shorter) time-spans are proving appropriate. A degree of modest chronological overlap between volumes covering a particular nation, state or region is acceptable where justified by the historical experience.

Each volume in the series is written by a commissioned European or American expert and, while synthesizing the latest scholarship in the field, is invigorated by the findings and preoccupations of the author's original research. As works of authority and originality, all contributory volumes are of genuine interest and value to the individual author's academic peers.

Even so, the contributory volumes are not intended to be scholarly monographs addressed to the committed social historian but broader synoptic overviews which serve a non-specialist general readership. All the volumes are therefore intended to take the 'textbook dimension' with due seriousness, with authors recognizing that the long-term success of the series will depend on its usefulness to, and popularity with, an international undergraduate and postgraduate student readership. In the interests of accessibility, the provision of notes and references to accompany the text is suitably restrained and all volumes contain a select bibliography, a chronology of principal events, a glossary of foreign and technical terms and a comprehensive index.

Inspired by the millennial watershed but building upon the phenomenal specialist progress recorded over the last quarter-century, the eventually multi-volume 'Social History of Europe' is dedicated to the advancement of an intellectually authoritative and academically cosmopolitan perspective on the multi-faceted historical development of the European continent.

Raymond Pearson
Professor of Modern European History
University of Ulster

Acknowledgements

Writing a comprehensive social history of late medieval and early modern Spain means borrowing heavily from scholars who have long toiled in reconstructing the Spanish past. My gratitude for their work – which I cite often in my notes or in the bibliography – is great indeed. I am aware that my labour has largely been to weave and interpret their accumulated wisdom and insights. But I have also incurred a great debt to those who directly, through comments and suggestions, or indirectly, through their example and work, have played a significant role in the formulation of this book. I am most thankful to Hilario Casado, Paul Freedman, Xavier Gil Pujol, Manuel González Jiménez, Denis Menjot, David Nirenberg and Adeline Rucquoi for their comments, suggestions and support. Chapter 4 was presented for discussion at the University of California Medieval Seminar at the Huntington Library, where I received comments from participants, above all Jason Glenn's detailed suggestions. Chapters 5 and 6 were presented to the UCLA European History Seminar and to my own graduate seminar on the social and cultural history of late medieval and early modern Europe. I benefited immensely from the questions of graduate students and faculty alike, above all from Lynn Hunt's perceptive observations. Professor Raymond Pearson, general editor of the series in which this volume appears, has helped me with his adroit comments and suggestions. I am most thankful for his understanding and support. All throughout the process of bringing this book to its final form, I had the pleasure of working with the editorial staff at Longman. Andrew MacLennan, Heather McCallum and Lorna Sharrock handled my manuscript with generosity and patience; Jane Raistrick, who copy-edited the book, saved me from embarrassing mistakes and helped to improve my text. To them, I am most grateful.

In thinking about social history in general, my ideas have long been shaped by Jacques Le Goff's personal and scholarly example and by the late Lawrence Stone's vivid interventions at the Davis Center (Princeton) for more than twenty years. His combative and uncompromising commitment to history has made an indelible mark on the way in which historians conceive of their *métier*. My wife and sister soul, Scarlett Freund, has laboured over every line of this text. The mistakes are all mine, but whatever is good and elegant here is due to her editorial skills and exacting critical mind. So much so that, in all fairness, this has been a truly collaborative enterprise. But then, this has been the case in every aspect of our life together.

This book is dedicated to Sir John H. Elliott, *doyen* of Hispanists all over the world. For many years, Sir John H. Elliott's generosity, sensitivity to the work of others, and scholarship have inspired and galvanized a whole generation of scholars. For almost thirty years, I have benefited from his advice and guidance and have incurred a great debt to his work and friendship. His generosity and that of his wife, Oonah Elliott, have been extraordinary. This dedication is therefore but a modest token of my enduring admiration and gratitude.

Teofilo F. Ruiz
Los Angeles

Publisher's acknowledgements

We are grateful to the following for permission to reproduce copyright material:

Map of the regions of Spain from Tom Scott, *The Peasantries of Europe* (Harlow, 1998), 48, © Addison Wesley Longman Limited 1998; Table 2.4 from Amelang, James, *Honored Citizens of Barcelona: Patrician Culture and Class Relations, 1490–1714* (Princeton, 1986), 17, © 1986 by PUP, reprinted by permission of Princeton University Press; Table 9.1 from Phillips, Carla Rahn, *Six Galleons for the King of Spain: Imperial Defense in the Early Seventeenth Century*, p. 241, © 1986, Reprinted with permission of The Johns Hopkins University Press.

Whilst every effort has been made to trace the owners of copyright material, in a few cases this has proved impossible and we take this opportunity to offer our apologies to any copyright holders whose rights we may have unwittingly infringed.

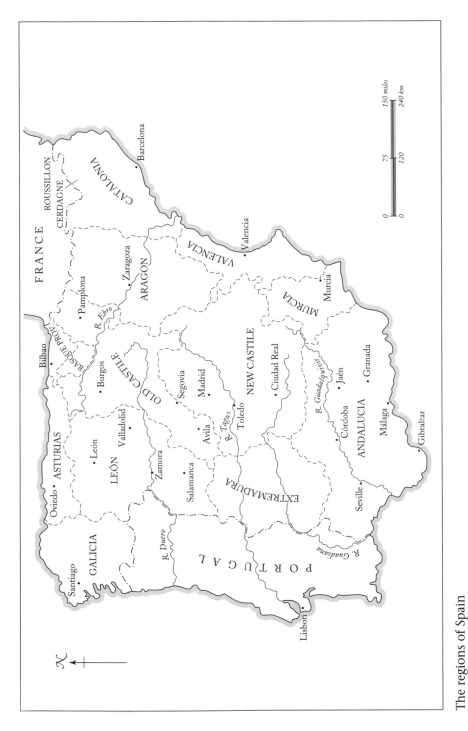

The regions of Spain

Source: Tom Scott, *The Peasantries of Europe* (Harlow, 1998), 48.

Introduction: from medieval to early modern

Historians of late medieval and early modern Spain have long seen the reign of the Catholic Monarchs (Isabella, 1474–1504, and Ferdinand, 1479–1516) as a watershed between two historical periods: the Middle Ages and the onset of modernity. To be sure, 1492 – *annus mirabilis* of the Castilian and Aragonese kingdoms; symbol of centralizing reforms – witnessed momentous events in the history of the peninsula. Nonetheless, the centrality assigned to the capture of Granada, the expulsion of the Jews, and the encounter between the Old World and the New have obscured far more enduring historical transformations.

Although some historians, most notably Sir John H. Elliott in his magisterial *Imperial Spain, 1469–1716*,[1] have noted a continuity between the late Middle Ages and the early modern period, most textbooks and monographs dealing with the history of Spain, whether in English, Spanish or French, faithfully tread the chronological path that splits the Middle Ages and the onset of modernity into discrete periods. This is the case for texts introducing students to the history of Spain as well as for those addressing the erudite.[2] The truth is that we remain prisoners of chronological constructs. Like other histories, Spanish historiography absorbed the positivism of leading nineteenth-century European historians and adopted the concept of iron-clad epochs and the view that prominent political events – *les grandes journées* – demarcate distinct historical periods.[3]

Nevertheless, 1492 did signal important landmarks in the political life of the Spains. The conquest of Granada, the expulsion of the Jews, the encounter with the New World were events of high historical significance, and collectively they had a dramatic impact on the mentality of Castilians, Aragonese, Catalans and other inhabitants of heterogeneous Spain.

The problem with these sharp chronological divisions, however, is that they arbitrarily separate the late Middle Ages from the early modern period. They also privilege political history over historiographical perspectives that are at least as important, or more so. Of course, I am referring here to the social and economic history of the Spanish kingdoms, conceived not as an appendage to a central political discourse but as manifesting a centrality of its own.

My aim in this book is quite straightforward. I wish to question the traditional periodization of the history of Spain, to suggest new ways of thinking

1

about the late Middle Ages and the early modern period, and to envisage social change as occurring independently of political watersheds. The dates 1400 and 1600, the chronological starting and ending points of this book, serve as arbitrary landmarks that link the social worlds of western Europe and signal the bridging of historical periods traditionally held apart: the late medieval and the early modern. One of my contentions in this book is that a history of the sixteenth century cannot be written without a thorough grounding in the preceding century, and vice versa.

Nonetheless, the extent to which formulations of social (and, by implication, economic) history have depended on chronological boundaries is evident in the pioneering and monumental *Historia de España y América*, written under the direction of the great Jaume Vicens Vives.[4] More than forty years after its original publication in 1957, this multi-volume work remains a model of how to organize a discussion of social history; at the same time, despite the originality and forward vision of Vicens Vives, the project did not escape the chronological impositions of a ruling ideology that conceived the history of Spain, and still conceives it, as a move from one significant date to another (1212, 1492, 1588, 1598, 1640, 1715, 1812) or as a record of ruling dynasties or systems (the Trastámaras, the Habsburgs, the Bourbons, the Republic). Thus, the second volume of Vicens Vives's collection closes arbitrarily (from the standpoint of social and economic history): with political events, such as the end of the reign of the Catholic Monarchs and the dissolution of the Trastámara dynasty, instead of with social or economic shifts such as the series of uprisings in Castile, Valencia and elsewhere in the 1520s, or the influx of American gold and silver from the 1530s onwards. And the formidable third volume ends in a similar fashion, with the dwindling of Habsburg rule in Spain, rather than with the more significant demographic and economic transformations of the mid-eighteenth century.

This criticism notwithstanding, one cannot but praise the efforts of Vicens Vives and of most of the historians who contributed to the *Historia de España y América* – in particular, the authors of volume III who delivered a history of *mentalités* and of marginality, topics still unexplored in Spain and in many other places outside of France in the 1950s.[5] We now have another excellent entry in the field of social history. As I was completing the last chapter of this book, James Casey's excellent monograph *Early Modern Spain: A Social History* appeared in print. After the initial scare of perhaps finding that the project I had spent years on had been pre-empted, I realized, after a careful reading, that our approaches to the social history of Spain diverge considerably. Casey's *Early Modern Spain* deals with a different chronological period. Although he makes revealing incursions into the period before 1500, the main thrust of his research is the early modern period, above all the seventeenth century, which anchors his earlier research. My book, on the other hand, emphasizes the continuity between the late Middle Ages and the early modern period. Moreover, Casey addresses topics other than the ones that are my main concerns. While he looks closely at religion and the family, I emphasize festivals, violence, and daily life. In the end, the two books provide complementary accounts of Spain's social history from 1400 to the end of the *ancien régime*, but from varying chronological and methodological perspectives. But the problem remains unsolved. Like the dates in Vicens Vives's *Historia de España y América*, those in Casey's narrative (1492 and 1500) remain a formidable wedge between epochs – the medieval and the early modern – and reinforce the strict boundaries set by political events.

When we cling to such chronological markers as 1492 and, therefore, to a specific kind of one-dimensional history, we become captive to a conception of history as politics. This deters us from studying historical transformations over *la longue durée*, from describing and explaining change over a long period of time – a task that is, after all, the fundamental duty of the historian. I should emphasize of course that social and economic history should not be studied or written without the proper political context. Nonetheless, in terms of underlying social structure, culture, *mentalité*, and the discourse of daily life, changes often occur imperceptibly; and in the case of late medieval and early modern Spain, whenever we perceive a sharp break, it bears no connection to 1492. If we could view and study the social history of Spain as a continuum, as a progression of social change that takes place over the course of centuries, then the distinctions between medieval and early modern would cease to be meaningful or useful.

Other aspects of writing social history are equally deserving of reassessment. Textbook after textbook describes Spain as a society of distinct orders (*la sociedad estamental*). They then give us a quick synopsis of these orders, almost always in a descending and fixedly hierarchical arrangement: nobility first, clergy second, the rest later. Missing from this analysis is the complex set of relations among different social groups, as well as the wide range of possibilities within groups. Let me offer a few examples.

Writing in the late 1320s, Don Juan Manuel (1282–c.1348), a prince of royal blood and one of the most troublesome nobles in late medieval Castile, described the social order of his day in *El libro de los estados* (*The Book of Orders*). Borrowing from well-established medieval notions of the tripartite division of society, Don Juan Manuel imagined a social hierarchy that was neatly divided into three broad orders (*estamentos*): those who pray (the clergy), those who fight (the nobility), and the rest, the immense majority of the population he defined as *labradores* (literally, those who work the land). An additional category acknowledged urban dwellers, who were, in turn, divided into three subcategories: the upper urban elite of the bourgeoisie, mercantile groups, and labourers (*menestrales*).

In adopting the tripartite division of society prevailing in medieval western Europe, Don Juan Manuel followed a tradition which maintained that felicity in this world and salvation in the next depended largely on accepting one's assigned place in the social hierarchy. Don Juan Manuel's convictions, however, ran counter to the changing realities of the late Middle Ages. His lofty views of the privileges of the noble estate, and his dismissive comments on those who worked, found their comeuppance in the urban militias that were manned by the very merchants and artisans he had branded as peasants, militias which defeated him time and again on the battlefields of northern Castile. Don Juan Manuel's normative categories may read well on paper and accurately reflect the mindset of an aristocrat in mid-fourteenth-century Castile, but they bear little relation to the fluid social world of late medieval Spain, where status was constantly being redefined by wealth and war.[6]

Writing more than a century later, in the 1470s, Jorge Manrique (1440?–1479) – by birth, a scion of one of the noblest families in Castile and Don Juan Manuel's social equal; by vocation, an indefatigable warrior and poet – presents us with a far more nuanced view of social structure. In his extraordinarily beautiful poem 'Ode to the Death of my Father' (*Coplas a la muerte de mi padre*), Jorge Manrique reflects on the levelling properties of death. Comparing our lives to rivers that flow into a sea 'which is dying', he notes that all rivers, large and small, run into the sea, and that all are equal, 'those who live by the [work of their] hands and those who are rich'.[7]

In a poem intended to praise the nobility of his father, this is indeed a remarkable statement. For Manrique, at least in these pages, society is divided into two distinct groups: those who work with their hands (the poor) and those who do not work (the rich). Thus, he somewhat sets aside the divinely inspired hierarchies presumed to sustain medieval life. Instead, it is wealth and work that define social categories. In the same vein, in Gutierre Díaz de Gámez's *The Unconquered Knight: A Chronicle of the Deeds of Don Pero Niño* (known in Spanish as *El Victorial*), written in the 1430s and 1440s, the true honour of knighthood resides not in birth, titles, or displays of arms, but in dedication and commitment to knightly ideals. 'Not all are knights who ride upon horses; neither are all knights to whom kings give arms. They have the name but they do not pursue the calling.'[8] Manrique, of course, would have agreed with that.

The sentiments expressed in these poems and in other literary works of the fifteenth and sixteenth centuries reveal confusion in the face of loosening social categories and the difficulty of discerning who was noble and who was not, who was a true Christian and who not, or, as was often debated in fifteenth-century Spain, who was a New Christian and who was an Old one. Thus, Miguel de Cervantes (1547–1616), writing in an ironic mode, could have Sancho Panza argue that since he was an Old Christian – meaning, a peasant who could brandish his 'purity of blood' as opposed to the merchants and nobles who bore *Converso* ties – he had the right to be made a duke. More to the point, in the second volume of *Don Quixote*, Sancho, quoting his grandmother, states that there are only two lineages in the world: those who have and those who have not (*el tener y el no tener*).[9] Similarly, the peasants of Lope de Vega's (1562–1635) many rousing plays, among them *Fuenteovejuna* and *Peribáñez y el comendador de Ocaña*, or the farmers of Calderón de la Barca's (1600–81) *El Alcalde de Zalamea*, embody nobility and faithfulness to the strictest code of honour, while their noble adversaries and tormentors epitomize villainy.

But right behaviour and Christian ideals were slowly eroding, as the influx of American silver and the birth of capitalism gave rise to new attitudes towards wealth. Many literary works touched on these economic transformations and the altered relations among social groups. 'More entailments [*mayorazgos*] are created by money and education than by the exercise of arms',[10] wrote Cervantes in *Don Quixote,* his numerous examples reflecting perhaps on his own troubled life. A similar though vitriolic indictment of the porosity of social classes appears in Francisco de Quevedo's (1580–1645) *Letrilla*, a poem about the role of money in early modern Spain. Money, Quevedo wrote, makes nobles out of inferior people, and Christians out of Moors; it buys favours, it buys love, it makes the ugly beautiful.

These literary depictions had real-life corollaries that illustrate the difficulties in discussing social hierarchies between 1400 and 1600. The old, 'feudal', tripartite social model was imported into the contemporary world as part of western European elites' idealized and self-serving representation of themselves; yet this official script was challenged daily by the radical transmutation of economic roles and the onslaught of money, war and politics. The perviousness of social boundaries, the role of wealth and work, and the growing secularization of society outpaced and eventually overthrew the elaborate social distinctions which, devolving from God downwards, had provided assurance to the few against the many and held the promise of order and salvation to the population at large. This is not to say, of course, that uneven relationships did not persist. They did, but were couched in the new idioms of class, education, and personal – as opposed to collective – achievement.

Modern historians, however, have not yet overcome the Circe-like fascination with estates and orders. These tidy categories have led to oversimplified accounts of complex and perplexing systems of social accommodation and conflict. The tripartite division of society has supplied an elegant explanation for the interaction between diverse social groups, but it has obscured or ignored countless variations within each order. A well-to-do merchant in fifteenth-century Burgos, a commercial centre in northern Castile, wore armour, proudly carried his heraldic colours, and lived in a well-appointed house in which he might even have hosted kings.[11] In spite of his commercial or professional pursuits, a sixteenth-century 'honoured citizen' of Barcelona had a far more aristocratic lifestyle and mentality than a destitute nobleman, barely scraping a living in some obscure corner of Spain.[12] The poor *hidalgo* (lower-level Castilian nobility) in *Lazarillo de Tormes*, a picaresque novel of the mid-sixteenth century, lived as marginal and hungry a life as did his socially inferior counterparts. Examples, and exceptions, abound indeed; they all point to the uncertain character of social classifications. This is doubly the case in Spain, where social filiation, family organization, terms of inheritance, economic conditions, and the relationship between those on top and those below varied dramatically and regionally.

Conventional descriptions of the social order thus leave a great deal to be desired. Perhaps the best way to describe a society in transition from orders to classes is to offer a typology of social filiation or positioning that is based on privilege, tax-exemption and power. For, ultimately, two broad categories held sway: those who, because of wealth, legal prerogatives and social standing, were part of the hegemonic order; and those who, lacking some or all of these attributes, were not. But such a typology cannot be dogmatic. The category of social and economic class is, after all, as problematic as that of ancient social orders. In devising such constructs – and we must remember that they are nothing but semantic constructs – we need to keep a careful eye on variations within each social category. Relationships of power, of hegemon to subaltern, are found not only across but within groups as well. A powerful *rico hombre* in fifteenth-century Spain had more in common with a semi-aristocratic merchant in Burgos, in terms of taste, lifestyle and power, than with a poor *hidalgo*. The opening of the second volume of *Don Quixote* offers a glimpse of the internecine struggles, animosities and envy that existed between *hidalgos* and *caballeros*. As might have been the case in real life, the *caballeros* of the unnamed village of La Mancha resented the use of the title *Don* by Alonso Quijano, the deluded man soon to become Don Quixote.

Conversely, types of marginality ranged widely, and we err when we lump together all *Conversos*, or all *Moriscos*. Although ancestry provided a common bond and served as a deterrent to integration into Spanish society, it is clear that rank, money, education, and place of residence accounted at least as much for the ease with which some individuals and families crossed over or assimilated into specific social niches in Spain.[13]

With these introductory remarks as context for the discussion that follows, this book opens with a short chapter on the geography and political life of Spain between 1400 and 1600. By providing a broad outline of Spanish history during this period, I try to address the economic, political and cultural history of these two centuries, and their links to social developments. I also take into account the discovery of, and encounter with, the New World as well as the impact of America on the social fabric and the demographic resources of Spain (especially in Castile). Part Two introduces the concept of orders (*estamentos*). This part includes three broad chapters organized around

Sancho's maxim on the haves and the have-nots. We begin with those who worked: the peasants and urban dwellers who did not enjoy the vast social and legal privileges of their betters. The following chapter examines in some detail the lives of nobles and clergymen. A third and final chapter focuses on those living on the margins of society. Part Three, on the tenor of life in late medieval and early modern Spain, explores a series of interrelated topics: violence and resistance; festivals and the character of daily life; diet and dress as sites for social exchange and as links between groups. How did these social groups interact? Under what terms? To what purpose? The forms of social exchange encompassed a wide range of public events: royal entries, religious spectacles, festive cycles, civil wars, mob violence. And on these occasions, boundaries – and connections – between social groups were forged, contested, negotiated. In the end, it was all about power: who had power, and how they contrived to exert it; who lacked power, and how they managed to endure.

Notes

1. John H. Elliott, *Imperial Spain, 1469–1716* (New York, 1964).
2. There are many examples of these types of textbooks and monographs. See, for example, Antonio Ballesteros, *Historia de España y su influencia en la historia universal*, 8 vols in 9 (Barcelona, 1918–41); Ramón Menéndez Pidal (ed.), *Historia de España* (Madrid, 1940–); or *La Historia de España Alfaguara*, 7 vols (Madrid, 1973–) which has the virtue of linking, in vol. III, the reign of the Catholic Kings to the early modern period. Similarly, in *Historia de España*, 13 vols (Barcelona, 1980–86), directed by Manuel Tuñón de Lara, vol. V integrates the late Middle Ages with the early modern period, but the chronological landmarks are always political.
3. There are many examples from traditional (and great) eighteenth- and nineteenth-century national histories such as the works of Guizot, Michelet, Croce, Carlyle, Ranke, Macauley, etc. For Spain see Modesto Lafuente, *Historia de España*, 30 vols (Madrid, 1850–66). See Peter Linehan, *History and Historians of Medieval Spain* (Oxford, 1993), and Hayden White, *Metahistory: The Historical Imagination in Nineteenth-Century Europe* (Baltimore, 1973).
4. Jaume Vicens Vives (ed.), *Historia de España y América: social y económica*, 2nd edn (Barcelona, 1971).
5. The differences between vols I, II and III are important even though, in principle, all three follow the same format. Volume III includes sections on marginality, a topic that is missing in earlier volumes.
6. On Don Juan Manuel and the *Libro de los estados* see José R. Araluce Cuenca, *El libro de los estados: Don Juan Manuel y la sociedad de su tiempo* (Madrid, 1976).
7. There are many editions of Jorge Manrique's greatest work. An English translation, not a very faithful or readable one, by Henry W. Longfellow can be found in *Ten Centuries of Spanish Poetry*, ed. Eleanor L. Turnbull (Baltimore, 1955), 23–77.
8. Gutierre Díaz de Gámez, *The Unconquered Knight: A Chronicle of the Deeds of Don Pero Niño* (London, 1928), 12.

9. There are many editions of *Don Quixote*. Throughout this book, I use *Don Quijote de la Mancha*, edited and annotated by Martín de Riquer (Editorial Juventud: Barcelona, 1955). For Cervantes's view of Old Christians as the origins of nobility see vol. I, ch. 21; for the two lineages in the world, vol. II, ch. 20.

10. *Don Quixote*, II, ch. 24.

11. See the illustrations depicting the merchant-knights of Burgos in the fifteenth century in *Regla de la cofradía de Nuestra Señora de Gamonal, de Burgos y libro en que se pintan los caballeros cofrades*, edición facsimile (Burgos, 1995).

12. On the 'honoured citizens' of Barcelona see James S. Amelang, *Honored Citizens of Barcelona: Patrician Culture and Class Relations, 1490–1714* (Princeton, 1986).

13. See Scarlett Freund and Teofilo F. Ruiz, 'Jews, *Conversos*, and the Inquisition in Spain, 1391–1492: The Ambiguities of History', in J.M. Perry and F.M. Schweitzer (eds), *Jewish–Christian Encounters over the Centuries* (New York, 1994), 169–95.

PART ONE

The geography and political setting

Chapter 1

Spain in the making

The social history of Spain, or, more precisely, of the Spains, must be placed against the variegated backdrop of Iberian geography, climate, language and economic patterns. To a large extent, village size, family structure and social position were governed by regional conditions, by what the land would allow to grow. Climate and topography thus determined the location of towns and villages as well as the amount of rent nobles could extract from their peasants.

Spain's ecological diversity is unmatched by that of any other country in Europe. Few places in Europe have suffered such adverse climatic conditions (extreme heat and severe cold) and so hostile an environment (thin soil, little water) as did parts of Spain (the Castilian plateau, western Aragon) in the late Middle Ages.

If we think of Spain in the plural – the Spains – it is not only because in 1400 or in 1600 a unified Spain in a true political sense had not yet come into being, but also because the country as a whole (that is, geographical Spain) was, and remains, sharply divided into distinct topographical and climatic regions. The availability of water in Aragon, Castile and Andalusia played a crucial role in creating starkly contrasting conditions of wealth and poverty. One cannot, therefore, accept the notion of a social history of Spain that privileges the history of one region over another. Castile may have become synonymous with Spain because of its demographic and political hegemony in the late Middle Ages and early modern period, but Castile was certainly not all of Spain. For the sake of convenience, however, historians often describe a region as normative and the rest as variations of or as parallels to that norm. This kind of 'history from the centre' regards politics as the prime mover of historical events and subordinates the study of social structure to that of political power. Geography teaches us otherwise.

Look at a map of Spain (p. xv), and you will see a series of subregions in which political, linguistic, social and cultural boundaries run parallel to the geographical contours of the land. Follow the slopes of the mountain ranges, the edges of the great high plains and the courses of the rivers, and you will find the topographical features sorting themselves into subdivisions which often (but not always) coalesce into particular political entities, or which, in an age of fragmented political autonomy, become individual Spains within the larger context of the peninsular state.[1]

Geography, climate and language[2]

Northern Spain

On the northern edge of the peninsula, running from Galicia in the northwest to the French frontier in the northeast, a fertile ribbon of land – green Spain, as it is called – stretches between the Atlantic ocean and the Bay of Biscay on its western and northern borders and the western spur of the Pyrenees mountains (the Picos de Europa) at its southernmost limit. With its bountiful rain, temperate climate, and small, numerous villages, the region as a whole has exhibited an age-old vocation for the sea and for maritime pursuits. Fishing fleets operated from Galician ports in the west as well as from the small bays (Guetaria, Gijón, Llanes, Fuenterrabía, Laredo, Castro-Urdiales, and others) in the central and eastern regions (Asturias, Cantabria and the Basque homeland). In the late Middle Ages and into the early modern period, the ports of the Bay of Biscay were, together with the Andalusian trade with America, the lifeline of the Spanish (by which I mean Castilian) economy. Iron, hides, honey, fat and other items were shipped to England and Flanders from these ports before 1350; and after the introduction of merino sheep, with their high-quality wool, a flow of mostly unprocessed wool found its way from central Castile to the northern ports and from there to the great textile centres of Flanders and Brabant. In a different direction another great but far more expensive supply of finished cloth and other manufactured goods poured into Spain through the same ports. But the people of the North were not limited to mercantile activities and seafaring; dairy industries, cattle – which sold well in the Castilian plains – and fruit trees complemented the economy of the region. Yet, one of the main staples of the region was men. Galicia, like the Basque country, was even then a land of migrants, its enterprising men pursuing work and business in central Spain or in far-away America.

Despite their congruities, this green Spain was divided further into very distinct subregions. In the period between 1400 and 1600, most Galician peasants and the poor in the countryside spoke their own language. The Galician language was older than Castilian, which eventually became the hegemonic language in the peninsula; it was also closer to its derivative language, Portuguese. In the central Middle Ages, the period before the rise of Castilian as a literary language (the twelfth and thirteenth centuries), Galician had been the chosen language of courtly poetry (the *cantigas*), but after the 1250s it declined precipitously and remained in decline until its brilliant renaissance in the late nineteenth century and re-emergence in the late twentieth century as one of the diverse languages of Spain's *autonomías*.

The economic structure of the region, which was dominated by ruthless lords with extremely fractured land holdings, differed considerably from that of neighbouring Asturias or of the faraway Basque country in the east. The mountains separating Galicia from Asturias, albeit unimposing, mark a veritable linguistic and economic frontier. Asturias, which, in the fifteenth and sixteenth centuries, did not experience the economic and political transformations that had touched most parts of the peninsula, is also quite distinct from its eastern neighbour, Cantabria. Though less widespread than Galician was in the west, the Asturian dialect was the lingua franca of the Asturian countryside and of the isolated villages located in the region's rugged mountains and high valleys.

Galicia and Asturias contrast vividly with the area known today as Cantabria, a region stretching roughly from San Vicente de la Barquera in the west to Castro-Urdiales in the east and the mountain passes of El Escudo in the south. Linguistically, politically and economically (but not geographically), Cantabria was fully integrated into the kingdom of Castile in the late Middle Ages and the early modern period; it only found its autonomous identity in the fever of regional patriotism which swept Spain after Franco's death in 1975.

To the east of Cantabria, the Basque provinces were a world unto themselves in the Middle Ages, just as they are today. If geographical differences among the regions of the green north are minimal, the Basques, who lived and still live on both sides of the Pyrenees, were able to sustain a separate identity in the face of centralizing pressures from the Castilian monarchs in the Middle Ages, and later from the kings and dictators of Spain. Basque was not a literary language in the period under consideration, and its many dialects and variations, spoken mostly in isolated mountain villages, were often incomprehensible even to native Basque speakers. Basque identity, contrary to Galician or Catalan identity, was thus far more centred on a sense of ethnic consciousness than it was on linguistic filiation. The fact that many of these differences resurfaced in the last two decades of the twentieth century (in Galicia, the Basque country, and Catalonia) reveals their original vehemence and underscores the historical, geographical and linguistic fragmentation of early modern Spain.

Central Spain
Below northern green Spain lie the two great plains of Castile. Early modern travellers, coming across mountain passes from the north, always remarked on the sharp contrasts between verdant Cantabria, Asturias, or the Basque country and the unyielding wastelands which, as transitional ecological habitats, led first into the high meseta of Old Castile, and later across the Central Sierras into the lower altitude of the meseta of New Castile.[3] Geographically, the plains of Castile are the central feature of the Iberian peninsula. Politically and economically, the cities on the northern plain (Burgos, Valladolid, Segovia) and those further south in New Castile and Andalusia (Toledo, Madrid, Seville) served as loci for the centralizing tendencies of the Castilian Crown and as centres for the spread of Castilian hegemony through language, culture, economic power and political leadership.

13

The high altitude of the northern plain created severe problems for agriculture and life in general. Intense cold in winter, scorching heat during most of July and August, hailstorms and snow showers as late as April and May, thin top soil, little rainfall (the rain in Spain, contrary to Professor Higgins's ditty, falls mainly elsewhere, not on the plain), and various environmental calamities made cultivating vineyards and growing corn and other staples of the medieval and early modern diet a trying enterprise.

Villages and towns clung to meagre rivers and rivulets that were separated from each other by wide open and arid spaces. Foreign travellers, upon crossing the great plains of Old Castile in the fifteenth and sixteenth centuries, plaintively decried its 'emptiness' and the 'lack of wooded areas'; in typical fashion of outsiders, they complained bitterly of the greed and behaviour of the natives and, above all, of the rapacity of tax-collectors.[4] Nonetheless, in spite of adverse conditions, the plains of Old Castile, and – after the Christian conquest of the regions south of the Central Sierras (Toledo in 1085, western Andalusia in the early thirteenth century) – the plains of New Castile and La Mancha, served together as a locus for the emergence of the hegemonic political entity in the peninsula: the kingdom of Castile-Léon. The language of the region, Castilian, became the dominant language in the peninsula by the sixteenth century; and it was transplanted by the conquistadors and Castilian settlers to the New World. In time, it became – though many continue, rightly, to object to this – synonymous with Spanish.

In the face of hardship, the peasants of Castile, through techniques of dry farming, extensive fallowing, transhumance, and above all laborious toil, produced enough food and generated enough income in taxes to enable the Castilian monarchs to pursue their policies of expansion in the peninsula, and beyond Iberia itself. Because of its rugged geography, harsh climate and economic structure, Castile was nonetheless ill-suited for its international role; and, as we shall see, its inhabitants paid a heavy toll for their hegemony in Europe.

We should not, however, think of central Spain (and many of the features described for this region here apply to parts of eastern Aragon as well) as a unified landscape. For Castile itself comprises many contrasting subregions – protected valleys, unyielding mountains, and subtropical ecological niches – where life differs markedly from the typical life of the plains. Even the hostile reports of foreigners are interspersed with glowing descriptions of bountiful areas, such as the Rioja.[5]

Southern Spain

How different was, and is, the south of Spain. Coming over the mountain pass of Despeñaperros, the old boundary between New Castile and Andalusia, and across the ancient road (before modern highways tunnelled through the mountains), one enters a very distinct landscape. The elevations of

Andalusia and Extremadura slope toward the sea, in search of their coastal destinies in the Atlantic and the Mediterranean. Like much of Spain, the south has rugged mountains, such as the Sierra Morena, the Serranía of Ronda. And, in the east, the imposing Sierra Nevada encircles Granada like strong walls in a fortress. There, in the Alpujarras, a mountain range south of the city of Granada and part of the Sierra Nevada, the *Moriscos* made their last stand in the 1560s.

Yet, for all their climatic and topographical advantages over central Spain, Andalusia and the south in general are not as green as the humid north. Nonetheless, the low altitude of the valleys, the long rivers, and the proximity to the Mediterranean allowed for fertile gardens and a culture of irrigation. Here, olive and orange trees, the vine, mulberry trees (which fed hard-working silk worms), spices, and semi-tropical plants (sugar cane in the area of Valencia, rice) served as the basis for economic (and social) structures entirely different from those in central Castile and the north. In Andalusia, gardens were created by Muslim rulers that looked like imaginary recreations of Paradise. The Alhambra, the palace of the last Nasrid rulers of Granada, and one of the most sensuous and beautiful buildings in Europe, is also a tribute to water: a demonstration in the precise and scientific use of water and its transformative powers. Wherever one turns in the Alhambra, the sound of running water, of fountains, provides a soothing counterpoint to views of arid, brown, and, at times, snow-capped mountains surrounding the city. In Valencia, one of the few places Christian conquerors of the thirteenth century did not completely spoil, the fabled *huertas* (gardens) *de Valencia* continued to be tended by *Moriscos* and their descendants throughout the late Middle Ages and in the early modern period. It remained – unlike Murcia and other parts of Andalusia which became wastelands because of the transhumance – a productive and beautiful landscape much admired by foreign visitors. Jeronimo Munzer, travelling in Spain in 1494, described the city and its environs in luminous terms.[6]

Because of the advance of the Christian reconquest in the mid-thirteenth century, and the ensuing precipitous demographic and economic decline, western Andalusia and Extremadura became the terminus for large migrations of livestock (the Mesta) from northern (summer) to southern (winter) grazing lands. Moreover, after the mid-thirteenth century and the expulsion of the Muslims from western Andalusia (1260s), the region became the site for latifundia in Spain. Large estates dominated the landscape, and its numerous landless peasants, a true rural proletariat, provided the conditions for social conflict (see Chapter 2).

Eastern Spain

Last, but certainly not least, each of the two eastern kingdoms featured their own geographical peculiarities. These differences in topography and climate

15

were parallelled by separate languages and political institutions, even though the kingdom of Aragon, the county of Barcelona (Catalonia), and, later on, the kingdom of Valencia shared a common political life as the Crown of Aragon. Both Aragon and Catalonia share a common northern border, the rugged mountain range of the Pyrenees. But in Aragon the mountains, moving south, give way to an arid, often unyielding plain, whereas in Catalonia they form a series of descending fertile valleys. Separated from Old Castile by the Iberian mountain range (*sistema ibérico*), which runs roughly north–south in the eastern borders of the latter region, medieval Aragon did not enjoy the natural advantages of Catalonia, except along the banks of the river Ebro. Away from the sea, it suffered the same extremes of cold and heat as its neighbour, Castile. Its plains remained almost deserted, as the meagre population cleaved to the banks of the Ebro river and other smaller streams. Zaragoza, the capital of Aragon, thrived on the life-giving water of the river. Its lands were carefully cultivated by Mudejars and, after their nominal conversion to Christianity in the early sixteenth century, by *Moriscos*. One could say that the Aragonese spoke two languages: a Castilian borrowed from their nearby neighbour and peppered with their own accents and Catalan words; and Arabic, the language of the largely submissive and exploited *Morisco* population. If travel accounts and literary works are reliable sources, the countryside of sixteenth-century Aragon, when not deserted, was inhabited by *Moriscos*.[7] Though Christians also lived in rural villages, they chose to make their homes mainly in the large cities and towns of the kingdom, Zaragoza, Calatayud, and others.

One may err off course in positing a seigneurial, rural, sparsely populated Aragon, as compared with a dynamic, urban (to the extent that we understand urban in late medieval and early modern Europe) and commercial Catalonia. But not by much. Most of Catalonia was blessed by a Mediterranean climate, whereby the harshness of seasons (winter and summer) was mitigated by the sea. But, as Fernand Braudel pointed out long ago, the Mediterranean can be quite cruel, and the lands on its shores are not lands of plenty. Nonetheless, Catalonia and its valleys sloping to the sea were far more fertile than their Aragonese counterparts (except for the Ebro basin), and its climate was more moderate along the coast.

Catalonia, in spite of economic and demographic reverses in the late Middle Ages, remained an enterprising region. It looked outward to its many Mediterranean holdings in Italy and the east. Its capital, Barcelona, dominated the entire region and imposed its commercial and entrepreneurial control on other areas of the county. Together with other regions of Spain, these geographical and linguistic entities formed the great puzzle that was medieval Spain, and is Spain today. Geography and climate moulded political and linguistic variations and led to the troubled and fractured character of the land.

Politics and culture

Spain in the fifteenth century

If the geography and climate of the Iberian peninsula show remarkable diversity, so does its political past. Lingering political divisions and conflicting cultural identities spawned an 'invertebrate' Spain, to invoke Ortega y Gasset's adroit term – invertebrate, in the sense of its geographical and political fragmentation. Ortega y Gasset had employed the term to lament the absence of 'feudalism' in the peninsula (about which he was partially wrong), an absence to which he attributed Spain's failure to develop a central unifying core.[8]

Castile

In 1400, there was, as indicated before, no Spain. In most of the western region of the peninsula (except for Portugal), the kings of Castile-León ruled over a vast realm, the aggregate of numerous annexations and conquests over the kingdom's 600-year history. Although the term Castile is used today to describe the most powerful and populous of the Iberian kingdoms in the early fifteenth century, the rulers of Castile knew better. They understood that Castile stood for a vast ensemble of far-flung, formerly independent political entities, each with distinctive social, political and economic institutions. In a letter to the municipal council of Avila in 1475, Queen Isabella opened her charter with the formulaic listing of her titles: 'Queen of Castile, of León, of Toledo, of Sicily, of Galicia, of Seville, of Córdoba, of Murcia, of Jaén, of the Algarbe, of Gibraltar, princess of Aragon and lady of Vizcaya and Molina'. With the exception of the titles of Sicily and Aragon, which she obtained through marriage to Ferdinand of Aragon, in 1469, and thus ruled only as a consort, all her other titles reflected the piecemeal formation of Castile by inheritance, family alliances and war. As late as the sixteenth century, Vizcaya, a part of the Basque country, insisted on preserving its particular relationship with the Crown and on safeguarding its ancient privileges and liberties, which new Castilian kings or their representatives had to respect by an oath pledged under the ancient oak at Guernica, the symbol of Basque identity.

By 1400, and certainly by 1500, the Castilian kings (and queen) had taken powerful strides to centralize their authority over their entire realm; but local traditions, ancient customs and different languages undermined centralization and fostered the regionalism and particularism that remain too vibrantly alive to this day. Although in theory the Castilian *cortes*, the equivalent of a parliament, represented the entire realm, in fact by the fifteenth century representation was limited to a few cities. In 1391, forty-nine towns sent representatives to the meetings of the *cortes*, but only seventeen had a vote in them by 1480. Most of the municipal councils sending procurators to the meetings of the *cortes* were located in Castile proper; by the 1480s, they were securely under royal control.

The population of Castile in the fifteenth century included a substantial number of Mudejars (Moors living under Christian rule), *Moriscos* (Moors living under Christian rule and nominally converted to Christianity), Jews, and *Conversos* (Jews who had converted to Christianity, or Christians with Jewish ancestry) (see Chapter 4). By the end of the fifteenth century, in 1492, Jews are supposed to have numbered between 80,000 and 150,000, with an equal number of *Conversos*, while the figures for Moors and *Moriscos* (who were essentially part of the same group) are very difficult to determine. Although their numbers in areas of northern Castile barely reached 20,000, the newly conquered kingdom of Granada, like most areas of rural Aragon and Valencia, was overwhelmingly inhabited by *Moriscos*. In spite of continuous defections to North Africa, the *Morisco* population grew considerably throughout the sixteenth century (one of the accusations hurled against them was their fecundity) until the eve of their expulsion in the early seventeenth century, when their number, for the entire peninsula, is calculated to have been around 319,000.[9] This religious diversity (see below), which was articulated as ethnic (or 'racial') difference by many contemporaries and foreign visitors, added to the complexities of Castilian social life. Religious affiliation and ethnicity often crossed social and economic boundaries, muddling even further the wishfully neat arrangement of Spanish society into orders.

Castile, as a political entity in the late Middle Ages and early modern period, has two distinct histories. Unlike its social history which presents no sharp breaks at the end of the fifteenth century, its political history is marked indelibly by the reign of the Catholic Monarchs: Isabella, queen of Castile (1474–1504), and Ferdinand, king of the Crown of Aragon (1479–1516). Their regime was, in fact, a political watershed. To begin with, the royal marriage led, eventually, to the rule of Isabella's grandson, Charles I of Spain (Charles V in Germany, 1516–56), and to Habsburg dominion (1516–1700) over the disparate political units that made up Spain; this occurred in spite of such great obstacles as Isabella's death in 1504, the vicissitudes of Joanna the Mad's rule, Ferdinand's second marriage and search for an heir of his own (which, if successful, would have caused further fragmentation of the peninsular kingdoms), and the vagaries of royal descent. Second, the reign of Isabella and Ferdinand brought to an end a century and a half of incessant civil wars, wanton noble violence, and continuous alienation of the royal domain into the hands of arrogant and spendthrift noble families and ambitious new men.

Throughout more than half of the fifteenth century, Castile was ruled by a weak and ineffectual king, John II (1406–54), whose favours wavered dangerously between his able favourite, the enigmatic Don Alvaro de Luna who controlled him for most of his life, and his ambitious and ruthless cousins, the Infantes of Aragon, Don Enrique and Don Juan. The Infantes of Aragon were among the greatest and richest magnates in Castile, children of the late king of the Crown of Aragon, Ferdinand of Antequera (1412–16), and brothers of the king of Aragon, Alfonso V (1416–58). Don Enrique was master of the Military Order of Santiago, with control over its vast financial and military resources, while his brother Juan (John) became king of Navarre through marriage and, eventually, king of Aragon at the death of his brother Alfonso V. Clearly, such powerful presences in the realm brought nothing but trouble. The political history of Castile throughout most of the first half of the fifteenth century, therefore, revolved around the conflict between Álvaro de Luna and the Infantes of Aragon for control of the king and the kingdom. Their unceasing struggles, and the excesses and cruelties of the magnates, had a nefarious impact on the life of the poor, mostly the peasantry. In the satirical poetry of the age, the nobility and the Crown are compared to wolves, and the poor people to lambs.

In the cities of the realm, the situation was not very different. Noble factions often used the populace as battering rams in their internecine struggles. In Seville and other Andalusi towns, for example, the followers of the great lords of Medina Sidonia fought those of the marquis of Cádiz throughout most of the second half of the century, before the Catholic Monarchs restored peace. A good number of the anti-*Converso* riots and the violence of the 1440s and 1460s can be seen, as Angus MacKay has shown, as part of a broader cycle of violence and social unrest.[10]

John II's death in 1454, a mere year after he had ordered the execution of his favourite, Alvaro de Luna, did not bring peace to Castile. His successor, Henry IV (1454–74), was as ineffectual as his father. Soon a tool of his favourites, all as greedy as Alvaro de Luna had been but none with Alvaro's cunning and desire to protect royal privileges, the Crown became much imperilled by magnate ambitions. Armed conflicts between noble factions, costly and indecisive wars against Aragon, and continuous skirmishes on the Granada frontier sank Castile into general anarchy and social discontent. The political unrest reached its lowest point in the so-called 'farce of Avila', in which a group of high noblemen and high dignitaries of the Castilian Church removed all the symbols of office from an effigy of Henry IV, kicked the mannequin off the stage, removed him symbolically, and then in fact, from the throne and elected his under-age and easily controllable half-brother, Alfonso, as the new king.[11] When Alfonso died, thwarting magnate ambitions, Henry IV wavered between his own daughter, Juana, and his half-sister, Isabella, in naming an heir. He changed his mind with such frequency that when he died, in 1474, leaving Juana on the throne, the matter escalated into war.

With the support of Ferdinand, whom she had married in 1469, and of most of the Castilian cities, Isabella challenged the rule of her minor niece, Juana (also known as la Beltraneja, because she was thought to be the daughter of Beltrán de la Cueva, Henry IV's intimate favourite). After a successful war against Portugal and against the noble factions that had supported Henry IV's daughter, the Catholic Monarchs restored order to Castile and curbed the excesses of the nobility with remarkable speed. The rule of Isabella and Ferdinand marked a dramatic change in Castile. By the 1480s, when they began to muster their forces for the final assault on Granada, the Catholic Monarchs had recovered most of the royal income that had been alienated to the high nobility during the late fourteenth century and most of the fifteenth. They turned the magnates from enemies of order and of the Crown into faithful servants of the realm. The nobility had no choice. They either obeyed and kept their social and economic privileges (which most did), or maintained their fratricidal political ambitions and lost their lives, went into exile, or suffered a severe diminution in their privileges.

Isabella and Ferdinand undertook a thorough reform of Castilian institutions by creating royal councils (of the Hermandad, of the Inquisition, of the Indies, of the Mesta) to administer different aspects of the kingdom's economic, political and religious life. Moreover, the Castilian Church, which had been mired in the most abysmal corruption (see below, Part II, Chapter 3), and whose members – above all the lower clergy – lacked a proper education, was turned into a militant Church, ready to advance the lofty claims of the monarchs.

Economic growth, educational reforms, an aggressive foreign policy, and the push for religious homogeneity – underscored by the establishment of the Inquisition in Castile in the 1480s and the decree of Expulsion of the Jews in 1492 – were important components of the overall programme of the Catholic Monarchs in Castile. The 'miracle year' of the Castilian monarchy, 1492, witnessed the surrender of Granada (1–2 January); the Decree of Expulsion (30 March); the actual exile of the Jews who did not convert, four months later; and Columbus's sailing across the Ocean Sea in his mistaken search for a westward route to the Indies.

Although recent historians have rightly questioned the nature of the Catholic Monarchs' reforms and the depth of Isabella and Ferdinand's centralizing policies, arguing that many of the reforms had precedents in an earlier period or that the monarchs' policies did not take real strides toward a 'modern' centralized monarchy, the reign constituted a substantial breakthrough in the political and religious life of the realm. Chronicles and other contemporary writings exude a sense of renovation, a feeling that their world had been drastically transformed.[12]

Granada and Navarre

The story of Castile, one of crisis and renewal in the fifteenth century, was not that of the two other smaller kingdoms, Granada and Navarre, which, together with the Crown of Aragon, shared the fragmented map of the Spains before 1500. In 1492, Granada was the last outpost of Islam in the Iberian peninsula, though the city and the kingdom had a long and fabled past. Already in the early thirteenth century, Granada was one of the largest cities in the peninsula, and its population rose to even greater numbers after the unsuccessful Mudejar rebellion in western Andalusia (1260s) and the subsequent expulsion of the Mudejars from Christian lands.

Against overwhelming forces, Granada's Nasrid rulers were able to preserve the independence of the kingdom for more than two centuries after the great Christian victories of the 1240s and 1250s. This was due partly to the surrounding rugged mountains which rendered military actions difficult, and partly to the steady flow of tribute which Granada's rulers paid to the kings of Castile to fend off aggression, but mostly to the internecine struggles and political anarchy besetting Castile between the 1270s and Isabella's ascent to the throne in 1474. A rich kingdom, Granada served as a link (through its great port at Málaga) between North African and Christian markets, while developing its own specialized economy as an agricultural centre and producer of silk and other luxury items.

By the late fourteenth century, the cultural splendour of the city crystallized in the building of much of the fabled Alhambra, a palace unmatched in its beauty by any other building in Iberia. Dynastic strife and the growing power of Castile, after Ferdinand and Isabella restored order in the 1470s, led to the final campaign against the city and its eventual fall to Christian troops on 2 January 1492. Although the terms of surrender guaranteed the Muslim population the right to practice its religion, intolerance set in directly, and harsh measures led to forced conversions and attempts at resettling areas in Granada's hinterland with Christians. The impact of these policies was to create an unstable political situation and social hierarchies based on religion, ethnicity and language, which eventually exploded (as we shall see later) in violent *Morisco* uprisings in the Alpujarras mountains in the late 1490s and 1560s.[13]

Navarre, a small kingdom uneasily perched between France and Spain, had a long and, for a brief period, successful history, one that predated that of its more powerful neighbours to the south, east and west. In the early eleventh century, under Sancho III the Great (1000–35), Navarre became the hegemonic Christian realm in the peninsula. Sancho's sons and grandsons became the rulers of other Iberian kingdoms, which quickly overtook the power of their ancestral homeland. Ruled in the thirteenth century by the counts of Champagne and effectively under French control throughout most of the fourteenth and fifteenth centuries, Navarre came to be governed by a member of the Aragonese branch of the Trastámara family, Juan (king of Navarre, 1425–79, of Aragon, 1458–79). Thus, Navarre became deeply enmeshed in the conflicts between Castile and the Crown of Aragon, and, later in the fifteenth century, in the conflicts between France and Spain. In 1512, the area of Navarre south of the Pyrenees was annexed to Castile. Another Navarre, a small and fledgling kingdom, remained quasi-independent on the French side. Henry of Navarre (or Henry of Bourbon, as the ruling family was known), the putative king of the mountain kingdom, became king of France in 1589. His descendants ruled France until 1789 (and briefly between 1815 and 1830); in a final ironic twist, and with Republican and dictatorial interludes, the Bourbons also ruled Spain from the early eighteenth century to the twentieth century, the present king included. These Albret-Bourbons, heirs to the kings who had lost their realm to the greater power of Castile, returned to the peninsula two centuries afterwards and, under the influence of French centralizing policies, forged a new Spain from its fragmented political components.[14]

The Crown of Aragon

East of Castile, running from the Pyrenees to the Mediterranean Sea, lay a strange and wondrous political entity, known in the late Middle Ages and in the early modern period as the Crown of Aragon (*la Corona de Aragón*). In many ways, the Crown of Aragon was paradigmatic of the fragmented nature of Iberian politics, geography and language. One of the early reconquest kingdoms, Aragon's origins date back to the early ninth century. Aragon's expansion eastward and southward into Muslim lands – coinciding with its newly gained autonomy from Navarrese tutelage – began in earnest in the eleventh century. By the twelfth century, Ramón Berenguer IV (1131–62) already ruled over the county of Barcelona and the kingdom of Aragon.

This is the putative birth of the Crown of Aragon and the beginning of a long line of count-kings (also known later as the 'Principality') ruling over Catalonia as counts and the kingdom of Aragon as kings. Thus, the kings of the Crown of Aragon ruled over two distinct political entities with different constitutional rights, different parliaments (*corts*) and languages. Under James I (Jaume I, 1213–76), Aragon-Catalonia embarked on active expansion and settlement of the Mediterranean and the southeastern Muslim frontier. The island of Majorca was taken from the Muslims in 1229, and Ibiza in 1235. Southern expansion culminated with the taking of Valencia in 1238. A rich prize indeed, Valencia received its own customs (the *furs*) and, like Aragon and Catalonia, had its own parliament or *corts*. Far more than in Castile, where the monarchs ruled over a fairly unified and centralized realm, the rulers of the Crown of Aragon (who were simultaneously kings of Aragon, counts of Barcelona and kings of Valencia) had to deal individually with the assemblies of each of these political units, with their different customs, systems of taxation, and, as pointed out earlier, languages as well.

The taking of Valencia marked, effectively, the end of Aragonese-Catalan ventures in the peninsula. The work of the Reconquest fell completely on Castilian shoulders, as the Crown of Aragon turned its back on further expansion south and westward and concentrated on its Mediterranean interests. In 1285, the Crown of Aragon annexed Sicily, and by 1311 Catalan soldiers and merchants had established their rule in what became the duchies of Athens and Neopatria, areas formerly held by the emperors of Byzantium.

Under James II (1291–1327), the Crown of Aragon became a formidable Mediterranean power. As the king restored peace throughout his realms, the *corts* of Tarragona (1319) decreed an end to the traditional practice of partitioning the kingdoms among the royal heirs, and the different realms forming the Crown of Aragon were never to be divided again.[15]

After Martin I (1395–1410) died without heirs, the Crown of Aragon faced a constitutional crisis. In the midst of considerable infighting for control of the crown and rising violence, representatives of the three parliaments composing the Crown of Aragon met at Caspe and elected Ferdinand of Antequera, a co-regent of Castile and uncle to John II of Castile, as the new king. Henceforth, the Crown of Aragon was to be ruled by Castilians, and the peninsular kingdoms, with the exception of Granada and Portugal, would be ruled by one family, the Trastámaras. As we saw earlier, however, close familial ties did not prevent internecine disputes and frequent open warfare between Castile and Aragon. Moreover, the Trastámara rulers of Aragon faced protracted disagreements with the Catalan *corts*. Ferdinand I and his successors were forced to acknowledge the *Deputaçio* (see below) of Catalonia (essentially based in and controlled by Barcelona) as the spokesman for Catalan liberties and privileges.

During the rule of Alfonso V (1416–58), who exiled himself to Naples where he preferred to live and from where he ruled his Spanish kingdoms through viceroys and royal representatives, and that of his brother John II (1458–79), the Crown of Aragon faced innumerable problems. Civil unrest, open warfare between contending factions in Barcelona (the *Biga* and the *Busca*, the former composed of 'honoured citizens' and landlords; the latter representing merchants, artisans and urban workers), and the neglect of John II of Aragon, who was always drawn to Castilian affairs, led to civil war. The most vivid manifestation of this conflict was a full-scale peasant uprising, known as the war of the *Remenças* (see below, Part Two, Chapter 2).

When Ferdinand II, John II's son and heir, married Isabella of Castile in 1469 and became co-ruler of Castile in 1474 and king of Aragon at his father's death in 1479, the two main political units of 'invertebrate' Spain were united under the dual kingships of the Catholic Monarchs. But if this was a marriage of equals, what each of them brought to the marriage was very unequal indeed. Castile, in spite of its century and a half of continuous political crises, was a fairly centralized monarchy even before Isabella's reforms. With a population of perhaps as many as 4–5 million inhabitants in the 1480s (demographic estimates vary greatly) compared to 1 million for the entire Crown of Aragon, with fixed political goals such as the re-establishment of order and the conquest of Granada, with a valuable commodity for export, wool, in almost unlimited quantities, and with an emerging and vibrant literary culture, Castile was by far the dominant power within the peninsula.

The rise of Castile coincided with the economic decline of the Crown of Aragon in general (with the exception of Valencia), and of Barcelona in particular. Many of the problems affecting the eastern Spanish kingdoms were not altogether of their own making. The slow decline of the Mediterranean economy, accelerated by the opening of the Atlantic trade and by the success of Portuguese trade in the Far East, negatively affected Barcelona and other Aragonese commercial centres. In truth, the Crown of Aragon was too difficult to rule, its different constituencies too hard to balance or to run harmoniously. There were too many parliaments and special interests to contend with on an individual basis. The Catalans, above all, jealously protected their ancestral liberties and institutions. Italy and the other Aragonese Mediterranean lands presented their own set of problems. Not surprisingly, Ferdinand II threw a great deal of his energy and cunning into the affairs of Castile. After all, the rulers of the Crown of Aragon, with the exception of some Italophiles such as Alfonso V, were Castilians in blood and heart. Besides Castile, Ferdinand II concerned himself with wider European issues, and especially with the ordering or recasting of the Italian political map after 1494. There, the troops and wealth that carried the day for Spain came from Castile. The neglect of the lands of the Crown of Aragon by its kings, benign neglect at times and not so benign at others, had dire consequences for the social and political history of Spain.

Last but not least, the Catholic Monarchs also promoted an aggressive policy in the Atlantic. Castile had a long interest in the western seas. The occupation of the Canary Islands by Castilian troops in the early fifteenth century highlighted Castilian interest in the Atlantic and Africa before Columbus. Although further Castilian ventures on the western coast of Africa were effectively checked by the Portuguese, who had an earlier jump in settling a network of factories and in controlling the southward sea lanes, Castile never relinquished its Atlantic ambitions. Christopher Columbus's voyage in 1492, in his misguided effort to find a route to the 'Indies', opened, nonetheless, a fabulous new world to Castile. Although the American enterprise did not bear real profits until the conquest of Mexico in 1521, the discovery of – or encounter with – first the islands of the Caribbean and later the mainland of America shifted the centre of Spanish history and economy from the Mediterranean and Africa to the New World. The Aragonese, initially excluded from trading or settling in America, were further removed from the centres of power and economic gains.

Spain in the sixteenth century

By the early 1500s, the map of the Iberian peninsula had been dramatically reshaped. Granada and Navarre had been annexed to Castile. Portugal had found its true vocation in maritime ventures along the coasts of Africa, India and Brazil; but between 1580 and 1640, it, too, fell under Spanish rule. The two other large political units, Castile and the Crown of Aragon, which had split apart briefly after Isabella's death, were once again under a single king,

Charles I (Charles V, emperor of the Holy Roman empire), heir to the peninsular kingdoms through his maternal grandparents. But again, one must emphasize that this unity was only fulfilled in the figure of the king and that the deep political, economic, social, cultural and linguistic differences of a previous age remained almost unchanged. For the administrative and legal unity that is the landmark of true centralization, Spain had to wait until its French masters, the Bourbons, turned the plural entities of Spain into a single realm, a nation, in the eighteenth century.

The political and economic life of Spain in the sixteenth century can be discerned, in its briefest outline, through a series of themes or problems, which deeply affected the social structures of the kingdoms. These pivotal issues were: 1) the conquest and settlement of the New World from 1492 onwards and the impact of the New World on the Spanish and European economy, society and culture; 2) the establishment of the Habsburg dynasty, the birth of Imperial Spain, and the role of Spain in European affairs and in the Wars of Religion that were fought, primarily in central and northern Europe, throughout most of the sixteenth and first half of the seventeenth centuries; 3) the internal political organization of the Empire in general and of Spain in particular; 4) the rebellion of the Alpujarras.

America and Spain

When Ferdinand and Isabella decided to sponsor the rather adventurous request of Christopher Columbus in 1492, they could not have suspected the extraordinary consequences of their action. They went to their tombs – Isabella in 1504, Ferdinand in 1516 – with little understanding of what lay ahead or of how the discovery of this New World would transform Spain. In 1516, when the Aragonese king died, the Spanish enterprise in the Indies and its sparse settlements were mostly restricted to the islands of the Greater Antilles and to tentative incursions into the mainland. By then two things were becoming clear. First, there seemed to be no great profit in this affair. Hispaniola, Cuba and Puerto Rico had little or no gold, and none of the fabled spices of the East. Moreover, the native populations were dying at an alarming rate, the result of colonial abuse and disease; and the Spaniards themselves had great difficulty adapting to the diet and ecology of the Caribbean. Second, these islands and the mainland nearby were not the Indies proper. And, as most of his critics and contemporaries had argued, Columbus had erred in calculating the circumference of the earth. If this was not the Indies, if the wealth of China, Japan and the Spice Islands was nowhere to be found, what was this place? And what gain was there to be had from it?

By the mid-sixteenth century, after Cortés conquered the rich and powerful city of Tenochtitlan, the capital of the Aztec empire, in 1521, and Pizarro equally obliterated the extensive and well-organized Inca empire in the 1540s, Spain came to rule immense territorial expanses, with large native populations and untold wealth – silver mines in Guanajuato (Mexico), the fabled mines of Potosí (in today's Bolivia). A river of silver, transported to Seville by two annual fleets, found its way into the altars of churches in Extremadura and elsewhere in Castile; but, more often than not, it went to pay for the wars waged by the Habsburgs in Italy, central Europe and the Low Countries.

The impact of America was not limited to its wealth, or to the effect of that wealth on the politics and economy of the Spains and Europe. In many respects, the income from the New World was smaller than that collected from the Castilian peasantry – and here it is convenient to remember, once again, that the taming of America was a Castilian, and not a Spanish, enterprise. The inhabitants of other regions of Spain (Catalonia, Aragon, etc.) were often forbidden to migrate to the New World. Along with plentiful lucre, the encounter with a vast continent inhabited by a heterogeneous population – some highly civilized, such as the Aztecs, the Mayas, and the Incas; and some not, such as the natives in the Caribbean – presented the Spaniards with complex legal, moral, social and logistical dilemmas. The political and intellectual debates of early and mid-sixteenth-century Spain revolved around the following problems: how to make sense of the humanity of America's indigenous people, and how to treat its natives; how to settle and administer such vast territories from a distant, overseas metropolis; how to fend off the frequent forays of English, French and Dutch rivals. These concerns became important issues for the Spanish monarchy and affected its policies and behaviour at home.

America introduced a new dynamic element into Castilian and Spanish life. It siphoned off a population that Castile, for all its problems of drought and famine in the sixteenth century, could ill afford to lose. It led to a wholesale transfer of Spanish institutions, religious practices (and intolerance), social mores and culture, as well as the Castilian language, to the New World. Such large-scale colonization, beyond the borders of the Old World, had never before been undertaken by a European power. The demands of America, and the example of America, brought about a restructuring of social categories and social relations within the peninsula itself. A good number of the conquistadors, men of very humble origins, rose to positions of great prestige and power within colonial society, and even within Spain. American gold and silver, as Quevedo pointed out in the poem cited in the introduction, made nobles of lesser men, and provided the ugly with astonishing make-overs.

The flow of bullion from the New World into Europe also triggered a rise in prices in Spain and elsewhere in the European world; it had a nefarious impact – together with the growing deficit of the monarchy that was triggered by the extraordinary expenses of war and the cost of court ceremonials – on the Spanish economy. Twice in the sixteenth century, at the end of the rule of Charles I and at the conclusion of that of Philip II, the Spanish monarchs had to declare bankruptcy. The peasants, most of all, suffered immensely from these economic upheavals. Unlike their better-off counterparts, few of them had the option of migrating to America.

America – with its exotic flora and fauna, its variegated people, its paradisiacal ecology (which was already being devastated by the introduction of pigs, cows, and large-scale cultivation of sugar cane) – forced Spaniards and Europeans to rethink the world and to discard long-held notions about the nature of humanity and of their own faith. In short, the authority of such classical and medieval texts as Pliny, John of Mandeville, and others was demolished by the physical reality of the New World. Moreover, miscegenation, which became widespread in the Spanish and Portuguese colonies, and the introduction of African slaves into the New World, led to elaborations of racial constructs that attempted to preserve the privilege and power of the white colonizers. Spain, which already had a long history of dealing with both ethnic and religious heterogeneity, was forced once again to face the issue of racial plurality, not only in the Americas, but in the metropolis as well.[16]

The Habsburgs in Spain

The political history of Spain in the sixteenth century was the outcome of political alliances set in motion by the Catholic Monarchs in the late fifteenth century and of what Machiavelli described as *fortuna*, which we can translate loosely as luck or fate. The well-laid plans of Ferdinand and Isabella to achieve peninsular unity by marrying their eldest daughter, the Infanta Isabel, to João II, heir to the Portuguese throne and later king of Portugal, and to encircle France by matrimonial alliances with England (Catherine's marriage to the English heir and Joanna's marriage to Philip the Handsome, heir to Flanders), yielded very different results from those intended. The premature deaths of Isabel and her son, and the well-known difficulties of Catherine and her famous divorce from Henry VIII of England, left Joanna and her consort, Philip the Handsome, as heirs to Castile. After Isabella the Catholic's death in 1504, Ferdinand withdrew, or was forced to withdraw, to his Aragonese lands, married again, and sought a new heir for the Crown of Aragon. When Ferdinand died without issue in 1516, Charles, the son of Joanna and Philip, became the foremost heir in Christendom. Through his mother Queen Joanna, who allegedly went mad soon after the death of her husband in 1506 and was confined to a castle until her death in 1555, the young Charles, born with the century in 1500, inherited Castile and all Castilian possessions overseas. From his grandfather, Ferdinand of Aragon, Charles inherited the lands of the Crown of Aragon, the Balearic Islands, and the Aragonese claims in Italy and in the eastern Mediterranean. Through his father, Philip the Handsome, the young Charles inherited from his paternal grandmother the Low Countries (with fabulously wealthy Flanders as the centrepiece) and claims to the rich Burgundian tradition as well. Finally, from his paternal grandfather, Maximilian, the young king inherited Bohemia and the claims to the imperial title.

When in 1517 Charles travelled to Spain to claim his crowns, he spoke no Castilian (or Catalan) and came surrounded by a bevy of Flemish advisers. He was not welcomed in either Castile or Aragon, and the parliaments of both kingdoms made their granting of new taxes or subsidies conditional on various demands – among them, that the new ruler learn Castilian, dismiss his foreign retinue, and take up residence in Spain. In 1521, discontent exploded into armed insurrection, as members of the urban oligarchies and lower nobility in Castile rose up in arms in what is known as the *Comunero* movement (from community or communal). In Valencia, artisans and urban workers (*Germanías*) took violent action against authority and property. When Charles crushed the resistance in Castile at the battle of Villalar and over-powered the rebels in Valencia, he established his undisputed rule through-out the diverse kingdoms (see below). At the same time, he bribed the imperial electors into choosing him as emperor of the Holy Roman Empire.

The Habsburg inheritance, for better or worse, drew Spain into the wider affairs of Europe. Through its intervention in Italy and conflicts with France, Spain had in fact already experienced the labyrinthine antagonisms of Euro-pean dynastic politics before Charles came to the throne, but never to the extent that it did after 1521. The Habsburgs' stake in central European affairs and the rising moral and political challenges of the Reformation entangled Spanish interests, wealth and manpower in endless religious wars far away from the peninsula. Even after Charles V's abdication in 1556 – when Charles's son Philip II (1556–98) inherited Spain, the overseas empire, the Low Coun-tries, and Italian possessions; and Charles's brother Ferdinand was handed Bohemia, the German lands, and the imperial title in 1558 – Philip, the new king of Spain, was still obligated by family protocols to support Habsburg political pursuits in central Europe, a policy which in the next century would prove fatal to Spain's well-being.

The Habsburg inheritance brought more than just political complications. The social history of Spain, above all of Castile, has to be seen against a back-drop of endless wars that Castilians, mostly peasants, paid for with their taxes and, often, with their lives. The Habsburgs – or the 'Austrias', as they were known in Spain – also brought a heightened sense of ceremony, and the colours of Burgundy (black and white). Most of the things we identify today as emblems of Spain's pride of place in sixteenth-century Europe made their way into the peninsula in the coffers of the Habsburg interlopers and their advisers. But Charles V, and his son Philip who grew up in Flanders, also brought to Spain the teachings of Erasmus, a taste for Flemish art, and the paintings by Hieronymus Bosch, Pieter Brueghel and others that today play their part in making the Prado one of the greatest museums in the world.

The policies of the Habsburgs opened deep rifts in the social fabric of Spain, bringing economic collapse in the mid-sixteenth century and worsening social conditions late in the century and throughout most of the next one. The Habsburgs' political and religious policies in central Europe, even if not consciously designed against Spain, nonetheless had dire consequences for the history of the Spanish realms. And the Castilians, though always respectful and even loving of their monarchs, knew it.

There is a famous anecdote, retold by Juan Reglà in one of the volumes of Vicens Vives's *Historia de España y América*, which describes a peasant engaged in conversation with Charles V. The peasant does not know he is speaking to the emperor and complains bitterly about how the subjects of the king have ruined themselves paying taxes to sustain a foreign policy which, as the story implies, has done very little for the Castilian peasantry, or for Spain as a whole. In a satirical poem of the early seventeenth century, also cited by Reglà, Quevedo addresses the Spanish monarch more directly: 'In Navarre and Aragon / there is no one who contributes a *real* [a monetary unit] / Catalonia and Portugal are of the same opinion / Only Castile and León / and the noble Andalusian kingdom / carry the cross on their shoulders / Catholic majesty [the title of the king of Spain]'.[17]

The administrative and political organization of Spain and its empire

In this brief account of what Spain was like in the sixteenth century, some attention must be given to the institutional structures that allowed for the running of Spain and its empire. A good number of the administrative practices of sixteenth-century Spain can be traced to the reforms the Catholic Monarchs carried out in late fifteenth-century Castile, though many of the new institutions harkened back to earlier medieval precedents. The councils (of the Inquisition, of the Santa Hermandad, of the Indies, etc.) served as the equivalent of ministries today and oversaw the conduct of affairs within their well-delimited jurisdictions. The Habsburgs adopted, without too many alterations, many of these late medieval administrative practices to run their burgeoning empire. But they also introduced significant changes.

The contrasts between Charles V and his son Philip II were enormous. The former accompanied his troops to the battlefield, and still issued personal challenges to rival kings. The latter worked tirelessly at his desk. Charles V was one of the last medieval kings who remained captive to a code of chivalry and courtliness. Philip II was certainly courtly as well, but he was first and foremost a master (and servant) of the nascent state. Surrounded by a host of secretaries, Philip attempted to supervise and to run everything that pertained to his kingdoms. Such meticulous rule required a centre. The Castilian monarchy – unlike the Crown of Aragon, where kings had clearly defined administrative centres at Zaragoza, Barcelona and Valencia – had long been a peripatetic monarchy. Burgos, Valladolid, Toledo, Seville, Granada and other cities had served, at one time or another, as temporary administrative capitals and ceremonial centres for Castilian rulers. Philip II invented a new capital, Madrid. The city lay close enough to his beloved monastery at the Escorial; and in the mid-sixteenth century its insignificance as a city, its lack of powerful local lords (which Seville had) or powerful ecclesiastics (which Toledo had), rendered it the perfect site for a royal capital. Toledo desperately coveted the honour of being the capital, but its powerful Church posed an obstacle to Philip's jealous wish to rule, at least in Castile, without restrictions.

Madrid thus became the capital of a highly centralized kingdom, Castile, and of a rather 'invertebrate' empire, the Spanish Empire. Nothing really changed, except that now the Spanish kings remained in one place instead of constantly perambulating across the Castilian plain. Castile still ruled, while the rest of the empire – the Crown of Aragon, Italy, the Low Countries, and America – enjoyed some of the benefits (and suffered the great inconvenience) of having Castilian masters. As Quevedo's poem makes clear, the non-Castilian domains contributed little in terms of taxes (with the exception of America), and even less in terms of manpower. Castile thus carried an inordinately heavy burden – the cross of 'Catholic majesty' – upon its spindly shoulders. Its inability to continue carrying this burden unassisted brought about the catastrophes of 1640 and the demise of Spain as a great power in European affairs.

Castilian hegemony was not limited to politics, taxes and war, but extended to a wide range of cultural and spiritual matters. As will be seen later, the Castilian Church led the ecclesiastical reforms that were subsequently imposed throughout the Spains; the Inquisition headquarters resided in Madrid. Far more significantly, Castile imposed its language. It did so in pitiless ways, which offended the sensibilities of subjects throughout the empire. By the sixteenth century, advancement in the royal bureaucracy was not restricted to Castilians, though they enjoyed the lion's share of positions, but the Castilian language was a requirement. The proud viceroys, servants of the emperor-king, poured out of Castile into the rest of the empire to rule parts that were not Castile as representatives of the king, while Philip II, now safely ensconced in his austere rooms at the monastery of the Escorial, sat serenely at the centre of his vast web.

The rebellion of the Alpujarras

For the dynamics of social relations in Spain, the revolt of the Alpujarras was, in the sixteenth century, what the attacks against *Conversos* and the Edict of Expulsion of 1492 had been in the fifteenth: a litmus test of the ability of Spaniards to integrate people with different languages and customs into the national project. The terms of the surrender of Granada guaranteed the defeated Muslims the freedom of their faith. These terms, despite the policy of tolerance adopted by Hernando de Talavera, the first archbishop of the newly conquered city, were soon set aside. Around the turn of the century (1499), there was increased pressure on the Muslims of Granada to convert to Christianity. In 1499, the Moors in the rugged countryside south of Granada, the Alpujarras, rose up in arms against their Christian overlords. Quickly put down, the uprising, known as the First Alpujarras rebellion, gave added impetus to the Catholic Monarchs' long-held ambition of conquering North Africa and establishing Christian rule there. Ferdinand and Isabella recognized, as did their adviser, the archbishop of Toledo Ximénez de Cisneros, the bond linking North Africa and the Muslim population of Iberia. They sought to sever this connection by carrying the banner of Castile across the Mediterranean. The death of Isabella in 1504 and the new demands of war in Italy, however, limited Castilian operations in North Africa to a few territorial gains, such as Oran, and brought about a policy of accommodation, whereby the Moors were nominally converted to Christianity but were in reality free to practice their ancestral religion, to speak the Arabic language, and to dress as Muslims.

A complex set of economic and political factors – the decline of silk manufacturing, the mainstay of *Morisco* wealth, and internecine struggles between noble factions – served as context for heightened inquisitorial activities against the *Moriscos*. In 1566, when the forty-year truce and moratorium on repression against former Muslim came to an end, Philip II, seeing that little progress had been made in integrating *Moriscos* into Christian and Spanish life, ordered a series of punitive measures. These attacks against the *Morisco* religion, language and culture were fuelled by religious intolerance and by fears of a Turkish invasion linking up with a *Morisco* fifth column. In Chapter 7, we will examine in greater detail the violence that resulted from these measures, but for now it suffices to say that Philip II's actions led to a second violent uprising in the Alpujarras. The war to subdue the rebels was carried out with unusual savagery on both sides, and the eventual defeat of the *Moriscos* led to their relocation throughout small towns in Castile and to the migration – over 50,000 strong – of Christian settlers into the now emptied lands around Granada. The consequences for the history of social relations in Spain were considerable, as was the resulting endemic violence, which continued to plague the mountains of southern Spain into the modern age.[18]

Culture

Even if briefly, we must examine the cultural developments of Spain in the period between 1400 and 1600. In fifteenth-century Spain, the three great literary languages, Galician, Catalan and Castilian, followed very different courses. Galician, which in the twelfth and thirteenth centuries had been the preferred language of courtly poetry, had, for all practical purposes, ceased to be a literary language. Poets such as Alfonso Alvarez de Villasandino (1345–1424?) and others, though Galician by birth, wrote in Castilian and made their living from the patronage of great Castilian lords. The geographical isolation of Galicia and its increased economic backwardness made it a secondary cultural centre by the late fifteenth century and kept it outside the main currents of Spanish culture until the nineteenth century.

In Castile and in the Crown of Aragon, the story was very different indeed. The political ties to Naples and the familiarity with Italy made fifteenth-century Castile, Aragon and Catalonia lively cultural centres. The embrace of Italian humanism and the translation of Italian literary works were parallelled by the production of vigorous Catalan and Castilian works of theatre, poetry and chivalrous romances. Such distinguished works as Fernando de Rojas's play *La Celestina*, the poetry of Jorge Manrique, and the romances of Martorell indicate the high degree of sophistication achieved by a small literary elite. Nobles became patrons of the arts, collected books, and, like Jorge Manrique and Iñigo de Mendoza, wrote great works of art. The so-called 'arms vs. letters' controversy was, by the fifteenth century, a phantasm; arms and letters defined nobility throughout most of the lands of the Spains (see Part Two, Chapter 3).

This cultural revival was not limited to those of high rank. The growing needs of the nascent state, above all in Castile, required a well-trained bureaucracy. Universities became, by the fifteenth century, and much more so by the sixteenth, avenues for social promotion. The children of the urban elite and of the lower nobility, and the university-trained *letrados,* came to occupy an important place in Spanish society as servants of the Crown and members of the professional classes. Moreover, by the end of the fifteenth century, the extensive reforms of the Catholic Monarchs included a renewal of educational zeal. The work of Nebrija – above all his *Arte de la lengua castellana* (*The Art of the Castilian Language*) in 1492, the first grammar of a modern European language – established Castilian as the 'language of Empire'. In addition, the philological work sponsored by Cardinal Ximénez de Cisneros, founder of the University of Alcalá de Henares (1508), led to the fabled polyglot Bible – an edition of the Bible with parallel versions in Hebrew, Chaldean, Greek and Latin – a major contribution of pre-Golden Age Spain to European culture.

The ascendancy of Castilian, now associated with the centralizing policies of Castile and with the discovery of the New World, marked the demise of Catalan. In sixteenth-century Spain, Aragonese, Valencian and Catalan authors, many of whose works were crucial to the development of the Golden Age of Spanish letters (one of the best examples is Juan Boscán, who wrote poetry in the style of Petrarch), now wrote exclusively in Castilian, even though at the local level Catalan remained the language of business in the eastern part of the peninsula for both oral and written transactions.

By the early sixteenth century, coinciding with the poetry of Garcilaso de la Vega (1501?–36), the *Siglo de Oro* (the Golden Age) of Spanish literature and art was well under way. For the next 120 years, Spain's output of literary, artistic and musical masterpieces equalled or surpassed that of any other European culture. The plays of Lope de Vega, Tirso de Molina and the incomparable Calderón de la Barca, the picaresque novels, the great novels by Cervantes, and the paintings of El Greco and others did more than just contribute to the dazzling cultural life of early modern Europe. Spanish high culture, its literature and art, was, perhaps more than in any other European culture, deeply embedded in the social fabric of the country, and in its social transformations.[19]

Conclusion

Between 1400 and 1600, Spain underwent important political and cultural transformations. Its variegated geography and climate dictated the fragmenting of its political organization. When our story begins, at the end of the fourteenth century, the Iberian peninsula was divided into distinct, often warring, political entities. Castile, lying in northwestern, central, and south-central Iberia, was the largest and most populated of the kingdoms, but the Crown of Aragon – a political unit comprising three independent realms (Aragon, Catalonia and Valencia) – cultivated its own political goals and fostered institutions that differed completely from those of Castile. In the southeast, the Muslim kingdom of Granada held its own until 1492, while on the opposite corner of the peninsula Navarre retained a fledgling independence until its final absorption into Spain in the early sixteenth century. Portugal, on the western front of the peninsula, completed the complex political mosaic of Iberia.

After Ferdinand and Isabella centralized power in Castile, their Habsburg descendants ruled a nominally united Spain throughout the sixteenth century. As we have seen, this unity was only superficial, and the assorted constituents – mainly Castile and the three branches of the Crown of Aragon – preserved their particular institutions. Culturally, however, Castile's supremacy in the sixteenth century led to the domination of the Castilian language and its literary forms over other regionally autochthonous forms. In many respects, the unrelenting pursuit of political and cultural autonomy in the last thirty years of the twentieth century has been an attempt to reverse the policies of late medieval and early modern Spanish kings.

Notes

1. John H. Elliott has already pointed out the importance of geography and climate in the development of early modern Spain and the limitations they imposed on the political aspirations of the Spanish monarchs. See his *Richelieu and Olivares* (Cambridge, 1984), 160; and his *Imperial Spain, 1469–1716* (London, 1963), introduction and ch. 1. See also the classic and wide-ranging study by Fernand Braudel, *The Mediterranean and the Mediterranean World in the Age of Philip II*, 2 vols (New York, 1975), especially vol. I.

2. This section on the geography and climate of Spain is taken from several manuals of geography. See Ruth Way, *A Geography of Spain and Portugal* (London, 1962); María de Bolos y Capdevila, Antonio Paluzie and Angela Guerrero, *Geografía de España* (Barcelona, 1969); Valentín Cabero, *El espacio geográfico castellano-leonés* (Valladolid, 1982). In addition, see Braudel, *The Mediterranean and the Mediterranean World*, vol. I, and Teofilo F. Ruiz, *Crisis and Continuity: Land and Town in Late Medieval Castile* (Philadelphia, 1994), Part I, ch. 1.

3. *Viajes de extranjeros por España y Portugal*, ed. José García Mercadal, 3 vols (Madrid, 1952), I: 295, 695, 898, et passim.

4. *Viajes de extranjeros*, I: 97, 117–18, 171, 218, 265–6, 268–70, 295–7, 424, 456, 606, 613–21, et passim.

5. For an excellent study of one of these subregions and the differences from the overall climate and topography of the plain of Old Castile see José Ortega y Varcarcel, *La transformación de un espacio rural: las montañas de Burgos, estudio de geografía regional* (Valladolid, 1974).

6. *Viajes de extranjeros*, I: 338–9.

7. *Viajes de extranjeros*, I: 291, 336–7, 342 (this was the case in Valencia as well), et passim.

8. José Ortega y Gasset, *España invertebrada* (Madrid, 1962), 23–66.

9. See John Lynch, *Spain under the Habsburgs*, 2nd edn, 2 vols (New York, 1984), II: 44–61. For the number of Jews in Spain and the historiographical controversy over their number see Henry Kamen, 'The Mediterranean and the Expulsion of Spanish Jews in 1492', *Past & Present*, 119 (1988): 30–55.

10. See Angus MacKay, 'Popular Movements and Pogroms in Fifteenth-Century Castile', *Past & Present*, 55 (1972): 33–67.

11. See Angus MacKay, 'Ritual and Propaganda in Fifteenth-Century Castile', *Past & Present*, 107 (1985): 3–43.

12. For the history of Castile in the fifteenth century, as well as other peninsular kingdoms, see Angus MacKay, *Spain in the Middle Ages: From Frontier to Empire, 1000–1500* (London, 1977), 121–212; Joseph F. O'Callaghan, *A History of Medieval Spain* (Ithaca, 1975), 521–676. See also Luis Suárez Fernández, *Nobleza y monarquía: puntos de vista sobre la historia política castellana del siglo XV* (Valladolid, 1975), 101–271.

13. On the history of Granada see L.P. Harvey, *Islamic Spain, 1250–1500* (Chicago, 1990) and Miguel Angel Ladero Quesada, *Granada: historia de un país islámico (1232–1517)*, 3rd edn (Madrid, 1989).

14. José María Lacarra, *Historia política del reino de Navarra*, 3 vols (Pamplona, 1973).

15. For this and the next section dealing with the Crown of Aragon in the late Middle Ages see Jocelyn N. Hillgarth, *The Spanish Kingdoms, 1250–1516*, 2 vols (Oxford, 1976–78); Thomas N. Bisson, *The Medieval Crown of Aragon: A Short History* (Oxford, 1986).

16. The literature on the relationship between the metropolis (Spain) and its colonies (America) is vast indeed. A few titles will suffice here. See Alfred W. Crosby, *The Columbian Voyages: The Columbian Exchange and their Historians* (Washington, 1987); Felipe Fernández-Armesto, *Columbus* (Oxford, 1991); William D. and Carla Rahn Phillips, *The Worlds of Christopher Columbus* (Cambridge, 1992); Inga

Clendinnen, *Aztecs* (Cambridge, 1991); John H. Elliott, *Spain and Its World 1500–1700: Selected Essays* (New Haven, 1993). See also Anthony Grafton, *New Worlds and Ancient Texts: The Power of Tradition and the Shock of Discovery* (Cambridge, MA, 1992).

17. Jaume Vicens Vives (ed.), *Historia de España y América. Social y económica*, 5 vols (Barcelona, 1972), III: 101, 155.

18. For the political history of the period outlined before see Elliott, *Imperial Spain*, and Lynch, *Spain under the Habsburgs*.

19. For the cultural and literary history of late medieval and early modern Spain see, *inter alia*, Otis Green, *Spain and the Western Tradition*, 4 vols (Madison, WI, 1968).

PART TWO

A society of orders

Chapter 2

Those who have not: peasants and town dwellers

'The world had peasants before it had nobles', said the peasant woman from the village of La Sagra, offering a nugget of popular wisdom to the officials who were collecting information for the *Relaciones histórico geográficas*, the great survey of Castilian customs ordered by Philip II in the late sixteenth century.[1] Historians, following traditional fifteenth- and sixteenth-century discourses, have nonetheless preferred to endorse the notion of a hierarchical order of nobles and of clergymen on top and of peasants on the bottom. Lacking access to the centres of power, the peasants were indeed outranked by the nobility, the clergy, and even the urban population. But their endless toil and financial contributions supported the entire edifice of society. As the Abbé Sieyes argued in his influential pamphlet *What Is the Third Estate?* (1789), without noblemen or clergymen, the French nation would still have endured; without the third estate, i.e. those who worked, it would not. In the fifteenth and sixteenth centuries, Spain would not have endured without its peasants.

In terms of numbers and economic output, those who worked the land, often under extremely harsh conditions and for very meagre returns, fed and paid for the upkeep of all of society. They were represented by the discourse of the period as vulgar and ignorant, as occasionally brutish and less than human. But even though they were viewed as objects of ridicule at best, and were more often than not despised and seen as degraded,[2] the peasants remained, for as long as they could, doggedly faithful to the working and tending of the land.

Peasants[3]

I have been using the term peasant to describe what in the late sixteenth century amounted to probably over 80 per cent of the entire population of Spain; but the term peasant is packed with strong ideological connotations that do not always fit the differential conditions and social standings of those who worked and lived on the land. In short, the social rank of those who engaged in agriculture varied and encompassed many different types of people. In the period under study, the social, economic and cultural distance between a well-to-do farmer – in many respects equal in standing to a member of the lower nobility – and an agricultural journeyman was forbidding indeed. The documents of the age and the language of the theatre use the term *'labrador'* (one who ploughs the field), but many *labradores* described in the sources never put their hands to a plough; others did it for them.

We are therefore confronted, at the very beginning of this enquiry, with the problem not just of defining social subsets within a variety of social and economic niches which the people we call peasants occupied, but of considering regional differences, varying agricultural practices, and the different types of settlements that covered Spain from corner to corner. How are we, then, to classify the peasants? And how did the diverse social levels in Spain operate and interact in the late Middle Ages and early modern period? There are several ways to establish a typology of the Spanish peasantry. A regional approach would group the peasantry according to areas of inhabitation. Peasants in verdant Cantabria (northern Spain) had different lifestyles, lived in smaller villages, and engaged in agricultural pursuits and livestock activities that differed from those of Andalusia or Valencia in the south and southeast of the peninsula. In the small and numerous villages of the north, many peasants enjoyed full ownership of their lands or most likely had long-term or life leases. They engaged in dairy farming, tended to livestock, and grew fruit trees and some grain. In the south, large villages were settled quite at a distance from one another. The peasants who lived there laboured as daily journeymen in large latifundia and engaged in the typical agricultural tasks of the south: the cultivation and care of vineyards, olive trees and cereals in Andalusia, and the irrigation and care of produce gardens in Valencia.

In the end, however, the boundary between different types of peasants – or between those we call peasants and other kinds of farmers – was defined by how much land was owned or held in emphyteutic leases; from whom the land was held and under what terms (i.e. the outlay of rent and/or tithes); the size of the family; the productivity of the holding; the type of inheritance; and myriad other factors. A complex blend of rural components yielded in each instance very different groups of peasants. Their economic well-being, or lack thereof, determined not only their social status within the village community, but also their diet, health, education, lifestyle, hopes for social mobility, and the type of relationship they could aspire to with their betters, and with regional and kingdom-wide officials. As we move into the late sixteenth century, we find local and royal authorities imposing ever greater fiscal demands on both affluent and struggling peasants.

Economic standing, however, was not the sole determinant of social position. Historical circumstances also affected social status. In general terms, one can argue that in spite of the widespread violence that plagued Castile and the Crown of Aragon throughout most of the fifteenth century, there was a marked economic recovery (much more so in Castile than in Aragon), which led to improved conditions for the peasantry. This economic recovery began to run out of steam by the mid-sixteenth century. Inflation (provoked in part by the influx of silver from America and the increasingly heavier taxes which the Spanish Crown imposed primarily on Castilian peasants to pay for wars in central Europe and the Low Countries), droughts and devastating plagues throughout most of the sixteenth century radically affected those who worked and lived on the land, and drove many fairly prosperous farmers into poverty. This led (again, mostly in Castile) to a large migration from the countryside to city.[4]

Nevertheless, even if we take into account these historical factors, the decisive criteria for determining types of farmers/peasants remain, I want to emphasize, the categories mentioned above: whether peasants owned or held land in long-term usufruct; and whether peasants, having little or no access to land, hired themselves out at harvest time. The impoverished majority in fact possessed no land at all, and either owned or rented, which, in southern Spain, in areas of Aragon, and in fifteenth-century Catalonia, meant a lifetime of hard economic choices and gruelling toil with little or no reward.

Owners, renters and journeymen

The census of 1792, though carried out long after the chronological limits of this book, provides support for the typology I have been suggesting. Although we cannot always extrapolate from a later period, fragmentary censuses of an earlier age exhibited similar classifications of peasants. The *labradores* – a general term for all those who cultivated the land – were subdivided in 1792, as they had been in earlier surveys, into three different categories: *jornaleros* (daily workers, journeymen); *arrendatarios* (renters holding the usufruct of the land and paying a *censo*, a fixed rent); and *propietarios* (owners). In 1792 – the averages may have differed in the fifteenth and sixteenth centuries, but not by much – *jornaleros* comprised 52.8 per cent, renters 30.6 per cent, and owners 16.5 per cent of the entire peasant population. This is very bad news indeed. At the end of the eighteenth century, less than half of all the peasants in Spain owned land, and the majority held so little land as to make their employment as agricultural journeymen an unavoidable necessity. Almost one-third of all the *labradores* worked the lands of others under complicated and diverse arrangements; less than one-sixth of the peasants owned their land outright.

These averages, however, varied from area to area; and in the late Middle Ages and early modern period, regional social and economic variations were more sharply delineated than in the late eighteenth century. Regional conditions affected not only the peasants' relation to the land and to their lords; they also dictated patterns of inheritance, family structure and demographic distribution.

Demography and patterns of inhabitation

We do not have reliable estimates of Spain's population until the late sixteenth century. The disasters of the fourteenth century (plague, war, famines, adverse climate) had a deleterious effect on the population of Spain. By the early fifteenth century, after a mild recovery, the population of Castile may have reached 4,000,000 people. Catalonia, and especially Barcelona, which had suffered a great deal of political disturbances and economic reverses, may have had only 300,000 inhabitants altogether, while Aragon and Valencia probably had around 200,000 inhabitants each. Mallorca had around 50,000 inhabitants, while Navarre's population may have reached 100,000. If these figures are correct – and medieval demography is, at best, a guessing game – then the lands that eventually became Spain in the early fifteenth century, just half a century after the disastrous crises of the fourteenth century and the plague, housed a population of around 5,000,000 inhabitants. This, however, may be a high estimate. The censuses of 1528/30 and 1591 yielded the approximate figures of 4,698,000 and 6,632,000 inhabitants respectively, pointing to an impressive rise in population in the sixteenth century. The figures are somewhat deceiving; for by the 1550s the demographic tide was turning, and the catastrophes of the late sixteenth century (again, a combination of plagues, famines, drought and high taxes) reduced the population to 6,000,000 by 1623.[5]

If, according to the censuses, approximately 80 per cent of this population were peasants, then as many as 5,305,600 peasants worked the lands of Spain in 1590. This figure may be conservative, since a great number of cities in Iberia were essentially large rural towns. In places such as Cuenca, a city with an important textile industry, 10 per cent of the active population (i.e. heads of household) were listed in the census as day-labourers engaged in rural work. Seville, the largest city in the peninsula and a bustling centre for the American trade, had neighbourhoods such as Triana, San Gil and others in which more than one-fifth of the active population worked in agriculture. Two points need to be made here: first, that many people who engaged in urban trades and who have been considered urban dwellers in fact laboured as rural workers, either full-time or on a seasonal basis; second, that the intimacy between urban and rural centres in most of Spain contravenes the notion of a dichotomous city–country relationship.

As despised as peasants were at times, peasant lifestyle, diet and mores pervaded the everyday life of the Spanish realms. Aragon, which in the sixteenth century had one of the lowest population density in the peninsula, was an empty, almost deserted landscape, dotted with a few settlements by the river banks. Inhabited mostly by *Morisco* peasants (see below), Aragon had two or three real urban areas, among them Zaragoza and Calatayud, but the rest of its towns and cities were semi-urban islands in a sea of rural communities. Only when we look at such cities as Seville (and we have already seen a strong rural presence in that city), Barcelona and Valencia can we speak of urban societies that are fairly distinct from the surrounding rural world. The point here, of course, is that, like most of Europe, Spain was an intensely rural world, and that the boundaries between its urban and rural spheres were vague indeed.

This large and motley peasant population was not always a stable one. The image of the immovable peasant, fixed upon the land and hardly ever abandoning his village, is very much a myth. As David Vassberg has convincingly shown, Castilian villagers were quite a peripatetic group, and the same can be said of peasants in other regions as well.[6] Moreover, a perceptible movement from centre to periphery – from the high, dry plains and the cereal-growing areas of Castile and Aragon to the rain-rich or irrigated areas of the Basque country, Catalonia and Andalusia – took place in Castile from the late fifteenth to the late sixteenth century, and accelerated after the mid-sixteenth century. These regions specialized in different types of agriculture – dairy farming, the tending of fruit trees in the north, and the cultivation of olive trees and wine crops in the south. Two other types of peasant demographic moves can also be discerned: from the countryside to the towns, as agriculture collapsed in the late sixteenth century; and from the metropolis to the American colonies, as the promise of the New World lured Spaniards away from their homeland. Those who owned, held or worked the land were thus not a static or stable population; to do them justice, we must view them in their great diversity and through the prism of social and economic transformations that radically altered their lives in this period.

Family structure and inheritance

The peasant family in late medieval and early modern Spain was a nuclear or stem one: that is, a couple and their children. This does not mean that single households or extended family groups did not exist, but on the whole more than 80 per cent of all peasant families conformed to the nuclear type. There were, however, regional exceptions. The Basque region and some parts of Old Catalonia, areas that were fairly similar in their topography, developed different ways of working and organizing the land. Known as the *caserío* in the Basque region and the *mas* in Old Catalonia (see below), these isolated, large households controlled fairly sizeable stretches of rural property surrounding the central house. Important departures from the normative type of village organization, the *caserío* and the *mas* often housed – because of the necessity of labour – extended families and dependents.[7]

Peasant life – its social organization, and the way in which the arable was cultivated – was governed by patterns of inheritance. Who would inherit the rights to the land? And under what terms? The need to resolve these urgent questions encouraged the development of different forms of organizing the soil. Although the great noble families and their bourgeois counterparts had embraced the principle of primogeniture – the favouring of the first-born male in the division of property – since the thirteenth century, the practice of partible inheritance was still regularly practised by Spanish peasants. These fairly egalitarian partitions of property acknowledged sons and daughters alike, though in locations such as Murcia men received land and women money. There were regional exceptions to this predilection for partible inheritance. In the *mas* and to a lesser extent in the *caserío*, inheritance rights were usually vested in the oldest male or, in the absence of males in Catalonia, in the oldest daughter. This type of legacy, however, carried with it the distinct obligation of providing for other siblings, either by paying for an education or apprenticeship or by funding dowries for the females. Partible inheritance ran counter to the individual peasant's desire to consolidate his or her holdings. The history of agriculture in pre-modern Spain oscillated precariously between expansion and/or consolidation of holdings through purchases and marriage – in what was a very lively market for land – and their eventual fragmentation through partible inheritance.

The peasantry: local and regional differences

Later on we shall see examples of the variety of peasant types in the village community, but at present I would like to draw a broad portrait of peasant life in late medieval and early modern Spain.

Northern Spain
As indicated earlier, there were, and still are, significant regional differences in how the peasants lived, worked the land, and related to those above them. Throughout most of Galicia, Asturias, the Basque country and Catalonia, peasants worked the land under different types of lordships, and were subject to particular rights and obligations. Lordships in the region – we cannot think of peasants without lords – ranged from distant and neglectful to predatory and oppressive; similarly, the peasantry enjoyed a wide range of freedom, from almost complete usufruct of the land they cultivated to servitude in some parts of Catalonia until at least the 1480s. In Galicia and throughout large sections of Asturias, ecclesiastical lords (large monasteries, cathedral chapters, collegiate churches) and lay lords held the peasants in their grip by means of ancient systems of land tenure and emphyteutic agreements (long-term or perpetual possession or usufruct of the land). More than anywhere else in Spain, property in these regions was progressively fragmented into smaller holdings through inheritance and subleasing. This kind of minuscule plot, the *minifundio*, has remained a feature of Galician life to this day. In the northwest of Spain, most peasants held small tracts of land from lords or from other peasants. These modest holdings barely allowed for a living and forced Galicians to take up seafaring activities (mostly fishing) and to migrate to other parts of the kingdom or to America.

East of Galicia and Asturias, in Cantabria and in parts of the Basque country, peasants 'owned' or, more likely, held lands in long-term, lifetime or 'forever' leases from a variety of lords. The dues they paid their lords or the king – even peasants who 'owned' their land held it, theoretically, from the king – varied from village to village; and even within the village itself, rents and obligations fluctuated from family to family, and from lord to lord. The mountainous northeast (Cantabria, the Basque homeland, northern Castile) thus did not experience the extreme fragmentation of property that plagued northwestern Spain. Scattered in small villages, some with scarcely more than sixteen *vecinos* (heads of household) or seventy to eighty inhabitants, the peasants engaged in subsistence farming, livestock tending, and the growing of fruit trees. Entrenched in their village communities, they were somewhat protected from the excesses of their lords by ancient customs and traditions. One such tradition, in the region of Oña during harvest time, was the limitation of time designated to working the lord's lands to four days per week.

In the already mentioned survey of 1792, Asturias shows an average of 3.1 per cent journeymen, 91.5 per cent renters, and 5.5 per cent owners; these figures constitute a middle ground between the considerably fragmented holdings of Galicia and the more stable ones in Cantabria. In northwest and north-central Spain, excepting the Basque homeland, lands were overwhelmingly occupied by renters with few journeymen. Demographic circumstances thus discouraged conflict from developing between the landed and the landless. This is not to imply that social differences did not exist, but they were predicated on the expanse of holdings rather than on the distinction of mere ownership.

One cannot, however, extrapolate from these circumstances to nearby areas. Each region, because of its peculiar history and local conditions, developed differently. As serfdom began to wane throughout the medieval West, with the expansion of the arable in the eleventh and twelfth centuries, servitude was imposed with a vengeance in parts of Old Catalonia, an area geographically similar to Cantabria or Asturias, where serfdom never prospered, even in an earlier age.

In 1400, close to a quarter of the entire population of Catalonia (and one-third of all its peasants) were serfs. This was at a time when serfdom had practically disappeared from other parts of the medieval West. Moreover, most peasants in the Spains, certainly throughout all of Castile and to a lesser extent in Aragon, were 'free'; they owed rents or payments to their lords but were not bound to the soil or subject to the humiliating dues (*chevage*, capitation fees) long associated with servitude. The story of the Catalan serfs, and their struggle for freedom in the fifteenth century, is remarkable indeed. How they came to be bound to the soil by predatory lords; how their servile condition was legitimated; and, more significantly, how these peasants gained their release from servitude – the only successful peasant uprising in western history – is a long and complex story.

Paul Freedman, in his excellent book *The Origins of Peasant Servitude*, provides a clear description and analysis of these events. According to Freedman, from 1000 to 1300 a considerable number of peasants in Old Catalonia were enserfed, as lords violently enforced their jurisdiction and power over them. At a time of weak royal control, the legislation of Catalonia's *corts* (parliament, assembly) sanctioned lordly violence against the peasantry, as well as the lords' economic and social control of the countryside. By 1400, the lords had imposed and legalized *mal usos* (arbitrary and abusive customs imposed on the peasantry), and required a redemption fee (*remença*) to free the peasants. After the Black Death and the crisis of late medieval society (which, as in other areas of Spain, should have improved the terms of peasant tenure and work because of labour shortages and the availability of better lands), the lords defied market forces and demographic decline and tightened even further their grip on the peasants. Moreover, throughout the fifteenth century, the lords enlisted lawyers, theologians and other learned people to provide moral, legal and historical (or pseudohistorical) arguments to validate serfdom. By 1462–72, with the Aragonese civil war raging in the background, the peasants, with the support of the Crown, waged a successful campaign against the nobility and their system of bondage. By 1486, the serfs of Old Catalonia had gained their freedom. These peasants, as Freedman shows, were different from the common stereotypes of serfs. Articulate and economically self-reliant, they sought liberty by a three-pronged startegy: they sent ambassadors to plead their case to the royal court in far-off Naples (and gained royal support for their demands in the process), purchased their freedom from their lords, and, when that failed, defeated the nobility in pitched battle.[8]

The case of Old Catalonia is even more remarkable when one considers that the circumstances of its peasants differed little from those of peasants elsewhere in Iberia. Shortly after the Black Death in 1350, the lords in northern Castile attempted to restrict the movement of peasants. The *fuero viejo de Castilla*, a compilation of customary laws, contained provisions to that effect; even so, the lords were not successful in having them enforced. In Aragon, on the other hand, the large *Morisco* population was in a state of semi-servitude under their Christian lords, even though by law they were deemed 'free'. Thus, similar conditions could lead to 'freedom' in one area, but promote serfdom in another.

Equally striking is the subsequent development of Old Catalonia's peasantry from servile to fairly well-to-do. From the sixteenth century onwards, a good number of peasants gained access to land by means of emphyteutic agreements. This was the *mas*, a homogeneous extension of farm land (between 100 and 200 hectares), with the household located in the centre of the farm. Through different strategies – late marriages, matrimonial alliances with female heirs (*pubilla*) – the *hereu*, heir and formal holder of the *mas*, sought to expand his patrimony. At the same time, it was not uncommon for the *hereu* to sublease portions of the *mas* to small farmers. In fact, in the region of Girona, the heartland of late medieval servitude, a quarter of all the cultivated land was divided into more than 30,000 small holdings and held by peasants through emphyteutic contracts in the eighteenth and nineteenth centuries.[9]

Central Spain

In central Spain, the mesetas of Old and New Castile were dominated by strong rural councils and by the sway of communal traditions. In these villages, communal practices and the use of common land (mostly for pasture) persisted against the onslaught of privatization. David Vassberg's wonderful book *Land and Society in Golden Age Castile* shows the durability of communal practices into the early modern period in the face of powerful urban interests.[10] The example of Soria, a small northern Castilian city close to the Aragonese border, and its extensive hinterland, illustrates the manifold conditions under which peasants lived and worked. In the mountains of Soria, most village lands were communal. The peasants held land individually, as well as having a share in the use of the commons. Patterns of landholding in the mountains of Soria parallelled those in Cantabria; peasants holding, or sometimes owning, a small piece of land was the norm. On the Castilian plains, however, the large domain, owned or held by ecclesiastical and lay lords or by the municipal council of Soria, dominated the landscape. Peasants rented lands from these lords – in long-term, but not necessarily advantageous leases – and paid their dues mostly in kind. This was, at best, a subsistence agriculture, with some specialization in the production of flax and saffron. But agriculture in the region of Soria, as in most of Spain, was already on the wane by the mid-sixteenth century.

The wealth of Soria consisted in livestock. It was the heartland of the Mesta (the guild of sheep-herders); the city itself was the terminus for one of the most important routes of the transhumance. The flocks of Soria travelled south to Extremadura, north to Navarre, and east to Aragon in search of pasture. In addition to long-distance transhumance, Soria and other Mesta locations organized local annual movement of flocks, and had large flocks that did not travel. As with land ownership or usufruct, sharp social differences existed among livestock owners. Those with large flocks were able to gain a significant foothold in the political and social life of Soria, thus wielding a great deal of influence on the organization and control of the rural landscape. Below them, a whole range of middling and small men followed. Their fortunes and social standing in their respective villages depended on the amount of livestock they owned. The lower we descend in the social hierarchy, the closer we come to the lowly peasants barely scraping a living, gaining part or most of their income by hiring themselves out as day-labourers.[11]

Eastward, across the Iberian mountains, in the kingdom of Aragon, the conditions under which peasants lived were radically different. In the

47

overwhelmingly rural world of this period, small settlements along river-
banks, mainly along the Ebro river, dotted an otherwise empty and deserted
landscape. This was a world of large lordships, and of lands held or worked
almost exclusively by *Moriscos* in semi-servile conditions. Though nominally
converted to Christianity, the *Moriscos* of Aragon held on tightly to their
religion and language – a form of resistance to crushing lordships. Their
ancestry and dependence on harsh lords secured the *Moriscos* the lowest rung
on the social ladder of the peasantry. Yet, because of their work habits, thrifti-
ness and agriculture expertise, the *Moriscos* did well with what little they
had. Foreign travellers almost always remarked on how well tended the lands
worked by the *Moriscos* were, how prosperous they seemed in comparison to
those of Christian peasants.[12]

Southern Spain

As we travel south, the landscape and the conditions of the peasantry change.
The broad arch of southern Iberia, which extends from the Atlantic to the
Mediterranean Sea, was a land of latifundia (large estates). Small peasant-
landowners could also be found here and there, above all in eastern Andalusia. Vassberg, for example, reports that in Lorca (Murcia) the irrigated plain
was 'largely in peasant hands and in an extremely subdivided state', and that
in the area of Granada, after the Alpujarras rebellion (1568), very small parcels
predominated.[13] Nonetheless, the latifundia, worked by a landless proletariat,
was the norm.

Miguel Artola, in his study of the latifundia, reports that landed estates in
western Andalusia (the regions around Seville, Córdoba, etc.) encompassed
over 63 per cent of all cultivated land and included two-thirds of the entire
population of the region. By the eighteenth century, *jornaleros* (day-labourers),
comprising more than 75 per cent of the peasant population, inhabited
the large villages of the south (western Andalusia), with their typical, whitewashed mud-and-straw houses. There is no indication that the proportion of
landless peasants was lower in the fifteenth and sixteenth centuries. Thus, in
the south, the breakdown of the rural population into day-labourers, renters
and owners was dramatically reversed. The census of 1792, which, as we have
seen, shows an average of 3.1 per cent day-labourers, 91.5 per cent renters
and 5.5 per cent owners for Asturias, yields 78.2 per cent labourers, 13.3 per
cent renters and 8.3 per cent owners for Andalusia.[14]

If we recognize that even after almost fifty years of rural reform, more than
half the peasant population in late eighteenth-century Spain possessed little
or no land, and were thus denied access to village communal holdings, then
conditions in the sixteenth century could not have been much better. The
sad truth remains that the majority of peasants barely subsisted as seasonal
workers and faced not only continuous economic uncertainty but crushing
dependence on avaricious masters.

The village community

As we have seen, owning or holding sufficient land was crucial. Without land, peasants had no rights within the village community. The rights to common lands, to graze animals, to use the woods, as well as other privileges vested in the village community, were essential to the well-being of individual peasants. To be denied the benefits of village rights meant having to face inescapable marginality, for the village community served as an all-encompassing context of peasant life. Every peasant or farmer lived within the confines of the village. By this I mean not just the physical contours, but – to use Ruth Behar's description – the web of rights, privileges and customs imbedded in the corporate character of the village.[15] Although villages throughout Spain differed considerably in size, types of housing, customs, and rights of inheritance – regionally, and within specific regions – the relation between village community and individual peasants or farmers remained fairly uniform throughout the peninsula.

The village community, however, was not a static entity. Many Spanish villages dated back to different stages of the Reconquest and to the slow settlement and/or resettlement of population on an advancing frontier. Over time, the contest over rights, jurisdictions and dues – an ebb-and-flow of grants and denials – wrought changes. It is worth emphasizing here that there were no peasants without lords; even well-to-do farmers were never released from their obligations, rental dues, and debts of allegiance to the lord of their lands. The lord could be distant and benign, or close-by and horrible. The lord could be the king, usually the most favourable arrangement, or a neighbouring monastery or cathedral chapter. Thus masters and peasants were enmeshed in complex networks of reciprocity, in links that bound the peasants to the land, to the village community, and to those who held and exercised economic and political power.

Villages in the Crown of Aragon and in Castile underwent slow but dramatic changes throughout the fifteenth and sixteenth centuries. Two developments were most significant. The first had its origins in the thirteenth and fourteenth centuries, but continued at an accelerated pace in succeeding centuries. This was the slow but inexorable transformation of the social structure of the village from relatively undifferentiated rankings to sharp social and class distinctions. I do not mean to say, however, that early medieval rural settlements were bastions of equality, far from it; nonetheless, there was a kind of rough equality in the social and economic status of peasants within the village, which tended to disappear in the early modern period.[16]

The egalitarian spirit idealized by later historians and playwrights was most evident in the village assembly, which in the late Middle Ages included petty-noblemen, the priest, artisans and *labradores*. Summoned by the tolling of the church bell, they gathered in front of or inside the village church and discussed matters concerning village life and community affairs. This cherished image has long exerted a powerful hold on historians of late medieval Spain and on the Spanish imagination as a whole, above all on the way Castilian playwrights conceived the rural world and the idea of freedom. Reality, however, had a different face. Already by the fourteenth century, this rough equality was being undermined by increasingly unequal conditions – one could almost call it class differentiation – sweeping through village life. A few well-to-do farmers began to monopolize most of the land, the rights to pasture, and other economic assets, taking control of political power as well. Part of this development, which did not occur evenly throughout Spain, resulted from the intrusion of urban capital into the countryside. Merchants and prosperous artisans invested their wealth in land, although the reverse also took place: wealthy farmers were able to break into the ruling groups of nearby cities. In Soria, as we have seen above, successful ranchers from the hinterland – people of peasant stock – rose to the ranks of the urban patriciate.

The move toward stratification also came from within the village itself. Some peasants, owing to such circumstances as number of children, inheritance, aptitude for work, and ambition, rose to prominence within their villages to the detriment of other peasants. These rich farmers controlled the affairs of their respective localities, imitated the nobility, often married off their daughters to impoverished local nobles, and sent their children to universities. They play prominent roles in the Spanish drama of the sixteenth and seventeenth centuries, appearing as heroes in Lope de Vega's *Fuenteovejuna* and Calderón de la Barca's *The alcalde de Zalamea*, and populate the pages of literary works. In Cervantes's *Don Quixote*, Dorotea, the young daughter of a rich peasant, guards her virtue and honour against the advances of her noble seducer as fiercely as a woman from the highest nobility would. And Camacho, a rich farmer, throws a lavish feast which becomes an emblem – in all of Spanish literature – of money's power. These *villanos ricos* (rich villains), albeit their pejorative appellation, succeeded in challenging the privileges of the lower rural nobility (the *hidalgos*). In the *cortes* of 1532, to mention just one instance, the *villanos* expressed their desire to obtain redress for grievances resulting from the excesses and privileges of their betters and requested that the lower nobility contribute to the maintenance of their villages.[17] Wealth could therefore create sharp social differences between peasants, but, paradoxically, it could also level social differences between rich farmers and the lower nobility.

The imbalance within the social world of the village was rendered visible by disputes between communal and private interests. The fifteenth century, and especially the sixteenth (above all in Castile), witnessed numerous violent attempts by lords, cities and rich farmers to seize land from the village community and to privatize communal pasture lands. The conflict between the desire to privatize communal lands and the move to preserve ancient communal structures was further complicated by struggles between the

Mesta and rural communities. The transhumance – the annual migration of livestock (mostly sheep) from northern summer grazing lands to winter pastures in Extremadura and Andalusia and then back to their original habitat – dated from much earlier times. It had received royal sanction in 1276, and it had prospered greatly after the initial failure to fully repopulate western Andalusia. The great Mesta herds moved along especially designated roads (the *cañadas*) which traversed most of the length of Spain on a north–south axis. Furthermore, there were local transhumances, such as in Soria (see above) and elsewhere, where local herds travelled between mountain and plain, from summer to winter pasture, within a specific region.

In the late fifteenth century, the Catholic Monarchs threw their support behind the Mesta. The Castilian economy became highly dependent on the export of the fabled merino wool to the textile centres in northern Europe (Flanders, Brabant). This very profitable enterprise, which benefited most of the aristocratic and ecclesiastic owners of large flocks, also brought huge income to the Crown, which collected taxes (in Spanish, *montazgo* and *portazgo*) on the annual movement of livestock and on rights of pasture. It brought mostly misery to the villages on or close to the roads of the Mesta, however, adding one further tangle in the conflict between private and communal rights. For though membership in the village community guaranteed the life-saving right to graze livestock in the commons and to let animals graze among the stubble after harvest, the reality of herds of sheep, cows and other livestock descending on a village, breaking through the fences, and leaving the ground bare was not a pleasant one to bear at all.

A typology of peasant life

In spite of all this information, it is hard to describe the life of a typical peasant in fifteenth- and sixteenth-century Spain. Part of the difficulty, as I have been arguing, lies in the fact that there were no typical peasants. Differences among regions and variations in social ranks of the peasantry make generalizations difficult. Nonetheless, some attempt should be made to provide a portrait of what peasants looked like and how they lived in most of Spain at the end of the Middle Ages and the beginnings of the early modern period.

One of the most detailed regional studies of Spanish peasantry is Francis Brumont's analysis of the Bureba region (northern Castile) during the age of Philip II. His work, and my own study of agriculture in northern Castile in an earlier period, form the basis of the discussion that follows.[18] Keeping in mind the exceptions noted before – the individual farmers in the Basque country and Catalonia; the overwhelming number of *jornaleros* in the south; the great number of renters and subrenters in Galicia and Asturias – here is what a 'typical' peasant might have looked like. In the Bureba and throughout northern Castile, the great monasteries (St Domingo of Silos, St Millán de la Cogolla, las Huelgas of Burgos, and others), lay lords, municipalities (which, in theory, were royal lands, since most towns came under royal jurisdiction), and the bourgeoisie held most of the *dominium*, the title over the land. Outright ownership by peasants was often fragmented by partible inheritance and thus made vulnerable to the ambitions of the Mesta, which was always seeking to expand its pasture land, or to seigneurial and bourgeois capital intruding into the countryside.

The peasants of northern Castile, whether renters or 'owners', cultivated the land in ways that harkened back to an earlier period. With few exceptions, the Roman plough – the preferred tool in the Mediterranean world – was used throughout Castile and the peninsula. This plough, far lighter than the heavy, wheeled plough of northern agriculture, was pulled by a team of oxen or sometimes by just one ox. In the sixteenth century, mules began to be used in rural work in greater numbers, leading to acrimonious debates on the advantages of one over the other. Oxen (and sometimes cows, as was the case in my family's village) were generally the animal of choice in the north, whereas mules made greater inroads in New Castile and the south.

The land was divided into two fields, conforming to the biannual system of field rotation (*año y vez*) common to southern lands: one field remained fallow, while the other was cultivated. With rare exceptions, the three-field system, which revolutionized northern agriculture, never prospered in Iberia. With thin soils, a harsh climate (in the central plains), and a perpetual dearth of manure, the fallow had to be ploughed repeatedly and often allowed to rest for two years. The village livestock – by which I mean the animals owned by the *vecinos* – grazed in the arable after the harvest and in the fallow and common lands during the rest of the year.

The arable was made up of mostly open fields – not in the long straight furrows of the north, but in a kind of quilt-work. At certain times of the year, close to harvest time, the arable might be fenced to keep the livestock out, whereas vineyards were almost always fenced or guarded. Most of the arable was reserved for the growing of cereals. Wheat was the preferred crop, essentially because lords demanded most or, at the very least, half of the peasants' payment in wheat. Barley was the second most popular crop, though in some regions of Castile barley production easily surpassed that of wheat. Rye was limited to areas suited, by climate and topography, to its growth. My own impression, however, is that the cultivating of rye, with its higher yield, was far more widespread than our sources indicate, and that rye – the dark bread – was the basic staple of the poor. Oats are rarely found in rural accounts, and maize, transplanted from the New World in the sixteenth century, was accepted slowly as a suitable crop in Galicia and in specific areas of the north. By the sixteenth century, money payments began to replace dues in kind; but in general, northern villages, which had been settled in the early phases of the Reconquest and enjoyed generous charters, kept up full or partial payment in kind longer than the larger villages of central and New Castile.

In northern Castile, the peasants grew other small crops to supplement their limited diets and incomes: legumes, some flax, vegetables in the gardens attached to their houses, and fruit trees. Everywhere, unless the climate or soil were exceedingly hostile, the peasants tended the vine for profit, for nutritional value, for pleasure, for gift-giving and hospitality. Monasteries spent large sums of money to cultivate vineyards, which were not always very productive or profitable. Certain regions of Spain – the Rioja, some areas of Catalonia and Andalusia – became highly specialized in the production of wine. From the thirteenth century onwards, these regions sent their wine to other areas of Spain and abroad. Similarly, olive oil from the south and wheat from the Tierra de Campos and the plains of Castile fed Spanish cities and the American colonies. The mixed peasant economy also depended on livestock. A large part of the Spanish flocks did not travel in the annual transhumance, but grazed close to home.

Agricultural tools and work animals were scarce in medieval Spain. Rural inventories testify to the asymmetry between cultivated land and the number of ploughs and oxen or mules. In a 'typical' village, the *yugero* (the ploughman) – the owner of a plough and team of oxen or mules who hired himself out to plough the fields in return for one-fifth of the crop – was a fixture of rural life and often played an important role in the village social structure, as the identification of *Don* in period documents indicate.

Beyond the village were the woods (*montes*), which in central Spain did not mean dense forests. Since an earlier age, most of Iberia (with the exception of most of the verdant north) had undergone a dramatic deforestation. Wood was very dear, and foreign travellers crossing Castile often complained of the absence of trees and the high price of wood. In the scrawny brush, and in pens behind the house, peasants raised pigs, rabbits and pigeons, which provided another source of protein for their meagre diets.

In Part Three of this book, I will examine aspects of peasant daily life, diet, and interaction with other social groups. For the present, before we turn our attention to those who lived and worked in the cities, we may wish to recall, once again, the destructive potential of social stratification within the village community. In villages with fragmented arables and insufficient ploughs or oxen, most peasants either worked together or died separately. Greed fostered individualism, privatization and social differences; need fostered communal practices and a semblance of equality.

Urban Spain

In Spain, at the end of the Middle Ages and the dawn of modernity, the boundaries between rural and urban were not as sharp as they may have been in other parts of Europe, or as they are today. Nonetheless, Anton van den Wyngaerde's splendid collection of drawings commissioned by Philip II and undertaken between 1562 and 1570 depicts cities and towns throughout Spain in which the physical separation between urban spaces – clearly defined by, and encircled within, walls – and cultivated fields was sharp indeed.[19] Earlier, we have seen the rural occupations of many urban dwellers – people who engaged in some form of agricultural work through most or part of the year but lived in large cities such as Seville, or in smaller ones such as Cuenca. Moreover, many towns in Castile and Aragon were agro-towns: large, overgrown villages whose particular economies revolved entirely around agricultural or livestock pursuits. The small, predominantly transhumant towns in the Segovian hinterland – Sepúlveda, Cuéllar, Pedraza and others – are good examples of this type of agro-town. Yet, urban dwellers and urban workers differed from their rural counterparts in significant ways; their social standing, economic activities and relation to other social groups – that is, the social structures within which they lived, worked and died – were unlike those of peasants.

Urbanization in Spain

In fifteenth- and sixteenth-century Spain, only a handful of what may be described as large cities or true urban centres existed. By the end of the sixteenth century, when demographic decline had already taken its toll, very few cities in Spain surpassed 25,000 inhabitants. Seville, because of its primary role in the American trade, housed nearly 100,000 inhabitants, but only Toledo, with a population of around 50,000 people, approached Seville's grandeur. And Toledo lost any hopes of further growth after Philip II chose Madrid as the capital of his empire. Catalonia, both the principality itself and its most important city, Barcelona, had long been on the decline, a reflection of long-term political strife within the Crown of Aragon and of the shift in the European economy from the Mediterranean to the Atlantic. Around the mid-sixteenth century, Barcelona barely reached 30,000 inhabitants, but no other Catalan town had even 10,000 people. (See Table 2.1.)

Social structure

Like their rural counterpart, the urban population ran the gamut of social categories, with city dwellers and working conditions ranging widely from place to place. These differences – manifested in and reinforced by forms of housing, dress, eating and civic rituals – underscored structures of social, economic, political and cultural inequality. Clearly, the distance between those on top and those below was far more entrenched and visible in urban centres than it was in the countryside. Nevertheless, as we shall see in Part Three, cities proved more conducive to interaction – violent as well as festive – between diverse social groups than did rural towns. For now, however, such a discussion must be postponed as we examine the social composition of sample Spanish towns.

Table 2.1   *City population in early modern Spain*

	1510s	1520s	1550s	1560s	1570s	1580s	1590s	1600s	1640s
Barcelona	30,000 to 35,000 (1516)								40,000 (1640)
Cuenca			16,000 (1550)						
Granada				50,000 (1561)					
Madrid			20,000 (1558)		35,000 (1571)		60,000 (1598)		
Málaga				15,000 (1564)					
Salamanca				25,000 (1561)					
Segovia				22,000 (1561)			28,000 (1594)		
Seville						130,000 (1580)			
Toledo				56,000 (1561)	62,000 (1571)		55,000 (1591)		
Valencia		60,000 (1520)						60,000 (1609)	
Zaragoza				30,000 (1563)					

Sources: Richard L. Kagan, ed., *Spanish Cities of the Golden Age: The Views of Anton van den Wyngaerde* (Berkeley, 1989); Jordi Nadal, *La población española (siglos XVI a XX)* (Barcelona, 1976).

The social structure of Spanish towns or cities depended, to a large extent, on their economic basis, geographical location, role in trade, and whether they served as a centre for regional, kingdom-wide or international exchanges. Cities in Spain, as in most parts of late medieval and early modern Europe, maintained a symbiotic relationship with their surrounding countryside. The size of these hinterlands, often containing many small villages under the direct jurisdiction of the city, varied depending on historical circumstances and evolved or expanded over long periods of time. The city of Avila, for example, exercised its lordship over an extensive *alfoz* (the Spanish equivalent of the Italian *contado* or urban hinterland), even though Avila was not at all important, either in size or as a commercial hub. Burgos, on the other hand, an important centre for the distribution of international trade until its decline in the mid-sixteenth century, had jurisdiction over only about

55

380 km^2, and a population in its hinterland of just over 5,000 in 1528. This represented a small territory, especially when compared to the immense lordships held by cities and towns in the region south of the Duero river and in Andalusia.[20]

The point here, of course, is that the boundaries of the city, notwithstanding the imposing limits of its walls, were fluid indeed. This fluidity involved more than the employment of urban people in agricultural labour and their migration to the surrounding countryside and farther afield during the high points of the rural calendar. It also affected the urban rural elites. The patrician elites, whether noble or not, owned land, often large estates, around the cities. There they lived for a great part of the year, often between St John's Day (23 June) and Michaelmas (29 September), during the period when it was convenient to supervise the planting and harvesting of their crops and to escape the smells and heat of the cities.

This fluidity extended to the political realm. In the vast hinterland of Segovia, a community of *villa y tierra* (that is, a community of city and country), citizens of villages (*vecinos*, peasants holding property) had rights in the city itself and political representation in the *cortes* as part of Segovia's delegation. In attempting to construct a typology of urban social groups, one must always keep in mind that in Spain they were never very urban.

Seville

There are cities in Spain for which we have excellent monographs and good sources. These works provide us with a vivid recreation of urban history over a long period of time and allow us to see the changing social and economic structures of urban life. Antonio Collantes de Terán's excellent study of Seville provides a careful examination of Seville's population in the fifteenth century and the first third of the sixteenth.[21] The largest city in Spain, Seville was already an important mercantile centre, with a large Genoese colony long before the discovery of the New World. After 1492, its Atlantic connections – Seville was the only port permitted to transact the Atlantic trade – made it a vibrant and dynamic cosmopolitan centre in the succeeding century. Certain areas of Seville today – the neighbourhoods around the cathedral, the neighbourhoods of Santa Cruz, Triana and others – still retain a late medieval and early modern look: narrow, tortuous streets in densely populated areas; whitewashed walls contrasting sharply with reddish tiled roofs and with bright windowpanes and doors; black iron fences guarding flame-coloured blossoming plants. Such snapshots of the past – with different types of houses, materials and colours – can be seen to this day in the old parts of cities such as Toledo, Avila, Barcelona, Girona and others.

In fifteenth- and sixteenth-century Seville – despite frequent epidemics (twenty-two widespread outbreaks of illnesses in two centuries), famines and

Table 2.2   *The population of Seville, 1384–1594*

Date of census	Number of vecinos	Total population
1384	2,613	around 12,000
1426–51	4,893	22,018*
1483–89	6,896	31,032
1533	9,161	41,224
1594	—	90,000

Sources: A. Collantes de Terán, *Sevilla en la baja Edad Media: la ciudad y sus hombres* (Seville, 1977);
J. Vicens Vives, *Historia de España y América: social y económica*, 5 vols (Barcelona, 1972).
Note: *I have used a 4.5 coefficient per *vecino*. The censuses did not include the truly indigent,
foreigners, slaves, or other marginal people; so the population was certainly higher than the numbers
given here.

other natural catastrophes which slowed down demographic growth – the
population of the city grew at a rapid rate (see Table 2.2).

The profits from the Atlantic trade and the richness of the Sevillian hinterland attracted immigrants from all of Andalusia, from other parts of Castile,
as well as from abroad. Seville's heterogeneous population ranged from illustrious high noblemen, the *ricos hombres* or grandees of Castile who kept houses
and extensive establishments in the city, to slaves, delinquents and people
on the lowest social rungs. In his extensive study, Collantes de Terán puts
together typologies of the city's different social and economic groups. His
typologies turn on three dominant criteria: 1) function (the old feudal division
of society: those who work, those who pray, those who fight); 2) income; 3)
tax dues or exemptions (a fiscal distinction).

By employing a mix of these three categories, Collantes de Terán comes up
with a complex breakdown of Seville's population – and by implication of
similar cities in Spain during this period – into broad categories, each subdivided into smaller and more closely defined groups. Table 2.3 provides us
with an approximation of social categories in cities throughout the peninsula.

My main focus here is on the non-exempted and partially exempted taxpayers, who constituted more than 80 per cent of the population of Seville.
In the next two chapters, we will examine the lives of the privileged classes as
well as those of the lowest strata of the population. As for religious minorities, Jews disappeared almost *in toto* from Seville after the pogroms and forced
conversions of 1391, which were the most virulent in all of Spain. The number
of Moors was also quite low, given their expulsion from Andalusia in the
late 1260s.

In Seville, as in other Spanish cities and rural areas, wealth was concentrated in a few hands. Although in the late fifteenth century only 42 per cent
of all the citizens of Seville were listed in the survey of individual wealth (the

Table 2.3   *A typology of urban social groups in Seville*

Category	Subgroups
Ecclesiastics	a) regular
	b) secular
	About 1 per cent of the population
Religious minorities	a) Moors
	b) Jews
Immigrants	a) from other parts of Castile
	b) from abroad
Privileged groups (full tax-exemption)	a) magnates
	b) knights
	c) *hidalgos* (lower nobility)
	d) squires
Tax-exempted groups	a) those employed in shipyards
(partial exemption)	b) those engaged in seafaring activities
	c) those employed in the royal palaces of Seville
	d) those employed in the royal hunt
	e) weavers
	f) *farfanes* – immigrants from North Africa (ten altogether)
	g) municipal employees
	h) familiars (those working for the Inquisition)
Taxpayers (no exemption)	Most of the city's population
Slaves	a) mostly Muslims captured in war
	b) an increasing number of Africans brought to Europe after the Portuguese sailings on the west coast of Africa
Marginal people	a) the poor
	b) criminals

Source: A. Collantes de Terán, *Sevilla en la baja Edad Media: la ciudad y sus hombres* (Seville, 1977).

rest of the population was either too poor to be considered liable for taxation or too privileged to be taxed), almost 95.5 per cent of these were found at the lowest economic scale, paying small tax amounts. Some 4.5 per cent of those listed as taxpayers held 44.7 per cent of all the wealth owned by this group. For most urban people, therefore, the difference between scraping a living and destitution was essentially a matter of a few *maravedíes* (*mrs*), while the gulf between those above and those below kept growing wider. It is important to note that here we are not even considering the really monied citizens of Seville, the top aristocratic elite, many of them lords of fabulous fortunes. They, of course, controlled and monopolized most of the real wealth of the city and its hinterland. They paid no taxes.

Wealth also appears to have been unevenly distributed by neighbourhood, a point that highlights the segregation of the urban populace by trade and income. In the censuses of 1486–89, the parish of San Miguel had an average income more than six times that of the neighbourhood of Santa Cruz and almost 22,000 *mrs* higher than that of Santa Lucía, the closest parish in terms of wealth. In Burgos, to give another example, the patrician elites resided almost exclusively on streets surrounding the cathedral and adjacent to the road to Compostela, the main commercial thoroughfare of the city. Whether in Seville, Burgos, Barcelona or elsewhere in Spain, housing, dress and diet (see below) created sharp contrasts between the different social groups sharing urban spaces.

As for the working population of Seville, what did they do? The research of Collantes de Terán offers a vivid picture of the different occupations found in the city. We know that the arsenal, or royal dockyards, employed around 400 men in 1427 and that their number must have increased considerably after the opening of the Atlantic trade. Textile production, however, provided the largest source of employment in the city. In parishes such as Genoa and Francos, more than 30 per cent of the population worked in some aspect of textile production. In Cuenca, one of the most important textile centres in Castile during this period, the proportion of textile workers was even higher.

In Seville, urban dwellers also worked in the metal, leather, building and seafaring trades, but a substantial number of taxpayers (*pecheros*), mostly those living in the northern parishes of the city, engaged in agriculture and livestock tending. Equally, a large number of Seville's citizens engaged in commerce, either in long-distance trade (655 persons in 1533) or in local shop-keeping, pub-tending, and the like (499 persons in the same year).

Other Spanish cities

In other areas of the Spanish realms, the social and employment structure of urban society was similar. Just down the river Guadalquivir from Seville, Cádiz – with 400 citizens (males heads of household) at the beginning of the seventeenth century or a population of around 2,000 inhabitants – benefited from the Atlantic trade, when the river silted and ships were prevented from sailing up the Guadalquivir to Seville. According to Sancho de Sopranis, who has studied the city and the census of 1605 in detail, the population included 44 noble families, 50 middling sorts, and 306 families of lower social groups. Thirty-one of the latter were employed as sailors, and there were at least eleven publicans, pointing perhaps to the long-established link between seafaring and drinking. Excluding the noble families and the utterly destitute, the working groups of the population represented 89 per cent of the citizenship of Cádiz, though some of the upper echelons of the middling sorts wielded the levers of economic power as handily as some of the nobility and even married off their daughters into noble ranks. The lower strata of the workers were just a step ahead of dire marginality.

The examples of Seville, for which we have such ample information, and even of Cádiz, overlook the grey areas in which different social groups met and interacted. In Burgos, a city with a long mercantile history, merchants at the top joined confraternities such as the Knights of Gamonal (founded in 1285 but still active in 1605) or the Real Hermandad in which the distinctions among mercantile activities, titles of nobility and municipal offices were, for all practical purposes, obliterated. Burgos, which for all of its commercial hegemony in northern Castile had probably fewer than 10,000 inhabitants in 1530, attracted peasants from the immediate hinterland, and artisans, merchants and artists (to work in Burgos's many churches) from other areas of northern Castile and from abroad. This was somewhat countered by a significant number of Burgalese merchants and their dependents setting up shop elsewhere, mainly in the commercial centres of Flanders or the ports of the Bay of Biscay, through which most of the Castilian trade flowed.

In Burgos and elsewhere, the urban oligarchs – merchants and municipal officers – purchased most of the land around the city and extracted considerable profits from agricultural production, especially in times of dearth. A substantial number of Burgalese citizens, those in less advantageous economic positions, engaged in agricultural pursuits. These were people who, as in Seville, Cuenca and elsewhere, lived in the city most of the year and travelled to the countryside to be hired as day-labourers or to work seasonally in the estates of the urban patriciate. For Burgos and other Castilian cities, we do not have the statistical information that is available for Seville or pre-modern Cuenca. Nonetheless, the social distribution of the population followed along the lines noted above. Nobles and tax-exempted oligarchs were on top. My rough estimate of the number of knights (lower nobility as well as non-noble) and their families in the fourteenth century is around 3 per cent of the city's population. High noblemen, high ecclesiastics (the bishop, dean and canons of the cathedral), their families and exempted servants, altogether made up around 6–7 per cent of the entire population of the city. Below them, in varying degrees of partial tax-exemption and wealth, came the *pecheros* (the taxpayers), the largest sector by far, comprising a motley group of artisans, small shopkeepers, those employed in the transport and handling of Burgos's main export staple, wool, and workers engaged in limited manufacturing and the service economy. They may have accounted for between 65 and 73 per cent of the population. And still below them, as elsewhere, we find the very poor and the marginalized. Of the latter, some undertook seasonal work and menial occupations; others lived off the charity given by ecclesiastical institutions and, increasingly in the sixteenth century, by the municipal council. Their numbers fluctuated between 20 and 30 per cent of the entire population, going up or down with the changing economic fortunes of the city. With some variations in the composition of the taxpaying group and in the economic pursuits of the ruling urban elites, the cities of the Castilian meseta had similar social structures.

Barcelona

When we turn eastward to the lands of the Crown of Aragon, two cities stand out, dominating their respective regions. One is Barcelona, capital of Catalonia and the traditional mercantile centre of Mediterranean Spain; the other is Valencia, ruling over a rich agricultural hinterland and thriving as an important commercial centre. In the fifteenth and sixteenth centuries, the former was on the wane, above all in the fifteenth century, reeling from endemic political strife and from its inexorable decline as a centre for commercial enterprises. The latter was very much on the rise, enjoying the boon of its privileged position on the western Mediterranean and its links to the interior.

In 1516, Barcelona had between 30,000 and 35,000 inhabitants, and only 40,000 a century later. In spite of pestilence, above all in 1589–91, the city enjoyed a modest demographic growth through the sixteenth century, thanks to immigrants from its own countryside and from southern France. They compensated somewhat from the onslaught of plagues and other demographic reversals. Barcelona was, in many respects, unique in the Iberian peninsula. The strength and political muscle (or ambitions) of its guilds created a sense of social stability and permanence unlike that of other urban centres in Spain. A comparative study of the censuses of 1516 and 1716–17 by Jordi Nadal and Emili Giralt shows negligible change in the working population of the city, and sons taking up their fathers' trade with little or no variation (see Table 2.4).

One should note the relative importance of agricultural activities, even in a city as emblematic of urban life in the Iberian peninsula. The number of widows is also significant, and it confirms the European-wide presence of widows as head of households. How this affected social relations, family networks and economic roles is a question that needs to be examined in greater detail, if we are truly to understand the social structure of Spanish cities. What is clear from these figures is that Barcelona's economic structure changed little over the long sixteenth century and that its social base remained, on the surface, fairly stable. This apparent stability, however, obscured the frantic political conflicts that agitated Barcelona throughout most of this period. Enjoying municipal privileges and a political autonomy that were becoming rare in late medieval and early modern western Europe, Barcelona, as capital of the principality of Catalonia, ruled the political and economic life of the

Table 2.4   *Changes in trades in Barcelona, 1516–1717*

Sector	Heads of household, 1516 (per cent)	Heads of household, 1717 (per cent)
Agriculture/husbandry	432 (6.7)	474 (6.1)
Fishing/maritime	284 (4.4)	297 (3.8)
Construction	329 (5.1)	542 (7.0)
Hides and leather	465 (7.2)	510 (6.6)
Cloth	979 (15.2)	949 (12.3)
Metal	229 (3.6)	361 (4.7)
Glass/ceramics	48 (0.8)	77 (1.0)
Victualling trades	230 (3.6)	427 (5.6)
Commerce and transport	530 (8.2)	602 (7.8)
Liberal professions	254 (3.9)	344 (4.5)
Public employees	117 (1.8)	173 (2.2)
Widows	1,118 (17.4)	1,122 (14.6)
Others	1,420 (22.1)	1,839 (23.8)

Source: James Amelang, *Honored Citizens of Barcelona: Patrician Culture and Class Relations, 1490–1714* (Princeton, 1986), 17. Copyright © 1986 by PUP. Reprinted by permission of Princeton University Press.

region. Within its walls, it housed all the diverse levels of governance for the city and the region. This institutional layering conferred a political importance to the city, which it retains to this day; it also created internal and external antagonisms, which affected the social fabric of its urban population. Although these diverse and often conflicting institutional bodies were many, two of them, together with the representative of the Crown in the city, dominated Barcelona's political life and helped shape its social structure: the municipal council, or municipal government, composed of the Council of the Hundred (Consell de Cent) and the five councillors who served as the executive body of the council; and the Generalitat (or Diputaçio), a permanent standing commission of six deputies, which represented the parliament of Catalonia.[22]

Unlike other parts of Spain, where patrician elites had monopolized most municipal offices and enjoyed tax-exempt status and economic hegemony from the thirteenth century onwards, in Barcelona, because of the remarkable strength of artisan groups, the guilds were able to challenge the existing oligarchy. Guilds, it should be emphasized, were either non-existent or of little importance throughout Castilian cities, and they exerted little influence (as opposed to quasi-religious confraternities) on the social, political and economic life of other Spanish urban centres.

Throughout the fifteenth century, as Catalonia and the Crown of Aragon suffered civil wars and peasant rebellions, the popular elements (merchants, masters of guilds) in Barcelona (known as the *Busca*), with support of the Crown, clashed with the 'honoured citizens' (the term that described the members of the urban elite) for control of municipal offices. A royal decree of 1454 allotted seats to merchants, guild masters and artisans (*menestrales*, i.e. masters from the lesser guilds) in a newly expanded council. For the next three decades, the 'honoured citizens' and their aristocratic allies (known collectively as the *Biga*) fought, often violently, against the newly gained privileges of the *Busca*. In the late fifteenth century, King Ferdinand's reforms restored the 'honoured citizens' to a position of privilege and power, without excluding merchants and artisans from municipal government. Ferdinand's grant of noble privilege to the 'honoured citizens', and the enforcement of a system of *insaculación* (a lottery) for the selection of public offices, restored a semblance of peace.[23]

The social division of Barcelona's population (and of other cities in eastern Spain) followed the lines delineated for Seville and Burgos: 1) a small noble or quasi-noble rich elite on top (the 'honoured citizens' and their aristocratic connections); 2) a large group, ranging from well-to-do merchants, often connected by familial and economic ties to the ruling elite, to master craftsmen with a political say in the affairs of the city, to artisans and urban workers, some on the fringes of poverty; 3) the poor and marginalised segments of the population. Nonetheless, in Barcelona, the middling sorts, because of the power of the guilds and the political history of the city and of Catalonia, were able to retain a stake in Barcelona's civic life and to defend their position and privileges against the ambitions of the few.

In spite of antagonisms and spatial segregation, the distance separating the different social groups in Barcelona was not very wide. Anyone who has walked through the streets of the city's old medieval and early modern centre (the *Barrio Gótico*), where sixteenth-century houses still stand, will have noticed the proximity of the quarters of the 'honoured citizens' to those of the nobility and the popular (artisanal) classes – a proximity that often added to the contentious character of the city but also enriched Barcelona's social life.

Valencia

The great city of Valencia was one of the urban jewels of the Spains. A centre for silk manufacturing and crafts, Valencia drew its sustenance from its surrounding gardens and, until the expulsion of the *Moriscos* in 1609, found a valuable and inexpensive labour force in the thrifty and industrious Muslim converts. Valencia, however, did decline, as did most urban centres in the peninsula in the seventeenth century. James Casey, in his remarkable book *The Kingdom of Valencia in the Seventeenth Century*, shows how the region, both its agricultural sector and urban economy, paid dearly for the expulsion of the Moors and the economic dislocations of the seventeenth century.[24] But the seventeenth century was an invisible mote in the eyes of foreign travellers, who, two hundred years earlier, had praised the city for its prosperity and beauty. Jerome Munzer, travelling throughout Spain in the late fifteenth century, described a large city, with sumptuous buildings, a German mercantile colony, civic services (a mental asylum among them), and other amenities. Outside the walls of the city, Munzer delighted in the *huerta*, the gardens which supplied the city with an endless variety of produce.[25]

As for social structure, Valencia, as we shall see in a later chapter, had a volatile and aggressive lower class. On the one hand, some of the great noble families of the region, in typical Mediterranean fashion, kept palaces and great houses in the city; on the other hand, a large artisanal population engaged in bitter struggle with Jews (and later with *Conversos*) and Moors (*Moriscos* after 1504) over business and employment practices. These antagonisms exploded in the 1520s in a revolutionary rising called the *Germanías* (see Part Three, Chapter 8). Valencia was thus one of the few places in late medieval and early modern Spain where urban popular groups mounted a serious challenge to the society of orders.

The *Germanías* represented a clear watershed in the social history of Valencia. The defeat of the artisanal and popular uprising in 1521 marked the ascendancy of aristocratic and rural interests in the city. Joan Reglà's early work on the region of Valencia has been thoroughly revised by Ricardo García Cárcel, who, through careful examination of royal tax records, has provided us with a closer estimate of the social breakdown of the population of the city. From the figures given by Joan Reglà of between 50,000 and 60,000 inhabitants in the first half of the sixteenth century, García Cárcel argues that around 60 per cent of the population were urban workers with no franchise. Some 4 per cent of the entire urban population lived from rents (mostly rents collected from rural property), among them a large number of clergy members. Reglà reports more than 1,000 beneficiate clergymen living in the city and receiving income from lands worked on by *Moriscos*. He also estimates a bourgeois population of around 10 per cent, with a large group of peasants living in the city and its suburbs and engaged in agricultural work in the Valencian hinterland. As in Seville, Burgos and elsewhere in Spain, neighbourhoods or parishes were fairly segregated. Nobles and landholders inhabited the parishes of St María and St Nicholas; members of the bourgeoisie (the mercantile and entrepreneurial groups) lived in sections of the parishes of St Martin; their counterparts who gained their income from rents concentrated in the parishes of St Stephen and St Andrew. City officials, royal bureaucrats, and administrators preferred the parishes of St Thomas, whereas artisans, the great majority of the population, chose the parishes of St Catherine, St Michael, St Creu and St Martin. Shopkeepers lived in St John, and peasants and other agricultural workers found housing in sections of St Martin, St Andrew and St Stephen, i.e. in the same neighbourhoods as their masters. Few cities were so residentially divided by social filiation; this segregation points to the clear social rifts – in religious worship, social identification, housing and other markers of difference – of early modern Spanish cities. Because of the social and economic impact of the *Germanías* and the loss of artisanal groups, by the sixteenth century Valencia became a city 'of widows, of those who collected rents from the surrounding countryside, and of workers'.[26]

Conclusion

In dividing the social order into two broad categories – those who have and those who have not – one risks overlooking the variety of categories within each specific social group. In this chapter, I have grouped peasants and some urban dwellers together, but, as we have seen, each of these categories included distinct social types. Peasants or farmers in this period ranged from servile subjects, as in some areas of Old Catalonia until the late fifteenth century, to prosperous and influential landholders often superior – certainly in terms of wealth – to their impoverished noble neighbours (the *hidalgos*). The distinction between owning land, renting land, or working as a journeyman determined rank within the social world of the peasantry. Geographical location, crop rotation, and other factors shaped family structure, peasant–lord relations, and types of tenancy. Significant changes occurred over time. By the late fifteenth century, the last isolated remnants of serfdom gave way to freedom. Peasants in sixteenth-century Castile, overburdened by heavy taxation, plagues, droughts and conscription, began to migrate in large numbers to urban centres, to the periphery of Iberia, and to America. Religion also played a role. Large numbers of *Morisco* peasants in Aragon and Valencia toiled under conditions of dependency and exploitation which approached serfdom. Their social organization and village structure differed markedly from those of Christians.

In the towns of late medieval and early modern Spain, lower social groups also showed complex social gradations, ranging from urban indigents to prosperous artisanal masters to oligarchs, many of them noble, who dominated the political life of most Spanish towns. The latter group will be examined in the next chapter. Within the cities, the distance between the privileged class and the petty-bourgeoisie was far smaller than the gulf separating masters of a trade from the poor. Each city had a particular form of social organization, which was determined, to a large extent, by geographical location and economic structure. Relations among urban groups depended as well on socioeconomic and regional considerations. Valencia and Barcelona, for example, enjoyed a great deal of political autonomy, even in the sixteenth century, and were dominant mercantile players. They also experienced more volatile and fractious social relations than Valladolid and Burgos, Castilian cities under strict royal authority. More importantly, wealth and social mobility made for fluid gradations among the peasants, urban workers and lower bourgeoisie of late medieval and early modern Spain. Often, the differences within each particular social order were far more significant than the distinctions between social groups themselves.

Notes

1. Cited in Manuel Fernández Alvarez and Ana Díaz Medina, *Historia de España: Los Austria mayores y la culminación del imperio (1516–1598)* (Madrid, 1987), VIII: 82–3. This is one of the best general histories of Spain.
2. See Paul H. Freedman, 'Cowardice, Heroism and the Legendary Origins of Catalonia', *Past & Present*, 121 (1988): 3–28; also his 'The Return of the Grotesque in Medieval Historiography', in Carlos Barros (ed.), *Historia a debate: Medieval* (Santiago de Compostela, 1995), 9–19.
3. For this entire section on peasants I depend on my article, 'The Peasantries of Iberia, 1400–1800', in Tom Scott (ed.), *The Peasantries of Europe: From the Fourteenth to the Eighteenth Centuries* (London, 1998), 49–73.
4. On the economic context of the late Middle Ages and the sixteenth century see Jaume Vicens Vives, *Manual de historia económica de España* (Barcelona, 1959). There is an English translation published by Princeton University Press. See also Jordi Nadal's classic work, *La población española (siglos XVI a XX)* (Barcelona, 1984), 19–85; Bartolomé Bennassar, *Recherches sur les grands épidémies dans le Nord de l'Espagne à la fin du XVIe siècle* (Paris, 1969).
5. See Ruiz, 'The Peasantries of Iberia', 53, Table I.
6. See David E. Vassberg, *The Village and the Outside World in Golden Age Castile: Mobility and Migration in Everyday Rural Life* (Cambridge, 1996).
7. For a more detailed discussion of these themes and the relevant bibliography see my 'The Peasantries of Iberia'.
8. Paul H. Freedman, *The Origins of Peasant Servitude in Medieval Catalonia* (Cambridge, 1991), 154–223.
9. See my 'The Peasantries of Iberia', 61–2.
10. David E. Vassberg, *Land and Society in Golden Age Castile* (Cambridge, 1984).
11. On the rural history of Soria see Máximo Diago Hernando, *Soria en la baja Edad Media: espacio rural y economía agraria* (Madrid, 1993), 121–8.
12. See *Viajes de extranjeros por España y Portugal*, ed. José García Mercadal, 3 vols (Madrid, 1952), I: 322, et passim.
13. Vassberg, *Land and Society in Golden Age Castile*, 122.
14. See Miguel Artola et al., *El latifundio: propiedad y explotación, ss. XVIII–XX* (Madrid, 1978).
15. See Ruth Behar, *Santa María del Monte: The Presence of the Past in a Spanish Village* (Princeton, 1986), 131–2, 191–4, et passim.
16. On the class transformation of late medieval and early modern villages see T.H. Aston and C.H.E. Philpin (eds), *The Brenner Debate: Agrarian Class Structure and Economic Developments in Pre-Industrial Europe* (Cambridge, 1985).
17. Fernández Alvarez and Díaz Medina, *Historia de España*, VIII: 84.

18. Francis Brumont, *Campo y campesinos de Castilla la Vieja en tiempos de Felipe II* (Madrid, 1984); Teófilo F. Ruiz, *Crisis and Continuity: Land and Town in Late Medieval Castile* (Philadelphia, 1994), chs 1–5.

19. Richard L. Kagan (ed.), *Spanish Cities of the Golden Age. The Views of Anton van den Wyngaerde* (Berkeley, 1989). This is a formidable and most useful book. It includes a chapter (IV) by Kagan on cities in the Golden Age and another on city planning in sixteenth-century Spain (ch. V) by Fernando Marías, which are the best guides to urban life and urban organization in early modern Spain.

20. On Avila see Angel Barrios García, *Estructuras agrarias y de poder en Castilla: el ejemplo de Ávila (1085–1320)*, 2 vols (Salamanca, 1983–84); Carlos Estepa Díez et al., *Burgos en la edad media* (Valladolid, 1984).

21. Antonio Collantes de Terán, *Sevilla en la baja Edad Media: la ciudad y sus hombres* (Seville, 1977).

22. On the history of Barcelona (and Catalonia) see James Amelang *Honored Citizens of Barcelona: Patrician Culture and Class Relations, 1490–1714* (Princeton, 1986); Thomas N. Bisson, *The Medieval Crown of Aragon: A Short History* (Oxford, 1986); Ferrán Soldevila, *Historia de Catalunya*, 2nd edn (Barcelona, 1963); Carmen Battle y Gallart, *La crisis social y económica de Barcelona a mediados del siglo XV*, 2 vols (Barcelona, 1973).

23. See note above and Amelang, *Honored Citizens*, 3–101.

24. James Casey, *The Kingdom of Valencia in the Seventeenth Century* (Cambridge, 1979), 4–78.

25. *Viajes de extranjeros*, I: 339–42. His description included pejorative representations of Jews and Moors.

26. Joan Reglà et al., *Història del país Valencià*, 3 vols (Barcelona, 1975), III: 47–66; R. García Cárcel, 'Notas sobre la población y urbanismo en la Valencia del siglo XVI', *Saitabi*, 25 (1975): 133–55.

Chapter 3

Those who have:
nobility and clergy

The nobility

The boundaries between social orders in late medieval and early modern Spain were, as pointed out earlier, permeable. This was especially so when it came to the noble estate. Well-to-do merchants not only claimed the status of nobility, as did the 'honoured citizens' of Barcelona and the commercial elite of Burgos, but they also fully shared in the lifestyle and military ethos of the Spanish nobility. At the lower end of the ladder of prestige and power, the distinctions between rural *hidalgos* (petty-nobles) and fairly prosperous *villanos* or *labradores ricos* (rich farmers) were almost imperceptible. When the *hidalgo* Quixote argues about novels of chivalry with a village curate, a barber, and the university-schooled peasant *bachiller* Sansón Carrasco, we witness a discussion among social equals, despite Quixote's own view of the nobility's superiority. Both clerical and noble status, or claims to such status, presented an extensive and complex range of possibilities. The few magnates (the high aristocrats or grandees) and their ecclesiastical counterparts (the cardinals and archbishops of powerful dioceses) moved in a rarefied world to which other lesser noblemen and clergymen had access only as retainers or servants.

Nonetheless, the noble ethos – an honour code deeply intertwined with the exercise of arms – was a formidable force in the construction of identity. What constituted the ideal nobleman and how one became one were questions hotly debated throughout Spain during this period.[1] Because the aristocratic ideal was varied and its influence pervasive, it touched the lives of people who elsewhere in Europe would never even dream of calling themselves noble. In one of *Don Quixote*'s many hilarious passages, Sancho Panza announces that since he is an Old Christian – that is, a peasant untainted by Jewish blood – he deserves to be made a duke, and that his daughter is entitled to marry high noblemen. Only his wife's sharp retort, that one should marry one's equal and not aim too high above one's station, reels him back to reality.

Cervantes's ironic and deeply felt exploration of his countrymen's claims to nobility was part of a more general discourse on blood and descent. This focused on two themes: references to Gothic blood and Gothic descent in the fifteenth century, and an acute and often morbid concern with purity of blood in the sixteenth century. The first theme was based on the notion of an uninterrupted line of descent from the Visigoths. This cultural myth was spun by poets, especially Jorge Manrique in his wonderful poem *Coplas a la muerte de mi padre . . .* , and by chroniclers and other learned men in fifteenth-century Spain. The Visigothic lineage, which played a significant role in legitimating kingly power and the Reconquest from the ninth century onwards, was appealed to with a vengeance again in the late Middle Ages. In short, descent from the Visigoths – as opposed to mixed descent from Moors or Jews – conferred nobility. It gave those who could claim Gothic ancestry a clean and pure bloodline, which then became associated with valour, honour, and other chivalric virtues in the fifteenth century. Those with claims to Gothic descent, regardless of how spurious, could thus imagine themselves as being above the rest of the population.

Gothic descent, or Gothic blood, became a powerful element in shaping the collective identity of Iberians (as 'pure' Castilians or Spaniards). Sancho, the humble peasant who boasted a lineage that was free of ethnically mixed blood-relations and therefore 'pure', had a far more substantial claim to nobility – Cervantes is at his sardonic best here – than a high-born nobleman descended from Jews and/or Moors. The second argument for nobility thus manifested itself as a preoccupation with blood and race; and these concerns took their most peculiar shape in the statutes of *'limpieza de sangre'* (cleanliness, or purity, of blood) of the late fifteenth and sixteenth centuries. Essentially, these laws banned anyone of Jewish descent from certain public or ecclesiastical positions, even though they might have been faithful Christians for more than a century. This happened in Toledo in the 1440s, when the city authorities sought to exclude candidates of Jewish ancestry – the terms often used in Castilian were 'of the blood of the Jews, of the race of the Jews' – from holding municipal offices. Later, purity of blood became the criterion for admission to religious orders, to the *colegios mayores* of universities (endowed colleges, providing free room and board to those admitted), and to the prestigious and ennobling Military Orders.[2]

As Sir John H. Elliott observed long ago, only in a society as heterogeneous as Spain could such a discourse of difference have prospered. For the obverse of the exclusionary concepts of nobility and purity of blood, of pristine race and Visigothic legacy (regardless of how seriously most of the population took this racial construct), was the actual heterogeneity of Spain's population, the mixing or miscegenation (if such term can be applied to Spain) of the different ethnic groups living in the peninsula for many centuries. Considerations of race and blood, though powerful determinants in the social imagination of late medieval and early modern Spain, were often cast aside, neglected, or ignored by those who ruled. A good number of the great noble families of Spain had *Converso* (i.e. Jewish) 'blood' running through their veins. Ferdinand of Aragon, the great king himself, had *Converso* ancestors, and foreign visitors to Spain commented on the 'Jewishness of Isabella's court and of the Queen herself'.[3] In the Americas, the Spanish conquistadors often married 'noble' native women as a means of social promotion in the New World and of connection with powerful native kinship groups. The best example of a descendant of such union is Garcilaso de la Vega, one of the foremost writers of his age and the son of a Spanish soldier and an Inca princess. The irony of Sancho Panza's claim to nobility (which validated his peasant origins and insularity) lies precisely in the fact that many nobles in Spain protested vehemently about their purity of blood and 'race', but in reality had little or no grounds for doing so. Of course, then, as now, good lawyers and plenty of money produced impeccable genealogies.

Arms and letters

In fashioning the noble ideal, no requisite held greater weight than the exercise of arms. In the introduction to *El Victorial*, an account of Pero Niño's deeds of arms in the early fifteenth century, the author, Gutierre Díaz de Gámez, compares knights to angels, but emphasizes that not all so-called nobles are really noble. What confers nobility, for Díaz de Gámez, is the selfless exercise of arms. 'They are not all good knights who ride upon horses; nor are they all knights to whom kings give arms. They all have the name but they do not pursue the calling.'[4]

In medieval Spain, 'a society organized for war', the exercise of arms was not limited to nobles, however.[5] In theory, and very often in fact, most groups in society, not just the nobility, were expected to perform military service. This was certainly the case for the bourgeoisie and the artisan groups that served in the city's militia. Often, nobles died fighting urban contingents during the fratricidal wars of the fifteenth century. Peasants also took arms, and quite successfully at that. In the late fourteenth century, Castilian peasants erected walls around their villages and defended them against noble incursions. And the Catalan servile peasantry, the *remenças*, waged war against an oppressive nobility; in alliance with the kings of the Crown of Aragon, they dealt the nobles crushing defeats in the fields of battle.[6]

The exercise of arms did not necessarily confer nobility by itself; nonetheless, it was an important element in the making of a noble. Great success in the field of battle brought, if not an actual title of nobility, a sense of belonging to an exalted warrior class. Many of the conquistadors, men of humble social origins such as Francisco Pizarro or Hernán Cortés, rose to the equivalent of high noble status by their deeds of arms and valour. That dream, of success and promotion through glorious feats, died a hard death indeed in early modern Spain.

From the late fourteenth century onwards, the exercise of arms was slowly transformed in two distinct ways. On the one hand, to be a warrior was clearly no longer enough. To be a noble meant – at least in the models supplied by period romances and books of chivalry – a distinctive style of living (a lifestyle, in today's terms), a particular perception of the social world, an ethics of knighthood, and a new sense of aesthetics. The revival of courtly culture in late medieval Europe in general, and in Spain in particular, produced an image of nobility that had little to do with the realities of everyday life or with the untold cruelties nobles perpetrated against other groups and against members of their own social order. Yet, its divorce from the real world did not prevent this courtly concept from becoming a standard by which all nobles were measured.

Courtly norms included forms of dressing and active participation in the festive cycles that were enacted throughout the realms of the Spains (tournaments, *pas d'arms*, theatrical representations); courtly culture privileged romance and knight-errantry as exalted codes of conduct.[7] When Don Quixote argues that 'religion is knight-errantry', he touches on a leitmotif that was of great significance to many noblemen throughout the fifteenth century and early parts of the sixteenth (though their actual lives, in all likelihood, veered far from the ideal).[8] Take, for instance, Jorge Manrique's poem *Coplas a la muerte de mi padre . . .*, which I have often mentioned above. A mirror of the nobility's self-image, it catalogues the ideal noble's courtly behaviour, manners and ethics. A true nobleman – or a true good man, for in Manrique's work a chivalrous identity is subsumed into a Christian life – transcends Gothic blood and lineage, goes beyond the excesses and fatuous displays of the Spanish nobility in the fifteenth century. The true knight is, above all, a loyal supporter of friends, a brave fighter of enemies, but he is also sensible, kind to his servants and relatives, and generous to those below him.

> To friends a friend; how kind to all
> The vassals of this ancient hall
> And feudal fief!
> To foes how stern a foe was he!
> And to the valiant and the free
> How brave a chief!

The equivalent of the great Roman paragons, as described by the poet, and a real noble, Jorge Manrique's father (the Master of the Military Order of Santiago and a man deeply engaged in the civil wars of the late fifteenth century) – whose death the poem describes – left no great wealth behind; instead, he waged war against the Moors, conquered their fortresses and towns, and, most of all, served his true king faithfully. In the end, Don Rodrigo Manrique died the good Christian death, embracing death with nobility and turning his back on the material world. The rewards of nobility, i.e. of behaving nobly rather than of claiming noble lineage, is life-everlasting and memory. To be remembered well – another name for fame and evanescent glory – is this world's counterpart to heavenly glory. And indeed, for all the protests of humility found in the *Coplas* and in other fifteenth-century literary works,

71

remembrance and the pursuit of earthly fame remain important components of the noble ideal.[9]

Emphasis on posthumous fame is also evident in the chronicles of the fifteenth century. Royal and private chronicles (of the latter, the best example is the *Hechos del condestable Don Miguel Lucas de Iranzo*) focused almost exclusively on the deeds of valour of their main protagonists – their piety and faith, their courtly behaviour, how fashionably they dressed, how splendid were their feasts. Their goal, that of the chroniclers as well as of their protagonists, was always posterity: the willing of memory, the construction of a persona that would transcend the ravages of time and the cruelty of enemies. Hence Jorge Manrique's plaintive reflection on the passing of Alvaro de Luna and the demise of the Infantes of Aragon, great lords of the first half of the fifteenth century who (according to Manrique) left no enduring memories or worthy examples as his father had done. Manrique's catalogue of noble attributes and other similar writings of the age, however, overlook culture, or letters, in the Spanish usage, as complements to the martial deeds and ritualized displays of valour that defined noble status.

Jorge Manrique himself was a man of letters. One of the highest-born men in the land and a warrior who lost his life at the age of thirty-nine serving the Catholic Monarchs at the siege of one of the castles of the marquis de Villena, he was found at his death to be carrying within his vest his last poem, 'Couplets against the world'. The marquis de Santillana (1398–1458), one of the most powerful magnates in Castile, was a book collector and an accomplished poet. Such noble-warrior-literati were customary in the fifteenth and sixteenth centuries. For to be a nobleman now also implied to be literate, to be open to the new wave of humanist learning and aesthetics that flowed from Italy to the rest of western Europe. The kings of the Crown of Aragon ruled in Naples as well. The most notable among them was Alfonso V (1416–58), the uncle of Ferdinand the Catholic and a ruler deeply involved in the humanistic learning of his age, who resided in southern Italy almost exclusively. From Naples, through Barcelona, Italian lyrical forms and Renaissance adaptations of classical learning made their way to the rest of Spain, where they were widely imitated by Castilian and Aragonese writers. Under this cultural influence, Juan de Mena (an important fifteenth-century writer) wrote a fabled but rather dull *Laberinto de fortuna*, in imitation of Dante.

Long before Castiglione's famous *The Courtier* served as a model for the genteel life in the early sixteenth century, the nobility of Castile and Aragon made the pursuit of letters, authorship, the patronage of the arts, and the inscription of learned motifs in festive cycles a central aspect of their self-fashioning. The nobility could not exist in the fifteenth century without letters. Don Quixote dreams of deeds of arms, but mostly he reads books about chivalrous adventures and seeks to recreate them in his daily life. It may be hard for us, living as we do in an unromantic age, to comprehend the extent to which romances in the late fifteenth and early sixteenth centuries – by then, printed and widely circulated throughout Spain – created a context for the creation of what may be called a culture of nobility. In Catalonia, knights challenged each other on long broadsheets that were posted in the squares of Barcelona, a genre that qualified as both literature and courtly bravado.[10] The period was filled with nobles who, through their deeds, sought to mimic art and fiction. But fiction also imitated and borrowed from life, so that the boundaries between the real and the fictional were blurred indeed.

Not every nobleman, of course, lived the beautiful life so magisterially described for the Low Countries by Huizinga in his *The Autumn of the Middle Ages*. But when Bernal Díaz del Castillo, a man of humble origins and one of the young soldiers in Cortés's army, stood at the gates of the great city of Tenochtitlan, he imagined it – he later wrote in his recollections – as a magical city out of the pages of *Amadís of Gaul*, the great romance published in Barcelona early in the sixteenth century and exceedingly popular among the conquistadors in the first colonizing stage of the New World. Bernal Díaz's words convey the sense of magic and the cultural and class associations of that particular moment:

> Next morning we came to a broad causeway and continued our march towards Iztapalapa. And when we saw all these cities and villages built in the water, and other great towns on dry land, and that straight and level causeway leading to Mexico we were astounded. These great towns and *cues* and buildings rising from the water, all made of stone, seemed like an enchanted vision from the tale of Amadis.[11]

Was Bernal Díaz del Castillo, despite his humble origins and lack of fortune in his youth, a nobleman? He certainly was a warrior, having fought hard battles in Mexico and Central America. In the style of noblemen, he wrote a 'true history of the conquest of Mexico', a history written late in life with an eye on posterity and his own enduring fame. He lived the life of a noble in his estate in Coayacán (outside the city of Mexico) during the second half of the sixteenth century. He looked like a noble, acted like one, and thus, for all practical purposes, was one.

The divorce of arms and letters

The combination, however, of a warring life and an intense literary career became more difficult to sustain as the Middle Ages came to an end. Exceptions remained, of course, of which Cervantes is a very good example. He fought at the battle of Lepanto (1571), where he lost the use of his left hand. Captured by pirates in 1575, he spent the next five years in captivity in Algiers until he was ransomed. He then returned to Spain to a hard life as a minor royal official. Seeking to change his circumstances, Cervantes applied to migrate to the New World in search of adventure and wealth; when he was refused permission to travel, he embraced a literary career.

Nonetheless, letters was often disassociated from arms and proved a far more certain road to wealth and nobility than the life of the warrior. The nature of warfare in the sixteenth century and the military reforms undertaken by Gonzalo Fernández de Córdoba, the Great Captain, in the late fifteenth and early sixteenth century radically diminished the opportunities for single combat and individual heroism. Fernández de Córdoba's emphasis on discipline and on the role of infantry, as well as joining pikes and firearms in combat (the heart of the fabled Spanish *tercios*), led to Spanish dominance in the battlefields of Europe and America for almost a century and a half. Knights-errant had no role to play in these new disciplined killing venues; nor were muskets, pistols and cannons the ideal knightly weapons. Not surprisingly, there are no firearms in *Don Quixote*. What an execrable age this is, Don Quixote remarks, in which warriors fight and kill each other, from afar, with firearms. More to the point, and a comment on the decline of knight-errantry and chivalric ideals, is the comparison Cervantes makes between a rich and honoured judge, riding his mule through the fields of Castile, and his heroic but destitute warrior brother, who lives off his family's largesse to fend off poverty. 'More entailments', Cervantes wrote, 'result from letters than from arms.'[12]

The military revolution of the late fifteenth century, with its dramatic impact on the social life of Spain in general and on the nobility in particular, was paralleled by a similar revolution in learning. A new social group, the *letrados* (university-trained men of letters), rose to prominence and broke into the ranks of the nobility with a vengeance. The needs of the nascent state provided ample opportunities for learned men in the ever-expanding bureaucracy. University training became a precondition for government employment and a fairly easy avenue for social and economic promotion and for ennoblement. This was a nobility that depended not on the exercise of arms, but on service to the Crown and on the ability to accumulate wealth. And these things, wealth and material possessions (land, most of all), were often the deciding factors in determining who was a nobleman or not.

Wealth

Lack of wealth, or non-ownership of land, did not necessarily mean exclusion from the privileged ranks of the nobility. The starving knight in *Lazarillo de Tormes*, the great mid-sixteenth-century picaresque novel, stands in the middle of the street picking at his teeth and pretending, in his great pride, to have eaten a sumptuous meal. In reality, he fed on the scraps his servant, Làzaro, collected. He is a fictional character, but one that reflects reality. The poor rural *hidalgos* put their hands to the plough in their ancestral villages in order to survive. Nonetheless, they decorated their humble village houses, as my ancestors did in a small village in northern Castile, with their formidable shields of arms. They also jealously safeguarded their lofty, if meaningless, status against encroachment by non-nobles. Yet, wealth and financial privileges still went a long way towards the making of a noble.

In Quevedo's satirical poem *Letrilla* (early seventeenth-century), money makes nobility. The Spanish term for petty-noblemen (*hidalgos*, meaning literally the son of someone who has something, or property) was a word deeply imbedded in the discourse of property. Nobility could hardly be conceived without property. To have no property was to fall into the lamentable condition of the knight in *Lazarillo de Tormes*. Moreover, in Castile, if one's family was exempted from taxes for three generations, one had the right to claim noble status. This was the case of the non-noble knights of Castilian cities (mounted bourgeois soldiers). In the mid-thirteenth century, non-noble knights were exempted from most taxes as a reward for their military service and for making horse and weapons available to protect their cities and the king. By the late fourteenth century, the non-noble urban knights entered the ranks of the nobility *en masse*. It did help that they – or at least a good number of them – also used their commercial gains to purchase rural estates, and that they sent their children to universities and into the Church. Thus, the combination of longstanding tax-exemption, service to the Crown, and wealth proved a sure road to nobility.

Tax-exemption also worked as a social boundary between nobles and non-nobles. The Basque, because of special privileges received from the kings of Castile-Léon in the Middle Ages, and because of their claims to ancient customary liberties, argued that they were all nobles, i.e. that every Basque, regardless of economic standing or education, was exempt from taxes and enjoyed noble status and privileges. The remarkable thing, of course, is not that they claimed such rank – after all, claiming some form of group exemption was an old medieval practice – but that they sometimes succeeded in their claims. In a society where the criteria for nobility were so vague, the boundaries between noble and non-noble were indeed easily crossed. Not everyone could take the road that led to nobility; certain prerequisites were necessary: money, 'blood', service, education and luck. But many did. In this they were abetted by the Spanish Crown's penchant for selling patents of nobility to those willing and able to pay.

It may be useful to look at one specific legal case, which ran from the late fifteenth century to the second half of the sixteenth, to see what kind of evidence was deployed to secure noble status and what kind of material advantages pertained to such a position.

Hernando Mexía de Cherinos (or Chirinos)[13]

A beautiful sixteenth-century illuminated manuscript in the Bibliothèque Nationale in Paris (Espagnol 435) summarizes a long and trying litigation, which the Chirinos family initiated to prove their nobility and therefore claim exemption from municipal taxes.[14] The black leather-bound manuscript, written in an impeccable and very readable hand, illuminated by a genealogical tree that glorifies the Chirinos line and links it with the Virgin and St George, is hardly unique. Spanish archives contain numerous examples of litigation undertaken by individuals and families seeking to assert their noble status and privileges. In many of them, as in the Chirinos brief, we can trace the history of a particular family (or at least the history they wish us to believe) over a period of almost a century; and, far more importantly, we can see what kinds of arguments were advanced to sustain claims to nobility, and how these arguments changed over time.

What, then, gave an argument for nobility credibility and legal standing? In the Mexía de Chirinos case, the litigation to prove nobility was prompted by the insistence of the municipal councils of Ubeda and Jaén to collect taxes; municipal officials refused to accept the Chirinos as nobles or to exempt them from taxation. The actual process began during the reign of the Catholic Monarchs in the late fifteenth century – though appeals were made to events that had taken place during the reign of Isabella's father, Juan II, in the mid-fifteenth century. The final decision on the case was not reached until 7 February 1567, when the manuscript was originally drawn.

Through the narrative of the document, we follow the peripatetic careers and lives of the Chirinos family. We begin with Pedro Alminial (or Almirante, or Almíndez) de Chirinos, a citizen of the town of Guadalajara; his son, Alonso de Guadalajara; and his grandson, Hernando Alonso de Guadalajara. The list continues with the great-grandson of Pedro Alminial, Hernán Mexía (de) Cherinos, and ends with Hernán's daughter, Doña María de Narváez. Altogether six generations of the family are invoked (including references to deceased ancestors), plus a good number of collateral branches and others related by marriage. In the century covered by the litigation, the family moved from Guadalajara (a small town east of Madrid) to Cuenca (in southern New Castile–La Mancha), to Ubeda (near Granada), and finally to Jaén (north of Granada), a larger town, when compared to Ubeda. This legal brief thus sheds light on the possibilities of geographical and social mobility in late medieval and early modern Spain; but, in this particular case, the perambulations of the Chirinos family may have been prompted, as I will argue later, by other, more unpleasant reasons.

Numerous witnesses were called to testify, either to support the Chirinos' claims or to back the municipal councils of Ubeda and Jaén. Most of the witnesses were old. Alonso de la Mula was seventy years of age. Another, Diego de Arriaga, was seventy-five ('more or less'). Gil Núñez, canon of the church of Cuenca, was seventy-three. The witnesses were clearly middling sorts (an archpriest, a canon), but lower middling sorts, pointing to the lesser status of the Chirinos and their clients. The testimonies of the Chirinos' supporters were fairly uniform, except that as the family kept failing to win their case in court, the witnesses advanced new and stronger claims until the litigants finally succeeded in 1567.

The reasons most often given to justify the Chirinos' claim to noble status were as follows. First, they had never, in their history as a family, paid taxes. They remembered that the great-grandfather, the grandfather, or the father of the claimant (depending on which stage of the litigation we draw our information from) had not paid taxes, had in fact been exempted from them, and had never been inscribed in the tax rolls in either Guadalajara or Cuenca; therefore, the claimants argued, they ought themselves to be exempted in Ubeda or Jaén. This was, as mentioned earlier, a very Castilian arrangement: a family that was exempt from paying taxes for three generations in a row achieved the privileges of nobility.[15]

The second most used argument for noble status in the depositions was the claim of a lineage that originated in the mountains. Though this argument is not fully deployed in the witnesses' testimonies of the fifteenth century, by the sixteenth century the Chirinos argued (and the witnesses were willing to corroborate) that the family originally came from the mountains, that is, from areas in northern Castile and the Basque country where there had never been Jews or Moors. The 'mountains' was a kind of code word for a heritage untarnished by Jewish or Moorish connections. Therefore, those born in the 'mountains' came from the fountain of *hidalguía* (knighthood) in Castile. This was indeed a common and widespread strategy, the tracing of family roots to a region never conquered by Islam and with little or no Jewish population. This argument was, in fact, a replay of the Gothic-blood and purity-of-descent arguments described earlier.

The third most common reason given by the witnesses to explain why they believed the Chirinos were noble is that the family had owned great houses in Guadalajara and in Cuenca. Alonso Hernández, an archpriest in Cuenca, swore that Pedro Almíndez de Chirinos 'was a generous and principal inhabitant of Guadalajara'. He stated that he had known Hernando Alonso Chirino in Cuenca as 'a knight' (an *ome hijodalgo* 'who carried a sword') and that his wife, he added as if to denote her wealth and importance, wore a gold ring. Their residence in Cuenca, the witness testified, was an important house, with an extensive retinue of servants. Moreover, Hernando had also been a *regidor* (a city official) for life. These arguments, or most of them, were given for most of the Chirinos as they litigated unsuccessfully to fend off the fiscal demands of municipal councils in southern Spain. Wealth, social prominence and municipal service – the legal and material markers of nobility – were conjured to confirm noble status.

Next the witnesses emphasized the military deeds of the family. According to one witness, Hernando Alonso de Guadalajara Cherino fought in the wars against Granada during the reign of John (Juan) II (1406–54). Hernando's brother had been, another witness testified, one of the defenders of Cuenca during the civil wars, before the ascent of Isabella. Other members of the family had also served the Crown or the municipality, which attested to their martial history. Another point made by the witnesses, who, because of the uniformity of their statements, had obviously been well prepared by lawyers or by the Chirinos themselves, was that there was no illegitimacy in the family. All of the Chirinos had been married in church; their children were all legitimate.

In the sixteenth century, one final proof of nobility was offered. Francisco Tebaeca, an elderly citizen (*vecino*) of Ubeda, taxpayer, and neighbour of the parish of San Pablo, testified that the Chirinos did not descend from the male line of 'plain men [*hombres llanos*, taxpayers], or from Jews, or Moors, or *Conversos*; nor had they or any of their ancestors . . . ever been prisoners of, or been punished by, the Holy Office of the Inquisition' (f. 34). Their main claim to nobility, Tebaeca argued, was that they came from a lineage of *fijosdalgo* (lower nobility).

The financial stakes in this long legal process were not significant. The original tax dues in dispute amounted to 500 *sueldos*, a meagre sum in late fifteenth-century Spain. Litigation and manuscript-related costs far exceeded the total amount of taxes being contested. Consider not only the great expense of carrying out a lawsuit for such a long time, but the high cost of drawing a document as elaborate as the one Hernando Mexía de Cherinos and his daughter commissioned to certify their noble status. The family tree, which illuminates the front page of the manuscript, placed the family under the protection of the Virgin and of St George. The claim was about money, but it was far more about status. And, in that sense, the stakes were high indeed. I am not a betting man, but I would be willing to wager a small fortune that the Chirinos were *Conversos*. In fact, it is not possible to establish this for certain, but there is strong evidence to suggest it. Their frequent moves – from Guadalajara to Cuenca, to Ubeda, to Jaén (the latter town was a stronghold of *Converso* artisans and shopkeepers) – are strong clues. They bespeak an attempt to carve out a new life, a new identity, in different towns, where old connections and familial ties would have been unknown or less known. Their marriages also suggest probable Jewish origins and *Converso* filiation. One of their relatives, named Mosén Diego de Valera, may have been the well-known *Converso* intellectual in the court of the Catholic Monarchs. And, although some of the female members of the family seemed to have married into the nobility, one Hernán Mexía de Cherino married Doña Isabel of Murcia, daughter of a *bachiller* (university-trained man) of Murcia. Her name, although this cannot be stated conclusively, hints at *Converso* origins.

There is more internal evidence pointing to the probability of *Converso* origins in this 58-folio brief, and one needs to return to the local archives to follow up on the more than seventy names mentioned in it. Our purpose here, however, is to answer the question: what makes a noble? Clearly, family ancestry, place of origin, wealth, purity of blood (after 1492), military and municipal service, and a history of tax-exemption were essential components in the making of a noble. These prerequisites, either individually or as a group, applied to all those wishing to attain noble status. Some Muslim knights, studied by Ana Echevarría, crossed over from being enemy soldiers to being faithful defenders of the Crown and Christianity. Their military prowess and their conversions served as avenues for social promotion.[16] Moreover, being a noble was of utmost importance, if one wished to overcome *Converso* ancestry and to attain social distinction. Although the Chirinos had a hard time obtaining their noble patent from the royal court, they, and others like them, ultimately achieved their goal. Social mobility was possible, if one had wealth, determination, and a good lawyer.

The nobility in Spain
Unlike in England, where the ranks of hereditary nobility were quite small, in Spain the ranks of the nobility were vast. In the Iberian realms families such as the de Chirinos (Cherinos) could also enter claims to noble status. Even *Conversos* with close relatives severely condemned by the Inquisition, such as the Bernuy family (see Chapter 4), could rise to the highest ranks in the land. And the nobility kept on growing throughout the early modern period, even as its role in warfare, politics and the economy diminished. Thus an inverse relation was obtained between the importance of nobles in the affairs of the realm (though a few grandees still exerted great influence) and the self-aggrandizing representations of their own standing. With the exception of the *validos* (the kings' favourites) such as the duke of Lerma under Philip III (1598–1621) and the Count-Duke of Olivares under Philip IV (1621–65) and their levy of dependants, a great deal of the business of government was conducted by secretaries, men of humble origins who owed their livelihood and eventual ennoblement to the king or to other powerful noblemen.

Some questions remain to be asked. How many nobles were there in Spain? What role did they play in Spanish society? And what was their territorial and hierarchical distribution throughout the Spains? Most estimates of the number of nobles in Spain in the fifteenth and sixteenth centuries range from the high figure of 13 per cent to a lower estimate of 10 per cent of the entire population, the latter being a more probable approximation. Even the 10 per cent figure, however, represents the highest percentage of aristocrats in a western European country and reveals the passionate commitment of a large segment of the Spanish population to a noble life. Beyond prestige and vainglory, noble status carried with it specific advantages, above all tax-exemption. We have already seen to what an extent the de Chirinos family was willing to litigate and spend money and energy to secure such a privilege. In addition, nobles had special legal rights and faced lesser penalties for criminal charges. Members of the privileged groups, the nobility and clergy alike, could not be sent to row in the galleys as common criminals; they could also not be imprisoned for debts; and they were entitled to special prisons and the right not to be tortured. Such advantages, which also exist in our world today, are clearly associated with class privileges; they were certainly worth the money and effort that many in Spain expended in purchasing a patent of nobility, or in marrying off a daughter – and paying huge dowries – to an impoverished *hidalgo*.

Noblemen were plentiful in the peninsula, but they were not evenly distributed throughout the land. The percentage of nobles was higher in Castile than in the Crown of Aragon, and higher in some regions of Castile than in others. Moreover, as I have indicated above, the distance between the high nobility – the so-called *títulos* (lineages) or grandees – and the rural lower nobility was wide indeed. At the pinnacle of the great lineages were the Velasco, La Cerda and Manrique families in Old Castile; the Medina Sidonia and Ponce de León families in Andalusia; the Paredes-Cardona and Cabrera families in Catalonia; the Hijar, Castro and Bolea families in Aragon; and the Borjas in Valencia. These constituted the most important noble groups among the thirty-five *títulos* (the number had been set at thirty-five in 1520 but rose to over a hundred by 1600) that formed a close and powerful elite. Each of these families in turn had their own extensive constellation of dependent nobles, and multitude of servants and peasants working their lands and enhancing their fabulous wealth and ostentatious lifestyles.[17]

For the few noblemen and noblewomen at the top, the partial loss of political power and the dwindling of their role in the making and unmaking of kings was more than compensated by an increase, through royal largesse, in their lordships and income. We may not find it too difficult to visualize great differences in income – for they exist in our world as well – but these sharp contrasts divided not only nobles and peasants but also different levels of the nobility. Through entailment (which was regulated and sanctioned by the *cortes* of Toro, 1504), primogeniture, and with full acquiescence of the Crown, this narrow elite, between thirty-five and a hundred families altogether and deeply intertwined by marriage, secured their privileges. In 1536, the count of Benavente, a great lord in the Tierra de Campos, had an annual expenditure of over 18,000,000 *mrs*, of which more than one million *mrs* went for personal expenses. His castle inspired awe in foreign travellers, as did his private zoo. The duke of the Infantado ruled over 800 villages and 90,000 peasants or vassals (which is more than some small countries today).[18]

A most remarkable example of aristocratic privilege is Doña Leonor, the daughter of Sancho, brother of Henry II, who was known as the *rica hembra*, the rich woman, and whose affluence equalled that of the *ricos hombres*, the highest nobility in early fifteenth-century Castile. Her fabulous wealth and family connections led to her marriage to her nephew, Ferdinand of Antequera, and eventually to the throne of Aragon as consort to her husband.

It is told that she could walk or ride from the border of Aragon to the border of Portugal, clear across Castile, without ever stepping out of her own lands. Inconceivably rich, the niece of a king, the wife of another, the mother of kings, a pious and learned woman, a peacemaker, Leonor also exemplifies the way in which wealth and family ties could overcome the social restrictions imposed on those of her sex. From her and others like her, Queen Isabella would learn about the right to rule. Yet, here at the end of this section, it is proper to compare the lavish lifestyles of these aristocrats with the average salary of an agricultural worker, around 16 *mrs* a day, and to recall as well the meagre income and diet of Quixote, who spent one-third of his income on 'suspicious stews and lentils', and the vain *hidalgo* in *Lazarillo de Tormes*, who did not even have enough to eat.

The clergy

If there were more nobles in Spain, as a percentage of the general population, than anywhere else in early modern western Europe, the same can be said for the clergy. Enjoying most of the financial, legal and social privileges that were held by the nobility, the clergy swelled to unprecedented numbers. Exact figures are not easy to come by, and historians' estimates have fluctuated between 80,000 and 200,000 in the mid to late sixteenth century. This places the ecclesiastical population at somewhere between 2 and 3 per cent of the total population of Spain, without taking into account the numerous secular individuals who were attached to ecclesiastical establishments and claimed the same privileges as the churchmen. The impression of a Spain overrun by nobles and ecclesiastics, both of them enjoying tax-exemption and excessively conscious of their social distinctiveness, has always been exaggerated; nonetheless, it has a kernel of truth.

The ecclesiastical world had its own internal hierarchy. Beyond the separation between a regular clergy (monks, nuns, mendicant friars, i.e. those who lived in monasteries and followed a rule) and a secular clergy (those who lived in the world, i.e. priests, bishops, etc.), the Military Orders (which in theory followed a monastic rule) bound together the noble and ecclesiastical ideals and were bastions of economic and social privilege. In addition, the Inquisition purportedly combined the interests of the state with those of the Church and integrated a vast network of lay people, the *familiares*, into the ecclesiastical order. We shall revisit the Inquisition in some detail later on, for its impact on the social life of Spain was great indeed.

The regular clergy was, by all accounts, far more numerous than the secular one. The *cortes* of 1626, for example, estimated the number of convents in Spain to be 9,088. Nonetheless, despite its lower numbers, the wealth of the secular clergy was overwhelming. Sir John H. Elliott mentions that the income of the entire Spanish Church in the early sixteenth century was 6,000,000 ducats. Of these, the regular clergy received 2,000,000 ducats of income and the secular Church received the remaining 4,000,000.[19] This immense income came from different sources, most of it originating in the vast domains the Church had accumulated in an earlier period. From the tenth to the thirteenth century, noble and royal testaments, donations and privileges, often 'for the remedy or salvation of one's soul', had added considerably to the wealth of the Church. Even though contributions to the Church declined in the late Middle Ages, pious donations still brought vast sums to the Church's coffers. In addition, the tithes and rents from its sizeable rural holdings provided a fabulous income. But these financial gains were attainable only in an economy that successfully resisted radical transformations, i.e. in an economy that privileged income derived from rural rents and from the export of raw materials, mostly wool from large flocks travelling in the annual transhumance. The Church, like the nobility, became defenders of the status quo and jealously guarded against economic changes and innovations.

For all the Church's wealth, its benefits did not reach all churchmen equally. Indeed the same sharp differences that existed within the nobility were widely present within the clergy. At the top of the ecclesiastical hierarchy, fifty or so bishops and archbishops enjoyed extraordinarily large incomes and lived in luxury. Yet, even within this narrow group, differences existed. The archbishop of Toledo, the Primate of the Spanish Church, received an income that was smaller only than that of the king in the early sixteenth century. At the bottom end of the social hierarchy, the lives of poor curates in remote rural areas were barely distinguishable from the desperate existence of their flocks. But these are commonplaces that must be questioned. The history of the clergy and their ecclesiastical affiliates and dependants changed radically over time, and so did their social interaction with the laity. These transformations must be examined against the background of political change in the kingdom of Spain and within the context of burgeoning religious life and spirituality in late medieval and early modern Europe.

The Church in Spain

Up until the marriage of Ferdinand and Isabella, national churches, i.e. the Castilian, Aragonese, Catalan and Navarrese churches, had their own histories, ambitions and programmes. From the thirteenth century onwards, the new mendicant orders, Dominicans and Franciscans above all, successfully challenged the power of older and more established monastic establishments (Benedictines, Cistercians). Within the cities – in the expanding universities, at the royal court, in the administering of the Inquisition – the mendicants gained an unassailable position. This varied somewhat from realm to realm. Geography and economic power had a great deal to do with the social standing of all clergymen and religious women, including the mendicants. Nonetheless, until the reign of the Catholic Monarchs, the Spanish churches were mired in deep corruption and embroiled in the fratricidal wars that were fought throughout the fifteenth century. High ecclesiastical dignitaries, almost all of them members of great magnate families, took an active role in the Castilian and Aragonese civil wars. The most notable example is the so-called 'farce of Avila', superbly studied by Angus MacKay. At Avila, on 5 June 1465, an effigy of the king, Henry IV, was placed on a stage outside the city and ritually de-crowned and dethroned. The archbishop of Toledo and other high ecclesiastics and noblemen played the most significant roles in the symbolic debasing of royal authority.[20]

Besides their political machinations – most of them aimed at advancing their own and their families' fortunes – the high clergy and other lesser clergymen lived ostentatiously and engaged in sexual misconduct. For the fifteenth century, we do not have the racy accounts of clerical misbehaviour that Peter Linehan has uncovered for thirteenth-century Castile; but if anything is certain, it is that the fifteenth century, as we will see in a later chapter, was even worse.[21]

The middling ranks of the Church, its cathedral chapters, the wealthy monasteries and well-endowed churches, before 1500, were mostly a world of greed. A great deal of the anti-*Converso* agitation in Toledo in the 1440s stemmed from the fierce competition between old patrician Christian elites and new urban elites of Jewish origins over the profitable benefits in the cathedral chapter.[22] Since the thirteenth century, the urban oligarchs had maintained a strong grip on middling positions within the Church and, for all practical purposes, monopolized the benefices in cathedral chapters and collegiate churches, as they did municipal offices. The children of the urban oligarchy flocked into new religious orders, into the universities, and into the ranks of the Inquisition; and the profits derived from these offices, more often than not, went to enhance the social standing of their clans rather than to furthering the mission or well-being of the Church. These middling ecclesiastics, men and women alike, were not noted for their piety or virtuous conduct. There were no saints in Spain in the early part of the fifteenth century, and not until the very end of the fifteenth do we find paragons of Christian life, most notably St Ignatius of Loyola.

At the bottom of the social ladder, rural curates, poor parish priests, impoverished monks and nuns were often uneducated, barely capable of performing the liturgy, and lax in enforcing ecclesiastical precepts and in curbing their personal conduct. The differences – in wealth, education, forms of dress, political power, and perspectives on the realm and world at large – between high ecclesiastics and this latter group were immense indeed.

The reforms of the Catholic Monarchs and the Council of Trent

The broad reforms of the Catholic Monarchs also affected the Church. Queen Isabella of Castile surrounded herself with pious and reform-minded religious men. A good number of them were of humble origins, and not from the high nobility, which, to a large extent, had opposed Isabella in the civil war for control of the throne. Once the Catholic Monarchs were victorious, they put the same energy that they had shown in reforming the political and economic structures of the realm into reforming the Church and disciplining the clergy, educating them and curtailing their most strident behaviour. Isabella was prompted not only by the political benefits of a reformed and united Church that would be fully supportive of the Crown's policies; she was also a devout Christian – one may even describe her as fanatical – deeply committed to cleansing the Castilian Church, and, by implication, the Aragonese churches as well. Her close advisers, Ximénez de Cisneros (1436–1517), a very learned cardinal and royal administrator, and the pious Hernando de Talavera (1428–1507), archbishop of Granada, worked as hard as the queen to accomplish these ends.

Although historians have exaggerated the extent of Isabella's reforms – as part of the mythification of the Catholic Monarchs – one can certainly speak of a reformed Catholic Church in Spain *before* the Protestant Reformation. In fact, the well-merited complaints, which dissenters hurled against Rome in the 1510s and 1520s, had already been met and redressed in Spain a quarter of a century or so before Luther's dramatic call for a renewal of the Church at Wittenberg on 31 October 1517.

The Catholic Monarchs' ecclesiastical programmes galvanized the clergy, as did the new opportunities for preaching and proselytizing in the New World. Many Dominicans and Franciscans, most notably among them Fray Alonso de Montesinos and Fray Bartolomé de las Casas, the latter known as the defender of the Indians, became the public conscience of Imperial Spain and fought bravely to protect the natives and to assert their common humanity against the greed of colonists in the Americas and against the objections of some scholars in Spain and of many Spaniards in the New World. And not only well-known figures stood up for the plight of the natives. The Bibliothèque Nationale in Paris and various archives in Spain house countless travel narratives and letters to the king or to the general of their respective orders, in which mendicant priests and, later on, Jesuits rallied against the exploitation of the natives and the lack of a benevolent policy from royal authorities.[23] The heroism and partial success of these friars reflected the growing militancy of most of the Spanish Church and a renewal of the Church's spiritual mission. That the monarchy, in the laws of Burgos (1512) and later in the *Leyes nuevas* (New Laws of 1542), recognized the rights of America's natives and their unassailable humanity was, in part, a testimony to the Church and to the lofty ideals of many of its clergymen.

In the early and mid-sixteenth century, the Spanish Church – backed by Imperial armies – was poised to play an enhanced role in European spiritual affairs. The Spanish Church, by which I mean the Castilian Church, plus the

Jesuits and the Reformed Discalced Carmelites (religious orders founded by the mystics Ignatius of Loyola and St Teresa of Avila), became the spearhead of the Catholic Reformation, of Catholic initiatives against the Protestants, and of far-flung missionary activity in Asia, Africa and the Americas. At the Council of Trent – a series of meetings held at Trent between 1545 and 1563 which established the Catholic doctrinal position *vis-à-vis* the Protestants – Spanish cardinals and theologians, most notably among the latter the Jesuits Lainez and Francisco de Torre and the Dominican Domingo de Soto (some of them of *Converso* origin), often guided the Church's complex agendas. To a certain extent, they imposed their political views (favourable to Spain) and the reformed programme of the Spanish Church on the rest of Catholic Europe. After Trent, there were serious attempts throughout Spain and its colonial empire to enforce ecclesiastical discipline (above all in sexual matters), to educate the clergy, and to set more stringent standards for the laity. It would be foolish to imagine that the reforms always worked, but, clearly, after the reforms of the Catholic Monarchs and after Trent, there was greater pressure to conform – both for ecclesiastics and for laymen – to these newly defined guidelines of a Catholic life. The impact of these measures on the social life of towns and villages and on the mores of the population at large was extensive indeed. Later, when we look at aspects of daily life, we will have an opportunity to explore the nature of these religious and social transformations. For now, it is enough to view the growing Inquisitorial activity against heretics (Protestants), *Moriscos*, gypsies and natives in Spain and in the New World as one of the consequences of Trent's far more rigid religious stance.

Military Orders

Two other aspects of the structure of the Spanish Church merit attention because of their significance in the social life of Spain and its colonies. The first of these two is the role of the Military Orders in Spanish society. Founded in the Central Middle Ages, the Military Orders sought to carry out the same task of fighting the Infidel in the Iberian peninsula that their better-known counterparts had undertaken in the Holy Land. Mostly a Castilian phenomenon – there was a military order in Portugal (Avis), and the Templars had had houses throughout the peninsula – the great Military Orders of Santiago (founded in *c.*1160), Alcántara (1166), Calatrava (1158) and, with the demise of the Templars in the early fourteenth century, the Orders of Christ and Montesa (1317) had, in their earlier incarnations, a quasi-ecclesiastical organization and a semblance of clerical discipline. The Military Orders and their vast financial resources came under royal control in the late fifteenth century and therefore lost their former political influence as well as religious purpose; yet, membership in one of these orders continued to be (and became even more so) an important social marker and a proof of purity of blood. Throughout the sixteenth century, the Military Orders retained their significance as a sign of difference and defined not only social position (i.e. the nobility of members) but also racial and religious status.

The Inquisition
The second institution, a Church within the Church in Spain, was the Holy Office or Inquisition. The great and jealous guardian of spiritual and racial purity, the Inquisition was established in Castile, and assumed its Castilian form throughout Spain, in the early 1480s. There had been a general Inquisition, either papal or episcopal, in Aragon and elsewhere in Europe, dating back to the early thirteenth century, but it had never been allowed to operate within the kingdom of Castile. The Spanish Inquisition was, from its inception, a different institution from that of its European counterparts. It was firmly under royal control, serving the needs of the state as well as those of religion. Its vast apparatus, which included ecclesiastics (mostly Dominican monks), quasi-religious followers, and secular employees (the *familiares*), cut across the political boundaries that separated the various kingdoms. The Inquisition was the only truly national institution in Spain until the eighteenth century; and, in a perverse way, one could say that in many respects the Inquisition *was* Spain, for it sought to define a national conscience and set of beliefs. At the same time, the Inquisition became indelibly associated with Spain – in recurring, and pejorative, representations by foreigners – and shaped the way the country was perceived abroad in the early modern period and into the present.

The Inquisition also bridged the boundaries between the secular and the religious. Although it purportedly sought to weed out heresy – mainly 'judaizers' (those suspected of secretly practising Judaism) in the first forty years of its existence, and Protestants, blasphemers, *Moriscos* and other heretics and dissenters throughout the rest of the sixteenth century – the Inquisition functioned as an effective means of social, political and economic control. Enjoying vast popular support, and acting hand-in-hand with a powerful state most of the time, the Inquisition articulated, through the staging of theatrical *autos-de-fe* (the public humiliation and judgment of heretics), an ideology of power and a policy of conformity to time-honoured social and economic norms. Since the Inquisition was sustained by an economy that was based on landed estates and land rents, it did not look favourably upon economic innovation or change; and it sought to preserve a hierarchical society and to uphold the policies of the Catholic king. The Inquisition persecuted Protestants and *Conversos*, but it also often persecuted those men who sought to transform Spanish economic structures.[24]

Inquisitors, saints and mystics
In the previous pages, emphasis has been placed on institutions rather than on individuals. The history of the Church in Spain, as brief as I have sought to make it, does not provide us with the understanding of social mobility and

relations between different social groups that the study of individual lives and case studies makes possible. A few vignettes afford us a glimpse into a whole range of social experiences and allow us to see that people of humble rank or motley background could exert deep influence on the Church and on society as a whole. While money, blood and other factors promoted noble status, mystic raptures, sanctity (or hypocrisy), and sheer determination were the paths chosen by some very singular people in the late fifteenth and sixteenth centuries to gain an influence disproportionate to their social rank. The following vignettes, drawn from the lives of well-known historical figures, show how, in the spiritual economy of the late medieval and early modern Church, a preferred currency was the claim of direct access to, or direct experience of, God. On the other hand, the period was filled with people who were brought in front of the Inquisition and either paid with their lives or suffered other severe punishments for making claims, expressing ideas, or engaging in behaviour that was not too different from that which led to canonization in other cases. In fact, some of the paradigmatic saints of the period had to weather perilous encounters with inquisitors or with Church authorities. From the aristocratic Ignatius of Loyola (1491–1556), born in the family castle at Loyola in the Basque country, to John of the Cross (1542–91), the destitute child of a humble family, we can see the workings of sanctity in creating social equality and mobility.

Ignatius of Loyola was a man of the world: a courtier who engaged in the usual pleasures of the age, and a soldier who was wounded during the siege of Pamplona in 1521. His well-known return to his ancestral castle to recover from his wounds, and his reading of *Saints' Lives* (The Golden Legend), in the absence of his beloved romances, led to Ignatius's spiritual conversion. This in turn led to a failed attempt to journey to Jerusalem, a spiritual retreat in the caves of Manresa (Catalonia), the beginning of the writing of his influential *Spiritual Exercises,* and the eventual foundation of the Society of Jesus (The Jesuits). Throughout his life Ignatius retained the aristocratic and military values of his upbringing, and they were firmly inscribed in the forging of the Society of Jesus and in the later activities of the Jesuits throughout the world. Yet, in spite of Ignatius's inheritance and his early taste for romance and chivalry, the Society of Jesus was the only Spanish monastic order to welcome *Conversos* among its ranks; and, when it became untenable to do so in Spain, the Society advised Spanish *Conversos* to join the order abroad. The Jesuits were also one of the first religious orders to care and do something about primary education for the lower classes (as they of course already did for the powerful).[25]

Ignatius's aristocratic background contrasts sharply with that of St Teresa of Avila (1515–82). Born in the old frontier town of Ávila, Teresa grew up in a wealthy, urban, semi-aristocratic household – at least, the aristocratic emphasis is present in Audair's laudatory biography and in the exemplary life constructed by contemporary biographers – but her grandfather, Juan Sánchez de Toledo, was a *Converso*, and a relapsed one at that. The family had fled Toledo – a place of bitter anti-*Converso* riots in the 1440s and of significant inquisitorial activity in the last two decades of the fifteenth century – for the safer confines of Avila. In the latter city, there had been no anti-Jewish pogroms in 1391 (see Chapter 4), nor had there been anti-*Converso* riots or unusual activities by the Inquisition. Avila, with an aristocratic ruling elite that derived its income from land rents and livestock, had always had a sizeable Jewish and Moorish population active in petty-trade and artisanal pursuits.

Teresa's father, Alonso Sánchez de Cepeda, was, as Teresa herself tells us in her autobiography, a man 'fond of reading holy books . . . [and] charitable to the poor', a man who would not keep slaves in a society where slave-holding by the wealthy was the norm. But Teresa as a child, not unlike Ignatius of Loyola or Don Quixote, preferred a different kind of reading. With the encouragement of her mother, a scion of the Dávilas, one of the most important and truly aristocratic lineages in Avila, she fed on a steady diet of romances, from *Amadís of Gaul* to *Palmerín*. She also read the lives of saints, always impressed by chivalric deeds and tales of martyrdom. Moved by her heroic readings, Teresa left home as a small child to fight the Moors, and again, very much like Don Quixote, to seek adventures. But she found her adventures and heroic deeds elsewhere. What followed, after such an ideal childhood, was her taking of the veil in the Carmelite Order at the age of twenty-one, her illness, her conversion to a spiritual life at the age of forty, her mystical experiences, and finally her energetic reform of the Carmelites and founding of the Discalced Carmelites. In between, besides facing fierce opposition and dangerous suspicions from the Inquisition, Teresa authored some of the most cherished books of the Spanish Golden Age: her autobiography, accounts of her mystical experiences and of the foundation of new Discalced monasteries, and other inspirational works, all written in a simple and direct Spanish that effectively reached out to her contemporaries and to posterity as well.[26]

I will not attempt to provide a full biographical sketch of Teresa's life; rather, I wish to flesh out the diverse social contexts from which saints, mystics, inquisitors and, as we shall see later, heretics emerged. Against the supposedly impassable barriers of ancestry and blood – what Spanish society misguidedly called race (*raza*) and the restrictions imposed by the statutes of cleanliness of blood (see Chapter 4) – there were many cases, not just among ecclesiastics, of social permeability. Teresa of Avila was only one of many *Converso* descendents who made a mark in Spanish society and who, because of their intellect, unusual spiritual gifts and good fortune, were able to transcend the narrow confines of their social order or the limitations of ancestral filiation.

This is not to say, of course, that it was easy to move back and forth across the markers of social distinction or to brush aside the prevailing discourses of difference. It was not. Yet, in Spain there were always many exceptions which signalled, especially among the clergy, a far more fluid society than in northern European countries. No example is more dramatic than that of Solomon Halevi, a member of a rich and prestigious Jewish family of Burgos (and whose life we will explore in greater detail in the next chapter), who converted to Christianity in 1390, studied theology in Paris, and returned to his native city to become its bishop, Pablo of Burgos or Pablo de Santamaría. His brothers and children, the fabled families of the Santamarías and the Cartagenas, played a significant role in the intellectual, political and religious life of fifteenth-century Castile as bishops, scholars, chroniclers and royal advisers.

In the case of Teresa of Avila and Solomon Halevi, unsuitable religious ancestry and beliefs were somewhat outweighed by considerable wealth, but the humble could also rise within the Church to positions of influence and moral command. This was the case of John of the Cross (1542–91), an orphan of peasant origins and of little manual dexterity, someone apparently targeted for failure and marginality. His early ventures into artisanal pursuits, as a means of securing a living, met with failure, but his sensitivity and natural intellect led him to an education, to a fateful encounter with Teresa of Avila, and with the Inquisition as well, then to a life as the greatest mystic of his age, and to eventual sainthood.[27]

But it is not only among saints, mystics and scholars that we find examples of swift social promotion or, more accurately, of advancement beyond ancestral or social thresholds. The Inquisition also provided an assured way up the social ladder. This was the case of Tomás de Torquemada (1420–98), the fabled Grand Inquisitor, whose name has become, not always correctly, a synonym for the cruelty and excesses of inquisitorial practices. Tomás's uncle, Juan de Torquemada (1388–1468), converted to Christianity, entered the Dominican Order, studied theology in Paris, and rose to become prior of the Dominican monastery in Valladolid. He became an important intellectual within the Order of Preachers and carried out several important missions for the Spanish Church abroad. His far better-known nephew, Tomás de Torquemada, also entered the Dominican Order. After rising to prominence within the Order and gaining royal favour by the late 1470s, Tomás became one of the eight inquisitors chosen by Rome in 1482 to reorganize the Spanish Inquisition after its initial rough years. Tomás became the main force in shaping the tribunal of the Holy Office. As inquisitor general for the lands of the Crown of Aragon, he prepared a series of ordinances (*Ordenanzas*, 1484–85) which established the judicial foundations of the Inquisition for years to come. He became, for later historians, the symbol of the Inquisition, of its harshness and abuses. For our purposes, what is significant here is the complex web of social relations and personal ambition that made his soaring trajectory possible. An unimpeachable *Converso*, Torquemada was able to place himself beyond the reach of the reproaches and suspicions that were destroying the lives of other *Conversos* attempting to prosper in Spain at this time. His education, his pedigree, his fervour and his ability granted him the premier position of guardian of orthodoxy, even though his family had been Jewish within living memory. These are the contrasts and contradictions that make Spanish social history both difficult and intriguing.

Although far more opportunities for social ascent seemed to exist within the Church than within other social groups – the Church after all encompassed all social groups – I do not wish to overemphasize the openness of Spanish societies. The protagonists whose biographical vignettes I have just sketched were exceptions, many exceptions I will grant, in a social milieu of fixed horizons. The truth lay somewhere in the middle. Within each social group, whether of peasants, merchants, nobles or clergymen, enormous differences of wealth, prestige and/or pedigree prevailed. But conversion, wealth, good connections and luck could be enlisted to enable upward mobility within one's own group or class, and beyond one's group. This was true, though much more difficult, even for the people who lived on the margins of society. It is to them that we turn in the next chapter.

Conclusion

As was the case with the peasantry and the lower urban social groups, the Spanish nobility and clergy ranged over wide social gradations. In contrast to other parts of Europe, nobles and clergymen were quite numerous in Iberia. Access to noble status was quite open, and entire groups of people, entire regions in fact, claimed noble privileges. Various qualifications – tax-exemption, place of birth, lineage, deeds of arms, royal service, education, 'purity of blood', orthodoxy and wealth – could, individually or collectively, raise families to the noble rank. Being a noble was all important, and wealthy merchants, farmers, *Conversos*, and other groups went to extremes to attain such a privileged state. But there remained a huge gulf between the grandees – the one hundred or so families who owned huge estates and exercised immense influence on the social and political life of the kingdom – and the multitude of other nobles, many of them close to starvation. From time to time, after centuries of successful negotiations, some families, such as the Bernuy (see Chapter 4), were able to break into the upper ranks of the nobility. But they were the exception that proves how tightly shut the high ranks of the aristocracy were to social climbers.

The same provisions applied to the clergy, but with some caveats. Although there was a strong connection between the high nobility and the highest ecclesiastical offices in the land, from time to time, saintliness, the favour of the mighty, education, and other factors could lead to a bishop's see, a cardinal's hat, or a prominent role in the Supreme Council of the Inquisition. The examples of St John of the Cross, St Teresa of Avila, and Torquemada show that someone without a family pedigree or wealth could confidently aspire to such positions.

Ultimately, the economic changes of the late fifteenth century and the onset of the early modern period often erased or mitigated social differences, and made privileges accessible to some who, according to the traditional ordering of society, had no right to them.

Notes

1. See Jesús D. Rodríguez Velasco, *El debate sobre la caballería en el siglo XV: la tratadística caballeresca castellana en su marco europeo* (Salamanca, 1996), 275–382.
2. On the questions of purity of blood see Henry Kamen, *Inquisition and Society in the Sixteenth and Seventeenth Centuries* (Bloomington, 1985); and, above all, Albert A. Sicroff, *Los estatutos de limpieza de sangre: controversias en los siglos XV y XVI* (Madrid, 1985).
3. *Viajes de extranjeros por España y Portugal*, ed. José García Mercadal, 3 vols (Madrid, 1952), I: 319. See also the frequent depictions of Spaniards by foreign travellers as being mostly Jewish or Moors, in I: 262, 265–6, 268–9, 296, 298, 446, 613, 843, et passim.
4. Gutierre Díaz de Gámez, *The Unconquered Knight: A Chronicle of the Deeds of Don Pero Niño, Count of Buelna*, trans. and ed. Joan Evans (London, 1928), 12. See pp. 9–10 for Díaz's comparison of the knights to angels.
5. See James F. Powers, *A Society Organized for War: The Iberian Municipal Militias in the Central Middle Ages, 1000–1284* (Berkeley, 1988).
6. See Paul H. Freedman, *The Origins of Peasant Servitude in Medieval Catalonia* (Cambridge, 1991), 179–202; Powers, *A Society Organized for War*.
7. For the importance of chivalry and courtly behaviour see above, note 1, but also the far more engaging and delightful book by Martín de Riquer, *Caballeros andantes españoles* (Madrid, 1967).
8. Miguel de Cervantes y Saavedra, *Don Quijote de la Mancha*, ed. Martín de Riquer, 2 vols (Barcelona, 1955), II, ch. 8: 'many are the roads that lead to God, religion is knight-errantry [*caballería*]; holy knights can be found in heaven [caballeros santos hay en la gloria]' (my translation).
9. The translation of the entire poem, a very poor one at that, is by Henry W. Longfellow, a bilingual edition in *Ten Centuries of Spanish Poetry*, ed. Eleanor L. Turnball (Baltimore, 1955), 48–77.
10. De Riquer, *Caballeros andantes españoles*, 142–7.
11. Bernal Díaz, *The Conquest of New Spain*, trans. J.M. Cohen (London, 1963), 214.
12. *Don Quixote*, II, ch. 24. Though, of course, for Cervantes a life dedicated to the exercise of 'arms' was always superior to one dedicated to letters.
13. The document uses different spellings of the name: Chirino, Cherinos or de Cherinos. This was not, actually, the family name. The names of grandparents and fathers differed from those of their descendants. Last names were only beginning to be established for the 'middling sorts' in the late Middle Ages and the onset of the early modern period.
14. All the references are to Bibliothèque Nationale, Paris (BN), Espagnol 435.

15. See my 'The Transformation of the Castilian Municipalities: The Case of Burgos', *Past & Present* 77 (1977): 3–33.

16. Ana Echevarría, 'La conversion des chevaliers musulman dans la Castille du XVe siècle', M. García Arenal (ed.), in *Conversion religieuse dans l'Íslam méditerranéen* (Paris, 1999).

17. For a review of the history of the nobility in Spain up to 1500 see Marie-Claude Gerbert, *Las noblezas españolas en la Edad Media, siglos XI–XV* (Madrid, 1997), 275–387.

18. John Lynch, *Spain under the Habsburgs*, 2nd edn, 2 vols (New York, 1984), I: 13.

19. John H. Elliott, *Imperial Spain, 1469–1716* (New York, 1964), 88.

20. Angus MacKay, 'Ritual and Propaganda in Fifteenth-Century Castile', *Past & Present*, 107 (1985): 3–43.

21. See Peter Linehan, *The Spanish Church and the Papacy in the Thirteenth Century* (Cambridge, 1971) and, above all, *The Ladies of Zamora* (University Park, PA, 1997).

22. See Angus MacKay, 'Popular Movements and Pogroms in Fifteenth-Century Castile', *Past and Present*, 55 (1972): 33–67.

23. BN, Espagnol 325, Espagnol 29, Espagnol 174. See also Lewis Hanke, *The Spanish Struggle for Justice in the Conquest of America* (Philadelphia, 1949).

24. There are a myriad of books on the Inquisition. See Kamen, *Inquisition and Society*; Benzion Netanyahu, *The Origins of the Inquisition in Fifteenth-Century Spain* (New York, 1995); Scarlett Freund and Teofilo F. Ruiz, 'Jews, *Conversos*, and the Inquisition in Spain, 1391–1492: The Ambiguities of History', in J.M. Perry and F.M. Schweitzer (eds), *Jewish-Christian Encounters over the Centuries: Symbiosis, Prejudice, Holocaust, Dialogue* (New York, 1994), 169–95 and the bibliography therein.

25. On Ignatius of Loyola and the Jesuits see A. Astrain, *Historia de la compañía de Jesus*, 7 vols (Madrid, 1912–25). There are numerous editions and translations of Ignatius's *Spiritual Exercises*, one of the influential books in early modern Europe. References to the religious history of Spain and to sixteenth-century mystics are found in the bibliographical notes at the conclusion of the book.

26. On Teresa of Avila see her wonderful autobiography, *The Life of Saint Teresa of Ávila by Herself* (London, 1957). See also Jodi Bilinkoff, *The Ávila of Saint Teresa: Religious Reform in a Sixteenth-Century City* (Ithaca, 1989).

27. On John of the Cross see E. Allison Peers, *Handbook to the Life and Times of St Teresa and St John of the Cross* (London, 1954).

Chapter 4

On the margins of society

Marginality, a concept of recent vintage, cannot always be fully applied to the medieval or early modern world. In its all-encompassing embrace, Christianity assigned a task or place to every individual and/or group within its moral economy of redemption, no matter how humble or degraded. In a sense, one that may seem ruthless or misguided from our modern perspective, medieval society was inclusive, each person fulfilling a role in the harmonious working of a divinely inspired history. So much for ideal formulations. In reality, numerous groups and individuals were excluded, persecuted and humiliated (what today we might call marginalized), and lived perilously on the margins of society.[1] The notion of marginality is therefore relevant to the medieval context, for exclusion meant debasement, endangerment and ostracism for those who were its targets.

The late Middle Ages and the first stirrings of modernity also coincided with a powerful drive to define a collective national identity. Throughout Europe, but most vividly in Spain, with its greater religious and ethnic diversity, literary, historical and iconographic representations of self and others helped stiffen the criteria for social belonging and banishment. Although social formations are always sustained by processes of exclusion and inclusion, the conflation of sudden economic, social and political upsets in the late Middle Ages and early modern period accelerated change and created conditions that were qualitatively different from those of a previous age. The genesis of the nation-state in the aftermath of late fifteenth-century feudal anarchy in England, France, and the kingdoms of Castile and Aragon, the rise of capitalism, and the discovery of the New World served as catalysts for the creation of new and harsher discourses of difference. Through them, individuals and whole sets of people could be placed not just below, on the lower rungs of an idealized social ladder, but outside, or on the margins, of society itself.[2]

What led a man, woman, or group to be placed apart from the mainstream of society varied in Spain from time to time and from place to place, depending on a whole set of historical circumstances. The degree of marginality also varied within specific groups and depended, to a large extent, on class and social prestige. In fifteenth-century Spain, to give a preliminary example, all Jews lived – in theory – on the margins of society; yet, clearly, a wide gulf separated a Jewish artisan in Briviesca or Avila, just before the Edict of Expulsion of 1492, from a great Jewish scholar at the royal court such as Abraham Seneor, the last official Grand Rabbi of Castile and trusted friend and adviser to the Catholic Monarchs who converted to Christianity in 1492. Not only did these two individuals live entirely different lives (albeit sharing the same religion), but their interaction with Christian Spanish society was sharply different. While, before 1492, Jews such as Isaac Abravanel and Abraham Seneor could move in and out of royal circles with ease and could – as Seneor and his family in fact did – cross over into the same or an even higher rank by converting, such bridging across religion and class was far more difficult for Jews in the lower ranks. For the latter, exile often led to significant loss of property, and conversion entailed life as a second-class citizen, always under the careful watch of the Inquisition and the endless suspicion of neighbours. In fact, in the late fifteenth century, most of the early *Converso* victims of the Inquisition came from artisanal and petty-mercantile groups.[3] For the elite Jews who chose exile over fortune and prestige in Spain (as Abravanel did in 1492), wealth and leadership may have helped to ease the transition to exile, but they constituted of course little consolation for the bitter removal from ancestral homes or for banishment from Sefarad (the Hebrew term for Spain).

With these variations and exceptions in mind, one may attempt to provide a typology of groups living on the margins of society. In Spain, class, wealth, region, time-period and ethnicity – or what Spaniards in the Middle Ages called 'race' (*raza*) – determined the different categories in social position and marginality.

In terms of religion, which was often perceived as the sharpest divider in what was at least in theory a Christian society, Jews, Muslims and heretics (*Conversos* still practising or accused of practising Judaism, Protestants, *Moriscos*, former Muslims still practising Islam) formed the largest group outside the dominant Roman Catholic persuasion. Neither Jews nor Muslims could be classified as heretics, but after 1492 for Jews and 1504 for most Muslims, both groups were nominally converted to Christianity. Deviance from their new faith, clinging to their ancestral culture, and particular ways of eating and dressing made these converts (*Conversos*) targets for the Inquisition. *Conversos*, therefore, formed an important subset – or at least some of them did – of religious marginalization, though as I have argued elsewhere, class had a great deal to do with the social acceptance and integration of *Conversos* into Spanish society.[4]

Socially and economically, beggars, the extremely poor and physically disabled, those suffering from certain illnesses (leprosy above all), slaves, the *pícaros* (scam artists, swindlers, etc.), prostitutes, vagabonds, and criminals were marginalized and/or persecuted for a variety of reasons. Clearly, the degree of marginalization changed from group to group and within groups themselves. A *pícaro* – the quintessential example is the fictional protagonist

94

in *Lazarillo de Tormes* – could have a 'marginal' life turned, at least on the surface, into an 'honourable' life. A criminal, as is the case today, could successfully escape the arm of the law and obtain respectability. Certain illnesses, poverty, and even begging could become emblematic of piety and pathways to power and sanctification. On the other hand, poverty and begging could also be markers of low status and expendability. Here the boundaries are blurred, and the distance between the marginal and the divine, between saint and heretic, are minuscule indeed.

Finally, because of language, behaviour, appearance and way of life, the Roma (usually referred to as Gypsies) lived, and live to this day, on the margins of society. The subjects of romantic idealizations, but more often of pejorative representations, the Roma suffered (and still suffer) endless persecution and punitive measures in Spain and elsewhere. But these preliminary observations do not convey the distinct character of marginalization and persecution experienced by each particular group and/or individuals. A brief sketch of each of these groups will permit us to see their differential location within the Spanish social order.

Jews

Jews had inhabited the Iberian peninsula since the beginning of the Christian era. Persecuted by the Visigoths, after their conversion to Roman Catholicism in 589, Jews prospered under Muslim rule and reached dazzling heights in literature, scholarship and in their economic and social standing. The Golden Age of medieval Spanish Jewry (eighth to twelfth century) produced such accomplished poets as Solomon ibn Gabirol (*c.*1020–58), philosophers such as Moses Maimonides (1135–1204), a native of Córdoba, and many other distinguished scholars and artists. This is not to say that there were no sporadic persecutions and conflicts, but, on the whole, the period between 711 and the early twelfth century was one of peace. The fall of the Caliphate in the early eleventh century, however, and the successive invasions of Muslim fundamentalist groups from North Africa shook (but did not breach) the longstanding relationship between Muslims and Jews.[5]

As the Christian Reconquest advanced south, large numbers of Jews either migrated to Christian lands, attracted by new economic opportunities, or found themselves under Christian rule as Muslim cities were defeated. One of the driving paradigms of Spanish medieval history has been the idea of *convivencia*, that is, the idea – as expressed in its most idealized form – that Jews, Muslims and Christians lived in fairly amicable terms in the Iberian peninsula and that subsequent intolerance was an aberration from the understanding and respect that abided between these diverse religious groups. Few, I think, still hold such exalted views today. I, for one, have never accepted this rosy picture. Rather, I argue that a complex set of relations, fraught with mutual antagonisms, brightened by small rays of conviviality and friendships, and driven by issues of power, material interests and religious strife, characterized the interaction between the three religious groups in the peninsula.

One must admit, however, that in what eventually became Christian Spain (the kingdoms of Castile and the Crown of Aragon) Christians, Muslims and Jews shared a geographical space and interacted in matters of business, politics, sex, crime, culture, and in the numerous conversions that flowed from one belief to another – not just from persecuted minority religions to the dominant one. While Jews were expelled from England in the late thirteenth century from most of France a few years later, and were battered in Germany during the first crusade-pogroms and afterwards, they lived in relative security – if not always in tranquillity – in Iberia until the late Middle Ages. At the same time, the usual commonplaces about Jewish life do not apply to Iberia. Under the jurisdiction of the Crown (which meant that they were subject to royal, not municipal, taxation), Jews were often employed as tax-collectors, and were themselves a very important source of income for the royal fisc; but they also pursued all kinds of economic activities. As farmers (yes! Jews could own land in Spain), artisans, merchants, shopkeepers, translators, royal advisers, physicians, tax-collectors, and, yes, money lenders, Jews enjoyed a fairly free range of professions and economic pursuits throughout most of their history in Christian Spain. I have shown elsewhere in my work how the economic structure of Jewish communities in northern Castile before 1350 was not determined by legal impediments or religious intolerance; rather the economic and social position of Jews was determined by the structure of Christian urban elites. For example, in Burgos, where the Christian oligarchy controlled trade, artisanal pursuits and money lending (again: yes! Christians also actively engaged in usury), Jews were excluded from these activities and concentrated instead on medical practice and kingdom-wide finances. In Avila, where the Christian ruling elite depended on livestock and land rents for its livelihood and power, Jews and Moors engaged in a large share of local artisanal production, shopkeeping and petty-mercantile activities. And they did so to the very tragic end of Jewish life in the peninsula.[6]

Moreover, at least until the end of the fourteenth century, Jews enjoyed their own autonomy. The Jewish *aljamas* (local independent communal governance, also known as *juderías*) in Castile and the Crown of Aragon were self-governing and often exempted from municipal jurisdiction and taxes, though the latter was an endless source of conflict with local governments. Jews were also not segregated to specific neighbourhoods. There were no ghettoes – a sixteenth-century invention – even though predominantly Jewish or Muslim neighbourhoods could be found in most Spanish cities. Similarly, wealth was unevenly distributed within Jewish society. Although some Jews – and later *Conversos* – amassed immense fortunes, Jewish communities showed the same breakdown by wealth and social status as their

Christian counterparts. There is ample evidence of Jewish poverty, criminal behaviour, and marginalization within their own marginalized society.[7]

This brief history of Jewish life in the peninsula tells us very little about their place on the margins of society. This indeed is part of the problem. Although in theory Jews were to be segregated and to wear distinctive clothing and markings (a yellow star or patch) as a sign of their difference and separation from Christian society, the very nature of the legislation in Castile and elsewhere indicates the failure in enforcing such repressive edicts. In truth, it was very difficult to distinguish at first glance who was who in Spain. Wealth, appropriate dress and speech, political connections, and ease of movement from one community to another permitted a kind of melting-pot environment – most noticeably among the elite and the 'middling sorts' – which alarmed many people in Christian society, above all the lower classes, but also some in Jewish circles who saw these signs of assimilation as a turning away from Judaism.[8]

The question of marginality or, better yet, of the degrees of marginalization is most obvious with reference to the Jews. Because of the ever-present anti-Judaism of medieval Europe and Spain, the Jews were set apart from Christians and branded with all-encompassing pejorative representations that became part and parcel of medieval life. According to popular lore and to the diatribes of learned clerics such as Andrés Bernáldez, a chronicler of the late fifteenth century, Jews had a peculiar smell, were lazy, greedy, sexually promiscuous, killers of Christ, necromancers, sodomites, ritual child-murderers, and guilty of other equally nasty practices.[9] If these accusations have a familiar ring, it is because western society has continually cast such aspersions to impugn minority groups or individuals. Similar acts of vilification were undertaken by witch hunters in the early modern period and by totalitarian leaders in the twentieth century.

False charges and denigrating perceptions notwithstanding, many Jews in Spain led lives that were almost indistinguishable from those of their Christian counterparts. This is why crossing over, once conversion had taken place, was so easy for the Jewish elite. Nonetheless, eroding social, political and economic conditions in the troubled fourteenth century had a negative impact on Jewish life as a whole. Indeed, the two centuries before 1400 witnessed growing antagonism against Jews and other marginal groups. This resulted, in part, from a downturn in the economy (which began around the 1250s), unstable political conditions (civil wars, royal minorities, when the Jews could not count on the king's protection), Christian victories in al-Andalus (which led to a triumphalist feeling among the ruling Christian majority), and an escalating rhetoric of difference among distinct groups. This latter phenomenon, as mentioned before, emerged from the forging of distinct Castilian, Aragonese and Valencian national identities – though still in an embryonic stage. The construction of national communities entailed exclusionary self-definitions: representations of self were predicated on, and bolstered by, representations against others. The rationale went somewhat as follows: I am a Castilian or an Aragonese, because I am not a Jew or a Muslim. But it affected other marginal groups in society as well.[10]

This growing tension and other social and political events (the minority of Henry III in Castile in the late fourteenth century, civil conflicts in the Crown of Aragon throughout the fourteenth and fifteenth centuries, and the inflammatory preaching against the Jews by some mendicant friars) led to widespread violence against the Jews in 1391 and afterwards. The end of the fourteenth century and the beginning of the fifteenth were watersheds in the life of the Jews in Iberia. It is here that our story begins in earnest. Throughout a good number of Spanish cities and towns, the populace rose up in arms against their Jewish neighbours. Most of the violence came from the lower classes: urban workers, petty-merchants, the poor. In most cases, royal officials, bishops and even the high bourgeoisie, as was the case in Barcelona, sought unsuccessfully to protect the Jews from these attacks. Clearly, there was a great deal more at stake in 1391 than just anti-Jewish violence, for the riots signalled deep social and fiscal unrest. Resistance to authority was mostly articulated in attacks against the Jews, who, in the popular imagination, were identified with the Crown (as tax-collectors and royal agents) and who had always been a traditional scapegoat.[11]

Regardless of the reasons for the uprisings – we will revisit these events in a later chapter – thousands of Jews were killed as they refused conversion, and many more thousands converted, either forcibly or voluntarily, to Christianity in 1391 and throughout the next three decades. The massive conversion of many Jews was an unprecedented event in Jewish history. Some like Solomon Halevi (mentioned earlier) or Joshua Halorqui, the leading Jewish scholars of their generation, converted without violence, and, as newly minted clergymen, Pablo de Santa María and Jerónimo de Santa Fe respectively, took to engaging their former brethren in bitter and successful polemics.

The consequence of the events of 1391 and of the subsequent conversions after the Disputation of Tortosa (1413–14) was the disappearance of Jewish communities – through conversion, exile, or death – from cities such as Jaén, Seville, Ciudad Real, and others. After 1400, the Jews in Spain became, with some notable exceptions, a truly marginal group. Their numbers had been drastically reduced, and their financial well-being battered by the rise of their former co-religionists, the *Conversos*, who now took over the economic roles formerly reserved for Jews. Those who remained faithful to their ancestral beliefs became segregated minorities in those Spanish cities or towns where their presence was still tolerated. They were now confined to specific gated neighbourhoods, and their access to other parts of the city was restricted, a development that was new to Castile although not to the kingdoms of the Crown of Aragon. After the political conflicts between the kings of Castile and the Crown of Aragon and their respective unruly nobility in the 1440s and 1450s – conflicts that were punctuated by anti-*Converso* riots – many Jews abandoned the cities and sought refuge in small towns, seeking the protection of powerful lords in the absence (because of the civil wars) of effective royal protection. Thus, in the 1440s one finds important Jewish communities in such towns as Briviesca (more of an overgrown village), under the lordship of the count of Haro, one of the most powerful lords in Castile.

This exodus to small localities and appeal to seigneurial protection produced negative results for the Jews: their withdrawal from important economic centres to financial and cultural backwaters; further fragmentation of Jewish communities, now under the protection of a diversity of lords who, more often than not, were engaged in open warfare with each other and with the Crown for the spoils of the kingdom; and, finally, their separation, at least until the restoration of order under the Catholic Monarchs, from the only reliable bulwark against persecution and popular violence – an effective and forceful monarch. This is not to say that Jews in the fifteenth century did not continue to play an important role at court. They did. But we must not confuse a few mighty financiers in the entourage of the king (and queen) with the diminishing role of Jews in the day-to-day affairs of the kingdom. As Ladero Quesada has shown, Jewish participation in tax-collection and tax-farming in fifteenth-century Castile was now shared fully, and sometimes less than fully, with Christian bureaucrats, many of them *Conversos*.[12]

By the 1480s, after the establishment of the Inquisition in Castile, the Jews of Iberia played a marginal role in the economy of the realm. They were often in open conflict with *Conversos*, whom they branded as non-Jews or worse, were segregated within the few cities where their presence was still allowed or were forced to inhabit less attractive localities. Because Christians associated Jews with backsliding *Conversos*, they came under increasing attacks and vitriolic depictions. Many synagogues, as in Toledo, were turned into churches; but the faith of those who chose to remain Jews had also been reinvigorated and strengthened by the disasters of 1391 and the travails of succeeding decades. It may be useful at this point to take a closer look at the fate of some of the Spanish Jewish communities in the fifteenth century.

The decline of Jewish life in the fifteenth century

The most obvious sign of the downturn that Jewish social, economic and political life took after the catastrophic pogroms of 1391, the subsequent numerous conversions, and the Disputation of Tortosa can be found in the precipitous decline of Jewish contributions to the royal fisc. The tax records of Jewish payments to the Castilian kings and to the monarchs of the Crown of Aragon – in 1281 for the latter, and 1291 for the former – reveal prosperous Jewish communities in both kingdoms. Their contributions reflect the large number of Jews living in Spain and their relative financial well-being. By contrast, the Castilian tax records of 1474 show an impoverished and diminished community. The Jews of Burgos, of the city proper, had contributed 109,921 *mrs* to the royal coffers in 1291. Almost two hundred years later, the amount was only 700 *mrs*. By 1474 there was only a handful of Jews left in the city. Those of Avila contributed 74,142 *mrs* in 1291 and only 12,000 *mrs* at the later date. This is indeed surprising because, unlike Seville, Burgos and other towns, Avila was one of the few cities in Spain that did not foster widespread violence against the Jews.[13] What this indicates, as noted above, is that Jews fled large towns. The latter were beset by civil strife as a result of the endemic civil wars of the period, and Jews sought refuge in small towns which did not have a previous history of Jewish life, and in the security of lordly protection. There were exceptions, nonetheless.

Segovia's *aljama*, or Jewish neighbourhood, remained fairly undisturbed throughout most of the fifteenth century. Occupying a particular corner of the city, the Jewish quarter (not a ghetto) had its own stores and services. María Asenjo, a distinguished historian of the city, has identified butcher shops, ovens, three synagogues, a bath and a cemetery. The fiscal contributions of the Jews remained fairly even from 1464 to 1478, indicating perhaps the stability of the city and of Jewish life there. Since Segovia was the hometown of Abraham Seneor (see above), its Jews gained a strong advocate of their interests in the royal court and were able to protect themselves from the virulent preaching of Dominican friars such as Francisco de la Peña. As they had done from time immemorial, the Jews of Segovia engaged in a diversity of trades, but more and more, as we come closer to the Edict of Expulsion of 1492, they were restricted to usurious activities or to tax-collection.[14]

All the efforts of the Jews to maintain a 'normal' life in the face of increasing pressure were, however, to no avail. On 31 March 1492, fresh from their victory in Granada, the Catholic Monarchs announced the Edict of Expulsion, granting Jews ninety days to choose between converting to Christianity and disposing of their property and leaving Spain. It was a hard and cruel choice indeed. Historians are not of one mind as to what led to the Edict of Expulsion. Some point out that the Catholic Monarchs, Ferdinand and Isabella, were personally friendly to Jews. Other historians accuse the *Conversos* of pushing for expulsion as a way to protect their own lives and wealth, now threatened by the Inquisition; yet others point to the heightened religious and national fervour, which was fuelled by Inquisitorial practices and by the achievement of national unity after the conquest of Granada. Whatever the reasons, the Edict of 1492 and the final expulsion brought an end to Jewish life in the kingdoms of Spain after almost a millennium and a half of uninterrupted Jewish presence and myriad contributions to Spain's culture, economy and society.[15]

In the same manner in which historians disagree on what prompted the expulsion, they disagree on how many Jews were left in 1492, how many chose exile, and how many returned from exile and embraced Christianity to recover their longed-for homes. The figures vary widely, from a preposterous one million Jews in Spain in 1492 to Henry Kamen's recent low estimate of around 80,000. According to Kamen, close to 40,000 Jews left, refusing to accept conversion, though a good number returned within the next five years to convert. How deeply 'Spanish' these Jews were, in spite of their uprooting, was evoked most poignantly in the pride in Spanish identity that Iberian Jews demonstrated in their exile throughout the Mediterranean and in the Low Countries. Their longing for Sefarad remains etched in those large keys, jealously preserved and passed on from generation to generation, which once, long ago, opened the gates and doors to their lost homes in Iberia.[16]

Muslims

The history of the Muslims in the diverse kingdoms of Spain differs significantly from that of the Jews. After enjoying four centuries of almost undisputed hegemony (military, cultural, economic and religious), by the late eleventh century the tide began to turn. The signal moment of this change was Alfonso VI's conquest of Toledo in 1085; and Toledo is a very good example of the ambivalent attitudes of Christian rulers and their subjects towards the Muslims in their midst.

The Muslims had been, with some occasional lapses, quite tolerant of other religions. As people of the Book, Jews and Christians lived under and profited from Muslim protection, albeit at a price. Christian and Muslims had shared the peninsula and fought over it for too long not to learn ways of accommodating each other in defeat and of respecting the life, property and even religion of the vanquished. It was a practical quid pro quo: today, you spare me; tomorrow, I will spare you.

Alfonso VI came to Toledo in 1085 as the emperor of the three religions, firmly determined to allow Muslims (and Jews) to retain their houses of worship, to practise their religions, and to conduct business freely. The clergymen who accompanied the king – most of them Cluniac monks from France imbued with crusading fervour – had other ideas. They began by turning the main mosque into a church and by trying to bully the Muslim and Jewish population. They did not succeed fully, but in Toledo – as in Aragon and Catalonia in the same period – large numbers of practising Muslims came under Christian rule. Free to practise their religion, they were nonetheless pushed to the margins.

There is a reason to begin so far away from 1400. The events that followed 1085 determined the fate of Muslims in Iberia in two very distinct ways. In the two decades following the battle of Las Navas de Tolosa (1212), the kings of the newly created Crown of Aragon (Aragon, Catalonia and Valencia) relinquished their role in the Reconquest. They turned their attention instead to

Mediterranean ventures and to the conquest of the Balearic Islands. More importantly, when James I conquered Valencia, the last great adventure and conquest of the Catalan and Aragonese in the peninsula, the Aragonese chose to allow its Muslim population to remain on the land, to engage in horticulture and silk work, and to continue servicing the complex irrigation network that had turned Valencia, under Muslim control, into a fabled garden. As had been the case in central Aragon, large numbers of Muslims remained on the land, but now as rather oppressed and exploited agricultural labour. They retained their religion, their language and their customs, but their economic and social standing deteriorated. This is not to say, of course, that there were no well-to-do Muslims. We find them in the documentation, not just in eastern and southeast Spain, but throughout Castile and Andalusia as well. Working in the silk industry, as itinerant merchants, as masons, physicians, dyers, shopkeepers and in other pursuits, they made immense contributions to Spanish life.[17]

In Castile, the developments were quite different from those of the eastern kingdoms. Away from the embattled frontier, in cities such as Burgos, Avila, Toledo and others, we find *morerías*, neighbourhoods inhabited by Muslims (known as Moors in Spain). In the North, a world of dry farming that was too cold for silk worms, we find few Muslims farmers. Working the land in most of northern and central Castile was, as we already know from Sancho Panza, a Christian occupation.

In the South, however, after the conquest of most of western Andalusia by Ferdinand III (1217–52) and Alfonso X (1252–84) and after a failed rebellion of the Mudejars (Muslims living under Christian rule) in 1264, most of the Muslims were expelled from the land, migrating to the kingdom of Granada or to North Africa. Thus, in 1400, we also find a wide range of life experiences and situations in the Muslim communities of Spain: North African and Granadine captives working as slaves throughout most of the South and the Balearic Islands; peasants in Aragon and Valencia tilling the land in a state of semi-servility; small communities of relatively successful artisans, silk merchants (in places where silk could be produced), masons, and physicians in the cities of the Crown of Aragon, northern and central Castile and in some localities in eastern Andalusia; and, finally, a free and quite vibrant Muslim life in the kingdom of Granada.

As to the latter, Abd-al-Basit, who visited Granada and its environs in 1465–66, describes a splendid and lively city, surrounded by abundant gardens, fig and almond trees. From a centre of active cultural and pious life, Granada's merchants travelled onwards to Christian Córdoba and elsewhere in Christian Spain to ply their trade and to maintain a link between North African markets and the peninsula.[18]

The independence of Granada and the free practice of Islam in Iberia came to an end in 1492. After harsh and protracted warfare, Granada surrendered on 1 January 1492, and, in spite of promises of tolerance made by the Catholic Monarchs, the Muslims of Granada and elsewhere throughout Spain felt the harsh blows of the Spanish drive for religious uniformity. By 1504, all the Muslims in Spain were forced to convert or to leave Spain.

Conversos and cleanliness of blood

Although nominally converted to Christianity, the *Moriscos* (the name given to Muslim converts to Christianity), unlike Jewish *Conversos*, proved mostly intractable to the new beliefs and language imposed on them by the Christians. Jewish *Conversos*, on the other hand, were often made victims of racial stereotypes. Although *Converso* families might have been Christian for more than a century, suspicion and belief that their blood was tainted remained part of Spain's social fabric and mentality throughout the early modern period. Positions in universities (admission to the great colleges) and cathedral chapters, and access to military orders, with their profitable economic privileges, required evidence of purity of blood and proof of non-Jewish ancestry. Eventually, this process of racialization became the litmus test for admittance to the high levels of Christian society. A descendant of a Jew, regardless of how sincerely Christian or avowedly faithful to his or her king, remained a Jew in the minds of Old Christians, unless lawyers, money, or recognition of a saintly life could erase or conceal the stain (see Chapter 3 and below).

Having said all this, however, the true history of the *Conversos* is still to be written. As William Monter argued a few years ago in a review of Benzion Netanyahu's book, the history of the Jews in Spain is a history of assimilation, that is, a history of the successful integration of thousands of *Conversos* and their families into the ranks of Spanish society. The examples of Pablo de Santa María and his extraordinarily talented and successful progeny, of the Caballería family, of St Teresa of Avila, the mystic, monastic reformer and doctor of the Church, all of them *Conversos* or of *Converso* origins, are only the best examples; but they pale when compared to the thousands of lesser-known cases who had fully crossed over into Christian society by the seventeenth century. Moreover, the statutes of cleanliness of blood (or purity of blood), demeaning as they were, could always be circumvented by money and social connections; for the most part, they came to function more as a class than as a religious (or racial) sieve. The example of the Bernuy family, studied in magisterial detail by Hilario Casado, is illustrative of the roads open to *Conversos* with means and ambition, regardless of origin.

The case of the Bernuy family
Hilario Casado Alonso, a gifted historian of early modern Spanish economic history, is presently at work on a monographic study of the Bernuy family. Although he focuses on the commercial activities and trajectories of the

different branches of the family (in Antwerp, Toulouse, Burgos and elsewhere) – some became Calvinists, others devout Catholics – his study allows us to see how successfully some *Conversos* negotiated social promotion in Spain.[19] From the Jewish neighbourhood (*judería*) to the highest dignity of the nobility (*grandeza*), Casado Alonso traces the history of the family from the fourteenth to the nineteenth century. His research provides us with yet another example of how wealth, ability and the right connections overcame the liabilities of birth and religion. It shows, once again, the permeability of Spain's late medieval and early modern social boundaries. Caution, however, is required. Though the Bernuys were not unique – we have already mentioned the successful cross-over of other great *Converso* families – they were also not typical.

The Bernuy were originally a Jewish family (their Hebrew name is unknown) from the region of Avila. In the mid-fifteenth century, one of the members of the family converted to Christianity, taking the name of Diego de Bernuy. As Casado Alonso explains it, the name Bernuy comes from a hamlet in the region of Avila, Bernuy de Zapardiel, perhaps indicating his place of birth. By the 1450s, Diego de Bernuy was settled in the city of Avila as a wool merchant and dyer. In addition, Diego and his brother, Alonso González de Bernuy, had long-distance commercial interests. The latter traded in Toulouse and Flanders, and Diego had business ties with merchants in Medina de Rioseco, one of the great fair sites in Castile. By the late fifteenth century, Diego de Bernuy was a very rich man and, according to Casado Alonso, one of the most important merchants in Castile. His newly gained status and wealth led to marital ties with a member of a respected Old Christian family of Avila and acceptance into the ranks of the local oligarchy. Other members of the Bernuy family, however, as was usually the case with *Converso* families, married endogamously, that is, they married other prominent *Conversos*.

By 1492, however, as the Inquisition turned its attention to rich *Conversos*, Diego de Bernuy was brought to trial, found guilty of 'judaizing' (of practising Judaism in secret), and forced to wear a *sambenito* (a distinguishing yellow or saffron garb) as a humiliating symbol of heresy. Diego's problems did not end there. Shortly afterwards, he was burned by the Inquisition, though it is unclear whether he was burned alive, or whether his effigy and/or bones were burned after his exile or natural death. But before he died, Diego was able to transfer most of his wealth to his children and friends; and the family escaped the Inquisition's trial fairly unscathed financially.

By the early sixteenth century, members of the Bernuy family had settled in the main commercial centres of Europe – Bordeaux, Toulouse, London, Bruges, Antwerp – and in the Spanish cities of Burgos, Seville, Medina del Campo and Avila. Their commercial activities reached into every corner of western Europe and the New World, establishing relations with the French court, as well as with the Spanish kings. In Burgos, Diego de Bernuy's son, also named Diego, was *regidor* (a high municipal post) in 1513 and his son,

Hernando, also held the post in 1517. By the mid-sixteenth century, the Burgalese branch of the family had become immensely rich, devout Catholics, and exemplary philanthropists. By the 1580s, the Bernuys had invented a new history for their family, in validation of which witnesses testified, as they had for the de Chirinos (Chapter 3), that they could never have been Jews.

In the late sixteenth century, the Bernuys of Burgos owned extensive properties in the area of Córdoba, and by the next century, one of the Bernuys became bishop of Jaén and another, Don José Diego de Bernuy, became marquis of Benameji (named after their Córdoba estate). One hundred years later, in 1789, the title of marquis was raised to the rank of grandee of Spain, the highest level of nobility. The transformation of the Bernuys, from *Conversos* burned at the stake to grandees of Spain, shows – as does the saga of the de Chirinos – that wealth, royal and municipal service, the right marriages with noble families, and above all the hiring of good lawyers and intellectuals to reinvent one's origins, could erase social boundaries.

Life after conversion: the *Moriscos*

Even before the conversions of 1391 or 1492, many Jews were already well integrated into Spanish life in terms of language, daily life, dress, and other material aspects. This was not the case with the *Moriscos*. The reluctance of *Moriscos* to become part of Spanish society, or, to put it more accurately, to become part of Spanish society as constructed by Christians, was remarkable indeed. As long as they were allowed to retain their ancestral language (Arabic or forms of Arabic) and practise their religion (Islam) with impunity – even after the forced conversions in 1504 – the *Moriscos* continued to live in Spain in relative peace and to contribute significantly to the Spanish economy and society. Munzer, a German travelling in southern Spain at the end of the fifteenth century, always drew, in the narrative of his voyage, favourable comparisons between the *Moriscos'* tended fields around Valencia, Murcia and Granada and those of their Christian counterparts, and between the *Moriscos'* diligence and work habits and, by implication, those of the Christians.[20] Nonetheless, by the sixteenth century, the political and social context in which *Moriscos* lived changed dramatically. Several factors affected *Morisco* life and led to their persecution, pejorative representation, and eventual general expulsion from Spain between 1609 and 1611. The first was the growing Ottoman threat in the western Mediterranean and the flourishing of North African piracy. Whether real or not, most of Mediterranean Spain lived, even after Lepanto, in constant fear of Ottoman invasion, landings, and Muslim raids. Watch-towers built on the Spanish Mediterranean coast kept a vigilant eye on presumed invaders. The real fear of these attacks resonates in the literary works of the late sixteenth century, above all in Cervantes's *Don Quixote*. Cervantes himself was captured and imprisoned in

North Africa, and his personal experiences in and subsequent release from captivity form the core of some of *Don Quixote*'s most engaging (non-protagonist-related) stories. Therefore, the *Moriscos* were perceived as a fifth column, ready to join invaders and give information to the enemy, and part of a huge conspiracy to destroy Christendom. Even after the naval battle of Lepanto (1571), when a coalition of Christian navies defeated the Turks and barred them effectively from the western Mediterranean (Cervantes fought, and lost an arm, in this battle), the fear of the Turk and of the *Moriscos* remained. This was not altogether an unfounded fear.[21]

Part of the perception of *Moriscos* as the enemy, as the 'other', had to do with the growing intolerance in Spanish society from the late Middle Ages onwards. I should hasten to add that this was a European-wide phenomenon and that with the exception of small pockets of tolerance, most European countries descended into a frenzy of persecution. Think of the witch craze which swept most of Europe (but not Spain) between the 1490s and the 1650s, or of the endless religious wars and religious persecutions which almost destroyed European society in the sixteenth and early seventeenth centuries.

In Spain, once the Inquisition's campaign against 'judaizers' began to run out of steam in the 1520s and 1530s, the Holy Office began to pay closer attention to the *Moriscos*. As I indicated earlier, the fears of heresy and dissent were not unfounded, for as the evidence from the Inquisition's tribunal of Cuenca and elsewhere shows, most *Moriscos* – notwithstanding their conversion – lacked even the most basic knowledge of Christianity. In the former kingdom of Granada, where memories of independence remained alive, the confrontations between Christians and *Moriscos* reached a boiling point. In 1567, frustrated by the inability to destroy Muslim culture, Philip II banned the use of Arabic, the traditional *Morisco* garb (the veil for women; certain types of hats and garments for men), and manners of eating (types of food, table etiquette, etc.) that identified *Moriscos* with Islamic culture. In a more extreme move, the Crown decreed that *Morisco* children were to be taken away from their parents and brought up as Christians and Spaniards. This was a two-pronged attack in which the Church and Crown combined in pushing the *Moriscos* to assimilate into Spanish society. Two years earlier, in 1565, a Church council in Granada had enacted a series of punitive measures against 'new Christians [originally] of the Mohammedan sect', which restricted their use of Moorish clothing, questioned the *Moriscos*' Christianity, and showed extreme mistrust of these new converts.[22]

The *Moriscos* in the mountains of the Alpujarras (near the city of Granada) rose up in arms in a bloody and hard-fought insurrection in 1568. After their defeat in 1570, the remaining *Moriscos* of Granada were dispersed throughout most of Castile. This was a cruel fate indeed, for it sought to destroy *Morisco* solidarity and sense of community and to isolate *Moriscos* in a hostile and alien world. In spite of the Crown's efforts to assimilate them into Castilian life, these policies did not fully work. (No such policies were even considered in the Crown of Aragon, where, as long as the *Moriscos* continued to work seigneurial lands and pay their seigneurial dues, they were left fairly free to practise their ancestral religion and to speak Arabic.) Instead, Castilian *Moriscos* migrated to cities, tended gardens, which became the main supply of produce to the burgeoning Castilian cities, or became itinerant merchants and peddlers, and rather successful ones too. By keeping alive the links between dispersed communities, some *Moriscos* thus found ways to subvert and counteract the royal wishes for assimilation. But stereotypes, which are so often applied to those who are somewhat different, were immediately mobilized by the Christian population as tools for the subjugation of *Moriscos*. Accused of greed and stinginess, of having too many children, of being versed in sorcery and necromancy, of speaking a foreign language, the *Moriscos* were pushed to the margins of society (imaginarily if not economically) long before they were expelled from the peninsula. In some respects, this discourse of difference is not unlike that which new immigrants confront in the United States or in Europe; and it is not surprising to find that it went on to push the *Moriscos* from the margins of society to permanent exile.

To what an extent they were marginalized can be seen in *Love After Death*, a remarkable play written by Calderón de la Barca around 1632–33 – that is, almost a generation after the expulsion of the *Moriscos* from Spain in the early seventeenth century. Set in Granada at the onset of the Second Alpujarras rebellion of 1568, the play, though sympathetic to the *Moriscos*, nonetheless includes all the markers of difference that make them appear an alien people, in spite of their new Christian faith. The *Morisco* protagonists, though nominally Christian, wear typical Muslim garments (short jackets and trousers for the men, white doublets for the women). One of the characters, Alcuzcuz (a reference to cous-cous, a staple of Muslim diet), is described as fat and a drunkard, in clear contravention of the precepts of Islam. He speaks in pidgin Castilian, providing a comic relief to the play. Even as it gave expression to *Morisco* complaints and depicted *Morisco* heroic deeds, *Love After Death* served to remind audiences in the 1630s of the distance that existed between them and the exiled *Moriscos*. The reconciliation and generous forgiveness scene that closes the play was little more than wishful thinking; it masked the unrelenting refusal of most Spanish Christians to admit in their midst those different from themselves.[23]

Gypsies (Roma)

At the outermost margins of society were the Gypsies or Roma (Romany) people. A world unto themselves, unwilling to give up their wandering lives and to settle within the confines of Spanish society, the Roma, despite their small numbers, played and still play a significant role in the Spanish imagination. Their wandering lives, their exotic *modus vivendi* and dress, their peculiar languages – exotic and peculiar, of course, only from the perspective of the dominant culture – made the Gypsies (the *gitanos*) objects of cruel persecution, discrimination, and derogatory representations, but objects also of long-standing fascination and idealization, the latter most powerfully in the Romantic imagining of Gypsies in the nineteenth century.[24]

In many respects, as despised as they were and unfortunately still are, the Gypsies provided and still provide Europeans and people elsewhere in the world with a vicarious release from their own sedentary and formal lives. Who among the readers – and certainly the writer – has not dreamt, at least once, of 'running away with the Gypsies' (a popular expression in Spanish) and wandering the roads of the world without acknowledging frontiers or laws? The ugly counterpart to this was the tarnishing of Gypsies in fifteenth- and sixteenth-century Spain as congenital thieves and tricksters, as kidnappers of children, as practitioners of the black arts, as irreligious, lascivious and other defamations which in early modern Spain or twentieth-century Europe could get one into a lot of trouble. Even the great Cervantes, who could write so wittily and passionately about Moors and Jews, drew the line at Gypsies in his novel *La gitanilla* (*The Gypsy Girl*, 1613). Nonetheless, as Leblon, Vassberg and others have shown, the Roma people occupied a useful economic niche. As wandering people, they carried goods across the land, often illicitly as contraband, thereby making them more desirable for isolated villagers. Coming through small villages and towns, the Gypsies read palms, told fortunes, and entertained the people with sensuous dances and songs – as they still do today. They were itinerant tinkerers, small traders and con artists; their constant roaming helped them somewhat escape the harsh policies of expulsion that were carried out against Jews and Moors, *Conversos* and *Moriscos*.

But they escaped at a very high price. As William Monter has pointed out: 'The Gypsies were total pariahs, who never intermarried with Old Christians; their mobility and their private language protected them from the Holy Office. Consequently, only a handful of them were ever arrested and none was executed, despite their well-earned reputation for blasphemy, irreligion and superstition'. On the other hand, precisely because they were Gypsies, from 1539 onwards 'all male Gypsies between the ages of twenty and fifty were ordered to serve on the royal galleys for six years'.[25] One had to be very hardy indeed to survive rowing in the galleys for six years, but finding and capturing the Gypsies, getting them to the galleys, and keeping them there was no easy task either.

On the criminal margins

In a later chapter on violence, we shall meet in fuller detail a whole gallery of rogues, people who lived fully outside the bounds of the law or who strode perilously the criminal boundaries of society. Here, I wish to provide just a brief typology of these criminal and marginal types. These included a motley collection of vagrants, thieves, hardened criminals, bandits, tricksters, conjurers, prostitutes, procuresses and, finally, *pícaros* (swindlers), those irrepressible protagonists of the great Spanish picaresque novels. The lives and shady activities of *pícaros* – often conflated with those of Gypsies – can be found in novels, most notably the anonymous *Lazarillo de Tormes* (1554), Quevedo's *La vida del buscón* (*The Swindler*, 1608) and Mateo Aleman's dark *Guzmán de Alfarache* (1599). Other works, such as Cervantes's *Rinconete and Cortadillo* and *Don Quixote*, as well as Fernando de Rojas's *La Celestina*, introduce the reader to go-betweens, prostitutes, thieves and other marginal social figures.[26]

Criminal records and civil and inquisitorial proceedings also give us glimpses into the activities and lifestyles of these individuals. These are fragmented perspectives, however, for they show us only those who were caught, or those whose activities, for some reason or another, drew the attention of the authorities. The writings of social reformers and the legislation of the *cortes* and of municipal governments, nonetheless, attest to a society in which crime and criminals, trickery and violence, permeated everyday life.

But, then, like other social groups, criminals or semi-criminals filled a wide range of social roles, not all of them negative. As William Christian describes it, necromancers, conjurers, tricksters and scam artists plied their trade in sixteenth-century rural New Castile and elsewhere throughout the land. Surprisingly, many were members of the clergy or religious orders, claiming the ability to chase hail-bearing clouds, for example, or to deal with locusts and other agricultural pests.[27] In some respects, the travelling conjurers served a useful social function: their services allayed the fears and anxieties of villagers. Despite run-ins with the Inquisition and civil authorities, they seem to have circulated throughout the Spanish countryside without too much impediment and to have been accepted as reasonably respectable purveyors of protection from natural and demonic disasters.

Similarly, procuresses – those shady old women who acted as go-betweens, repairers of maidenhood, and madams in brothels – also blended in and were associated in the popular imagination and in literary works such as Fernando de Rojas's *La Celestina* with two very distinct social types: on one extreme the witch; and on the other, the *beata*, the pious old woman who went from church to church in her daily devotions, and who followed charismatic priests and preachers in ways not too different from groupies of modern rock stars. Although it was better to be branded a *beata* than a witch – an old woman's very life might well depend on such semantic distinctions – the term *beata* had pejorative connotations, and *beatas* were, in some circumstances, marginalized as well. Perhaps what I am attempting to describe here is the systemic discrimination against and marginalization of the old, above all of old, unattached and poor women. Elsewhere in western

Europe, persecution of women in general, and of old women in particular, was articulated through the witch craze, that is, through the widespread prosecution of women as witches and their condemnation to burning and/or hanging. While between 80,000 and 100,000 people, mostly women, were executed for witchcraft, such accusations and executions were not numerically significant in Spanish inquisitorial trials. Nonetheless, the identification of old women with witchcraft remained a powerful social weapon for keeping certain groups on the margins of society.

Again, however, the point to be emphasized here is that of fluidity across social categories. Celestina, the old go-between in the eponymous work mentioned above, gained access to the houses of the well-to-do under the veil of her piety – that is as a *beata* – while back in her own abode in the outskirts of town she kept a stable of prostitutes, repaired maidenhoods, and plotted malevolent schemes.[28] Likewise, Lazarillo, the hero or anti-hero of *Lazarillo de Tormes*, son of a whore and of a thief who was hanged for his crimes, rose, through trickery, deceit, and the adulterous pimping of his own wife, to a position of relative honour and prosperity in his town. 'Things are not always what they seem' is the refrain of sixteenth-century picaresque novels. Social position and dignity could be purchased with gold and gained through dishonest means.

Nowhere, however, was the ambivalence between crime and legality more vivid than in the case of prostitution. In Spain almost every large town or city had established official brothels by the sixteenth century.[29] Antoine de Lalaing, travelling in Spain in 1502, reports on the neighbourhood of prostitutes in Valencia: 'like a little town, encircled by walls and a single gate, with a gate keeper. Inside in around three or four streets, there were small houses with richly dressed women in silk and damask (between two hundred and three hundred women altogether) plying their trade. The fees were set by the municipality at four *dineros*, and the little enclave of prostitution had two doctors who visited the women on a weekly basis.'[30]

Prostitution and brothels had long been seen as necessary evils, as ways to avoid, in the eyes of the dominant Catholic society, the greater sins of promiscuity, adultery, homosexuality, and crimes of passion. Prostitutes, therefore, whether or not under the legal supervision of a municipal council such as the one in Valencia and almost every other Spanish city, served an important function in the social life of the community. Yet, prostitutes had to wear distinguishing clothing that branded them as sinful and fallen women; and, in the moral economy of late medieval and early modern Spain, they represented all the negative aspects of womanhood. After the Council of Trent (1545–63) and the upsurge of Counter-Reformation Catholic spirituality, pressure mounted to regard prostitution, whether legalized or not, as an evil to be eradicated and prostitutes as lost sheep to be converted, reformed and cloistered in safe monasteries. Elizabeth Perry, in her excellent book *Gender and Disorder in Early Modern Seville*, paints a vivid portrait of the evolution of attitudes towards prostitutes in Seville. As Perry argues of municipal control of prostitution: 'the paternalism of this system of legalized prostitution [by eliminating pimps as middle-men and monitoring the prostitutes' health] served important social functions. It reinforced the power position of officials and clerics who could play the role of authority in rituals that portrayed their power as acceptable because it was compassionate . . . as well as neutralized the anger of prostitution.'[31]

For all that, prostitution represented a significant source of income for municipal councils. The heightened threat of syphilis, which raged throughout the peninsula after 1550, gave greater impetus to the policing and regulation of prostitutes. Surveillance, in turn, made prostitution part of the 'official' social body of the community; for the surveillance of prostitution meant the policing of all of society as well. Here, in the regulation of sexual commerce and the state-controlled commodification of women, we see a glimmer of the geometry of power, sexuality and the law that would become part of the apparatus of the nascent nation-state in early modern Spain and in western Europe.

More transgressive than female prostitution, male prostitution (monetary sodomitic transactions) operated on the fringes of society and completely outside the law. There are a handful of references to male prostitution, all of them cases brought in front of the Inquisition. Religious and cultural prejudices and animosity were directed at various kinds of transgressive sexual behaviour. Sodomy (which is how late medieval and early modern men and women conceptualized what today we call homosexuality or, to be more accurate, same-gender sex, and which was punishable by burning to death), lesbianism, the use of artificial phalluses by consenting females, cross-dressing, and other unusual sexual acts served as categories for marginalization. Jeronimus Munzer reports having seen six Italians, accused of sodomy, hanging from their feet outside the wall of Almería. After hanging from their necks to death, their genitals were cut off and the bodies were hung upside down to illustrate their distorted nature (against nature). This form of punishment, however, was replaced by an edict of the Catholic Monarchs (22 August 1497) by which sodomites were to be burned and their property confiscated.[32]

There were, however, some prominent cases of women who dressed as men and gained a reluctant acceptance from society. In the early seventeenth century, Catalina de Erauso, a nun, fled her convent, dressed as a man, and joined the army in the New World. After killing another soldier in a bar brawl, Catalina revealed herself as a woman and escaped nun to avoid execution. Instead of punishment, Philip IV granted her a pension and, more surprisingly, the right to dress as a man.[33]

As with other types of marginality, unacceptable sexual behaviour could be rendered acceptable, or at least permissible, by royal fiat, wealth and social

111

position. Male homosexuality, effeminate behaviour and dress were often severely punished by death, unless high rank protected the offender from the Inquisition and the law, in which case the damnable offence became simply an expression of fashion and delicacy (see Chapter 6). Social class and, above all, wealth, as Quevedo satirically argued, were powerful lords indeed.

Slaves[34]

At the very edge of marginality were the slaves. As with every other social group, the conditions under which slaves lived and worked ranged widely and depended, to a large extent, on where the slaves lived, in what kind of labour they engaged, and who their masters were. The nature of slavery also changed substantially from the early fifteenth to the mid-sixteenth century in the Spanish world. In the earlier period, most slaves – except for a handful of African slaves – were captured Muslims (Moors) employed in a variety of pursuits and trades. By the sixteenth century, several developments led to a radical transformation of the institution and to a change in the types of slaves brought to Spanish soil and to the colonies. First, the opening of equatorial Africa by the Portuguese led to the growth of the slave trade as a highly profitable enterprise; second, the establishment of the plantation system, mostly dedicated to the growing of sugar cane, created economies of scale and world-wide markets. This led to new forms of slavery – a slavery quite distinct from the traditional slavery of the Mediterranean world – and to a nefarious impact on Black Africans, both in Africa and throughout the western world. The conditions of slaves in the ships engaged in the Atlantic crossing and in the plantations were harsh indeed. Many died along the way, and those who survived suffered the obliteration of their cultures – or the attempts by their masters to obliterate their culture, though many aspects of African religion, language and culture survived in Brazil, Cuba, the Caribbean, and parts of the United States. They also suffered untold brutalities, killing labour, sexual abuses, and other inhumane excesses.

In this regard, the native populations of the New World, although not legally slaves (despite Columbus's recommendation to the Catholic Monarchs to enslave the Caribs after his second voyage), were either decimated by illness (measles, yellow fever), which Europeans brought with them and to which natives had no immunities at all, or died from being overworked. In Cuba, the island's entire native population was wiped out within a few generations. In Mexico, Peru, Bolivia and elsewhere, natives were conscripted by the Spanish colonists through a series of legal or semi-legal arrangements (*encomiendas*), often against the wishes of the Crown, into backbreaking work in agriculture or in mining for precious metals. The silver, which like a running stream flooded Europe in the sixteenth century, was dug up from the earth in the mines of Guanajuato (Mexico) or Potosí (the viceroyalty of Peru) by natives whose worlds had been destroyed by the Spanish conquistadors, and who had been turned into *de facto*, if not legal, slaves.

In Iberia, slavery and forced labour had a somewhat different face. Slaves came from different sources. The most important one was Spain, where Muslims were captured in war, first during the wars against Granada and later in the endemic conflict against North African pirates. When Málaga was taken in 1487 after a stiff resistance, its entire population was enslaved and dispersed throughout the kingdom – mostly through western Andalusia.[35] Munzer, travelling in Valencia, reports having seen men, women and children captured after the rebellion in Tenerife (Canary Islands) in 1486–87, and sold into slavery. Eighty-seven had made the crossing from the Canary Islands in the Atlantic, off the west coast of Africa, to Valencia in the eastern shores of Spain. Fourteen died along the way, and the rest were enchained, sold, and put to 'heavy work'. Munzer describes the Guanches (the inhabitants of the Canary Islands) as 'beastly'; implicitly, he is providing a rationale for their enslavement.[36]

After the fall of Granada in 1492, raids on the North African coast and the capture of Muslim ships at sea or in naval battles – the battle of Lepanto (1571), for example – provided a substantial number of slaves. But it should be added that slaves flowed both ways, for Christians were also captured at sea or on coastal raids and taken as slaves to North Africa. I have already mentioned the most vivid example of such an occurrence, that of Cervantes, who lived as a slave in Algiers before writing *Don Quixote*. Other slaves came from equatorial Africa, brought into the peninsula by Portuguese merchants throughout the fifteenth century and by Spanish and Portuguese slave traders in the following centuries. The conservative estimate for the number of slaves in Spain at the onset of the early modern age is around 100,000, although recent scholarship, most notably Bernard Vincent's, puts the number much higher. Regardless of the figure we accept, slaves represented a significant percentage of the population (100,000 out of around 5,000,000 inhabitants in 1500 and of 7,000,000 in 1600). Divided roughly equally between 'Blacks' from equatorial Africa and 'Whites' from the Barbary Coast, the Ottoman empire, and regions of North Africa, their presence in Spanish society was rendered even more visible by their concentration in urban centres and in certain occupations as household servants, hired out by their masters as artisans and daily labourers (both urban and rural) and as part of the retinue of great houses. In this respect, slavery in Spain was far less brutal than in the New World. Manumissions, the ability of slaves to purchase their own freedom or to be ransomed (in the case of Muslim slaves), were instrumental in freeing and integrating many slaves into Spanish society. In places like Seville, with a large slave population, freedom and integration, however, were often limited. Because of their 'racial features' and experiences of isolation and discrimination, former slaves were restricted to the lower levels of the social order and employed as stevedores, masons, street peddlers, and the like. But, although some slaves gained freedom in early modern Spain, not all of them did. Slaves were chattel, property, and it was not uncommon to brand them, even on their foreheads, with the demeaning words: 'I am the slave of such and such'.

Finally, a substantial number of criminals and heretics (whether found guilty by Inquisitorial or by civil tribunals), Gypsies, and other marginalized groups trekked in chains along the roads of Spain to serve their time in the royal galleys. From the perspective of what they did and of their future life expectancy, once they got to the galleys their fate was incommensurably worse than that of any other group in Spain.

Conclusion

Defining marginality in late medieval and early modern Spain is not an easy task. Categories of marginalization (or what we understand today as marginal) depend on a number of variables, all of which could be altered rapidly. Race, religion, economic class, peculiar behaviour, gender and age were the most common vectors along which exclusion, oppression, exile and even death could occur. Race, as has been seen, did not mean in fifteenth- and sixteenth-century Spain what it means today. Race was often synonymous with religion, as in the case of *Conversos* and *Moriscos*. In Spain, as in most of late medieval and early modern Europe, religion was a key element in marginalizing certain groups, though wealth could diminish or even eliminate discrimination. Poverty and certain forms of behaviour also led to the margins of society. In a country such as Spain, where a large number of non-Christians lived and prospered, the dominant religion could and did deal quite harshly with those holding different beliefs.

Some other groups, such as Gypsies, slaves, galley prisoners, natives in the New World, prostitutes and homosexuals, also suffered increased isolation and classification as alien to the slowly emerging notion of who was a Spaniard. In many respects, although what we call marginalization has always existed, exclusionary and repressive policies reached an unprecedented level in Spain and the rest of western Europe during this period. Emerging national identities and the growing centralization of the nation-state resulted in discourses of difference and exclusion and, more importantly, better methods of repression and surveillance. Those left on the outside paid a heavy price, in lives and in suffering, for the painful birth of modernity.

Notes

1. Most of the most interesting and pioneer work on marginalization in the Middle Ages has been done by Bronislaw Geremek. See his *The Margins of Society in Late*

Medieval Paris (Cambridge, 1987) and his *Truands et misérables dans l'Europe moderne, 1350–1600* (Paris, 1980). In addition, see Michel Mollatt, *The Poor in the Middle Ages* (Chicago, 1986).

2. This is a much debated topic. The classical works by Jean Delumeau, *La peur en Occident* (Paris, 1978); R.I. Moore, *The Formation of a Persecuting Society* (Oxford, 1987); and Carlo Ginzburg, *Ecstasies: Deciphering the Witches' Sabbath* (New York, 1991) have now been criticized by David Nirenberg, *Communities of Violence: Persecution of Minorities in the Middle Ages* (Princeton, 1996). See also the review of Nirenberg's book by Philippe Buc, 'Anthropologie et Histoire (note critique)', *Annales HSS* (Nov.–Dec., 1998): 1243–9.

3. Teofilo F. Ruiz, 'The Holy Office in Medieval France and in Late Medieval Castile: Origins and Contrasts', in Angel Alcalá, ed., *The Spanish Inquisition and the Inquisitorial Mind* (Highland Lakes, NJ, 1987), 33–51 and, in particular, 43–46.

4. See Scarlett Freund and Teofilo F. Ruiz, 'Jews, *Conversos*, and the Inquisition in Spain, 1391–1492: The Ambiguities of History', in J.M. Perry and F.M. Schweitzer (eds), *Jewish-Christian Encounters over the Centuries: Symbiosis, Prejudice, Holocaust, Dialogue* (New York, 1994), 169–95.

5. For the history of the Jews in medieval Spain see Yitzhak Baer, *A History of the Jews in Christian Spain*, 2 vols (Philadelphia, 1966).

6. T.F. Ruiz, *Crisis and Continuity: Land and Town in Late Medieval Castile* (Philadelphia, 1984), 272–82.

7. See Nirenberg, *Communities of Violence*, 127–99.

8. On this see Benzion Netanyahu, *The Origins of the Inquisition in Fifteenth-Century Spain* (New York, 1995), 3–213.

9. Andrés Bernáldez, *Historia de los Reyes Católicos* (Biblioteca de autores españoles, LXX, Madrid, 1953), 599.

10. See T.F. Ruiz, 'Representación: Castilla, los castellanos y el Nuevo Mundo a finales de la Edad Media y principios de moderna', in Carlos Barros (ed.), *Historia a Debate: Medieval* (Santiago de Compostela, 1995), 63–77.

11. See Philippe Wolff, 'The 1391 Pogrom in Spain: Social Crisis or Not?', *Past & Present*, 50 (1971): 4–18; and Nirenberg, *Communities of Violence*, 230–49.

12. Miguel Angel Ladero Quesada, 'Los judíos castellanos del siglo XV en el arrendamiento de impuestos reales', in *El siglo XV en Castilla: fuentes de renta y política fiscal* (Barcelona, 1982), 143–67.

13. See J. Amador de los Ríos, *Historia social, política y religiosa de los judíos de España y Portugal*, 1st reprinting (Madrid, 1973), 915–31, 996–1003.

14. María Asenjo, *Segovia: la ciudad y su tierra a fines del medievo* (Segovia, 1986), 322–9.

15. This debate is summarized in Freund and Ruiz, 'Jews, *Conversos*, and the Inquisition', 185–7.

16. See Henry Kamen, 'The Mediterranean and the Expulsion of Spanish Jews in 1492', *Past & Present*, 119 (1988): 30–55. Also see Freund and Ruiz, 'Jews, *Conversos*, and the Inquisition', 186–8.

17. For a general history of Islam in Spain see Richard Fletcher, *Moorish Spain* (New York, 1992).

18. *Viajes de extranjeros por España y Portugal*, ed. José García Mercadal, 3 vols (Madrid, 1952), I: 251–7.

19. 'De la judería a la grandeza de España. La trayectoria de la familia de mercaderes de los Bernuy (siglos XIV–XIX)', paper given to the annual meeting of the Society for Spanish and Portuguese Historical Studies in Minnesota, 1996. Here I summarize some of Casado Alonso's findings that relate to the family in Spain. I wish to thank Professor Casado Alonso for his help.

20. *Viajes de extranjeros por España y Portugal*, I: 337–68.

21. On *Morisco* life see Antonio Domínguez Ortiz and Bernard Vincent, *Historia de los moriscos: vida y tragedia de una minoría* (Madrid, 1978); also Henry Lapeyre, *Geografía de la España morisca* (Valencia, 1986); María J. Viguera, *Aragón musulmán* (Zaragoza, 1988) for a background to Muslim life in Aragon before 1400.

22. The edict is published in Domínguez Ortiz and Vincent, *Historia de los moriscos*, 268–72.

23. The play has been translated and can be found in Eric Bentley, ed., *The Classical Theatre*, vol. III: *Six Spanish Plays* (New York, 1959), 315–405.

24. On the Roma people in Spain see Steven Hutchinson, *Cervantine Journeys* (Madison, WI, 1992), which deals with literary representations of Gypsies in Golden Age Spain; Louis Cardillac, 'Vision simplificatrice des groupes marginaux par le groupe dominant dans l'Espagne des XVIe–XVIIe siècles', *Les problèmes de l'exclusion en Espagne (XVIe–XVIIe siècles): idéologie et discours* (Paris, 1983), 11–22; and the excellent summary by David E. Vassberg in his *The Village and the Outside World in Golden Age Castile: Mobility and Migration in Everyday Rural Life* (Cambridge, 1996), 143–6.

25. William Monter, *Frontiers of Heresy: The Spanish Inquisition from the Basque Lands to Sicily* (Cambridge, 1990), 323–33.

26. There is an accessible English translation of two picaresque novels: *Two Spanish Picaresque Novels: Lazarillo de Tormes and The Swindler*, published by Penguin (Harmondsworth, 1969 and many reprints).

27. William A. Christian, Jr., *Local Religion in Sixteenth-Century Spain* (Princeton, 1981), 29–30, 63, 191, 236 et passim.

28. See Fernando de Rojas, *La Celestina*, in Bentley, ed., *The Classical Theatre*, III: 1–95.

29. A list of brothels operating under either royal or municipal licence can be found in Angel Luis Molina Molina, *Mujeres públicas, mujeres secretas: la prostitución y su mundo, siglos XIII–XVIII* (Murcia, 1998), 77–98.

30. *Viajes de extranjeros por España y Portugal*, I: 478–9.

31. Mary Elizabeth Perry, *Gender and Disorder in Early Modern Seville* (Princeton, 1990), 140.

32. *Viajes de extranjeros por España y Portugal*, I: 350.

33. Perry, *Gender and Disorder*, 128. For a far more detailed discussion of Erauzo's life, see Mary Elizabeth Perry, 'From Convent to Battlefield: Cross-Dressing and Gendering the Self in the New World of Imperial Spain', in J. Blackmore and G.S. Hutchenson (eds) *Queer Iberia: Sexualities, Cultures, and Crossings from the Middle Ages to the Renaissance* (Durham, 1999), 394–419. Of great interest is also the case of Eleno/Elena de Céspedes, a hermaphrodite, the daughter of an African slave, and the victim of Inquisitorial prosecution in sixteenth-century Toledo. See Israel Burshatin, 'Written on the Body: Slave or Hermaphrodite in Sixteenth-Century Spain', in ibid., 420–56.

34. For a description of slavery in Spain see Vassberg, *The Village and the Outside World*, 146–50; and Antonio Domínguez Ortiz, 'La esclavitud en Castilla durante la Edad Moderna', *Estudios de historia social de España*, II (Madrid, 1952), 367–428. See also the enchanting book by Bartolomé Benassar, *Les tribulations de Mustafa des Six-Fours* (Paris, 1995).
35. Vassberg, *The Village and the Outside World*, 147.
36. *Viajes de extranjeros por España y Portugal*, I: 339.

PART THREE

The structures of everyday life

Chapter 5

Festivals and power: sites of inclusion and exclusion

From the general description of social orders and brief case studies of particular social groups in the previous section of this book (Part Two), we turn now to a different perspective of Spain's social history. Here, and in the other chapters of the third part of this book, I will explore specific aspects of social interaction, or, to borrow Braudel's title for his great three-volume study of early modern European society, the structures of everyday life. My aims in this concluding section of the book are twofold. First, I wish to describe the tenor of late medieval and early modern life in Spain, to attempt to determine how social and cultural manifestations changed over time, and why. Second, I wish to focus on specific social and cultural manifestations: festivals, violence, diet, fashion and attitudes towards the sacred as sites for the encounter of different social orders, as places for social exchange. Although the study of such cultural and historical phenomena as festivals, violence, etc. is in itself a valid concern for social historians, my interest here goes beyond the merely descriptive. Rather, I wish to raise questions as to how different social groups interacted through festive and/or violent exchanges. What was the effect of these performative events on different groups? How did each group participate? What did they bring to these events? What did they take out of them? This chapter and the next one examine the role of festivals in the social history of Spain before proceeding to other cultural and social aspects (violence and daily life) in late medieval and early modern Spain.

Festivals

We begin with a series of vignettes that take us on a wide-ranging tour of Spain's festive tradition (both secular and religious) from the early fifteenth century to the latter part of the sixteenth. Our first example comes from a magnificent cycle of festivals, jousts, *tableaux vivants* and other ludic events, which were held in Valladolid in May 1428. Most of the events were 'public'; that is, they were performed in the main square of Valladolid, attracting the whole population of the city and the surrounding countryside. What follows is a paraphrase of the description of the feast, as recorded in several of the chronicles of the period.

On Thursday, 29 April 1428, the Infanta Doña Leonor, sister of the king of Aragon, of the Infantes of Aragon, of the queen of Castile, and cousin to John II, king of Castile, came to Valladolid on her way to Portugal, where she was to marry Don Duarte, heir to the Portuguese throne. Accompanying her were her redoubtable brothers, the fabled Infantes of Aragon, Don Enrique and Don Juan (the latter was also the king of Navarre), sworn enemies of their cousin the Castilian king (John II). The king of Castile rode on horseback to the outskirts of the city to meet Doña Leonor and her cortège and to bring her into the city with great honour, the king leading the Infanta's horse by the reins within the walls of Valladolid.[1]

The actual cycle of celebrations began with a joust or *pas d'armes* held by the constable, Don Alvaro de Luna. Forty-five knights, all Don Alvaro's men, dressed in garments of gold and silk trimmed with sable and ermine, rode to the field of combat to sustain the honour of their master. After fierce jousting in which the king, the Infantes of Aragon and Don Alvaro participated in spirited fashion, the constable hosted a lavish banquet. The Infante Don Enrique followed with a fantastic production. An Italian craftsman in the service of the Infante built a large castle of wood and canvas, with a high tower, a belfry, twelve other lower towers, and an outer wall encircling the castle. High over the belfry, a golden griffin held a large banner of red and white, and twelve other smaller banners, also of red and white, flew from the other lower towers. From the gate of the imaginary castle to an arch flanked by two towers ran a railing of reeds, dividing the field for the joust. At the arch or ceremonial entry gate to Don Enrique's castle a sign announced to all comers: 'This is the arch of the dangerous pass of hard chance [risk]'. On top of each of the flanking towers stood a man with a leather horn, and, nearby, a golden wheel, *'la rueda de la aventura'* (the wheel of Fortune) reminding those entering the *pas d'armes* of the unpredictable and changing nature of the goddess Fortuna.

The fictitious castle was the setting of a fictitious war. Outside its walls, in front of the mighty and the people of Valladolid, the Infante Don Enrique danced as a prelude for dressing for combat. After eating and drinking, the Infante retired to his lodgings to arm himself. Upon return to his fictitious castle, he brought with him an *entremés*, a short theatrical skit or *tableau vivant*. The chronicler describes it for us: 'Eight young maidens, riding on noble horses, all very well dressed, followed by a cart with a woman dressed as a goddess (Fortuna), and twelve singing maidens accompanied her in the cart, as well as many minstrels'.

Upon arriving at the gate, the goddess, surrounded by her maidens, sat at the foot of the golden wheel of fortune to witness the combat. Dressed now in armour, the Infante Don Enrique and five of his knights rode to the railing to hold the ground against all challengers. To the sound of horns and the tolling of a bell from the belfry of the fantastic castle, a lady on a small mare rode, in the company of a herald, to meet the knights attempting to enter the *pas d'armes*. 'Lords, what adventure has brought you to this dangerous pass called Pass of the Strong [meaning difficult or adverse] Fortune? Return, for you cannot pass without jousting'. To this challenge rose first the king of Castile, with twenty-four of his knights dressed in green garments. John II wore gold, silver and ermine (white and black), and his helmet carried a large plume and a diadem of butterflies. The king fought 'as such an accomplished knight that it was a marvel', breaking two strong lances. He was followed to the joust by the king of Navarre – who broke only one lance – with twelve knights dressed as windmills. The day concluded with a sumptuous dinner hosted by the Infante Don Enrique in the lodgings of Don Alfonso Enríquez, admiral of Castile.

Once the feast of the Infante Don Enrique concluded, it was the turn of his brother Don Juan, king of Navarre. On 24 May, Don Juan and five of his knights rode to the joust to hold a *pas d'armes*. A rich tent was set up in an open field, and the host stood surrounded by thirteen attendants, dressed in silver (white) collars and red caps. To this feast, the king of Castile came with ten knights in garments of olive-brownish green. On his back John II carried a javelin and a horn and, preceding him, the king's huntsmen and hunting dogs drove a chained lion and a bear. John II took two turns in the list, breaking a 'very strong lance'. He was followed by the Infante Don Enrique, with five of his knights dressed in brown and blue. The Infante also broke a lance, but then withdrew to his lodgings, only to return soon after, alone, without any fanfare and richly garbed in clothes embroidered in gold with a placard that read *Non es* (meaning: he is not [king], as his cousin and brother were). After the tournament, the royal family dined at the king of Navarre's lavishly appointed tent, which was decorated with French tapestries and a ceiling of red, white and blue.

Finally, in the beginning of June, John II held his own festivities in honour of the Infanta Doña Leonor. This feast, like the previous ones, revolved around a tournament or *pas d'armes*. In the main square of Valladolid, the king's men set up a covered stand with eighteen rows of seats that were adorned with rich golden cloth. The railing for the joust was red, and at the end of the list stood a platform decorated with rich French cloth. The king of Castile rode to the mock battle, all dressed in white, as God the Father. Twelve knights, also in white and dressed as saints and with 'a symbolic token of each saint's martyrdom in their hands', followed the king into the joust. Their horses were fitted with red cloth, and each man carried an emblem that read '*Lardón*' (*Galardón*). The Infante Don Enrique answered the call to arms and courtly deeds with twelve of his men, six dressed as 'flames, that is, in colours imitating flames'; the garments of the rest were covered with mulberry leaves. His brother, the king of Navarre, also rose to the challenge. Within an artificial rock, he rode to battle, and one of his men, standing on top of the rock, waved the king's banner. Fifty knights, twenty-five in front, twenty-five behind, surrounded the king of Navarre, making thunder-like noises (*lanzando truenos*). After jousting until 'the stars appeared in the sky', the king took the entire gathering to his lodgings for a feast.[2]

This cycle of feasts held the popular as well as literary imagination for many years. Echoes of its magnificence and bizarre displays still resonated in the poetry of Jorge Manrique more than four decades later. They contrast vividly, because of their marked aristocratic air, with other more popular types of festivals, such as Jaén's carnival celebrations in the 1460s, Philip II's royal entry into Zaragoza in 1585, the numerous inquisitorial *autos-de-fe* performed in Madrid's Plaza Mayor, in Toledo's Zocodover and elsewhere throughout the Spanish Empire, or, finally, with the increasingly important feast of the Corpus Christi throughout Spanish urban centres. Elsewhere in my work, I have already studied in detail the feasts of Valladolid and shown their political meaning and the manner in which John II and his constable, Alvaro de Luna, deployed colours and other symbols to enhance the power of the king against their enemies, the Infantes of Aragon. This feast concluded with the exile of the Infantes from Castile and the temporary victory of the constable's policies.[3]

In the following pages we turn to different manifestations and examples of ludic performances in late medieval and early modern Spain. My concern, however, in these two chapters is not all type of festivities. The private celebrations of rich and poor, such as the wedding of Camacho described in Cervantes's *Don Quixote*, will be treated in the last two chapters. Here, my concern is with communal festivities. With this caveat, a few general observations are necessary to place festivals within their social contexts and to examine how festivals worked and to what purpose.

The history of festivals goes back to the very beginnings of history, and they have always been an integral part of the human social and cultural need for play. They also served as ways of articulating prestige, social difference and power. In the medieval Spanish kingdoms, there were, by the fifteenth century, well-established cycles of festivals. In addition, special events, or unique circumstances, were often legitimized by celebratory performances. The long summary of the festival cycle of May 1428, with which this chapter began, is an example of the latter.

Calendrical feasts

In a sense, one can posit two distinct categories of festivals: calendrical and non-calendrical. Calendrical festivals were closely tied to the liturgical calendar and most often celebrated the landmarks of the Christian year. The chronicles of the period include either passing references or elaborate descriptions of the festivals held at Christmas, the Epiphany (6 January), Candlemas (2 February), Easter, Ascension Day, the feast of St John the Baptist (24 June),

St Michael's Day (29 September), St Martin's Day (11 November) and the numerous feast days given to the Virgin. Let us not be deceived by the religious character of these festivals. The chronicles often highlighted the secular attributes of the celebrations – the jousts, the *juego de cañas* (a peculiar Spanish diversion, borrowed from Moorish culture, in which men galloped against each other at great speed and fought with wooden lances), the *tableaux vivants*, the elaborate meals, the dancing and other such demonstrations – while passing quickly over their devotional aspects. This was certainly the case of the account produced by Don Miguel Lucas de Iranzo's chronicler, who, in recording the festivities of Jaén in the 1460s, downplayed their religious features to promote the secular enterprises sponsored by his master.[4] Similar descriptions, emphasizing secular celebrations, are found in the Castilian chronicles of the fifteenth and sixteenth centuries, as well as in their Valencian, Aragonese and Catalan counterparts.

Calendrical celebrations – i.e. those repeated every year and thus part of ritual performances – included ancient festival traditions which had been co-opted by the Church and secular rulers. Carnival, and the festivities associated with May Day, probably had origins that pre-dated Christianity but that became linked with Church festivities: Carnival as a prelude to Lent; May Day celebrations as part of the month-long tribute to the Virgin Mary.[5] Both of these calendrical festivals, despite their liturgical associations, retained enough pre-Christian and subversive elements to make them quite distinct from other festivals in the traditional religious calendar.

Non-calendrical feasts

Non-calendrical feasts commemorated special occasions of a non-repetitive nature. Royal and princely entries, the ascent of the king or queen to the throne, the birth of a royal heir, the weddings and funerals of the powerful, and the celebrations of great victories engendered festivals that were distinct from the year-long iterative liturgical celebrations. A word of caution, however, is necessary. Although these non-calendrical activities lacked the repetitive nature of calendrical ones and were not fixed to specific dates, they were rituals nonetheless and part of a complex network of symbolic and performative codes. As such, they embodied, and helped define, the dominant social and political discourse.

Royal entries, the feasts marking the beginning of a new reign, and royal weddings followed carefully choreographed scripts that borrowed from precedents and imitated historical as well as literary models. No king would have deviated radically from the traditional entries of his ancestors. The repetitive nature of ludic events – even when not following a liturgical cycle – provided continuity. They inscribed ritual and social negotiation – in this case, the political displays of the monarchy – into the everyday life of the populace.[6]

From the perspective of social history, festivals, whether calendrical or not, were familiar, comforting, entertaining events that crossed class boundaries while reiterating, by ritual performance, the differences between social groups. Festivals and other public ludic events thus functioned not merely as sites of power (that is, to legitimize the power of those who ruled), but also as generators of a manifold discourse of inclusion and exclusion.

There is yet another aspect of festivals that I should mention here briefly before looking in detail at issues of inclusion and exclusion. Festivals also played an important economic role in the life of the realm as a whole and of cities in particular. Although this is not a book about the economy of late medieval and early modern Spain, the frequent distribution of food at formal festivals added greatly to the caloric intake of the poor. In many respects, these celebrations provided a necessary part of the diet of lesser social groups and helped maintain hierarchical relations between different social orders. In addition, the planning and staging of these feasts, as well as the provisioning of the towns and the influx of visitors attending particular events, required a restructuring of supplies, special budgets, and the like, which affected the policies of the monarchy and of municipal councils. Behind social displays and festive symbols lay the harsh realities of economic exchanges, food distributions, and the lower classes' constant hunger.

Festivals of inclusion and exclusion: power and the binding of social groups

In 1440, the Infanta Doña Blanca, daughter of John, king of Navarre (whom we have already met as one of the Infantes of Aragon and who eventually became the king of the Crown of Aragon), came into Castile to wed the Infante Henry, heir to the throne of Castile. On the outskirts of Briviesca, a small town in northern Castile under the lordship of the count of Haro, one of the kingdom's greatest magnates, the Infanta was greeted with an elaborate cycle of festivities. These celebrations reveal how the occasion served as a display of power and as a means to bind the population into a legitimation of the existing order.

The first to meet the Infanta and her cortège were the count and his retinue, as she witnessed the spirited combat of one hundred knights, fifty dressed in red against fifty dressed in white. After this martial display, the Infanta continued on her way into Briviesca, where she was received 'by everyone' in the town. Among the sounds of trumpets, drums and other musical instruments, the members of artisan confraternities paraded with their banners, danced in the streets and performed short theatrical skits (*entremeses*) for the Infanta. The Jews danced in the streets of Briviesca carrying the Torah, while the Moors did likewise carrying the Qur'ān. This they did 'in the manner', the chronicler tells us, 'that was usual when kings from abroad come to rule Castile'. These public events were followed by banquets lasting four days, day-long dances, mummers, and the running of bulls and jousts. The feasts concluded with a theatrical and bizarre hunt held in a vast fenced meadow and performed for the Infanta and her ladies, who sat on a stage looking on the proceedings.[7]

One can easily reconstruct this cycle of festivities. It progressed from a noble reception, restricted to the powerful count of Haro, other magnates and the one hundred warring knights, to the entrance into the city, where it was received by artisans, Jews, Moors and the rest of the population. Although the scripting of the feasts followed a rigorous hierarchical order – nobility first, those below later, and then a return to the celebrations of the mighty – those of lower social standing were included in performances that brought together all social orders.

Although ruled by a powerful lord, Briviesca was a small town indeed. Castilian Jews in the 1440s lived in precarious conditions, their numbers were small, and they were economically marginalized. The same could be said of Moors, living so far north, deep into the Old Castilian heartland; yet, both groups are prominently mentioned in the chronicle as participants in these public displays. And they were not just casual but crucial participants in the established rituals of reception. In a society fraught with antagonisms between different social and religious groups, rivalries and mistrust, even open hatred and persecution, were temporarily set aside for civic spectacles and ritual performances.

How eagerly Jews, Moors, artisans and marginal groups in Briviesca, or in other towns where similar events took place, participated in these feasts is hard to tell. In the next chapter, we shall see how they were compelled to participate in the feast of the Corpus Christi. For now, one can say that there were rewards to be enjoyed: the dances, the mummers, the running of bulls, the exciting jousts, the excesses of free food and drink distributed throughout town. The chronicler lavishly describes the amount of food, the silver fountains that poured wine for all to drink. The beautiful garments of the noblemen and ladies, the well-appointed horses, the innumerable rich tapestries and banners – all of these brought temporary relief from the awful drabness of medieval life, from the squalor and shortcomings of the lives of the poor and the persecuted religious minorities.

For a brief period of time, they were included (albeit often forcibly) as festive participants in the social fabric of the town and kingdom; they played an important role in the ritual affirmation of power. It did not matter then, as it does not matter today, that these moments of elation, of binding social groups, also served to confirm their diminished status and their oppression. Today, cultural artefacts such as TV, football and carnival work in similar ways: by binding most people into a common experience, and by providing an outlet for the miseries of everyday life, they obfuscate *and* buttress class differences. This point deserves to be reiterated, and I will do so throughout these two chapters, for it goes to the very heart of how power is exercised and social distinctions are maintained.

City and countryside

Festivals also served other purposes. In Briviesca in the 1440s, in Jaén in the 1460s, in Seville during Holy Week from the sixteenth century onwards and elsewhere in late medieval and early modern Spain, the celebrations of the mighty bound country to city. These rites of inclusion helped urban centres, dominated by local oligarchs, to assert their hegemony over the surrounding countryside.

When Henry IV of Castile (1454–74) came to Jaén in 1464, he was met far away from the city by the constable of Castile and governor of Jaén, Don Miguel Lucas de Iranzo. Riding a white horse, with a scarlet damask banner in his hand and surrounded by a large contingent of knights, the constable escorted the king to the outskirts of the city. Half a league (around two miles) from the city gates, at that liminal point between urban and rural spaces, the king was met by a motley group, which included the canons of Jaén's cathedral chapter and municipal officials leading the procession. They were followed by five hundred knights, donning false beards (that is, disguised as Moors), thirty other knights dressed as Moorish women, playing tambourines and bells, four thousand children (the chronicler surely exaggerates the number) riding wicker horses, another thousand children armed with wicker crossbows and 'many other men and women'.[8]

As in other royal and princely entries, the entire population walked all the way out to the city's border to bring the king or royal prince back within the walls of the city. These city spectacles, therefore, linked urban centres to their hinterland. Throughout most of Spain (certainly in central and southern Spain), because of the topography and the historical peculiarities of the Reconquest, cities (in this case, Jaén) ruled over a vast and often sparsely populated countryside. Jurisdiction over distant villages was always in question throughout the fifteenth century and part of the sixteenth. Antagonisms within the city and its hinterland abounded. Almost every festival, certainly royal and princely entries, included a transposing of urban symbols of power – the seals and banners of the community, the parade of richly dressed municipal officials and ecclesiastics – to the countryside. Similarly, great feasts, whether noble jousts, rowdy carnivals or elaborate processions of the Corpus Christi in Seville, Valencia and Barcelona, drew peasants from faraway villages to the abundant food (often free), the novelty, excitement and splendour of the proceedings. They were entertained on these occasions, woven into the common body of the community and taught salutary lessons about social differences, hierarchy, obedience and power.[9]

In this sense, the feasts also showed a purposeful transition from 'public' to 'private', from exterior spaces to interior ones. Although public and private are quite modern concepts, and they do not fit fully the reality of late medieval and early modern life, there is no other way to describe the ebb and flow that occurred within each individual feast and that can also be discerned when we look at the history of festivals in Spain over a period of two hundred years.

Public and private

The great festivals organized by the mighty (jousts, entries, and other such feasts) always included performances and displays that took place in the main square of the town – as was the case of the great feast in Valladolid in 1428, the telling of which opened this chapter. Similarly, the feasts often took place in both urban and country settings. An example of this is the theatrical hunt organized for Doña Blanca in a fenced meadow outside Briviesca. It followed other elaborate celebrations within the town walls themselves. In Jaén, all of the feasts of the constable in the 1460s included public celebrations in the city, followed by lavish banquets and bear-baiting in the nearby countryside. What I wish to emphasize here is that these performances, to be effective, required an audience, and the larger the better. Beyond the obvious attempt to bind people into a community, to provide them with a collective identity defined by the power of the feast-giver, the *mise-en-scène* of Spanish festivals in this period, or at least until the late sixteenth century, required the inclusion of *all* social classes, all religious groups (except for Jews after 1492 and for Muslims after 1504) in public and communal participation.

With rare exceptions, the planning for these festive events was the work of the powerful or their agents. In the organization of festivals, there were, of course, many levels of participation and varying relationships of mutual empowerment and responsibility between diverse social groups. Artisan confraternities organized their own parades, practised and performed their *tableaux vivants* and theatrical skits. The audience, on the other hand, was always a motley group of the very important, as, for example, the Infanta Doña Blanca sitting on a stage and gazing in amazement at the bizarre celebrations of 1440, and the lower social groups, standing or sitting by the side. This is not to say that the 'audience', by which I mean the mass of the people, was passive. The feasts were highly successful as sites for social negotiations because of the high degree of participation they demanded. Those attending shouted their approval (or disapproval), danced, prayed and showed their devotion (in the case of the Corpus Christi and other religious events), ate and drank together or, until the mid-sixteenth century, almost together. And sometimes, when things got completely out of hand, they joined in rebelling and in wreaking wanton violence.

These communal and inclusive events, however, always gave way to private and exclusionary ones. At some point in the feast, entry, joust or procession, the 'people', that is to say the powerless, would be left out in the streets, albeit still celebrating the last revelry. The mighty withdrew to the interior of palaces or to well-appointed tents for lavish banquets. Earlier, we have already witnessed this pattern in the feasts of 1428. At the nocturnal celebrations, access was restricted only to those close to the royal family and high nobility. Similarly, the feasts of Don Miguel Lucas de Iranzo, the reception of Doña Blanca in Briviesca and Philip II's triumphal entry into Zaragoza show this progression from the all-inclusive 'public' celebrations to the more intimate and 'private' gatherings of those who ruled. This is, of course, nothing new. It is a pattern followed to this very day. As today, it served a social and political purpose in late medieval and early modern Spain. It reiterated the distance between social groups and the hegemony of one group over another. In ruling or in creating patterns of ritual observance – which in some respects is one and the same process – repetition is all important. In the tripartite division of society, those who worked in Spain and throughout Europe knew that the private circles of the mighty and their celebrations were not open to them.

In many respects, Habsburg Spain in the sixteenth and seventeenth centuries witnessed the progressive withdrawal of the monarch and his family from the public gaze. Clearly, from the mid-sixteenth century onwards the kings of Spain had little taste or inclination for frequent public displays. They preferred instead to isolate themselves, as Philip II did at the Escorial, from the kind of participatory kingship one finds in the realms of Spain from the twelfth century until the end of the Middle Ages. The Habsburgs, to a certain extent because of their Burgundian inheritance or because of new ways of conceiving of royal power and dignity, had no desire to be in the public eye.[10] Sometimes, however, it was politically unavoidable, as in the case of Philip II's entry into Zaragoza, but, on the whole, royal participation in public festival cycles declined.

Here we are faced with a social transformation that transcended the personal likes and dislikes of particular monarchs and magnates and their inflated sense of royal majesty. By the mid-sixteenth century, there was a noticeable shift in the use of festivals to unite the different orders of society in rituals of obedience to the Crown. This development was most certainly related to the growing centralization of political power, above all in Castile. It also reflected the growing prestige of the monarchy. Following the reforms of Ferdinand and Isabella in the late fifteenth century and the restoration of some semblance of order in the realms, a popular religion of the monarchy unfolded in (mostly Castilian) Spain which, unlike in France and England, did not depend on the sacralization of royalty.[11] Rather, the kings in Castile derived their popular support – despite some criticism and complaints – from the large reserves of goodwill they elicited from the people. Foreign travellers often reported the devotion and respect with which Spaniards throughout the land referred to their kings, often by uncovering their heads when pronouncing the king's name.[12] Literary works, *Don Quixote* most notably, often drew the line at attacks on the king, though there were exceptions, such as Quevedo's mordant satires. But, by then, Spain was beginning its disastrous descent.[13]

In many respects, what took place in most of Spain during the slow transition from the Middle Ages to modernity was a shift in the nature of festivals and a hardening of social differences, certainly a widening of the gap between the highest and lowest levels of society. Some of the social fluidity of the turbulent fifteenth century (more a matter of perception than reality) was replaced by a fierce competition for exclusive rights and entitlements among groups and an exaggerated sense of one group's prerogatives *vis-à-vis* those of others. The growing distance between those above and those below was not just a matter of ideology, literacy, or even economics; it was physical as well. Think of the popular feasts of 1428, which I have described above, when kings and royal princes fought, danced and acted out their political agendas while surrounded by a throng of the common people from Valladolid and its hinterland. Think of the theatrical skits performed in Jaén or Briviesca, as the mighty perambulated through the streets of the town, and compare them to the theatrical representations staged in the inner courtyards and rooms of the palace of the Retiro (Buen Retiro) or in the artificial pond (the Lake of the Retiro Palace) in Madrid. Although some of these theatrical performances date from the 1630s, just on the other side of our chronological terminus, they are emblematic of the greater social distance coming into play that I am attempting to trace here.

Private plays were frequently performed inside palaces to which the people of Madrid had no access. There were still performances that either a limited number of citizens or all the people of Madrid were allowed to attend. Yet, how they were allowed to do so was dramatically different from the previous centuries. The stage was set on a raft. The players faced the king and his court, who were lavishly installed on one of the shores of the artificial lake. On the other shore or in boats stood the people of Madrid, barely able to hear the dialogue or to see the faces of the actors.[14] They gazed upon the stage, and beyond – with the stage as a link between ruler and people – they gazed upon the king and his court. Here too we find inclusive moments. The citizens of Madrid, rich and poor, flocked into the gardens of the royal palace. They were entertained by theatrical productions, which bolstered Crown and Church and reaffirmed social differences and obedience to those on top. They were witnesses to the power of the king and his court and to the divinely sanctioned justice of a society of orders. But proximity to the king was now frowned upon. It was not allowed.

The removal of public performances by the powerful to more controlled physical spaces was distinguished above all by the increasing physical distance between the king and the people, and between great lords, churchmen and commoners. Whether by the (still incomplete) transition from public squares and city streets to the circumscribed spaces of the *corrales* or the floating stage of the Retiro, or by the partial (but noticeable) transition from 'secular' (jousts, carnival, banquets in the outskirts of the town, etc.) to 'religious' (*autos-de-fe*, Corpus Christi processions and other religious observances), theatrical performances in the sixteenth century lost their earlier spontaneity and openness and became subject to tighter official regulation and control. In them, the king was a towering but aloof presence. As in the great Inquisitorial displays of sixteenth- and seventeenth-century Madrid, he would just make an appearance on his balcony, content to be gazed at from below by the attending crowd. In the next chapter, I will return to this theme as well as to religious festivals, but now we must take up a very different and controversial topic.

Carnival in Spain, 1400–1600

In his remarkable and suggestive book *Rabelais and His World*, Mikhail Bakhtin, the noted Russian literary critic, argued that the late medieval and early modern carnival was the quintessential subversive celebration. According to Bakhtin, during carnival the social order was inverted, put upside down. During carnival celebrations, social rules were suspended; those at the bottom of society were able to ridicule and debase those in power. Even if for a brief period of time only, the 'popular script' replaced the 'official' one; and in the revelry and excesses of carnival, the status quo was challenged and, in exceptional cases, such as at the carnival in Romans chronicled by Le Roy Ladurie, those in power were physically and violently threatened.[15]

Following Bakhtin, the carnival stood in direct contrast to other types of festivals. Whereas celebrations such as royal entries, Corpus Christi processions, and the like confirmed the established order, carnival subverted it. Whereas the former served to enhance solidarity within the community in rituals of inclusion, the latter, through its inversions and debasing, pitted one social group against another and questioned the normative structure of society. Notwithstanding Bakhtin's wonderful insights and remarkable contributions to the study of carnival, ribaldry and humour in late medieval and early modern Europe, I have serious doubts about his assumptions on the role of carnival in the political and social life of fifteenth- and sixteenth-century Europe in general and Spain in particular.

Although the carnival is usually associated with the days preceding Ash Wednesday and the beginnings of Lent – above all the Mardi Gras or Fat Tuesday, the culmination of carnivalesque excesses – in truth, most of the

Spanish medieval and, to a lesser extent, early modern festive cycles included elements of carnival: inversion, cross-dressing, and the mocking of authority. That is, carnival elements, as shall be seen later, were not limited to the eve of Lent.[16] The presence of fools (*locos* in Spain), Morris dancers (the sabre or sword dances), mummers, *tableaux vivants*, food fights and disguises was evident in all type of celebrations throughout the year. Of these carnivalesque forms, the disguises – the almost obligatory dressing of Christians as Moors, sometimes as Moorish women – reflect not only the historical impact of Muslim culture in Spanish history but the central role played by representations and debasements of the 'other' (in this case Moors and Jews) in ritualized festivals.

The Christmas festivities celebrated in Jaén in 1463, under the sponsorship of the constable Don Miguel Lucas de Iranzo, included one hundred Christian knights disguised as Moorish knights. They engaged a similar number of knights, dressed as Christians, in mock combat. The feasts also included knights playing the roles of the king of Morocco, the erstwhile enemy of Christian Spain, and of Muhammad, who, when defeated, hurled the Koran first on the ground and later into a fountain. At the conclusion of the twelve-day celebration of Christmas, on 6 January, the Day of the Epiphany, twelve knights marched through the streets of Jaén with crowns on their heads and masks on their faces, followed by a fool dressed as the Master of the Military Order of Santiago, the sworn enemy of the constable.[17]

The rituals of carnival and its symbolic language could reach bizarre proportions. Nonetheless, like other types of festivals, it also bound, *pace* Bakhtin, different and antagonistic social groups into a community. Thus, rather than subvert norms, in many instances carnival – by providing moments of relief and entertainment and by articulating notions of power and hierarchy, even if through ribaldry – assuaged popular unrest and eased the task of ruling.

During the Jaén celebrations of Holy Week in 1461, the constable Don Miguel Lucas de Iranzo, after praying at the sanctuary of the Virgin in Guadalupe, returned to Jaén for further devotions at the cathedral on Maundy Thursday and Good Friday. On Easter Monday, once the solemnities of Easter Sunday had been left behind, the constable offered the city of Jaén a carnivalesque spectacle in which the people were both observers and participants. It also taught them salutary lessons about social status in a society of orders and power. After a public distribution of Easter pastries to the population of the city, the constable had built a huge wooden castle on wheels. The castle was dragged into the main square by the constable's guards, and those manning the castle – also the constable's men – attacked a tower defended by the constable and some of his court. A battle ensued in which eggs were used as projectiles. Nine to ten thousand eggs, the chronicler tells us, were deployed in the battle. This was followed by a sumptuous banquet given by Miguel Lucas de Iranzo and held outside the city walls. The entire population of the city was invited. The hosts, the constable, his wife, and

133

sister-in-law, danced to the delight of those in attendance. And there was still more that day: a bear-baiting show; a return to the city for a nocturnal joust, with the list (the arena of the tournament) lit by innumerable torches; abundant music; and yet another serving of food distributed to the population just before retiring for the night. This exhausting day allowed no time for thought about the very real problems facing Jaén, a city on a disputed frontier, or about the oppressive and predatory nature of the constable's rule over its people. What the latter probably remembered, as they put their heads on their miserable beds, was the constable, colourfully dressed, standing high over them on top of the tower, his dancing, the food, and the fun of the day.[18]

The private chronicle that depicts these events also provides many other examples of carnivalesque celebrations. Without an exception, however, they were scripted by the constable or his men, and the debasing and mockery were always directed at Miguel Lucas's enemies, whether lay or ecclesiastic. The constable, his family or allies were never targets of any of the carnivalesque ribaldry.

The carnival feasts in Spain

Julio Caro Baroja, in his delightful study of the carnival in Spain, describes the carnivalesque season as extending from Christmas or the Epiphany (6 January) to Ash Wednesday (the beginning of Lent), but carnivalesque revelry was present, as we have just seen, throughout the festive year. According to Caro Baroja, the carnival in Spain (and elsewhere) was recognizable by a series of paradigmatic events and deeds. Most were popular in character, having the rough, grotesque and vulgar excesses of popular humour so well described by Bakhtin;[19] some were given a polite veneer when appropriated by the elite and well-to-do. Carnivalesque play, however, even when scripted and used by the powerful, always retained evidence of its popular provenance. Carnival, then, was a site for the meeting of social groups, where the playing field – though perhaps not allowing for as much popular agency as scholars have often argued – was nonetheless more even than in other types of festivals.

One of the main characteristics of the carnival was carnality. Carnivalesque celebrations were dominated by food, excesses of eating and drinking, elements of the irrational, and jovial madness. Though not a Spanish painting, Brueghel's depiction of carnival or, rather, of the contrasts between the abundance and carnality of carnival and the austerity and leanness of Lent captures the quintessential notions of the celebration. In Spain, the fourteenth-century *Libro de Buen Amor* (the *Book of Good Love*) describes, in one of its most engaging sections, the struggle between Don Carnal (Lord Carnality) and *Cuaresma* (Lady Lent). The former's armies, composed of hams, pieces of bacon, succulent cheeses, kitchen utensils, game and abundant wine, are routed by Doña Lent's host of fishes and vegetables. Carnality is imprisoned, and thus begins the metaphorical withdrawal from the world during the forty days preceding Easter Sunday.[20]

Obviously, the carnal excesses of carnival also reflected the anxiety of the poor about food. Spain, and the Mediterranean as a whole, as Braudel has pointed out, was a land of scarcity. This preoccupation with food had its counterpart in mythical stories about a paradisiacal land (Cockaigne, *jauja* in Spanish) where there was no hunger, where partridges and hams flew through the air and landed directly in one's mouth. Paradise became a stomach filled with victuals and delicacies that in real life were eaten only by the rich. The food images of carnival and the actual distribution of food by the powerful during these and similar festivities erased, even if temporarily, one of the most important social boundaries separating rich and poor, powerful and weak: that is, how they ate. The 'armies' of carnival were composed precisely of the food items (with the exception of bacon) that the poor seldom ate, either because they were not affordable, or because, as was the case with venison and other game, they were reserved for the nobility by strict sumptuary laws.

Carnival was also marked by acts of irrationality (within the limits prescribed by those in power), by the presence of *locos* (fools, madmen), by satire, by verbal and physical abuse, by inversions and cross-dressing. As Caro Baroja points out, however, social and economic standing had a great deal to do with whether one inflicted the abuse or was a victim of it. The targets for derision were most often the poor and the weak. Cross-dressing, mostly men dressed as women, though the opposite can be found as well in the literature and in the daily life of the period, also provided a way in which to erase important gender boundaries. The woman who dresses as a man to redress attacks against her honour or to enjoy greater freedom of movement is a common figure in Golden Age literature. The best examples can be found in *Don Quixote*, specifically in the character of Dorotea, the protagonist of one of the stories within Cervantes's marvellous narrative. This is also the case of Rosaura in Calderón de la Barca's incomparable *Life is a Dream*. In both cases, cross-dressing helped overcome the liabilities of femininity in early modern Spain, but it also promoted social inferiors (Dorotea and Rosaura) to some rough equality with their deceivers. Cross-dressing in the other direction, that is, males dressed as women, appeared to many contemporaries as an excessive form of frivolity (unless performed in a specific same-sex scenario and thus punishable by law). Often harshly condemned by the Church, it was found mostly at court or in the plays of the elite, and, as the case of Jaén shows, it was used in carnival to debase the enemy.

Carnivals in the sixteenth century

We have already seen the carnivalesque excesses of Jaén. Were those of the following century any different, and why? An anonymous, undated document, most probably from the mid-sixteenth century, describes the festivities of Fat Tuesday, or Mardi Gras, in Madrid. The narrative is restricted to the outcome of a tournament held in front of the lodgings of the '*comendador*' and describes, in careful detail, the garments of the knights crossing lances and of the ladies witnessing the combat. We learn, in passing, that the prince and the cardinal of Toledo watched some of the events from a window, and that at the end of the day there was a feast in which the 'ladies and gentlemen danced as was the custom'.[21] Similarly, in the joust held during the first Sunday of Lent, 'because during Carnival there was no place to hold the tournament because of the many feasts that took place', the emphasis is on the clothing and dancing of the nobles in attendance.[22]

In fifteenth-century chronicles, especially in the private chronicle of Don Miguel Lucas de Iranzo, we find the same preoccupation with describing – sometimes in excessive detail – the clothing of the upper elite as well as their dancing. Missing from most brief accounts of carnival time in the sixteenth century, however, are the people and the intermingling of the powerful and the weak, of nobles and commoners. For all we know, the 'people', in this case the merchants, artisans and workers of Madrid, were there on the fringes of the celebration. The jousts were, after all, held in public spaces and remained high-quality entertainment. But although the people may have been present *in situ*, they do not appear in the narratives. Their public role of legitimizing power had diminished in the political world of Habsburg Spain, or at least in the context of carnival. In the account just cited, the prince, the cardinal, and the very high-born ladies looked from a window, silent but perhaps more than willing observers of the events performed in their honour.

Carnival and plays in sixteenth-century Spain followed a pattern in which performance served as intermediary between ruler and people; the king and the elite stood removed from the 'action' – that is, from the play itself – and from contact with their social inferiors. This pattern could also be seen in other types of performances that included carnivalesque celebrations. In the next chapter, we will look in detail at Philip II's ceremonial entry into Zaragoza in 1585, but a brief mention will suffice here. The chronicler of the event, Henry Cock, an archer in the king's guard, describes in just a few lines the celebrations of '*Carnestolendas*' (carnival) from 3 to 6 March 1585. We see the city of Zaragoza filled with masked men, 'knights as well as citizens [by which he means the rich bourgeois]', declaiming amorous couplets and humorous puns, throwing eggs filled with water to the ladies gazing upon them from their windows.[23] The 'low people, servants and maids', Cock tells us, 'throw flour to each other or snow balls (if snow was to be found on the ground) or oranges, as it is done in Andalucía'. The prince of Savoy, on his way to Zaragoza to meet his bride, was doing exactly the same thing – throwing oranges to ladies and passers by – in the streets of Barcelona. Spectacles (skits, *tableaux vivants*, etc.) were presented in the streets, as Cock had seen them performed by the students in Salamanca.[24]

What Cock's account describes was not an event exclusive to Zaragoza; rather, in his brief narrative, he makes comparisons to carnival celebrations throughout Spain. Obviously, the free-for-all of Jaén in the fifteenth century, even if scripted by the constable Don Miguel Lucas de Iranzo, had given way to a rather sharp separation of social groups and to different kinds of entertainment: one category for the well-to-do and one for 'the low people' (*la gente baja*). Philip II and his immediate family, whom we have already seen making their slow way to Zaragoza, are nowhere to be found in Zaragoza's carnival celebrations of 1585.

In 1637, an anonymous chronicler described, among other events, the celebration of carnival in the royal court in Madrid. Although beyond the chronological terminus of this book, the account illustrates the new modality of carnivalesque ribaldry and the further separation of social groups into well-defined spaces and types of celebrations. The carnival described here was confined exclusively to the court. We must assume that a popular carnival took place elsewhere in the neighbourhoods of Madrid, obviously with official sanction or at least benign neglect, but without participation of the elite. The anonymous narrative insists that this was the first time in which the celebrations were held in this specific manner to honour and entertain the king and his family.

On Sunday afternoon of *Carnestolendas*, that is the Sunday before the beginning of Lent on Ash Wednesday, masked people 'including many from the people' (the lower classes) entered the gardens of the Buen Retiro palace. The king, queen, foreign ambassadors and important royal councillors stood on a balcony to witness the spectacle. Three large and festively decorated floats entered the plaza in front of the royal palace. The first float was built in the manner of a galley, carrying a band and the *Carnestolendas* of Barcelona, a motley crew of masked revellers dressed in outlandish fashion. The float was surrounded by mounted knights masked and disguised in bizarre and diverse manner, making gestures and carrying cut figures. Their servants, on foot and equally masked, carried other festive representations.

The second float represented the Indies; its decorations and masked participants sought to invoke the wealth and the dependency of the New World. Horsemen and lackeys disguised in appropriate fashion also accompanied the float. The third and final float carried musicians and 'bizarre masks', which 'entertained the king [and queen] greatly'. This was followed in the early evening by dances, which, as implied in the account, the court enjoyed from the security and aloofness of the palace's balconies. On Fat Tuesday, the king and the court travelled to Madrid, where the city authorities entertained the king with a feast. We are not told by the chronicler the nature of these celebrations, but we are told that at these feasts, as at those of Carnival Sunday, the king and his court were mere spectators.[25]

We have another account of how the royal court spent the three days before the beginning of Lent in 1638, the year following the previous description. Again, it is a brief narrative, which mentions, without any details, the masks and entertainment of Carnival Sunday in the palace and gardens of the Buen Retiro. On Carnival Monday, there was in the palace a masque – a theatrical representation enacted by six men and an equal number of women, followed by a comedy. Members of different religious orders were present by a personal invitation of the countess of Olivares, the wife of Philip IV's prime minister, the powerful count-duke of Olivares. On Tuesday, the king and his court were in Madrid for the city's public celebrations. Upon their return to the palace, a skit (*entremés*) was performed in which members of the court, including the count-duke of Olivares, took specific parts. The skit represented a wedding in which an elderly and ugly (*de muy mala cara*) servant, lavishly dressed, played the bride to one of the royal buffoons acting as groom. With 'ridiculous and entertaining customs', the members of the high court enacted the fake marriage to some criticism from the attending clergy, 'because of the indecency of the dresses'. The narrative tells us, however, that not much harm was done because 'it was only among those of the court and the servants of their majesties'; thus, it 'was not so dissonant to some'.[26]

My aim, in these narratives, is to illustrate, as Bakhtin has done in describing the grotesque in early modern Europe, the fundamental change in festivities in general, and in the carnival specifically, as sites for social exchange between different classes. This, of course, was not a Spanish phenomenon alone. The transition from public to private ludic places and the withdrawal of the elite from public exchanges also occurred elsewhere in western Europe. In England, to cite just one example, the popularity of courtly Jacobean masques indicated a withdrawal of the court into the private spaces and the removal of the populace from courtly entertainment.[27]

The people still played an important role in such events as royal entries, ceremonial royal travel and other great spectacles of the monarchy, but only as spectators; they were no longer active participants (or not as much as they had been in the past). Nor would Philip II or his descendants be seen dancing among the people or taking part in a public tournament, as his fifteenth-century ancestors had done. The times had changed. The nature of power was different. Kings were far more jealous of their prerogatives, and wielded their offices in a new and more authoritarian manner. Culture itself was different, and the gap between 'official' and 'popular' cultures grew wider by the day. In this Bakhtin and Norbert Elias may be right: the somewhat homogeneous culture of the late Middle Ages had been fragmented into the distinct cultures of the early modern period. Signalled by forms of dress, eating, entertainment and language, the discourses of difference neatly divided social groups into separate entities: the vulgar and the courtly. But let us retain our scepticism as to the homogeneity of the medieval world. The social heterogeneity of the late Middle Ages, which had been rendered so visible in the rowdy commingling of cultures in festivals, was now being streamlined into two distinctive spheres: upper and lower, elite and so-called popular.[28]

Popular carnival survived of course and still survives to this day in Spain, Brazil, the Caribbean and elsewhere, though often toothless and without real subversive qualities. Does this mean that subversive intentions and activities have vanished? Again, our evidence is from the seventeenth century. In his book on the carnival Caro Baroja cites an odd and unusual event, published long ago in the *Memorial histórico español*. The event took place in Mérida (Extremadura) in February 1642. It is reported by the narrator, Father Pereyra, as a 'rare' event and thus not to be identified as a recurrent activity within the carnivalesque cycle.

A completely naked man with a paper crown on his head, a sceptre in his hand, a sword on his belt and a decorative chain on his neck marched through the streets of Mérida around ten o'clock in the evening. He was preceded by two men with lit torches and followed by another two men, also with torches. A group of musicians followed playing trumpets and clarinets to announce his progression through the city, but the music was such as to give the impression that the Corpus Christi (the viaticum) was making its way to someone on the edge of death. When women flocked to their windows and balconies to worship the consecrated host, the naked man turned towards them to expose his genitals, while his companions shouted obscenities. This they did even to the wife of the viceroy. The report was that the naked man, guilty of sexual and social misconduct and, even more important, of the sacrilege of impersonating the consecrated host, fell violently ill and was close to death. His partners in crime, a motley crew of servants and some well-to-do young men, were imprisoned in a room and put on a salutary diet of bread and water. Worse things, I am sure, awaited them.[29]

There are lessons to be learned from this performance, even if it was unusual. First, carnival or carnivalesque ribaldry, as tamed as it was by political power, always retained its potential for subversive display. In this case, the naked performance addressed several diverse political and religious agendas in one fell swoop: sexuality, religion and political power. The naked man, his phallic display and the sexual verbal play (insults and sexual harassment may be more precise) defied the enforced modesty and strict sexual mores of early modern Spain, where elite women were often restricted to the household. His paper crown was a challenge to what was, in 1642, after the secession of Portugal and Catalonia and the crushing defeats in central and northern Europe, an unstable monarchy. Lastly, representing himself as, or giving the

139

impression of being, the Corpus Christi, was a very serious transgression indeed in the morbid religious atmosphere of mid-seventeenth-century Spain. At court, in the intimacy of the royal chambers, a small group of courtiers, as we saw above, could get away with cross-dressing and play-acting, but in the streets, the agents of the Inquisition and the Crown watched carefully and menacingly.

Conclusion

In this chapter, I have attempted to provide a typology of festivals in late medieval and early modern Spain. Festivals, which ranged from royal entries to celebrations of weddings, births and funerals to carnival, played an important social role. As sites for the interaction of different social groups, celebrations also functioned as didactic cultural artefacts. Through them, the lower social orders (and the upper classes) learned about hierarchy, difference and power. Festivals played also an important economic role, providing a vehicle for the circulation of wealth through exaggerated distributions of food and expensive displays. Carnival, which has long been seen by cultural critics such as Bakhtin and others as the quintessential popular subversive event, was instead a highly choreographed event that, with some exceptions, tended to reassert the political dominance of the Crown, the nobility and the urban elites. Every aspect of festivals was pregnant with symbolic meaning, and the ritualized performances, which were the very embodiment of celebratory acts, were carefully managed by those above for specific political purposes.

Notes

1. For the political context of these feasts see Luis Suárez Fernández, *Nobleza y monarquía: puntos de vista sobre la historia política castellana del siglo XV*, 2nd edn (Valladolid, 1975), chs 7, 8, 9. A summary of the political life of Castile in this period can be found in Joseph O'Callaghan, *A History of Medieval Spain* (Ithaca, 1975), chs 22, 23.
2. This narrative is gathered from contemporary chronicles. The most important is that of Pero Carrillo de Huete, *Crónica del halconero de Juan II*, ed. J. de Mata Carriazo (Madrid, 1946), 19–27; other chronicles that describe the feasts of 1428 are: Alvar García de Santa María, *Crónica de Juan II de Castilla*, 2 vols, in *Colección de documentos inéditos para la historia de España*, vols C & CI (Madrid, 1891): C, 14–20; *Refundición de la crónica del halconero*, ed. J. de Mata Carriazo (Madrid, 1946), 56–67; *Crónica del rey don Juan II* in *Crónicas de los reyes de Castilla*, II, ed. C. Rossell, (Biblioteca de autores españoles, LXVIII, Madrid, 1953), 446–7.
3. For a reading of the feasts of 1428 see T.F. Ruiz, 'Festivités, couleurs et symboles du pouvoir en Castille au XVe siècle: Les célébrations de Mai 1428', *Annales ESC*, 3 (1991): 521–46; see also my 'Elite and Popular Culture in Late Fifteenth-

Century Castilian Festivals: The Case of Jaén', in B.A. Hanawalt and K.L. Reyerson (eds), *City and Spectacle in Medieval Europe* (Minneapolis, 1994), 296–318.

4. Ruiz, 'Elite and Popular Culture', 296–7.

5. There are still heated arguments on the origins of carnival, that is, whether the medieval and early modern carnival had classical roots or not. See below ch. 6 and Julio Caro Baroja, *El Carnaval (Análisis histórico-cultural)* (Madrid, 1965), 11–46.

6. For a general summary of royal entries in Castile see Rosana de Andrés Díaz, 'Las entradas reales castellanas en los siglos XIV y XV, según las crónicas de la época', in *En la España medieval*, IV (Madrid, 1984), 46–62. See also below, ch. 6.

7. *Crónica de Juan II de Castilla*, ed. J. de Mata Carriazo (Madrid, 1982), 398–400; *Crónica del rey Don Juan II*, 332–3. See also my 'Festivités, couleurs et symboles du pouvoir en Castille', 528–9.

8. *Hechos del condestable don Miguel Lucas de Iranzo: Crónica del siglo XV*, ed. J. de Mata Carriazo (Madrid, 1940), 189–96; see also Ruiz, 'Elite and Popular Culture', 304–5.

9. Ruiz, 'Elite and Popular Culture', 307–10.

10. See Jonathan Brown and John H. Elliott, *A Palace for a King: The Buen Retiro and the Court of Philip IV* (New Haven, 1980) and below, ch. 6.

11. On this point see T.F. Ruiz, 'Unsacred Monarchy: The Kings of Castile in the Late Middle Ages', in Sean Wilentz (ed.), *Rites of Power: Symbolism, Ritual and Politics Since the Middle Ages* (Princeton, 1985), 109–44; also Ernst H. Kantorowicz, *The King's Two Bodies: A Study in Medieval Political Theology* (Princeton, 1957).

12. *Viajes de extranjeros por España y Portugal*, ed. José García Mercadal, 3 vols (Madrid, 1952), I: 95 et passim.

13. There is always a great deal of reverence for king and monarchy in *Don Quixote*. One can compare this to Quevedo's satirical portrait of Philip IV: 'Filipo, que el mundo aclama / Rey del infiel tan temido / Despierta, que por dormido / Nadie te teme, ni te ama'.

14. Brown and Elliott, *A Palace for a King*, 203–6 et passim.

15. Mikhail Bakhtin, *Rabelais and His World* (Bloomington, IN, 1984); Emmanuel Le Roy Ladurie, *Le Carnival de Romans: De La Chandeleur au mercredi des Cendres, 1579–1580* (Paris, 1979).

16. See Caro Baroja, *El carnaval*, 151–390.

17. *Hechos del condestable Don Miguel Lucas de Iranzo*, 98–100; Ruiz, 'Elite and Popular Culture', 296.

18. *Hechos del condestable*, 63–5, 163ff.

19. Caro Baroja, *El carnaval*, 47–100; Bakhtin, *Rabelais*, 196–367.

20. Caro Baroja, *El carnaval*, 101; Juan Ruiz, *El libro de buen amor*, ed. M. Brey Mariño (Madrid, 1960), 199–211.

21. *Relaciones breves de actos públicos en Madrid de 1541 a 1650*, ed. José Simón Díaz (Madrid, 1982), 8–9.

22. Ibid., 9–11.

23. *Viajes de extranjeros*, I: 1312.

24. Ibid.

25. *Relaciones breves*, 450.

26. *Memorial histórico español*, 49 vols (Madrid, 1851–1948), XIV: 336–8.
27. On this topic see Leonard Tennenhouse, *Power on Display: The Politics of Shakespeare's Genres* (New York, 1986), 72–101; Stephen Orgel, *The Illusion of Power: Political Theater in the English Renaissance* (Berkeley, 1975), 65ff.
28. See Norbert Elias's suggestive analysis in his *The Civilizing Process*, 2 vols (New York, 1982), II: 229–33.
29. *Memorial histórico español*, XVI: 267–69.

Chapter 6

From Carnival to Corpus Christi: festivals of affirmation

In the previous chapter, I have argued that carnival and, to a lesser extent, other festive cycles in late medieval and early modern Spain were partially stripped of their function as sites for social exchange and rituals of inclusion. In the specific case of carnival, one also witnesses the waning of this feast as a locus for the articulation of social resistance by the powerless. Was there any other venue in which such social interaction – even though more restricted than in the Middle Ages – still took place?

Not surprisingly, two types of spectacle still required public participation as a way of legitimizing political and spiritual power. We may call the first category displays of regal power, and the second, celebrations or affirmations of faith. In Spain, however, the distinctions between the two were ambiguous; in the popular imagination and in the very scripting of the events the two forms of public display were often conflated. Essentially, no manifestation of state power lacked an ecclesiastical component, and vice versa. In many respects, religion in Spain in this period, by which we mean the Catholic Church, and the monarchy were one. It remained so, with some republican interludes, until shortly after Franco's death in the decade of the 1970s.

Displays of regal power

Among the displays of regal power that called for the presence of the people to legitimize the event were royal entries into a town – of which we have already seen an example from the fifteenth century in the previous chapter. Other such events included the reception of foreign princes (and princesses), funerals (the recent highly orchestrated funeral of Princess Diana is a vivid reminder of the permanence of these spectacles), births and other events in the life of the royal family and powerful magnates. Such festive occasions and their observances were significant social phenomena. Beyond their entertainment value, they advanced specific political purposes, bolstered social structures, and sustained the relations between different orders.

The municipality of Madrid commissioned master Juan López de Hoyos to write a detailed account of the funeral of Philip II's son, Prince Don Carlos (the fabled Don Carlos of Schiller's and later operas), who died in 1568, as well as one of the funeral of Philip II's third wife, his beloved Isabel of Valois.

In 1572, López de Hoyos also wrote and published an even more elaborate account (252 pages in the facsimile edition) of the reception into Madrid of Ana of Austria, Philip II's fourth wife. López de Hoyos's lavish descriptions and explications of the symbolism of the numerous triumphal arches erected at the gates of the city (all of which combined mythological scenes with historical events glorifying the Spanish monarchy), of the mock naval and land battles fought for the occasion, of the faithful homage paid to the future queen by Madrid's municipal officials and of the 'enjoyment' of the people served three very distinct purposes. The first was to link the public spectacle offered by the faithful city to the power of the monarch; the second was to bring into prominence the role of the municipal elites, which had after all organized and paid for the festivities; the third was to create a record for posterity, a written memory, of these communal celebrations.[1]

López de Hoyos's narrative is far too extensive to summarize here. A far better example of late sixteenth-century public displays articulating social hierarchy while accommodating the populace is Philip II's triumphal march from Madrid to Zaragoza (the capital of Aragon) in 1585. We have a brief narrative of this royal voyage from Castile to Aragon, the purpose of which was to meet the duke of Savoy, Carlos Emmanuel, who was coming to Zaragoza to wed Philip II's daughter, the Infanta Catalina of Austria. Far more important than the nuptials, the voyage gave the king an opportunity to present his young son and heir, Prince Philip (later Philip III), to the Aragonese *cortes* meeting at Monzón and to exact from the Aragonese procurators an oath of allegiance to the prince as rightful heir to the throne, and thus to the Crown of Aragon. The context of Philip II's voyage was the instability reigning in the eastern kingdoms and the continued resistance of the Aragonese to any Castilian encroachment on their liberties. The usually reclusive Philip II thus undertook an enterprise filled with pitfalls when he placed himself and the spectacle of royalty on parade.

The narrator, Henry (Enrique) Cock, an eyewitness and member of the royal guard, provides us with the unusual perspective of a foreigner who was nonetheless an insider. Henry Cock, an archer of the king, was physically close enough to the king to see these displays of power and the popular response to them from the centre of activities. As a non-Spaniard, he was removed enough – his loyalty to the dynasty notwithstanding – to report the response of the 'public' without excessive national pride.[2]

A royal entry in Zaragoza (1585)

We may follow the royal cortège as it slowly made its way from Madrid in the midst of winter to Zaragoza for carnival (see Chapter 5). Long before the royal voyage began, plans had to be made to secure provisions and lodgings along the way, and measures had to be enacted to prevent price gouging by merchants and innkeepers along the road. The year of 1585 was not, after all, an easy one. An important part of the royal financial resources was already committed to the building and provisioning of the Invincible Armada, which was to set sail against England three years later.

Philip II was a retiring king, and such a public promenade was quite a departure from his usual behaviour and style. Moreover, Aragon had been for a long time a troubled land, and its people were quite defiant about their vaunted independence. Undoubtedly, such personal exertion on the king's part and such a public display had very specific aims: to rally the people in support of the monarchy's foreign ventures, and to impress the Aragonese elites with the up-swell of popular support in Aragon itself. The royal voyage also sought to reinforce the social bonds that tied the people to the Crown, while reiterating, through rituals and displays, the distance between one and the other.

After lunch in the afternoon of 19 January 1585, the king on horseback, in spite of his years and illnesses, rode ahead of the royal carriages in which the Infantas and the young prince travelled. Henry Cock wrote of the large crowd of nobles and commoners gathered at the gates of Madrid to see the king depart the city. Philip II's first leisurely journey took him only as far as Barajas, around 10 km (a mere twenty minutes by car, and the site of the city's airport today) from the centre of Madrid. There, as was to be the case all along the way, the royal visit prompted weddings by members of the local aristocracy and municipal elites, dances, celebrations, pious visits to local shrines, royal largesse and rewards to local nobles and notables. The people were always present, coming out *en masse* to see the joyful spectacle of the king riding among his people.

We can imagine the impact of the royal cortège's slow movement along the dusty roads of Castile: the king on horseback, the sumptuous carriages of the royal princesses and prince, their fancily dressed bevy of ladies-in-waiting and maids. The people gazed at the smartly dressed German and Spanish guards, riding on both sides of the road, the motley company of nobles and ecclesiastics, the continuous bowing to and kissing of the king's hand in homage by local nobles and municipal officials at every designated stop. And along the road, the people also stood, their hats and caps humbly in their hands, shouting their love for and devotion to the king, their admiration of the finery of the ladies and gentlemen, though the king himself always dressed with the greatest simplicity, all in black. And the expression of their love and devotion was no less enthusiastic, even though this was the same king who had taxed them into starvation and led the country down the path of bankruptcy, even though this was the king who had taken their sons to die in incomprehensible wars in central Europe or on Flanders' fields.

We cannot follow the king throughout his long journey. It may be wise to restrict our summary to two specific moments: the royal crossing from Castile

145

to Aragon and the actual royal entry into Zaragoza. Both of them were pregnant with ritual and social significance. Upon arriving at the border between
Castile and Aragon, the king was received by the *Justicia* of Aragon[3], and 'many
people from the region, Castilians and Aragonese together, came singing and
dancing to see the crossing into Aragon'.[4] The border was signalled by stone
landmarks (*mojones*), and Henry Cock goes to great lengths to explain how
one jurisdiction ended and another began just on the other side of the line
(*raya*). The guards, the author observed, marked this crossing of boundaries
by discharging their pistols into the air. At the border of Aragon, the king of
Spain and his cortège engaged in festive demonstrations, which effectively
asserted the distinctiveness of the realms of Castile and Aragon while proclaim-
ing the rule of Philip II over all of Spain. Castilian officials had to relinquish
their symbols of office in what was in fact foreign territory for them. The
king, on the other hand, by simply crossing the border, shifted his jurisdiction from king of Castile to king of the Crown of Aragon. His passage through
that liminal boundary was dignified by celebrations and performances which
were well-grounded in the tradition of royal entries.[5]

Entering Zaragoza, and staying in the city throughout the month of March
for the celebration of the wedding, called for the most extraordinary displays of finery and celebrations. The *Justicia* of Aragon and the archbishop of
the city met the king outside the walls of Zaragoza. Together with other
'officials of the kingdom and the city', they dismounted and came to kiss the
king's hand in obeisance. Riding on horseback, the king entered the city in
a well-organized procession. Knights from Castile and Aragon led the march
into the city. They were followed by municipal officials dressed in red velvet
with gold trimmings. In third rank came members of the royal council
with mace bearers, all in scarlet cloth with trimmings of white velvet. Behind them, in clearly defined ranks, came the chancellor and the mace bearer
of the *Justicia* of the kingdom, followed by other judges and lawyers of the
civil and criminal courts of Aragon. Fifth in the order of the procession
marched eight deputies from the *cortes* of Aragon, representing the different
orders or estates of the realm. The mace bearers of the ecclesiastical and noble
estates held their maces high in the air to indicate their privileged rank. Among
them rode the grandees of Castile. Afterwards, at the end of the ceremonial
procession, the king came with the *Justicia* of Aragon riding on one side and
the archbishop on the other. The royal guards and the royal carriages followed with the Infantas and the royal heir. Huge crowds awaited outside
and inside the gates of the city. Throughout Zaragoza, along the route of the
royal procession, balconies and windows were decorated with silk and wool
tapestries. Stages were also set up throughout the city, where musicians and
other festive acts delighted the crowds.

That evening and on successive nights throughout the month, Zaragoza
was lit up with a profusion of bonfires and torches. Artisans, organized in

146

confraternities, marched with torches in front of the king's palace; knights engaged in mock battles in the Moorish fashion. Bulls, with lit torches tied to their long and dangerous horns, were let loose throughout the city. I could go on and on describing and glossing the different nuances of each day's celebration, but allow me to add just one more description before bringing this to a close.

Shortly after the king's arrival to the city, on 26 February 1585, a religious procession marched from the cathedral to the king's palace. In clearly defined ranks, and in ascending order of social status, the parade began, led by the '*mentecatos*', men and women who were mentally impaired and patients in a Zaragoza hospital for the insane. They were followed by orphans, residents of another of the city's pious institutions. Third in rank came the '*sambenitos*', those who had been found guilty by the Inquisition and condemned to wear distinguishing robes and hats. In an aside, Cock comments on the beauty of some of the women who had been found guilty of practising Muslim rites or of 'judaizing'. Their exquisite, brightly coloured dresses were, of course, intended as visual enhancements of the parade, but they also signalled, quite blatantly, the subservience of their wearers to all those who followed them in the parade. Behind the Inquisition's station came the artisans' confraternities, all of their members marching with lit candles. These were followed by a large number of friars and monks, representing the many monasteries of Zaragoza. Next came the secular clergy and the canons of the cathedral chapter, and closing the parade came the archbishop and the city officials. The procession lasted ten hours, and the king patiently observed it from his balcony.[6] No variation from the strict hierarchical arrangement was conceivable. The free-for-all carnival, which mixed high and low in entertainment, even if briefly, had now given way to clearly enforced groupings by social rank, mental competency, religious orthodoxy and wealth. The parade presented a visual equivalent to the rigid stratification of society.

At the beginning of this discussion on festivals and their role in the social history of late medieval and early modern Spain (Chapter 5), we saw, in the long evocation of the festivities of May 1428, the importance chroniclers placed upon the colours and garments worn by the participants. In 1585, more than 150 years later, the fabrics (silk, brocade, scarlet cloth), colours (a profusion of blacks, reds and whites), and martial displays of innumerable tournaments held in Zaragoza still taught valuable lessons to the populace. Festive events, especially those of a grandeur comparable to the ones held in the Aragonese capital, still required – as I have indicated earlier – the presence of the people. Thus, to emphasize the point again, these events remained sites for social display and exchange. But negotiations between the different social orders became more difficult as the distance between them widened. Kings and the ruling elites seldom came among the people any more. Instead they gazed, as Philip II did, from the remoteness and protection of their high windows and balconies. Something had changed radically in the transition from the late Middle Ages to the early modern period, and it was not just the physical space between the powerful and the weak in celebrations. Public spectacles were transformed from the loose arrangements they had been in an earlier age to more sophisticated and regimented productions. Ceremonial processions to honour the king were now carefully organized and choreographed to achieve greater social consent to the power of kings. This change occurred not only because resources were more plentiful, or because political power was more centralized, but also because more classical and renaissance models of rulership were available for emulation. Underlying the growing separation between the different social orders, whether in royal entries or Corpus Christi celebrations, were new concepts of power and rulership, new ways of thinking about the relationship between a king and his people, and new ways of envisioning the social orders themselves. In effect, we are confronted here with a process that Max Weber described long ago as the 'routinization of power', that is, the affirmation, by performative rituals, of social difference and political control. In the long parade in front of the king's balcony – how much did the king see? how long did he sit or stand at the window? – the whole of Aragonese society arrayed itself, neatly divided in ranks, both to participate in and bear witness to the apotheosis of royal power and the rightful, hierarchical ordering of society.

Affirmations of faith

There was a place, nonetheless, where, at least in theory, all social orders were and continued to be one, even into the early modern period. This was the world of belief; but equality here – the equality of all Christians in the face of God – was of course purely theological and not factual at all. Yet, even though strict hierarchical order was often preserved, religious or semi-religious public performances called for an emotional response and for forms of participation (prayers, adoration, singing, pious gestures) that bound all or most of the people into a community of faith.

Although there were many different categories of what, for lack of a better term, I call celebrations or affirmations of faith, ranging from the individual to the collective, from the public to the private, my interest here is in very specific celebratory performances. The focus is on festive or pious events, which called on people from all social ranks to participate, which transcended the boundaries between city and countryside, and which above all sought to foster a sense of community and inclusion in those present, whether, as shall be seen later, they did so as celebrants or victims.

One must not forget that throughout Spain, the celebration of the patron saints of small villages and large towns brought about well-orchestrated displays in which secular and ecclesiastical authorities worked hand in hand for the greater glory of their saintly patrons and the honour of their localities. On such days, as is the case even today, the usual antagonisms of small villages and towns were put aside or articulated in festive competition. Still, the religious processions, games, eating and other celebratory acts that marked these days also served to provide, as they did in larger cities, a sense of communal identity and even membership in larger and far more encompassing entities: the Catholic Church, the kingdom.

I would like, however, to add a word of caution. The celebrations or affirmations of faith described here were complex matters. Many factors beyond faith and religious fervour operated to make people join in processions, religious festivities and Inquisitorial trials (*autos-de-fe*). First, there was the issue of human curiosity and the desire for entertainment. Most public affirmations of faith were exceedingly theatrical and were performed with the most extraordinary pomp and displays of wealth. As such, they provided a rich source of entertainment. Second, there was the question of fear and the reality of coercion. Non-participation, rejection of the hegemonic Catholic discourse and absence from religious feasts, masses and communion could and did have dire results. Individuals paid a psychological toll for nonconformity, since by forgoing participation in these public events they in effect withdrew from the community of believers and belonged nowhere in the social world of sixteenth-century Spain. More severe consequences could follow in the form of an accusation of unusual behaviour by a neighbour, a bad recommendation from the local priest, or a summons to the Inquisition's court. Repressive religious systems – and most European countries, not just Spain, were religiously repressive – have ways of instilling conformity and displays of false (as well as real) piety from nobles and commoners alike. This observation, however, should not obscure the fact that many in Spain and elsewhere seemed to have truly embraced the public shows of religiosity and that popular devotions were expressions of deep, emotional fervour. One explanation for the attractiveness of these types of festivities and celebrations is their highly ritualized character. The repetitive nature of religious celebrations – and of royal entries as well – provided a sense of familiarity and security, and a sense of continuity that was cherished in the midst of life's uncertainties. With these caveats, we should proceed to examine two very specific types of affirmations of faith.

The first one is the feast of the Corpus Christi, and the second is the great public trials of the Inquisition, the *autos-de-fe* (the literal translation is deeds of faith, but it also meant, in the sixteenth century, to augment, to increase faith). The latter celebrations and their *mise-en-scène* have long captured the popular imagination, as well as film makers' taste for gory settings. They have also become emblematic (mistakenly, I should add) of Spain's harsh and morbid religiosity.

The Corpus Christi processions

Miri Rubin's *Corpus Christi: The Eucharist in Late Medieval Culture* provides an excellent study of the cult of the consecrated host as the central symbol of worship in late medieval Christianity and as the rallying point for the unity of the faith. Rubin also explores the manner in which the celebrations and processions associated with the feast of the Corpus Christi became, in time, a language for the articulation of communal order and power, but always allowing for private explorations of the soul and for the internal devotions of every Christian.[7]

In Spain, papal sanction of the feast of the Corpus Christi was granted in 1264. This was followed in the fourteenth century by conciliar and papal decrees establishing the manner in which processions of the consecrated host were to perambulate through the streets of cities and towns and to receive the adoration of the people. These were, from the very beginning, highly scripted celebrations, and the first reports of such festivities in Spain, dating also from the fourteenth century, followed the guidelines set by Church authorities.[8] Nonetheless, the feast itself did not reach its great standing among the people until the late fifteenth century, and its most sumptuous displays did not occur until the early modern period and the contemporary age.

In many respects, the celebrations of Corpus Christi – together with the great *autos-de-fe* – came to replace, in part, the whole cycle of late medieval festivals, which bound the powerful to the weak. Although, as we have seen before, carnivals, royal entries, the feasts of Christmas, Epiphany and the like continued to be celebrated throughout the early modern period and beyond, they paled when compared to the growing solemnity, pomp, scale and inclusiveness of the procession of the Corpus Christi. The former festivities were also no longer privileged in the chronicles and accounts of the period, as had been the case in the fifteenth century. Instead, these narratives turned most of their energies to the description of religious festivals. This transition is difficult to explain fully. Clearly, the conflation between politics and religion and the tighter control of the printed word by state and Church help explain this shift, but more is needed to provide a convincing answer. To this day, the feast of the Corpus Christi remains the most important procession in places such as Toledo, Córdoba and other Spanish cities. Today, as in the late fifteenth and throughout the sixteenth century, it can still command the undivided attention, curiosity, and sometimes even devotion of its spectators.

I have been unfortunate enough to witness the Corpus Christi procession under the Franco dictatorship. Led by the military (goose-stepping their way through the streets of Córdoba) and the civil authorities, with bands of music and different confraternities joining in the parade, the consecrated host, the actual body of Christ according to Christian theology, stood suspended within a large baroque gold reliquary (*a custodia*) for the adoration of all. In the late Middle Ages and early modern period, the planning of and participation in the procession of the Corpus Christi was a serious matter indeed. It required the most careful organization by municipal and ecclesiastical authorities and the harshest penalties for those reluctant to contribute to the devout and festive displays. The procession combined entertainment and devotion. It taught visually, and performatively, about social hierarchy, order and power, but it also allowed for an inclusive spiritual experience. At the Corpus Christi procession, all social ranks came and worshipped together. All, Christians and non-Christians, served as witnesses to the majesty and redemptive nature of the consecrated host and to the turning of bread into the body of Christ (transubstantiation). This was also, of course, the Catholic (and Spanish) response to the Protestant denial of transubstantiation, and was thus a public and *political* reaffirmation of faith by all social classes.[9]

In late fifteenth- and sixteenth-century Valencia, Madrid, Barcelona and other cities and towns in Spain, on the eve of the feast of the Corpus Christi, the streets were thoroughly cleaned and the balconies along the procession's route were gaily decorated with tapestries and silk hangings. In some instances, the streets along which the host would perambulate were also covered with rich carpets. In some cities, as is done in Toledo to this day, canopies were hung over the narrow streets. Flowers and colourful displays were present everywhere.

The Corpus Christi procession in Madrid
Javier Portús Pérez in his richly descriptive and interesting book *La antigua procesión del Corpus Christi in Madrid*, and Angela Muñoz Fernández in a short but comprehensive article, describe the processional order of the Corpus Christi celebration in late fifteenth-century and early modern Madrid. In the 1480s, city officials and nobles took turns, six persons on each side, carrying the canopy, or baldachin, under which the host was paraded through the town.[10] Royal entries, as we have seen, closely paralleled the processional patterns of the Eucharist. Kings also rode into cities underneath finely embroidered canopies. This point ought to be made once again. The conflation of the sacred and the political in these spectacles always involved salutary lessons for all social orders. It also served, in a monarchy without direct sacral attributes,[11] to sanctify political power and to equate the Corpus Christi with the king.

Both royal entries and Corpus Christi celebrations – as well as other religious and festive processions – followed on a double tradition. On the one hand, there was an increasing knowledge of the Roman military triumphal entrance, following the Renaissance revival of the classical past and the spread of humanism to Spain. Books on the subject were published throughout Spain in the fifteenth century.[12] On the other hand, and far more relevant to the

Corpus tradition, there was the yearly re-enactment of Jesus's tumultuous reception into Jerusalem on Palm Sunday.

Preceding the canopy and the consecrated host, members of the Madrid oligarchy marched with lit torches. Angela Muñoz mentions that in other Spanish cities the banner of the town led the procession rather than representatives of the elite. Behind the body of Christ walked most of the ecclesiastics of the town, dressed in their liturgical garments. They were followed by the trade confraternities. Each confraternity carried stages (some small ones on their backs and, later, movable stages), on which skits or *tableaux vivants* depicted the mysteries of the Corpus, scenes from the Old and New Testament and other hagiographical material. Participation was not altogether voluntary. A fine of 3,000 *mrs* was imposed on any confraternity failing to join in or to contribute to the pious entertainment. Those too poor to organize such displays individually were encouraged to pool their resources for the production of a worthy spectacle.[13]

Moors and Jews, before the end of the fifteenth century, were equally compelled to participate in the Corpus procession. A similar fine of 3,000 *mrs* was levied on these religious communities for failure to appear. A document of 1481, cited by Angela Muñoz, orders the Moors to bring out their *'juegos'* (games, but here meaning also representations) and dances. The Jews were also expected to contribute with dances or to incur the already mentioned fine. As David Nirenberg has shown, the feasts of Holy Week in the fourteenth-century Crown of Aragon (which in many ways paralleled the solemnities of the Corpus Christi) always included participation by the Jews. Although Jews (and Moors) were humiliated by being forced to witness and acknowledge a triumphal Christianity, the celebration, as Nirenberg points out, served also as an inclusionary gesture, bringing together Jews, Moors and Christians into a communal festival.[14]

But if in fifteenth-century Spain, Moors and Jews (coercive elements notwithstanding) joined in festive performances – as we have seen on the occasion of the Infanta Doña Blanca's entrance into Briviesca – by the end of the century, the presence of religious minorities in royal entries and Corpus Christi processions became a rare phenomenon. By then, Jews and Moors had been segregated in very specific areas within cities or banished altogether, because of their religious beliefs. By the early sixteenth century, neither of the two religious groups survived, at least officially, within the boundaries of Spain. In cities such as Burgos, as we saw earlier, the elite also clustered in certain sections of the city. Until the sixteenth century, therefore, these festivals provided a fleeting moment of unity and the possibility of crossing the unforgiving boundaries of neighbourhoods, class, rank and religion.

What about the 'people'? Unlike other festive occasions in which commoners had become mere spectators, in the Corpus Christi procession the great mass of the population played a dual role as participant and spectator.

According to Portús Pérez, half the people of Madrid participated directly in the procession, while the other half watched, from the streets and windows, as the Host marched through the city. After the official ranking of the dominant social groups in front, around and behind the Corpus Christi, people joined in the procession and walked behind the Host as it meandered through the city. One activity did not preclude the other. As is the case today, one could join the procession at various points throughout its route, both as a witness and as a participant. Both roles – and this is the main point I wish to make here – conferred agency, regardless of social standing. On the one hand, by following the Corpus Christi through the streets of one's city, one became part of a hallowed moment, an actor in a sacred play. On the other hand, the outpouring of devotion – whether one watched the procession, marched behind it, or did both – was overwhelming; it was impossible to remain unaffected by the sheer scale of religious fervour. The physical and emotive responses exacted by this mass phenomenon turned the viewer into an active participant. These sentiments, whether rehearsed or truly felt, created a sense of genuine belonging, of communal solidarity, which empowered the poor and the downtrodden while, paradoxically, reinforcing and legitimizing the structures of power (that kept them poor and downtrodden). In many respects, things have not changed. The carnival in Rio de Janeiro today fulfils more or less the same function of reiterating social differences while allowing a period of licence.

And, in a deep sense, the Corpus Christi was *like* carnival. This explains to some extent the waning of popular carnival, with its subversive tendencies, in early modern Spain, and the rise of the tightly controlled and ritualized performances of the Corpus Christi. The Corpus processions throughout Spain and certainly in Madrid by the early modern period included enough carnivalesque elements: figures of large-headed dwarfs and giants, devils, Moors, masquerades, Morris dances, devotional and not-so-devotional theatrical skits, and other grotesque elements. They provided an inverted image of the divinity of the consecrated host, but, unlike carnival, in the Corpus Christi processions all these representations of inversion, ribaldry and debasement were carefully regulated and served only as complements to the consecration of religion and of the state.

The Corpus Christi in late medieval and early modern Valencia

The Corpus Christi celebration and the Inquisitorial trials provided a unity in matters of belief and ritual performances that Spain sorely lacked in the political arena. In Valencia, another of the great capitals of the Spanish realms, the Corpus Christi followed along the general patterns already described for the Corpus processions in Madrid; but perhaps because of its Mediterranean context and its distance from the centres of political and religious power in far-away Madrid, the Corpus Christi in Valencia had an exuberance (by which

I mean more secular festive elements), which surpassed the processions in Madrid. Antoni Ariño, in his excellent study *Festes, rituals i creences*, pays close attention to the evolution of the Corpus Christi processions in Valencia from the fourteenth century to the present.[15]

When Valencia began honouring the Corpus in 1355, the celebration oscillated between being a city-wide affair and a parochial one, and was organized by the parishes on a rotation basis. According to Ariño, the Corpus Christi procession evolved from a fairly egalitarian ritual – in which men and women, artisanal trades, the well-to-do, and secular and ecclesiastical people participated freely – to a complex cultural phenomenon. By 1425, social orders in the procession were ranked in a clear hierarchical order. Moreover, the addition of masked actors, music, theatrical representations and carnivalesque figures in the fifteenth century marked a transition to more complex types of religious festivities. Among the long list of symbolic figures and characters represented, the sources for the early fifteenth-century processions mention angels, devils, patriarchs (Noah and his ark, Jacob and his ladder), prophets, the apostles, saints and virgins, other characters (the Virgin Mary and the child Jesus, the Magi, etc.), mythological and biblical animals.[16]

An important component of the feast of the Corpus in Valencia was the *entremeses* or *roques* (in Valencian). In the procession of 1528, some of the *entremeses* or theatrical skits included representations of the Last Supper, of the sacrifice of Abraham, of Hell, of the martyrdom of St Sebastian, of the Crucifixion and of other equally edifying or lugubrious events. Moreover, within each social rank participating in the Corpus celebrations, there were specific, well-defined hierarchies. Artisanal guilds or confraternities followed a well-regulated order of precedence; canons of the cathedral and other ecclesiastics also marched in a pre-arranged order, which clearly signalled, to themselves and to those in attendance (almost the entire population of Valencia), the proper social ranking of each group or individual. The same attention to status was evident in the procession of royal and municipal officials, city oligarchs and the nobility in residence.[17]

As early as 1416, the ruling elite (ecclesiastical as well as secular) of Valencia fixed the route of the procession to coincide precisely with the ceremonial route followed by the kings on the first royal entry into the city. Thus, as in Madrid and elsewhere, there was a convergence between religious and political festive performances. Both rituals, by their reliability and repetition, ensured the social order. Moreover, as Ariño shows, the Corpus was not only a representation of Christ on earth; the feast functioned as a powerful symbolic event, affirming the power of religion and the Crown on many levels: 1) visually, by the great display of rich tapestries, rugs and banners, which provided an explosion of colour within the city; 2) olfactorily, by the profusion of flowers thrown from the balconies and windows at the passing of the consecrated host; 3) musically, by the continuous playing of music throughout the city. Should we be surprised then that, in Madrid or Seville (where the feast of the Corpus reached unprecedented levels of frenzy), the population as a whole reacted with extreme forms of joy and devotion (tears, shouts, expressions of tenderness, etc.) at the sight of their living God? Antagonisms and violence were set aside at least for a day.[18]

Inquisition trials and *autos-de-fe*

As theatrical as the religious processions were (and still are), they did not match the performative power of the great inquisitorial trials held in Spain throughout most of the early modern period. The Inquisition's *autos-de-fe* functioned as theatres of power, attracting thousands of spectators: the wealthy and powerful watched from well-appointed balconies or from the stage itself (where the trials, punishment and reconciliation of heretics took place); the less well-off watched from wherever they could find a place. We must not imagine, however, that the great *autos-de-fe* were common occurrences. Their cost was exceedingly high, the preparations so elaborate, that they were held only intermittently. They lacked the cyclical nature of the Corpus Christi processions and similar religious festivities, which followed the liturgical calendar. But precisely because of their non-calendrical and infrequent character, the *autos-de-fe* had tremendous visual and psychological impact. In a strange and contradictory way, the elaborate public trials of the Spanish Inquisition functioned as sites for the inclusion of all social orders and at the same time as sites for the exclusion of certain individuals. One action was intimately linked to the other. The act of excluding some meant the inclusion of others. Definitions of self, collective or individual, and representations of membership in a community, religious or political – then as today – were always bound up with representations against others.[19]

The main purpose of the public *auto-de-fe* was to cleanse the Christian community from damning heretics. This was done by the trial and condemnation of those accused of heresy, and by the inquisitor's public preaching to those found guilty and to the audience in attendance. In a sense, the *auto* became, not unlike the Corpus Christi processions, a public and communal reaffirmation of faith. We must also remember that the execution – by either asphyxiation or burning, or a combination of both – of those found to be relapsed heretics did not take place at the *auto-de-fe*. The ceremony was not about the spectacle of torture and death (though it often did begin and end with these two scenarios, albeit in settings that were hidden from the public). After guilt had been determined, the condemned heretics were taken to another location, usually outside the city walls, and executed by the civil authorities. As members of the Church, inquisitors were not allowed to shed blood; it is my impression, however, that the Spanish monarchy was just too jealous of its power to allow the exercise of high justice to anyone but itself.

Let us return to the point I am attempting to make here. In their affirmation of faith, all of the people, powerful and weak alike, became participants, and therefore complicit, in the punishment of heretics. Through prayer, shouts of approval or condemnation, and gestures that shaped the ebb and flow of public trials, they took part in excising the heretics from the social body and in restoring to health the moral economy of their particular towns and realms. By casting out crypto-Jews, *Moriscos*, foreigners, Protestants, sodomites and blasphemers, they reaffirmed their own rightful place in Spanish and Christian society. The representation of 'otherness', which underpinned Inquisitorial trials, was also a *counter*-representation of communal identity, a reverse index of what it meant to be a Spaniard and a Catholic in the sixteenth century. One was granted membership in the community by participating and acquiescing in the exclusion of a targeted few, an old and well-known practice into our own age.

Yet the *auto-de-fe* – and here is the paradox – also sought to reconcile, and thus to include, those who were to be punished, even those who were to be put to death. Although it did not always work, quite often the cooperation of those indicted was a prerequisite for the *auto-de-fe*'s proper functioning as a cleansing and binding ceremony. This was made implicit in the processional march and in the trial itself. Those dressed in the humiliating garb of the '*sambenito*' (a yellow tunic with saffron-coloured crosses) marched in orchestrated processions to the site of the *auto-de-fe*. They attended their own trials with little or no resistance and made exemplary acts of contrition at the announcement of their guilt and punishment, even when the latter was death. This of course was accomplished through the pervasive forms of coercion we have seen before: the threat and/or infliction of social, psychological, moral, financial, and, above all, physical injury. The *sambenitos* were cogs in the machine, made to enact the dominant social and moral codes. There was a script, and those found guilty knew it and followed it to the letter.

The pressures and terrors applied to obtain such compliance may trouble our modern conscience. But for those orchestrating and witnessing the public spectacle in the sixteenth century, the hegemonic cultural values involved in punishing transgressors and in embracing that punishment were sacrosanct; and worked both to legitimize the Church and state's use of power and to bolster society's hierarchical character. More than that, the *auto-de-fe* served as a double-edged reminder to all, wealthy and poor, pious and sinner, that membership in the community of faith was conditional. What, then, was the *auto-de-fe* like?

Scholars working on the Inquisition have long noted that the Spanish *autos-de-fe* evolved from the spectacles invented by the medieval Inquisition in early thirteenth-century southern France.[20] Throughout most of thirteenth- and fourteenth-century Europe, trials of heretics were known collectively as *sermo generalis* (general sermon). Usually held on Sundays, the public *sermo generalis* attracted large crowds of people, including royal and municipal officials, and ecclesiastics. The accused stood on a high platform, open to the gaze and shouts of those in attendance. The inquisitor preached a sermon (hence the name) to the suspected heretics, but also to the audience. At the prompting of the speaker, the sermon was often interrupted by shouts from the crowd. This was a participatory ceremony, and the interruptions and clamour of those in attendance functioned as a choral response to the inquisitor's religious (and social) admonitions. Indulgences were granted to those in attendance; the accused were handed down their sentences. Many of those found guilty kneeled and repented their heretical deeds; thus, they were absolved and reinserted in the communal body. Those who refused to accept their guilt, or who remained faithful to their errors, were taken away to be punished or executed.[21]

From this rather simple ceremony, the Spanish *auto-de-fe* grew into an elaborate religious ritual charged with symbolic meaning and social lessons. As the great Henry C. Lea pointed out long ago, the *sermo generalis* first and the *auto-de-fe* later were physical enactments – one could say previews – of the Final Judgement, and thus laden with all kinds of frightful and redeeming associations.[22]

Autos were long in the planning. Local tribunals might propose holding a large inquisitorial trial or *auto*, but approval from the Supreme Council of the Inquisition had to be sought before proceeding with its organization. The date had to be chosen carefully. Feast days of important Christian saints, of saints of special relevance to Spanish historical events, or days dedicated to the adoration of the Cross (3 May, 14 September) were preferred. These dates inscribed the workings of the Inquisition within a liturgical and historical calendar, but they also allowed for a larger attendance.

Henry C. Lea's great work on the Inquisition in Spain, written more than a century ago, and Avilés's recent article on the *auto-de-fe* describe in detail the ritual structure of the ceremony and how it was organized. As Lea points out, the less frequent the *autos-de-fe*, the more elaborate they became. After approval to hold an *auto* was obtained from the Supreme Council of the Inquisition, early notices went out – as much as a month before the *auto*'s scheduled date. Invitations were sent to the authorities participating in the ceremony, securing their presence for the great event.

Long before the *auto* was held, special preparations were made. This included the making or fixing of the special garments to be worn by the accused (the *sambenitos*): the mitres (conic hats in reverse imitation of a bishop's hat), which covered the heads of the heretics; the effigies of those who had fled or died and were to be tried *in absentia*; the special boxes to carry the bones of those exhumed and brought to trial after their death and burial. A special box or coffer of 'crimson velvet with gold fringes and a gilt lock and key' held the sentences of those to be relaxed (put to death). Green crosses, to be

157

carried by the accused, had to be made. Other crosses were made and carried in the processional, which took place the day before the *auto-de-fe*. A Dominican prior marched with the large green cross of the Inquisition and a confraternity official proudly raised a white cross. The prosecuting attorney was assigned his own standard: a banner of red damask, with the royal coat of arms and the cross of the Inquisition, a symbol of the marriage of Church and state in the rooting out of heretics.

In the days preceding the ceremony, local Inquisition officials occupied the main square of the town. In Madrid, where some quite spectacular *autos-de-fe* were performed throughout the sixteenth century, the Plaza Mayor, the main square and the site for the acclamation of new kings and for the running of bulls, was the place of choice. In Toledo, the Zocodover, or the square in front of the great Gothic cathedral, was a preferred site. In these squares, two large stages were built. One was assigned to the 'penitents', that is, those on trial, and to their guards. The other was reserved for the Inquisition, municipal and royal officials and a bevy of other ecclesiastics. The windows and balconies of the houses surrounding the main square of the town filled with important people and their families. Although, as Lea indicates, ecclesiastical and secular authorities were most willing participants, their presence was nonetheless compulsory. This was done to forestall absences prompted by political antagonisms or by refusals to occupy, in the rigid hierarchy of the procession, an assigned position that was inferior to rival orders or officials. The *autos-de-fe* served as events in which the social ranking of the elite could not be contested, even by members of the elite themselves. The *autos-de-fe* thus strictly enforced a careful articulation of the gradations of social order and power. Familiars (officials of the Inquisition) on horseback, notaries and town criers, carrying the banner of the Inquisition and blowing loud trumpets, perambulated through the town. At strategic corners, they made stops and called all of the people of the city to attend the *auto-de-fe* to be held 'at such place and at such date'.

The *auto* began very early with masses held at the parish church and at the site of the *auto* itself, before the ceremonial procession began. Soldiers came first, as they do today in the procession of the Corpus Christi; then the heretics came in an ascending hierarchy of guilt. Those accused of lesser crimes, and thus liable for lesser punishment, appeared first; those to be executed marched last. They walked their painful and humiliating journey one by one, escorted each side by familiars of the Inquisition or by friars. The heretics followed the processional route through teeming and excited crowds, which shouted words of opprobrium and – in some locations – attempted to take matters into their own hands.

The *auto* lasted into the night, an exhausting, cathartic form of psychological theatre. It ended with the reconciliation of some of the accused and the taking away of the recalcitrant and relapsed heretics to be burned elsewhere.

The king, his court, and distinguished visitors were often present. Great *autos* were often made to coincide with signal political moments: the swearing of the heir to the throne, a gathering of the *cortes*, a royal wedding.[23]

What impact did such celebrations have on the mass of the people? How did they serve as sites for social exchanges? How did they erase, and at the same time reaffirm, social hierarchies? I think the answer is clear and easy, and I have already attempted to explain how this was so throughout this and the preceding chapter. Processions, *autos-de-fe* and other such religious manifestations – unlike carnival and tournaments, which eventually became segregated by class – occasioned a public outpouring of emotion, anger, physical and verbal gestures. These signs, a kind of performative text, inscribed the community in the worship of the Host, in the devotion of saints, and, in the case of the Inquisition, in the complicit trial and punishment of heretics.

A short anonymous narrative of events in Madrid in the early seventeenth century may serve as a fitting conclusion to these chapters on festivals and spectacles. The story tells of how, on 5 July 1624, a 'sacrilegious foreign heretic' (a Protestant?) entered the Church of the Monastery of St Philip in Madrid, snatched the consecrated host from the hands of the priest, tore it to pieces, threw the pieces into the fire and to the floor and stomped on the remaining fragments of the body of Christ. The unnamed desecrator also took the chalice, filled it with unconsecrated wine, spilled it on the floor and, drawing his dagger, attacked the priest. Those in attendance drew their swords (notice the carrying of weapons into Church) and sought to punish the heretic right on the spot. The priest interceded and prevented the swift execution of the attacker. Rather than remitting him to the Holy Office tribunal in Toledo, he had him brought to trial immediately. On Sunday 14 July of the same year, the foreign heretic was brought to a small *auto* held in the Plaza Mayor of Madrid. Even though there was such short time for preparation, all of the important ecclesiastical and civil authorities of the city, as well as a large crowd of common people, were in attendance.

The accused's parade through the streets of Madrid included passing in front of the royal palace, where the king saw him from a balcony as the procession made its way to the Plaza Mayor. There, the heretic was placed on a high stage and as his crimes were read the people broke into 'shouts, tears, . . . slapped and scratched their faces and bodies, pulled their beards and hair'. All of these are, of course, the traditional signs of mourning. In this case, it represented a collective and popular mourning for the sacrilege committed on the body of Christ.

The death sentence was announced; the accused was taken outside the walls of the city. There, on an empty field, he was asphyxiated (as a form of mercy) and his body was then burned to cinders and the ashes cast on the fields and streams of Madrid. The king and his court, dressed in mourning, attended masses at the monastery of St Philip. Together with the powerful, a

159

large throng of the poor and weak also came to mourn and to see the spectacle of their betters.[24]

Conclusion

From a general view of festivals in the previous chapter, I have focused here on very specific types of festivals. I have described them as affirmations of power and of faith, though in Spain political power and religious beliefs were deeply intertwined. In their elaborate royal entries, theatrical *autos-de-fe* and symbolically rich Corpus Christi processions, Church and state created ceremonial spaces in which the unity of Spaniards under one ruler and one doctrine was reiterated. As we have seen in the previous chapter, many of these ceremonial events – though clearly hierarchical and at times, as in the *autos-de-fe*, exclusionary – bound *all* social groups in rituals of inclusion and exclusion.

These affirmations of power and faith also confirmed the trend already described in the previous chapter. As we move from the late Middle Ages into the early modern period, the distance between high and low grew wider. The vision of kings and high lords dancing among the common people was replaced by the mighty looking on celebrations from secure and distant balconies. There was a 'privatization' of the ceremonial, a withdrawal from public celebratory spaces to private ones. In Spain, far more than in other European countries, this was most obvious in the distant character of the Habsburg monarchs and in the growing importance and complexity of the Corpus Christi celebrations. As a result, carnival, with its fiercely popular and subversive roots, was demoted to a festivity that was to be carried out in the peripheries of regulated life or carefully choreographed from above. Festivals became, therefore, yet another expression of the growing power and control of Crown and Church.

Notes

1. Juan López de Hoyos, *Real aparato y sumptuoso recibimiento con que Madrid (como casa y morada de S.M.) rescibio a la Serenissima Reyna D. Ana de Austria*, facsimile of the 1572 edition (Madrid, 1976). See also his *Relación de la muerte y honras fúnebres del S.S. Principe Don Carlos, hijo dela Mag. del Catholico Rey D. Philippe el Segundo Nuestro Señor* (Madrid, 1568).

2. *Viajes de extranjeros por España y Portugal*, ed. José García Mercadal, 3 vols (Madrid, 1952), I: 1295–1412, 'Anales del año ochenta y cinco, en el cual el Rey Católico de España, con el Principe Don Felipe, su hijo, fue a Monzón a tener las cortes del reino de Aragón', compuestas por Enrique Cock, notario apostólico y arquero de la guardia del cuerpo real.

3. The *Justicia* of Aragon was always a high nobleman, appointed by the Crown of Aragon to make sure that the liberties and rights of the Aragonese were not usurped by the king or by the high nobility. The *Justicia* was, therefore, an independent

and influential figure in the affairs of the Crown of Aragon. See John H. Elliott. *Imperial Spain, 1469–1716* (Harmondsworth, 1975), 29 et passim.

4. *Viajes de extranjeros*, I: 1303.

5. On the issue of liminality, here and elsewhere, I follow the work of Arnold Van Gennep, *The Rites of Passage* (Chicago, 1960), 15–25; see also Victor Turner's vast body of work, above all, *Celebrations: Studies in Festivities and Ritual* (Washington, 1982); *From Ritual to Theatre: The Human Seriousness of Play* (New York, 1992).

6. *Viajes de extranjeros*, I: 1309–11.

7. Miri Rubin, *Corpus Christi: The Eucharist in Late Medieval Culture* (Cambridge, 1990).

8. See Angela Muñoz Fernández, 'Fiestas laicas y fiestas profanas en el Madrid medieval', in J.C. de Miguel Rodríguez (ed.), *El Madrid medieval: sus tierras y sus hombres* (Madrid, 1990), 151–76; see also Javier Portús Pérez, *La antigua procesión del Corpus Christi en Madrid* (Madrid, 1993). See also below.

9. Political in the sense that so much of the foreign political programme of the monarchy was tied to the support, at least in theory, of the teachings of Trent. At the centre of the Catholic Reformation was the question of transubstantiation, that is, of the real physical presence of Christ in the host.

10. Muñoz Fernández, 'Fiestas', 166; Portús Pérez, *La antigua procesión*, 79ff.

11. See T.F. Ruiz, 'Unsacred Monarchy: The Kings of Castile in the Late Middle Ages', in Sean Wilentz (ed.), *Rites of Power: Symbolism, Ritual and Politics Since the Middle Ages* (Philadelphia, 1985), 109–44.

12. See Alfonso de Palencia, 'Tratado de la perfección del triunfo militar', in *Dos tratados de Alfonso de Palencia* (Madrid, 1876), 105–63.

13. Muñoz Fernández, 'Fiestas', 167–68. For a thorough description of these theatrical representations in Madrid see Portús Pérez, *La antigua procesión*, appendices, I & II, 295–331.

14. Muñoz Fernández, 'Fiestas', 168; David Nirenberg, *Communities of Violence: Persecution of Minorities in the Middle Ages* (Princeton, 1996), 200–30.

15. Antoni Ariño, *Festes, rituals i creences: temes d'etnografia Valenciana*, IV, ed. Joan F. Mira (Valencia, 1988).

16. Ibid., 365–74.

17. Ibid., 386, 395–6.

18. Ibid., 401–4.

19. On this point of how representations work to create 'otherness' see T.F. Ruiz, 'Representación: Castilla, los castellanos y el Nuevo Mundo a finales de la Edad Media y principios de la moderna', in Carlos Barros (ed.), *Historia a debate: Medieval* (Santiago de Compostela, 1995), 63–77.

20. On the Inquisition in general see Henry Kamen, *Inquisition and Society in Spain in the Sixteenth and Seventeenth Centuries* (Bloomington, IN, 1985); Ángel Alcalá (ed), *The Spanish Inquisition and the Inquisitorial Mind* (Highland Lakes, NJ, 1987); the old but still formidable work by Henry C. Lea, *A History of the Inquisition in Spain*, 4 vols (New York, 1906–07) is still an inexhaustible mine of information on the Inquisition trials and theatrical performances.

21. Miguel Avilés, 'The Auto de Fe and the Social Model of Counter-Reformation Spain', in Alcalá (ed.), *The Spanish Inquisition and the Inquisitional Mind*, 249–64; Lea, *A History of the Inquisition*, III: 200ff.

22. Lea, *A History of the Inquisition*, III: 200ff.
23. Ibid., III: 209–29.
24. *Relaciones breves de actos públicos celebrados en Madrid de 1541 a 1650*, ed. José Simón Díaz (Madrid, 1982), 93.

Chapter 7

The burdens of violence: sites of conflict

The nature of violence

Unlike festivals and communal affirmations of faith and identity that, regardless of their hegemonic intent, sought to bind the social orders into a harmonious whole, violence and its counterpart, resistance, led diverse social groups and individuals to fierce and often fatal antagonisms. Of course, not all violence pitted one group against another. Nor did resistance always mean the resistance of subalterns to their superiors. In late medieval and early modern Europe different categories of violence and resistance brushed against each other, ranging from individual acts of psychological and physical violence (what today we call street crime or domestic violence) to intra-group violence (factions of nobles and their retinues fighting other nobles; rural communities attacking nearby villages) to the victimization of those below by those on top and the resistance of the former against the excesses of their oppressors.

I do not wish to suggest that the nature of violence in late medieval and early modern Spain was exceptional, or that the violence of that period represents a unique moment in history. In general, one must admit that physical and psychological aggression (and resistance) in contemporary developed societies is less pervasive than it was before the onset of industrialization and compulsory public education in the eighteenth and nineteenth centuries. Nonetheless, the tandem rise of technology and modern nationalism has also produced extraordinarily violent excesses: to wit, the world wars, atomic terror, genocide, and ethnic cleansing of the twentieth century which have no parallel in human history. In Spain, the cruelties of the Civil War, 1936–39, most certainly surpassed any other tragedy in the national history of Iberia.

While the phenomenon of violence has endured, the categories of violence and the ways in which they are articulated and perceived differ altogether from what they were in the past. Johan Huizinga in 'The Violent Tenor of Life', the dramatic opening chapter of *The Autumn of the Middle Ages*, vividly captured the reality of violence in late medieval life.[1] Those who live fairly protected lives may find it hard to understand the brutality that governed the everyday life of medieval and early modern men and women (or, for that matter, to imagine the systemic violence that continues to plague our own inner cities and entire nations elsewhere in the world).

Pervasive violence in fact played a crucial role in constructing community. The examples in these two chapters will enable us to view the violence and resistance in late medieval and early modern Spain as crucibles, which shaped and cemented relations between different groups and individuals. Not unlike *autos-de-fe* and public executions – the paradigmatic examples of official violence – violence served, perversely, to reconcile one group with another, to include some by excluding others. Ever since David Nirenberg's challenging book *Communities of Violence* (1996), the power of ritual group violence to enact a distorted kind of social inclusion can no longer be overlooked.[2] Of course, the type of orchestrated social and religious antagonism that Nirenberg discusses did not always work. Far too often, ritualized or highly choreographed social violence descended into uncontrollable mayhem. This, in turn, led to truly exclusionary deeds: to the permanent removal, by execution or exile, of offending individuals and/or groups.

What categories of violence (and resistance) were discernible in late medieval and early modern Spain? What were the social consequences of such clashes? Did violence and resistance change over time? If so, how did they change? These questions are not always easy to answer. From one perspective, popular agitation against Jews and *Conversos* in fifteenth-century Spain, for example, can be seen as an extreme form of violence against a religious 'other' and against those suspected of being so. At the same time, this antagonism was also fuelled by concrete social and economic forces (anti-Jewish and anti-*Morisco* sentiments, famines, pestilences, etc.). In other words, the anti-Jewish violence reflected specific temporal and material conditions as well as a systemic tradition of violence. Moreover, the religious violence that was so peculiar to late medieval and early modern Europe was also, unquestionably, a manifestation of resistance to the Crown and to factions of the nobility perceived to be, not always correctly, allies and protectors of Jews and *Conversos*. In truth, most forms of violence revealed implicit (and, in some cases, very explicit) resistance to the constituted order. But our knowledge of violence is most often gleaned from clerical sources that echo the class interests of the powerful, and most records are generally hostile to the claims and resistant undertakings of the lower classes.

Towards a typology of violence: official violence

For the sake of clarity, a typology of forms of violence and resistance may prove useful. Violent acts can be divided into two broad, distinct, but not mutually exclusive, categories. The first is official violence, encompassing actions more or less sanctioned by law that those in power – kings, nobles, the Church – took against their subjects and vassals. In this category we find extreme forms of violent behaviour: noble attacks against villagers, open civil war, and lesser, though still harsh and punitive forms of violence. These included the irregular and biased enforcement of the law, of conscription, and of excessive taxation. The struggles of the ruling elite in the fifteenth century for control of the throne or for extension of their privileges were almost always waged by frequent appeals to legal, moral, or patriotic principles, which inevitably embroiled the rest of the population. The consequences for those caught in the middle, regardless of the legality of these struggles, were always misery and/or death. Since the Crown, the nobility and even the urban patriciate mobilized, or attempted to mobilize, the populace as combatants and shock troops in their endless battles, the exercise of violence crossed social boundaries, with members of each order playing the dual role of aggressor and victim. Nonetheless, as is the case today, social prominence and wealth went a long way toward pre-empting the possibility of victimhood and mitigating the impact of defeat.

The awful civil wars of fifteenth-century Spain parallelled similar outbursts of violence in England and France. As manifestations of violence from above, they created a climate for the exercise of official violence. By the same token, the inquisitorial *autos-de-fe*; the militant enforcement of orthodoxy; the pogroms against Jews in 1391 and against *Conversos* throughout the fifteenth century; the punitive measures against *Moriscos* in the sixteenth century; the repression and wholesale slaughter of natives in the New World – all these forms of violence also functioned as discourses of power. They reinforced specific structures of power and legitimated the hierarchical tiering of society.

Unofficial violence

Under the category of unofficial violence, one may group a whole set of acts of resistance and collective crimes, which, though intimately linked to official violence, emerged or were played out outside the boundaries of legality. Among them, the most obvious were organized movements of resistance. The most notable of these movements was the war of the *Remenças*, already outlined in a previous chapter; but collective eruptions of violence were not limited to such large-scale peasant wars. Similar movements occurred in the Spains (and in overseas colonies) throughout the fifteenth century and even in the supposedly calm late sixteenth century. In the latter century, the revolt of the Alpujarras (see above, Chapters 1 and 4) stands out as a rather remarkable disturbance of order and of a religious minority's resistance to the constraints imposed by a Christian majority. The brutal armed struggle brought savage reprisals from both sides and resulted in the dramatic displacement of property and in the social and demographic relocation of both *Morisco* and Christian populations. But the rebellions of the *Remenças* and of the Alpujarras have, to some extent, obscured other widespread antagonisms between the central authorities in Madrid and specific regional or social groups within the kingdom at large (Aragonese, Catalan and Galician peasants).

An important subcategory to be explored in some detail is banditry. Although embedded in the social fabric of the Spanish realms in earlier centuries, banditry became systemic in certain regions of the kingdom, above all in the south and in Catalonia, in the early modern period. As I will argue, banditry and other lesser forms of criminal activity – scams, *pícaro* activity, organized prostitution, gambling, false begging, and the like – functioned as sites for violent or semi-violent interaction between different social orders, as they do today throughout the world. Another form of violence that cut across class lines and public/private or individual/collective boundaries was the widespread phenomenon of sexual and parental violence against women and children in late medieval and early modern Spain. Although a great deal of this type of violence occurred within the confines of the household and the family (thus somewhat outside the scope of this chapter: see Chapters 9 and 10), the frequency and toleration of such behaviour played a significant social role. Indeed, violence against women and children – often enacted because of real or perceived transgressions against the honour of husbands and male relatives, or because of breaches of parental or familial authority – articulated and reinforced the iron-clad hierarchies of family and society. We ought not to forget that servants, dependents, natives in the New World, and slaves were generally feminized and/or thought of as children. This correlation with patriarchy's traditionally disempowered members made the subordination of social others seem 'natural' and justified. Women, children and social inferiors could not circumvent the rigid constraints imposed on them by husbands, fathers and masters without incurring violent repercussions, even death.

The violence of everyday life

In the introductory pages of this chapter, I made a comparison between the relative security and peacefulness of our present lives and the unstable and turbulent lives of most people in late medieval and early modern Europe. Even in today's Western democracies, we are vulnerable to street crime, domestic violence, and the occasional arbitrary and abusive demand of the state and its official agents. But we view such occurrences as departures from normality, as unusual and unexpected. In fifteenth-century Castile and Aragon, in sixteenth-century Spain, and in most of Europe, such events were the stuff of everyday life. Royal decrees, literary works – Cervantes's *Don Quixote* is paradigmatic of the genre – and the ordinances of the *cortes* are filled with complaints about and representations of daily violence. This was an intensely physical world: blows were often the aftermath of verbal abuse and violent language. The recourse to fists, arms, and group attacks – one village, fully armed, raiding another nearby because of a mere ironic insult, as jocularly described in *Don Quixote* – was a common occurrence. These acts of individual and collective aggression were part of a symbolic language, a violent form of communicating power. Whereas commoners fought one another with fists, knives and staves, noblemen cultivated jousts and tournaments as elaborate ritualizations of violence. Let us not be confused by Hollywood's glitz and by nineteenth-century romantic depictions: jousts were murderous encounters. Lives were lost, people were maimed. Yet this controlled mayhem received the sanction of Church and state; and deeds of chivalry and the warring life were seen, to paraphrase Huizinga, as examples of the life beautiful.

The exercise of state justice, especially the public execution of criminals and political enemies (what Max Weber correctly identified as the legalized monopoly of violence), was in its gory performance another display of officially sanctioned violence. Even at the stake, strict hierarchies as to the permissible manner of death were observed. Public executions – the beheading, garroting, or asphyxiation of nobles; the hanging or burning of commoners – functioned as theatres of power to the delight and edification of most of the population. They were, as shall be seen, not just exemplary forms of punishment but socially inclusive ceremonies as well. We may also regard the violence and physicality of late medieval and early modern Spain as an effect of the vulnerability of most Spaniards to illness and early death and an acceptance of life's tenuous embrace. With the exception of the well-to-do (and they were not always exempt either), most people in late medieval and early modern Europe were continually besieged by hunger, illnesses, lice, skin diseases, falling teeth, infections and other such problems. The vivid portrait of daily life that Keith Thomas paints in *Religion and the Decline of Magic* is a grim reminder that even in such places as England, which enjoyed a better general standard of living than most continental states, life was, for the immense majority of people, full of despair and misery.[3] And those who had more than enough to eat were not necessarily healthy as a result; they consumed excessive amounts of meat and other rich foods, little or no fibre, and few vegetables or greens. Gout, chronic constipation and other such pleasantries became their bane. Infant mortality and death by childbirth, which are great tragedies in modern developed societies, were normal events. They struck the rich and the poor with the same unforgiving harshness.

Physical violence in all its manifestations, therefore, has to be seen as an extension of the upheaval of daily life, of the cruelties and uncertainties of human existence. These were, of course, somewhat ameliorated by the festivities described in the previous chapters, by the comforts of religion, and by the constructions of imperial glory. There could be joy – as was the case for Sancho Panza and Don Quixote – in a piece of bread, a chunk of cheese, and a patch of grass beneath the stars in which to sleep after having been run over by a flock of goats and sheep.[4] Such amelioration however was no security for the downtrodden; violence for them lurked behind every tree and corner.

Official violence: civil strife

The chronicles as well as the ordinances of the different *cortes* or *corts* (parliaments or regional assemblies) in fifteenth-century Castile and in the Crown of Aragon read like extensive catalogues of official violence. They report, in vivid language, the mighty conflicts of the age and the unceasing strife of the Crown against a rapacious nobility. They also tell the story of internecine warfare among nobles, describing the march of lordly armies up and down the dusty roads of the peninsula. My purpose here, however, is not to relate the history of these political conflicts. In the introductory chapter, I have already outlined the course of political life in fifteenth- and sixteenth-century Spain. At present, I wish to examine specific instances of these violent encounters and show how the essentially political and social conflicts of the mighty functioned as venues for social negotiation.

Most of the civil strife that will be discussed in this section occurred mainly because of competition for political power and financial resources. It often led to armed conflict but also to a great deal of propaganda and justification, as the contending parties sought to legitimate their ambitions. Narratives of armed engagements seldom linger on the havoc such battles wreaked on the population as a whole, on the lives of peasants and urban dwellers. We often must read between the lines or mine a scant literature of protest to gauge the impact of civil warfare or to learn how the weak were forcefully conscripted (though sometimes they enlisted freely) into noble armies, or were assaulted and destroyed.

The civil wars of the reigns of John II (1406–54) and Henry IV (1454–74), and the ones waged in the early years of the reign of the Catholic Monarchs; the systemic strife in the Crown of Aragon throughout most of the fifteenth century; and the internecine struggles of noble bands in both kingdoms during this period generally comprised pitched battles between knightly hosts, but, more often than not, they were wars of attrition in which one side attacked the vassals of the other side. In Spain this meant the dependent peasants; and waging war meant robbing their animals and goods, burning their properties, raping their women, conscripting their sons or holding them for ransom. These are precisely the charges that peasants and urban dwellers of Galicia lodged against their lords and that we will examine in detail in the next chapter.

Violence against peasants: the cases of Ribafrecha and Leza

Let me begin with a vignette from a period before 1400, which reflects many of the issues I wish to explore at length here. The fourteenth century had also known its share of royal minorities (with the usual fighting among the great nobility for control of the regency) and civil wars. As in the fifteenth century, the absence of a stable central authority opened the floodgates to untold violence. In the face of reduced resources, the habitual solution in the fourteenth, fifteenth and sixteenth centuries was to squeeze harder on those below and to extract more income from people less and less capable of paying. This scramble for money and power, which was driven by a decline in income and population stemming from the late medieval crisis (climatic change, pestilence, noble violence), threw different social classes into abnormal relationships. When the nobility victimized its own peasants or peasants in general, it broke the ideal principles of the medieval social order. The defenders of society (knights, nobles, the king himself) were duty-bound to protect those who worked and prayed. In return, they were ceded the land's surplus to maintain their warrior lives and noble status. This divinely sanctioned contract was breached when violence erupted among those on top (especially since it was always manifested by violence against those below). But while violence may have helped the elite to defend their privileges, it also created spaces wherein certain groups were able to exercise roles beyond those prescribed by the official tripartite order. I am not saying anything particularly profound here. Simply, violence functioned as a catalyst for the breakdown of idealized social strata and introduced more complex and realistic ways for groups to negotiate and interact.

This is the story of a few small rural communities in the area of the Rioja (north-central Spain) in the first half of the fourteenth century. Most of these villages were under the lordship of Santa María la Real de Nájera, a powerful but besieged monastery in the decades of the 1320s and 1330s. The region was battered by civil unrest, in the aftermath of the high nobility's struggles to control the regency of the young king Alfonso XI (1312–50). Bad weather affected crops, causing a sharp demographic and economic downturn. The monastery's acerbic relations with the municipal council of Nájera did not help matters either.[5]

Conditions became so critical that the Crown agreed to lower the tax-assessment of several of the villages – that is, the contributions peasants owed the royal fisc (in addition to the many dues they owed the ecclesiastical lord – in view of the growing (noble) violence and devastation. In some cases, entire villages, the village of Ventosa among them, 'became deserted, their fields gone to waste, its inhabitants having fled to Navarre'.[6] Considering our stereotypes of medieval peasants and their static relations with their masters, this was pretty radical. Abandoning an ancestral village *en masse* in the late Middle Ages or in the early modern period was a deed of last resort. These peasants (all fifty or so of them) just picked up their tools, cattle, and personal goods and migrated to another kingdom. We do not know what their subsequent lives were like, but one expects that in Navarre they found a far more stable political scenario and a lord capable of protecting them from the depredations of other lords.

169

The peasants of Ventosa succeeded in resisting noble violence by fleeing and by removing themselves and their work from a tormented area. These peasants had agency and met the scourge and rapacity of noble violence as well as ruinous economic conditions with a communal act of defiance. Their counterparts in the sixteenth century, faced with a different kind of violence (fiscal abuse and military conscription), also opted for the road. Emptying out the Castilian countryside, they fled to the cities, to the peripheries of the empire, and to America.

Not all peasants fled, however. Between the early decades and the mid-point of the fourteenth century, numerous villages entered into defence agreements with their lords. Surviving sources show how entire village populations – often listed by name and occupation – came together to build ramparts around the perimeter of their communities and strong houses with iron-locked wooden gates. These rather elaborate barricades, built to contain rebellious nobleman and their retainers, were put up, watched over, and paid for by the peasants themselves. Violence thus served as a context for negotiations between lords and their peasants.

Walls and keeps erected against rural violence, however, often yielded outcomes opposite to their original intent. They deterred some noblemen, but others viewed fortified villages as opportune strongholds from which to terrorize the countryside. Such was the case of Ribafrecha, the village that was sacked in late 1315 or early 1316 by John Ferrández de Bezla, a rebellious magnate seeking to carve out an estate for himself amid the civil anarchy of the realm. John Ferrández de Bezla and his men burned the village, stole all the movable property and cattle, and destroyed the crops and gardens. When order in the region was somewhat restored by another magnate, John Alfonso de Haro, and the municipal militia of the nearby town of Logroño, the peasants had no choice but to move elsewhere. There was nothing to return to. In April 1316, the long-suffering peasants of Ribafrecha founded a new village, Oriemo, away from the desolation of Ribafrecha. They chose, perhaps unwisely, to build yet another wall around the village.

The question must be asked: what makes this violence 'official'? The answer is: not much. But one must remember that all of these actions were carried out on either side with innumerable claims to legality and to the well-ordering of the realm. Violence was, in fact, a political and social discourse. What is most interesting about these vignettes is the widening circle of those pulled into the maelstrom of violence: peasants, ecclesiastic lords, the high nobility and their retinues, the Crown, urban dwellers. This was most obvious in the case of Leza, a small village, also under the lordship of the monastery of Santa María la Real de Nájera, that was forcefully appropriated by Don John Alfonso de Haro. We have already met the count of Haro, who, two decades earlier, had acted in the name of the king as a defender of order; now, in 1334, he had become a usurper.

After the militia of Logroño (de Haro's former allies in the struggle against John Ferrández de Bezla) successfully campaigned to restore Leza to its rightful owner, Don Loys, prior of Santa María de Nájera, the entire male population of Logroño (the *vecinos* or citizens, i.e. the property holders and taxpayers of the town) gathered in the town's cemetery on 6 May 1334 to decide under what terms to support that measure. Numerous conditions were imposed on the monastery to ensure its ability to defend the village and its peasants from further noble attacks.[7]

The civil wars of the fifteenth century, in both the Crowns of Aragon and Castile, were the background to incidents similar to those occurring in the fourteenth century. With some alterations in the cast of characters and forms of violence, different social orders were drawn into close and perilous relations. The discourse of these relations may not have been as colourful as that of the festivals described in the previous chapters, but it was as significant. In these encounters meaning was conveyed through the grim tools of war and devastation. But the process was one and the same: like festivals, violence opened the door to new kinds of social interaction and, in many cases, to aggressive negotiations of power, prestige and survival among distinct social orders, religious groups and individuals.

The burdens of violence

Even as order began to be somewhat restored in the late fifteenth century, the conflicts of the mighty continued to impinge painfully on all social classes. We can follow the impact of the war between the armies of the Catholic Monarchs, on the one hand, and the alliance of Portuguese troops and disaffected Castilian noble allies, on the other, through a series of royal letters written by the queen and king to the municipal authorities in Avila. During the last stages of the war, in the late 1470s, the city of Avila was drawn forcefully and painfully into the fray. This meant mobilizing a great deal of its population and tapping into its financial resources to pay for the additional costs of war.

On 7 February 1475, the Catholic Monarchs summoned two representatives of the city to attend a meeting of the Castilian *cortes* at Segovia. The main purpose of the gathering was to recognize the newly born Infanta Isabel as heir to the throne, but the first issue addressed by the royal summons was that of violence. The vivid language of the royal chancery deserves to be heard, for it resonates with the anarchy and despair of the times.

> It is well known how, for some time now, there has been great disorder, corruption [and misconduct] among people of all social orders, as they engage in the vices and crimes of disobedience [to the crown], tyranny . . . carrying out many thefts and highway robberies, rebellion, sedition, factional wars [that cause] the death of many men and many other evils and damages. As a result many have changed and usurped

171

their manner of living [that is, live outside their own natural social order] and live in a manner alien to themselves.[8]

Perceiving that a corrosive violence was destroying the harmony of the social order, pitting one group against another, disrupting the realm, and – far more threatening – encouraging people to usurp the social prerogatives of those above them, the Catholic Monarchs ordered Avila and other Castilian and Leonese cities to send procurators to Segovia to discuss measures that would restore order.

These were not idle words or formulaic language. Just over two months afterwards, on 10 April 1475, Ferdinand and Isabella requested that Avila, Salamanca and other cities of the realm refuse to supply the nobles who had risen up in arms in Plasencia. Among these nobles were Don Alvaro de Zúñiga, the marquis de Villena and the master of the Military Order of Santiago, one of the most powerful men in the land. The Catholic Monarchs' letter to Avila and other cities was more than a simple request, for it ordered the confiscation of all goods intercepted on their way to the rebels, and the imprisonment of those engaged in such activities and, eventually, the penalty of death.[9]

A month later, on 16 May 1475, Ferdinand ordered every man in Avila over the age of eighteen and below the age of sixty, 'those on horse and on foot', to join him, with all their weapons, in resisting an invasion from Portugal. I doubt very much that *all* the men of Avila rallied to the king's aid; but, in all likelihood, a good number of the city's militia marched out to join the royal contingents, and Avila was duly rewarded for its efforts. A month afterward, when Isabella visited the city for her first visit as a queen – in what was, to the relief of Avila, a very subdued royal entry – she pledged to honour all the privileges of the city.[10]

But Avila and its citizens were not released from the exigencies of violence and warfare. The Catholic Monarchs kept up a steady stream of requests for supplies, new taxes, and men to carry on the war against Portugal. Once the affairs of Portugal were settled, requests for contributions to the campaigns against Granada began to pour in, and new restrictions were imposed on the city's autonomy. The men of Avila were commanded to guard the mountain passes near the city and to prevent rebellious noblemen from escaping the royal armies. These demands, while illustrating the shifting political relations between the Crown and urban centres in Castile during the late fifteenth century, point to the travails that open warfare and civil unrest enforced upon all social groups.

As I have indicated, the diverse social orders were so intimately linked that little occurred in the realms that did not affect the population as a whole, even if events affected each social order differently. When the urban militia was called to arms, it included proud urban knights who, for all practical purposes, were nobles. But the militia was also made up of *peones*, footmen, the petit-bourgeois, and taxpaying, well-to-do artisans and local farmers. Two hundred men of Avila's militia, a sizeable contingent considering the city's population, saw action in the Granada wars. The bishop of the city and a staunch supporter of Isabella, Don Alfonso de Fonseca, was granted the temporary lordship of the city. A new and elaborate tax-assessment (*repartimiento*) was to be collected from the city and villages of the land of Avila. The brunt of the contributions to the Catholic Monarchs fell most heavily on the peasants, who not only paid heavy subsidies they could ill afford but also gave their lives guarding mountain passes.

Literary representations of violence

The civil wars that plagued the Spanish kingdoms (Christian and Muslim alike) in the late fifteenth century were vividly depicted in the chronicles of the period. Civil disturbances and systemic violence also generated a whole literature of protest. Both a reaction to the violence and a critique of existing social conditions, this literature of protest articulated deep grievances against the breakdown of civil authority. Paradoxically, the most vehement critics of noble abuse were themselves members of the ruling groups perpetrating most of the violence. In a sense, a great deal of the satirical and critical poetry of fifteenth-century Castile and, to a lesser extent, the Crown of Aragon was issued from within the ranks of the nobility. Many of the authors belonged to its highest echelons or, as was probably the case with the author of *Las coplas de la panadera* (*The couplets of the baker woman*), had established ties to the political life and social patronage of the court.

These poems, written in the common language of the people, had many repeated refrains; they were thus easy to remember and to transmit orally. Most of them contained bitter attacks against the higher orders: against the greed, violence and concupiscence of the clergy and the nobility. This type of social critique, quite common in late medieval Europe, was often animated by the somewhat morbid spirituality and melancholic feeling of the age. Nonetheless, in Castile and in the rest of Spain, this literature addressed problems that were specific to the Iberian realms: the presence of large religious minorities and the fratricidal wars of the fifteenth century, particularly their impact on the lower social orders.

An early example of this kind of critical literature is the *General Dance of Death* (*La dança general de la muerte*). Although its European provenance is traced to the decade after the onslaught of the Black Death (1348), internal evidence in the Castilian version has allowed scholars to date it to the early fifteenth century.[11] In the poem all the orders of society – an entire catalogue of social types: young and old, rich and poor, male and female, urban and rural – are summoned to dance in front of Death. All, the powerful in particular, are exhorted to repent and to contemplate the coming of death. Popes,

173

emperors (kings), cardinals, archbishops, high nobles, patriarchs, rich merchants, doctors and usurers are accused of greed, gluttony, excessive displays, and taxing believers and subjects beyond measure. All who have lived in the pursuit of wealth will be punished in Hell. Only the humble peasant, 'who never took his hand from the plough, as he worked the lands of others . . . who eats bacon and sometimes mutton . . . and whose life is work and effort', and the good monk, are permitted to enjoy the blessings of Heaven after death.[12]

The cast of characters, which includes a rabbi and a Muslim *alfaquí* (a Muslim religious official), represents a complete gallery of Spanish late-medieval types. But even though the rabbi and the *alfaquí* receive no heavenly rewards, they are spared the bitter condemnations that are aimed at the upper classes and the impious mendicants. Thus, the *Dança general de la muerte* places the marginalised and the poor on one side and those who victimized them on the other. Poverty and hard work, as instantiated by the figures of the peasant and the pious monk, stand out as quint-essential Christian virtues against the unchristian violence of those on top.

This point is reiterated in Ruy Páez de Ribera's poem dedicated to Queen Catalina (1373–1418) in the early fifteenth century.[13] The poem bemoans the conflict among the great noble houses, the neglect of the land and its people during the wars of reconquest against Granada, and the waste of lives and energy in the fratricidal wars plaguing Castile. In it, most of the great noble lineages are deemed 'not worth a fig', and unbridled noble violence and factional struggles wear down the peasants who are oppressed by the nobles and knights whose very duty it is to protect them, pressed hard by rent-collectors and forced to sell their own clothes. Moreover, many *fijosdalgo* (petty-nobility) find themselves mired in conditions similar to those of the peasants: 'lost and abandoned [*desechados*]' by the breakdown of civil order.[14]

In the same vein, the anonymous *Coplas de la panadera* – attributed to Juan de Mena, a courtly poet, and imitated and reproduced in Catalonia, where the political scenario mirrored that of Castile – tells the story of the battle of Olmedo (1445), an important military engagement between John II of Castile and his constable, Alvaro de Luna, on the one hand, and the Infantes of Aragon and the rebellious nobility on the other. Told from the viewpoint of a woman baker (almost all bakers were women in late medieval Castile) and using salty and scatological metaphors, the *Coplas* mocks the fatuous exhibitionism of war-mongering nobles and ecclesiastics and denounces their cowardice and obvious renunciation of Christian and chivalrous virtues. Caught in the middle of noble strife, the peasants – who are also represented as cowardly and vile – flee a violence that is incomprehensible to them.[15]

In a far more poignant poem, *Coplas de Mingo Revulgo*, Fray Iñigo de Mendoza describes late fifteenth-century Castile under Henry IV as a place torn by civil war, famine and pestilence. Two sheep-herders, Mingo Revulgo and Gil Arribato, discuss the affairs of the kingdom. They compare the rebellious barons who inflict violence on the people to wolves, and the people to helpless flocks (of sheep): 'I see the wolves coming in / and the flocks bleeding'. The latter have been left unprotected by a weak and incompetent king. The author, whose blood ties connected him to both the great noble family of the Mendozas and the great *Converso* clan of the Santamaría, ends the *Coplas de Mingo Revulgo* with apocalyptic images of a war that 'does not allow mothers and their children to lie quietly in their homes'. Civil war finds its way into the most hidden of places, bringing endless disturbances to the land.[16]

The tormented vision of much of the protest poetry and literature of the fifteenth century paralleled the ordinances of the *cortes* (Castilian or Aragonese) and the chronicles of the period. All of these sources evoked, or depicted in graphic language, the deeds of violence, the civil unrest, and the impact of violence on the rest of society.[17]

The Catholic Monarchs and systemic violence

In principle, the sixteenth century brought a restoration of order and a taming of the nobility, despite the uprisings of the *Comuneros*, *Germanías* and *Moriscos* (the Alpujarras rebellion). Traditional historiography has viewed the reign of the Catholic Monarchs as a watershed, not only because it reformed the government of Castile but also because it ended the cycle of violence that bedevilled the peninsular kingdoms throughout the fifteenth century. During their reign, the internecine struggles of an unruly nobility were put down, and peace was restored. But recently historians have observed that, with or without royal sanctions, the systemic violence of those on top disrupted the idealized vision that had governed relations among the different social orders. In a paradoxical sense, the curtailing of noble excesses, and the turning of nobles into servants of the Crown, opened the door to different kinds of conflict. Whereas in the fifteenth century noble violence constituted a struggle for control of the Crown, in the sixteenth it involved a resistance to the encroachments and excesses of a centralized monarchy.

In the diverse regions and motley constituencies of the Crown of Aragon, the reforms of the Catholic Monarchs did not curb the most wanton excesses of the nobility, as they had done in Castile. Ferdinand and Isabella concentrated their quite remarkable efforts in Castile and did not attempt – or did not attempt in real earnest – to deal with the complicated and unyielding constitutional arrangements of the Crown of Aragon. Their heirs, whether Charles I or Philip II, ruled from Castile and dealt with Aragonese, Valencian or Catalan issues very gingerly. This was not a benign neglect, but a shrewd realization of how limited their power was in dealing with the diverse social, institutional and political issues of the eastern kingdoms.

The price paid for the imbalance in royal authority between Castile and the Crown of Aragon was an onerous one. First, a diminished royal authority in the kingdoms of the Crown of Aragon gave the high nobility a partial free hand to carry on their traditional factional struggles. This, in turn, created an atmosphere of violence that deeply affected the other social orders. Second, it allowed for violent private actions against unprotected minorities, specifically against the *Moriscos*, a thing unimaginable in sixteenth-century Castile. Third, it created a space for resistance to Castilian dominance and for challenges to royal authority. The best example of the latter is the Antonio Pérez affair.

Noble violence

We can briefly list some of the most salient examples of noble violence. In many respects, they represented a continuation of the appalling violence of the previous century that was contained but not extinguished by Ferdinand I's victories in the 1480s. Despite half-hearted attempts by the viceroys to restore peace, personal vendettas, assassinations and open factional warfare were common in the three eastern realms. In Aragon, the vassals of the count of Ribagorza engaged in a bitter war against their lord in the 1580s. The conflict drew knights from as far away as Catalonia, who hired themselves out to one side or the other, and allowed for the looting and sacking of villages and other egregious behaviour. Reaching unprecedented levels, the violence at Ribagorza became paradigmatic of what could happen when quarrels surpassed the usual noble or family feuds.

Ribagorza, a great seigneurial estate, occupied a strategic position close to the troubled frontier with France. Its location made the upheaval a serious concern for the Crown; yet royal intervention was of little avail. The conflict involved more than two hundred villages and localities and drew nobles and peasants alike into its rapidly escalating violence. Charles I, with the support of most of the inhabitants of the region, had already made attempts late in his reign to absorb the lands of Ribagorza into the royal domain. This led to the start of a war, as royal efforts to gain legal redress in the *cortes* of Aragon were thwarted by the Aragonese love for their intractable constitutional liberties. The lord of Ribagorza, Don Martín de Gurrea, and later his son, Don Hernando, insisted on taking possession of their title, and when faced with the resistance of their vassals, they hired the notorious bandit Lupercio Latrás to terrorize the region. Valentín Vázquez de Prada, in his excellent short summary of the violence in the region (which I follow faithfully in these pages), cites an eyewitness account of some of the violence. This eyewitness recounts how the mercenary bands of Latrás played ball (a kind of rugby or football) on Palm Sunday of 1588, using the heads of executed villagers to mark the boundaries of the playing field. This took place precisely in the year of the Armada, when the Spanish monarchy launched the largest fleet ever assembled in Christendom and mobilized very large armies indeed against England. Yet, the Crown could not restore peace on its northeastern frontier or prevent these kinds of abuses.[18]

The violence in the region of Ribagorza lasted almost four decades and ended only when Philip II purchased the county from its murderous lord in what was essentially the paying of a substantial bribe for his capitulation. For forty years the peasants in Ribagorza had been the victims of open warfare, but, whether in Ribagorza or elsewhere, peasants were also drawn into the fray as combatants. Here one cannot make a clear-cut distinction between social orders on the basis of oppression and victimization. Although those at the bottom were most often the victims of systemic violence, they also participated in it; either in response to real or perceived threats by the powerful, or when coerced to do so by those above them, or when the opportunity for monetary gain or the pleasure of revenge proved irresistible. In addition, there was always – in Spain and elsewhere in Europe – a floating population of displaced peasants and the poor ready to make a living through illegal and violent means. In Catalonia, lordly strongholds became refuges for the disaffected, places from which noble-led gangs scourged the countryside and carried out attacks against other nobles and against the helpless civilian population.

The region of Urgel, like Ribagorza, lay close to the border with France and was thus sensitive territory for the Crown. Valentín Vázquez de Prada describes the violence in Urgel in the 1590s as a 'veritable civil war'. The disturbances reached such a magnitude that the Crown had to send royal troops to lay siege to and destroy the castle of nobleman Joan Cadell in the village of Arséguel.[19] The mayhem in Urgel mirrored the widespread general violence of the Catalonian principality, a violence that increased in virulence in the second half of the sixteenth century. It exploded into a true civil war in the middle of the next century.[20]

Valencia, though far more prosperous than the other two kingdoms of the Crown of Aragon, was also plagued by internecine struggles among the principal families of the region. In the 1550s, the Rocafull and the Masquetá families fought each other, forcing the viceroy to take the extreme measure of executing one of the contenders. Later in the decade, the Pardo de la Casta clan fought the Figuerola family in a protracted feud lasting over a decade. The violence spread, as more families entered the fray.

As a corollary to the disputes between noble families and the waves of violence sweeping over Valencia and its hinterland, nobles often engaged in criminal behaviour in the expectation of being granted immunity based on their exalted rank. This was the case of Don Juan Folch de Cardona, admiral of Aragon and marquis of Guadalest. This high-born nobleman and ranking official in Aragon kidnapped two nuns from the monastery of the Immaculate Conception in Valencia. Despite his rank, he was executed in 1577 under orders of the viceroy.[21]

Noble violence eventually brought a reaction from the Crown and stern measures to contain these excesses. It was too late. The pervasive physical threat to the population at large and the psychological impact of entrenched conflict affected the social fabric of the Crown of Aragon and, by extension, that of Spain and its empire. The inability of the central authorities in Madrid to monopolize legal violence, to use Max Weber's terms again, or to maintain full control of legal and public vengeance left individuals and specific social groups very much on their own. In their attempts to negotiate peace with violent nobles or unruly bandits, to maintain order, and to preserve their lives and properties, these groups and individuals were continually thwarted by arbitrary and random violence. Illegal and unrestricted violence – very different from state violence, which was always somewhat predictable – functioned not just as a site for social interaction, as I have argued in preceding pages, but as a discourse, a language, that cut painfully across social boundaries.

Moriscos

The somewhat limited role of the Crown in the eastern kingdoms (limited only in comparison to its fairly efficient rule in Castile) also allowed for violent relations between the Old Christian population and the *Moriscos* in the Crown of Aragon. In Granada, the uprising of the Alpujarras, which has been outlined in some detail in Chapter 1 and which will be reviewed again below, was a bitterly contested revolt by the *Moriscos* against what they rightly perceived as an occupying and oppressive power. In the Crown of Aragon conditions were different indeed. Foreign travellers crossing Aragon proper in the fifteenth and sixteenth centuries noted again and again the many small villages along the way that were inhabited almost exclusively by *Moriscos*. From Antoine de Laligny in the early sixteenth century to Henry Cock, one of Philip II's guards, travellers viewed *Morisco* life as a salient feature of the Aragonese landscape.[22] Although they were repressed by lords who often exploited them mercilessly, the *Moriscos* devoted themselves to agriculture and thrived, much to the chagrin of their Christian rivals. Successful in resisting assimilation, with large growing families (their fertility was often perceived as an offence), and thrifty in their daily lives, the *Moriscos* became targets of popular hatred. Though nominally Christians, they practised their own religion, Islam, openly, spoke Arabic, and dressed in fashions that set them apart from the rest of the population. If they survived at all in the Crown of Aragon, it was mainly because they generated a sizeable income for the nobles they served. The nobles, in turn, sought to protect their *Morisco* dependent population from the threat of royal sanctions, inquisitorial persecution, and popular prejudice throughout most of the sixteenth century.

After the 1550s, however, the tide began to turn. Inklings of what was to come were already visible in the *Germanías*, the Valencian popular revolt of the 1520s (see next chapter), in which popular discontent was expressed through attacks on the *Moriscos*. The Alpujarras rebellion gave the Christian population a fright in its display of what *Moriscos* could do if pushed too far. The frequent attacks of Berber corsairs on the eastern shores of Spain (occurrences given particular prominence in the literature of the period), the real Ottoman threat, and the Spanish military failures in North Africa increased the level of fear of *Moriscos* and the perception of them as the enemy within. Cervantes had no love for them; nonetheless he depicted a *Morisco* who was expelled from Spain after a long, peaceful and productive life in a village of La Mancha in rather positive terms. Yet, in the narrative, Cervantes has Ricote, the *Morisco*, admit to the allegedly insidious and heretical character of most of his co-religionists.[23] All of these elements created a volatile situation that was not limited to pejorative literary representations or to popular hatred. Violence often erupted in extremely ugly fashion, both as part of the general context of violence and as manifestation of singular religious and racial (or what was defined as racial by contemporaries) intolerance.

Three years after Philip II made his triumphal entry into Zaragoza in 1585, *Moriscos* were massacred in the village of Codo. Prompted by the alleged killing of a livestock owner in 1585, mountain people descended into the plains and killed close to seven hundred *Moriscos*. Supported by the bands of the infamous Lupercio Latrás, these mountain villagers also attacked and killed a large number of *Moriscos* in the village of Pina.[24] The contemporary account of the violence at Pina reads almost like a newspaper report of ethnic cleansing in the Balkans. The same uncontrolled violence, the same fear and mistrust on both sides, are evident.

The case of Pina

Jerónimo de Blancas, chronicler of the kingdom of Aragon, provides a thorough account of the attacks on the *Moriscos* of Pina. In spite of his clearly expressed biases and hatreds, the *Morisco* victims are often described as 'sad'; some of the followers of Latrás are indicted as 'rabble' (*canalla*). The attack on the *Morisco* community at Pina, a village under royal jurisdiction on the outskirts of Zaragoza, took place within the context of the seigneurial strife in Ribagorza and the nefarious activities of the infamous Lupercio Latrás. What happened there?

In 1588, Lupercio Latrás, back from serving as infantry captain of the Spanish army in Sicily (where he had been sent with a pardon as a way of removing him from his criminal life in Aragon), returned to the region upon hearing the news that his lord, the count of Ribagorza, faced an open rebellion from his vassals. Arriving in Ribagorza with a troop of followers, Latrás marched south to relieve the lord of Pinilla, who was besieged in the castle of Benabarra, and to recruit soldiers for the conflict in Ribagorza. Caught in the animosity against the *Moriscos*, Latrás used them as convenient scapegoats to recruit the outlaws, the disaffected and the idle to his service.

Their first attack was carried out against Sástago, a village of almost three hundred *Morisco* households in the jurisdiction of the viceroy of Aragon. Sástago, reinforced by *Moriscos* from other localities in the region, put up a stiff resistance. Those who broke through the defences were swiftly killed or seized, and some of Latrás's followers (also known as mountaineers) suffered 'strange cruelties'. De Blancas describes how one of the mountaineers was cut to pieces by the *Moriscos*, boiled (after his death) in oil, buried in the ground up to his waist, and kept as an object of derision. His narrative allows us to see a world in which more than a thousand *Moriscos* lived alongside a handful of Old Christians, and in which *Moriscos* were armed to the teeth and knew how to defend themselves.

Defeated at Sástago, Latrás and his gang turned to Pina. In Pina, a larger village of four hundred households, the *Moriscos*, constituting only a quarter of the population (around one hundred households), lived at one end of the town in a segregated neighbourhood called La Parroquía, which looked like a town in itself (*'parecían . . . pueblo de por si'*). On 26 April 1588, Latrás's troops, around four hundred infantrymen and twenty cavalry, attacked the town. With some support from the Old Christians in Pina, including those troops sent to protect the town and the *Moriscos*, the rebels turned their wanton attack on the *Moriscos* into a religious crusade. With cries of 'long live the faith of Christ' and 'kill the Moors', they burned *Morisco* houses (while many of their inhabitants were within), killing with 'excessive cruelty', looting, and raping. Latrás's band scourged Pina, but the *Moriscos* who survived the initial attack fortified themselves in a few strong houses and held firm. Nonetheless, when a large number of *Moriscos* from Gelsa, a nearby town, were turned back from their aim of relieving those besieged at Pina, the doom of the defenders was at hand.

The chronicler, as noted earlier, renders a fairly sympathetic portrait of the *Moriscos* and their desperate fight against the superior force and cruelty of their enemies. In the end, after fierce resistance, some of the *Moriscos* escaped to Gelsa under the veil of darkness; others sought refuge in a nearby Franciscan monastery. The latter, however, found no safe haven there. Latrás's troops, joined by the Old Christians of Pina, came into the monastery, killing some and taking the rest to the main square of the town. There 'babies had their heads smashed against the walls in front of their mothers' and adults were cut to pieces, as the rabble tested their strength and accuracy with cutlasses. All of this took place just a few miles from Zaragoza, the capital of Aragon. But, of course, violence always breeds violence. A few months afterwards, on 21 October 1588, a company of Old Christians, including a monk, was set upon by a band of *Moriscos* on the road between Zaragoza and Calatayud – the same road Philip II had travelled in reverse for his royal entry in Zaragoza three years before. Seventeen of the Old Christian company were tortured, killed, and their bodies mutilated near the inn of la Romera. The atrocities described in these sixteenth-century accounts are like the ones recently reported in Bosnia and Kosovo.[25]

These, I should add, were not isolated incidents but part of a pattern of collective and individual violence committed against *Moriscos* simply because they were different. In the United States today, such actions would be classified as 'bias crimes'. Here again, we witness the complicated ways in which violence cut across social boundaries. Attacks on *Moriscos* were sometimes sparked by popular animosity. On these occasions, the nobility, the social order most responsible for violence, was often found defending its *Morisco* peasants from a rampaging mob.

We should not idealize the *Moriscos* nor depict them solely as victims, although to a large extent that is what they were. We have seen in the above descriptions how they could defend themselves and even go on the offensive. Royal and viceroyal edicts from the second half of the sixteenth century – above all in the kingdom of Valencia, a heartland of *Morisco* life – forbade them to carry weapons. These edicts also specified which types of weapons – mostly firearms – could not be owned by *Moriscos* or carried by them in public. In addition, the viceroyal ordinances imposed heavy fines and stiff penalties on those ignoring the ban. The frequency of these decrees and the urgency of their tone, however, suggest a world in which the *Moriscos* may not have been in open rebellion, but in which they were able to resist and, often through banditry and crime, go on the offensive against their Christian persecutors. But even though they did not resist always forcefully, the widespread belief among Christians was that the *Moriscos* constituted a clear and present danger.

In 1582, a royal decree to the city of Valencia prohibited recently converted *Moriscos* from going to sea or fishing without an official licence under penalty of being condemned to the galleys and a fine of 50 ducats.[26] That same year, those with lands near the sea could not work their fields without obtaining written permission from the justice, *'bayle'*, or juryman of their particular locality; they needed approval for their comings and goings to their own lands. Four years later, Philip II's decree forbade *Moriscos* in the Valencian region to move to the coast or to become vassals in coastal regions without prior royal authorization. In addition, they were forbidden to use their language (Arabic) or to give aid to the Moors (from North Africa).[27]

Clearly, the Spaniards, or at least the ruling groups, were convinced of the sinister ties among *Moriscos*, Turks and North African raiders. What these royal edicts did was to arouse popular misgivings and provoke violent acts, even far away inland, with predictably deleterious effects. After the bloody revolt of the Alpujarras and the threat of Muslim corsairs, the growing climate of mistrust in Spain provided a licence for official and unofficial violence against the *Moriscos* and ushered in new forms of social negotiations, uneven and one-sided as they were, between the Christian majority and a persecuted religious minority. These measures ranged from decrees restricting *Morisco* movement and regulating their dress and language – though the *Moriscos* were in theory (if not always in practice) Christians – to spontaneous and savage physical attacks by Old Christians and likely retaliations by *Moriscos*.

In 1608, the *Moriscos*, accused of not having really converted to Christianity, were blamed for a wave of crime in the Valencian region. They were charged with joining bands of armed men (the actual infraction was carrying flint rifles, pistols and other forbidden weapons) and with terrorizing the countryside. Lists of their names were posted. Eleven of them were condemned to death *in absentia*, and twenty-seven others were captured and tried for their crimes. A bounty of 50 pounds each was placed on their heads.[28]

In the next chapter, we will have the opportunity to examine banditry in greater detail. For the present, it is sufficient to note that in late sixteenth-century Valencia, and even after the expulsion of *Moriscos* in the early seventeenth century (for some obviously refused to depart), they were often branded as criminals and persecuted as such by the authorities. It is also clear from the documentation that they did not go quietly; nor did they suffer Christian violence, official or unofficial, patiently. Long after the expulsion and beyond the terminus of this book, some *Moriscos* took to arms and remained in the countryside as bandits or as hidden witnesses to a vanishing world. The rich *Morisco* Ricote, in the second part of *Don Quixote*, who returns home disguised as a German pilgrim in search of his Christian wife, his daughter, and his hidden treasure, could not have been just a fictional and isolated figure. The continuous presence of *Moriscos* – in the Alpujarras until the 1570s, and in Aragon and Valencia until the eve of the expulsion – generated social strife and uncertainty. It gave a unique character to the relations among different social and religious groups in Spain.

The Antonio Pérez affair

A great deal of the noble violence and popular disturbances experienced in the Crown of Aragon during the sixteenth century were linked to the uneasy relationship between the central authorities in Castile (finally fixed in Madrid in the 1560s) and the eastern kingdoms. The latter, above all Aragon and Catalonia, jealously sought to preserve their autonomy against what they rightly perceived as an encroaching foreign power. Even if Madrid was quite diplomatic in its dealings with other parts of the realm, its policies and imperial demands, and the claims of the Inquisition (the only truly national institution, but firmly controlled by Castilian interests), made for certain trouble. Part of the trouble derived from the clear territorial separation between the kingdoms, a separation that even Philip II did not dare challenge.

Henry Cock, in his narrative of the royal voyage and triumphal entrance into Zaragoza (discussed in the previous chapter), provides us with a dramatic description of the divide between one realm and the other and of the proud and stubborn manner in which the Aragonese reasserted their autonomy. The story is worth repeating. Upon reaching the boundary with Aragon, which was lined with stone landmarks (*mojones*), the royal cortège was received by the *Justicia* (or general ombudsman) of Aragon, and 'all the officials [*alcaldes, alguaciles, y toda la justicia*] of Castile were forced to put their staffs of office on the ground, according to ancient custom, since it was *another* kingdom'. Philip II's guards discharged their weapons into the air to mark the passing from one jurisdiction to another.[29]

This need to keep sharp distinctions between the different political jurisdictions of fragmented Spain was the context of the crisis kindled by the Antonio Pérez affair. It led to violent antagonisms between Madrid and the Crown of Aragon, creating a climate of social upheaval and resistance. In short, the Antonio Pérez affair provided a focus around which to articulate opposition to the central authorities in Madrid. Antonio Pérez was the trusted secretary of Philip II and thus privy to the most secret decisions of the Spanish monarchy. In the late 1570s, Pérez, besides engaging in the illicit sales of public offices, entered into a conspiracy that resulted in the death of Escobedo, the secretary of Don Juan de Austria, the illegitimate son of Charles I and hence Philip II's half brother. Don Juan, the hero of the great naval victory at Lepanto, was an ambitious man, with a penchant for political intrigues and for actions that could destabilize the monarchy. Whether with the king's knowledge or not, Antonio Pérez ordered Escobedo's assassination. The latter had threatened to expose Pérez's illegal transactions to the king. Taken prisoner in 1585 and tortured, Pérez confessed to his role in the murder, but claimed that he had had Escobedo killed by royal order. Condemned to death in 1590 on charges of *lèse majesté*, he escaped and sought refuge in Aragon, his birthplace.

With Pérez under the protection of the *Justicia* of Aragon, Philip II was forced to go through the Aragonese courts to bring him to justice. The Royal Audiencia of Aragon rebuffed the king's Castilian councillors and refused to extradite Pérez to Castile. Having failed in the courts, Philip II had Antonio Pérez charged with heresy and sodomy by the Inquisition. Although the Inquisition did bring to trial individuals guilty of these charges, sodomy, necromancy and heresy had long been a shorthand for dealing with those accused of political crimes. Now these charges were being invoked by the Inquisition to circumvent Aragonese resistance and the punctilious observance of its charters (*fueros*) and autonomy.

When in May 1591 Antonio Pérez was about to be transferred from the prison of the *Justicia* to that of the Inquisition, a popular revolt, in which members of the lower nobility and of the popular classes participated, prevented Pérez's surrender to the Inquisitorial authorities. In June of the same year, as the relocation of the prisoner was attempted again, but now under heavy guard, a far more serious revolt broke out. In the midst of all the disruptions, Antonio Pérez fled to a Protestant area of France (the Bearn), escaping altogether Philip II's justice. These acts of popular resistance led to the sending of a large contingent of royal (Castilian) troops to Zaragoza, to the putting down of a half-hearted Aragonese uprising, and to the execution of some of the leaders of the revolt, among them the *Justicia* of Aragon, Don Juan de Lanuza, in December 1591.[30]

As in other early examples, although expressions of 'national' loyalty, resistance to royal authority, and violent actions were undertaken mainly by the powerful in Aragon to protect their own interests and prerogatives, they nevertheless stirred up the passions of all members of society. Then, as today, social and political communities endured by defining themselves against other communities. In Aragon, the love of country and regional pride brought social groups together in opposition to a real or perceived foreign threat. These sentiments and passions – the engines of exclusion that conjure nations into being – could often be marshalled by those on top to mobilize the lower social orders, even the Church, in defence of the motherland. This is a recurring historical phenomenon. It should not surprise us that what today we call patriotism and nationalism thrived under different forms in the late Middle Ages and early modern period, and that these fiery commitments served to bind or pit different social groups in political and military endeavours that spanned across geographical and political boundaries.

Conclusion

In this chapter, we have gone from looking at festivals as sites for social interaction to looking at violence as occasions for periodic intergroup exchanges. My aim has been to provide a rough typology of violence in late medieval and early modern Spain, with a special focus on what I have described as official violence: that is, violence from above that was often sanctioned by the law or articulated as conflict among the upper classes. Through a series of vignettes, I have shown how lower social groups were drawn into the conflicts of the nobility, the Crown and middling sorts. The price for their involvement, whether voluntary or not, was always heavy. The plight of the poor and the excesses of the nobility reverberated in the literature of the period, as writers, turned social critics, deplored the widespread violence.

Certain types of violence, mostly in Aragon and Catalonia, must also be regarded as parts of regional or national conflicts, through which local elites resisted the intrusion of centralized power from Madrid (and the Inquisition). In their violent opposition to royal authority, local elites frequently appealed to ancient privileges and laws as a bulwark against Castilian and Habsburg ambitions.

A subset of these types of regional uprisings and waves of violence was the systematic attacks on the *Moriscos*. As in the case of anti-*Converso* riots, the attacks on the *Moriscos* could be read in a variety of ways: as religious antagonism; as resistance to certain lords (seen as protectors, and exploiters, of the *Moriscos*); or as yet another expression of interclass conflict. Whatever the interpretation, the numerous large-scale massacres of *Moriscos* signalled the extent to which violence pervaded all social orders in Spanish society.

Notes

1. Johan Huizinga, *The Waning of the Middle Ages: A Study of the Forms of Life, Thought and Art in France and the Netherlands in the Dawn of the Renaissance* (Garden City, NY, 1954). The new translation of this book has been re-titled: *The Autumn of the Middle Ages* (University of Chicago Press) in which the first chapter is different.
2. See David Nirenberg, *Communities of Violence: Persecution of Minorities in the Middle Ages* (Princeton, 1996), 3–17, 200–30.
3. Keith Thomas, *Religion and the Decline of Magic* (London, 1971), ch. 1.
4. Miguel de Cervantes y Saavedra, *Don Quijote de la Mancha*, ed. Martín de Riquer, 2 vols (Barcelona, 1955). The story of being overrun by a flock of goats and sheep occurs in vol. I, ch. 18. The description of their pleasure at some humble food and a good patch of grass in which to sleep is found throughout the book.
5. See Teofilo F. Ruiz, *Crisis and Continuity: Land and Town in Late Medieval Castile* (Philadelphia, 1994), 291–313; also T.F. Ruiz, 'Violence in Late Medieval Castile: The Case of the Rioja', *Revista de História*, 133 (1995): 15–36.
6. Archivo histórico nacional, Madrid (AHN), Clero, carp. 1033, no. 6 (26 May 1326).
7. AHN, Códice 106B, ff. 187–205a (11 May 1334).
8. *Documentación Real del Archivo del Concejo Abulense (1475–1499)*, ed. Blas Casado Quintanilla (Ávila, 1994), 15.
9. Ibid., 18–20.
10. Ibid., 24–7.
11. *Poesía crítica y satírica del siglo XV*, ed. Julio Rodríguez Puértolas (Madrid, 1981), 40–1.
12. *La dança general de la muerte*, in *Poesía crítica*, 43–70.
13. On Páez de Ribera see *Poesía crítica*, 91–3. The poem examined here is entitled *Dezir de Ruy Páez a la reina doña Catalina*, 94–7, written between 1406 and 1418, the year of Catalina's death.
14. Ibid., 96–7.
15. Ibid., 134–8 et passim.
16. Ibid., 223, 230.
17. See the *Crónicas de los reyes de Castilla*, III (Biblioteca de autores españoles, LXX: Madrid, 1953), 163, 167, 179, 309, 343ff. (violence in Aragon due to the rebellion of the count of Urgel), et passim; *Cortes de los antiguos reinos de León y Castilla*, 5 vols (Madrid, 1861–66), III: 16–17, 19, 33, 45, 63 et passim; for Aragon the published sources for the fifteenth century are extensive: see, *inter alia*, *Cortes de los antiguos reinos de Aragón y de Valencia y Principado de Cataluña*, 26 vols (Madrid, 1896–1922) and the bibliography in Santiago Sobrequés i Vidal and Jaume

Sobrequés i Callicó, *La guerra civil catalana del segle XV: estudio sobre la crisi social i econòmica de la Baixa Edat Mitjana*, 2 vols (Barcelona, 1973), II: 355–58.

18. V. Vázquez de Prada, 'Conflictos sociales en la Corona de Aragón en el reinado de Felipe II', in L.M. Enciso et al., *Revueltas y alzamientos en la España de Felipe II* (Valladolid, 1992), 41–64.

19. Ibid., 45.

20. See John H. Elliott, *The Revolt of the Catalans: A Study in the Decline of Spain* (Cambridge, 1963), 1–113.

21. Vázquez de Prada, 'Conflictos sociales', 44–9.

22. *Viajes de extranjeros por España y Portugal*, ed. José García Mercadal, 3 vols (Madrid, 1952), I: 476, 492, 1307–8. Henry Cock commented that in the village of Muel there were only 'three Old Christians, the priest, the notary and the innkeeper', the rest were *Moriscos*.

23. Cervantes, *Don Quixote*, II, ch. 54.

24. Vázquez de Prada, 'Conflictos sociales', 48–9. See also Antonio Domínguez Ortiz y Bernard Vincent, *Historia de los moriscos: vida y tragedia de una minoría* (Madrid, 1978).

25. These two accounts are found in Francisco R. de Uhagón, *Relaciones históricas de los siglos XVI y XVII* (Madrid, 1896), Relación XVIII, the account of Jerónimo de Blancas, 193–208; Relación XIX, 209–11.

26. Bibliothèque Nationale, Paris (BN), Espagnol 060, f. 74 v.

27. BN, Espagnol 060, ff. 90–3.

28. BN, Espagnol 317, f. 19 (1 December 1608).

29. *Viajes de extranjeros*, I: 1303 (the emphasis on 'another' is mine).

30. For the Antonio Pérez affair see John Lynch, *Spain under the Habsburgs*, 2nd edn, 2 vols (New York, 1984), I: 198–204, 322–4, 360–3; also John H. Elliott, *Imperial Spain, 1469–1716* (New York, 1964), 258–61, 271–8; and his *The Revolt of the Catalans*, 49–77. A witness account of the disturbances in Zaragoza, 24 May to 28 July 1591, can be found in *Colección de documentos inéditos para la historia de España*, 112 vols (Madrid, 1842–95), XII: 259–67. The best overall study of the revolt in Aragon in 1591 is the forthcoming work by Xavier Gil Pujol. An early preview of the impact of the 1591 revolts can be found in his 'Ecos de una revuelta: el levantamiento foral aragonés de 1591 en el pensamiento político e histórico europeo de la edad moderna', in *La Corona de Aragón y el Mediterraneo, siglos XV–XVI* (Zaragoza, 1997), 295–331.

Chapter 8

Resisting violence: the wrath of the poor

In the previous chapter, we looked at acts of violence that were fully, partially, or purportedly sanctioned by the law; for the sake of convenience, I have called such acts official violence. Here I wish to turn my attention to violence that operated below the bar of legal sanctions: the unofficial versions. As pointed out earlier, these terms, official and unofficial, are organizing devices, not exclusive categories. As taxonomies of violence and resistance, they allow us to examine social eruptions and gauge how social relations were negotiated and fought over. Bearing in mind that all forms of violence invoke legal, religious or moral principles to justify destructive actions, and that social disturbances are multivalent, boundary-shifting events that defy simple explanations, let us revisit the pogroms against Jews in 1391 and the attacks, mainly in Toledo, against *Conversos* in the 1440s.

From 1391 onwards, acts of extreme violence were committed in many cities and towns of Spain with the implicit, and sometimes explicit, imprimatur of ecclesiastical authorities. In some cases, as in Seville in 1391, the violence was fuelled by the incendiary preachings of a churchman (Ferrán Martínez de Ecija). Even though the Crown sought to put a stop to the attacks against the Jews (and against *Conversos* in the mid-fifteenth century), those engaged in violent and criminal behaviour did so confident that their actions had divine sanction – in their minds, they were doing God's work with the support, or at least the acquiescence, of local ecclesiastical and civil authorities. At the same time, the pogroms were also deeply rooted in social conflict. In their assault on royal power, the urban noble factions worked on the pent-up fears and rancour of their bourgeois and proletarian allies to settle scores and vie for power.[1] An example of this occurred in Jaén, where nobles opposed to Don Miguel Lucas de Iranzo, the ruler of the city, used anti-Jewish violence to thwart and eventually kill him.

One could go on peeling away the layered meanings of such events, but the point has been made: all social encounters, whether stately festivals or mass riots, served as cultural artefacts to define power relations between and within groups, and among individuals. In this chapter I will focus on the other side of the social equation to show how those in the lower echelons resisted power and sought to empower themselves as a social group.

In examining the weapons of the weak (to paraphrase James Scott's insightful phrase[2]), the tendency has been to idealize resistance from below and to depict it and its standard-bearers in heroic terms.[3] Though my sympathies lie with the resisters and their causes, I recognize that savagery and treachery have never been the monopoly of any particular class or group. A great deal of the violence can be attributed to those who held the greater share of power among the groups in contention. But abusive power practices infiltrated all social niches, often turning victims into victimizers; and oppressive power relations (to follow Foucault somewhat freely) regulated even the structure of family, regardless of social filiation. What then can be said about forms of resistance from below? How can one explain the illegal or unofficial violence that threatened the social order and sought, in one form or another, to transform the political, economic and social status quo?

Throughout the two hundred years under consideration, there were important explosions of popular discontent against authority. They ranged from large-scale regional risings to smaller, localized acts of violence and resistance. Acts of banditry and piracy pervaded Spain along the shoreline, but even more so in the South and in the eastern kingdoms; they were, in part, forms of protest against existing conditions. As segments of the population lapsed into waves of crime and revenge, the bandit emerged as a hero and an enemy of the wealthy in the popular imagination as well as in reality; over the course of two centuries, he became a stock figure in Golden Age and Romantic literature.

Other forms of resistance included individual or communal refusals to pay taxes or lordly dues; resistance to or evasion of conscription; desertion from the army; and similar deeds that may not have threatened the stability of the state but nevertheless thwarted and slowed it down. Let us not be too optimistic about the success of these forms of resistance, however. No matter how numerous the uprisings or how ingrained the resistance, the basic structure of the *ancien régime* in Spain and elsewhere was not altered. As Lawrence Stone has observed, radical change from below, in pre-revolutionary Europe, took place only when those who ruled were divided. The inversion of social order, if it ever occurred, lasted only until the ruling classes settled their differences and re-established control. Only at the onset of modernity – with a transformed European economy, industrialization, and compulsory primary education in the West – could some space be created for social change. And even then, as we can easily see all around us, the social orders – the two great families described by Sancho Panza, those who have and those who have not – remained pretty much an unchanged reality.

In late medieval and early modern Spain, there were several categories of resistance movements. For expediency's sake, we may list them as follows:

1. regional armed uprisings against the state, lords, social conditions, and/
   or the dominant religion;

2. local armed uprisings against specific local lords or specific local social conditions;
3. banditry, piracy, and other forms of organized criminal behaviour;
4. individual and communal actions against constituted power: slowdowns in the performance of duties; refusals or delays in paying taxes or seigneurial dues; and resistance to conscription.

Regional armed risings

Between 1400 and 1600 Spain witnessed significant armed risings against constituted authority. In earlier chapters I have mentioned some of these events, but it may be useful to list them again in chronological order. These risings included the long war fought by the servile population of Old Catalonia against their lords in the fifteenth century: the war of the *Remenças* that ended servitude in the region by 1486. In Galicia, the far-off region in northwestern Spain, widespread uprisings also occurred. Contemporary with the war of the *Remenças*, the Galician revolt of the so-called *Irmandiños* (literally, little brothers; in reality, the members of a *hermandad* or league of peasants, plus urban dwellers and representatives of other social groups) was not as successful as its eastern counterpart. Nonetheless, for a few years the *Irmandiños* struck terror in the hearts of their oppressors.

In the early sixteenth century, two significant armed risings took place. The first was the war of the *Comunidades* (*Comuneros*) in Castile in 1520–21. This was the armed resistance of certain Castilian cities – that is, of the urban ruling elites and their allies – against the young king Charles I and his foreign advisers. In the east, an analogue to the *Comunero* rising swept through Valencia between 1519 and 1523. In addition, there were two *Morisco* uprisings in the Granada region. The first was short-lived; it took place between 1500 and 1501. The second and far more serious one, the revolt of the Alpujarras, occurred between 1568 and 1570, though exiles and reprisals extended the unrest far beyond two years. Toward the end of the sixteenth century, the Aragonese revolt (1591–92) brought to an end, at least for the period under study, these widespread forms of violence and resistance. The seventeenth century, however, suffered such large-scale social upheavals (in Catalonia, Portugal and Andalusia in 1640) that for a while they threatened to undermine the unity and survival of Spain.[4]

Writing the social history of these rebellions is not an easy task. Basic narratives of these events and analyses of their political consequences abound, but the social aspects, the interaction and antagonisms between social orders, and the ways in which the populace voiced its grievances, sought allies among other groups, and fought to assert its demands have rarely been studied. For the history of these events was generally written from the standpoint of the elite, i.e. from above.

Each event, of course, had its distinct character. The servile population that rose up in arms in late fifteenth-century Old Catalonia, attempting to gain freedom from their pitiless masters, differed quite markedly, in social filiation, motives, strategies and sought-after allies, from the fairly well-to-do merchants and lower nobility of the *Comunero* uprising in the 1520s, or from the angry, urban lower class of the *Germanías* in 1520s Valencia. They differed as well, in religion if not in labour conditions and social status, from the *Moriscos* of the Alpujarras.

Below, I wish to examine two resistance movements and to re-assess their place within the social history of Spain in the late Middle Ages and early modern period. While other uprisings have spawned a more extensive historiography, these movements have remained in relatively obscurity.

The rebellion of the *Irmandiños*

Although little known when compared to the war of the *Remenças*, the rebellion of the *Irmandiños* has recently attracted the attention of historians. Unfortunately, the writing of this history has been mainly a local project; promoted by the revival of local patriotism and political autonomy in modern Spain, it has remained somewhat divorced from the wider context of the kingdom.

The *Irmandiños'* revolt can be told in a few words. As the Reconquest advanced southward from the ninth to the late fifteenth century, Galicia became increasingly marginalised within the political and economic life of the realm. With the exception of Santiago de Compostela, the shrine of Spain's erstwhile patron-saint and still a formidable pilgrimage site in the late Middle Ages, the region suffered the ills and neglect associated with peripheries. As discussed earlier, in the kingdom of Galicia – it had been a kingdom in the early history of Spain and remained nominally so in the motley titles of the Castilian and Spanish kings – peasant land-ownership and tenure had become fragmented beyond reason. Most of its villagers were impoverished and suffered under a relentless and predatory lordship. Galician cities, with the exception of Santiago, had not developed as rapidly as some of their counterparts in the Castilian plain, the Bay of Biscay area, or Andalusia. Galicia's maritime pursuits (fishing, trade), which held great promise in the fourteenth century, had now fallen quite behind the enterprising ventures of sailors and fishermen from the Bay of Biscay's coastal towns. The only sector that had grown as the region declined was that of lordship. Galicia was the paradigmatic land of lords (ecclesiastical and seigneurial), and their tenacious grip extended throughout the region.

With the decline of feudal rents in the fourteenth century, due to the disruptions of the plague and the civil wars, noble and ecclesiastical lords throughout the peninsula, above all in Galicia, redoubled their efforts to exact dues from the peasantry. What they could not get by legal means, they extorted by force. Strong houses, castles, and other noble lairs became the refuge for gangs of noble retinues. They scourged the countryside victimizing the peasantry and targeting small cities and merchants on the road. Coupled with a demographic upturn in the fifteenth century and a growing need for new lands, the social tensions between those below and those above reached a boiling point.

Rural and urban resistance to noble abuse, and frustration with a weak royal presence (the Castilian kings were busy fending off their own cadre of renegade nobles), became evident in the formation of the *hermandades*. As longstanding bulwarks of the monarchy against noble ambitions, the *hermandades* (brotherhoods or leagues of urban dwellers, small-town residents, peasants, lower nobility and lower clergy) held a venerable place in the political history of medieval Spain, playing an important role in restoring order during periods of turmoil. Their main purpose was to re-establish peace and justice by persecuting criminals and putting down rebellious noblemen.

In early fifteenth-century Galicia, several *hermandades* rose against oppressive lords and appealed to the king (John II) for support in their efforts. Most of the early disturbances in the 1420s and 1430s were local, but occasionally they presented a serious challenge to the established order. This occurred in the city of Orense, where urban rioters threw the bishop into the river Miño in 1421, and with the vassals of Don Nuño Freire of Andrade (known as the 'Bad'), who organized into a *hermandad*, waged war on their lord, and threatened to occupy Santiago de Compostela in 1431.[5] In depicting these insurrections, the contemporary chronicle of John II refers to the participants as *gente menuda*, or the small people, who were ultimately unable to hold their own against their better-equipped adversaries.

These two uprisings, as well as sporadic outbreaks of anti-noble violence in the next three decades, served as a prelude to the so-called 'second war of the *Irmandiños*', a widespread revolt throughout the kingdom of Galicia which, though rooted in peasant discontent, drew people from all social rungs. For almost two years, between 1467 and 1469, the *Irmandiños* waged a successful war on the noble and ecclesiastical lords. The Galician *hermandad* paralleled the formation of similar leagues in Castile whose function it was to stand up against a cruel and unruly nobility with the support of the Crown.

In Galicia, endemic anarchy, the plague and harsh economic conditions paved the way for the depredations of the powerful and the resistance of the weak. A motley alliance of peasants, artisans, shopkeepers, clergymen and lower nobility stormed and overthrew noble strongholds and castles. High nobles and powerful ecclesiastics were driven off the land. The members of ruling groups who fought back in the initial stages of the rebellion lost their lives. As in the Jacquerie (the great French peasant uprising of 1356) or the English Peasant Revolt of 1381, the leadership of the *Irmandiños* revolt came from the lower nobility, including some younger sons of illustrious noble houses. And like other peasant revolts, the movement went far beyond random

191

acts of violence. The *Irmandiños* took steps to restructure the social order of the Galician kingdom. Their demands included meting out stern justice to overbearing feudal lords, preserving urban rights, eliminating abusive taxes, restituting ecclesiastical lands that the nobility had appropriated, and other measures aimed at levelling social disparities.

But, as with earlier broad-based social upheavals, by the spring of 1469 the nobles who had fled to Portugal to save their lives joined their brethren in Galicia and, in encounter after encounter, thanks in part to their superior weapons and military prowess, they defeated the rebels. As the *Irmandiño* rebellion became more radicalized, the peasants and lower urban classes lost the support of most of their bourgeois and noble allies. They were left alone to taste bitter defeat and harsh reprisals.

Social heterogeneity and the *Irmandiño* revolt

Carlos Barros's excellent study *Mentalidad justiciera de los Irmandiños, siglo XV* views the *Irmandiño* revolt as a call for justice by a broad segment of Galician society.[6] In his focus on the rebels' pursuit of equity and retaliation, Barros incisively analyses intergroup exchanges and the revolt's ability to erase, even if only briefly, the barriers between social orders. This it did in two significant ways: by bringing together dissimilar groups, men and women from different geographical regions within Galicia, in a common cause; and by assembling the powerful and the weak on the battlefields of Galicia. Using a long judicial process (the Tabera-Fonseca case, 1526–27), which examined the events of the 1460s and included depositions from eyewitnesses to the *Irmandiño* revolt, Barros provides a careful breakdown by social class of the victims of noble abuse and a taxonomy of the crimes committed against them by those in power.

If, as indicated earlier, the revolt drew a wide range of social types, it was because the targets of noble excesses, raids, looting, rapes and murders ranged across a broad social spectrum. Peasants were, not surprisingly, the favourite prey. Attacks against peasants consisted of the habitual theft of cows and oxen, illegal imprisonment, the ransoming of captured peasants, torture, and the illegal collection of tribute. These deeds were the signs of predatory lordship; in more or less virulent forms, they defined the power relations between lords and peasants in western Europe from the central Middle Ages onward.[7]

Martín de Tarrio, a peasant of the village of Cruces, testified that the *alcalde* Alvaro Sánchez, a municipal official operating out of the fortress of Rocha Forte with a retinue of fifteen to thirty footmen (described as *malhechores*, malefactors), engaged in a wave of crimes – specifically rape, robbery, and the imposition of an illegal tribute of fish – in the area of Cruces. Among their victims were women, a butcher from the nearby city of Santiago of Compostela, and a citizen of Padrón (a small town in the region of Compostela) caught unawares on the open road. Although most of the witnesses who testified in the judicial proceedings many years after the actual events were peasants, *escuderos* (squires or lower nobility) appeared as well in the dual role of witnesses and victims. Gonzalo de Cardeleiro, a squire from Malpica, accused the knight García Martínez de Barbeira and his band (fifteen to twenty armed men operating out of the stronghold of Outes) of imprisoning him, together with a woman from Santiago de Compostela and an undetermined number of citizens of the towns of Noya and Muros, and of asking for ransom to restore their freedom.[8]

Besides the great mass of peasant victims, the records of the inquest show a significant number of assaults and captures of fishermen, town officials, lower clergy, and merchants on the road. After the peasants, travellers constituted the largest group of victims. These figures reveal a countryside of unsafe roads – most crimes were committed in rural areas – where commerce and the economic life of the region were becoming increasingly dangerous and impossible to sustain. Women, who put up with the lordly economic scourge as much as men, were further burdened by sexual violence. The rape of lower-class women by upper-class men or their minions in Galicia followed a pattern of sexual abuse that prevailed in other regions of Spain and the world. In times of political anarchy and open violence, women became convenient targets for lordly greed and desire.[9]

The revolt also attracted members from all social groups because the violence threatened not only the economic structures of Galicia; it also threatened its moral foundations. The sexual violence in particular impinged on complex patriarchal codes of honour, virtue, and rights over women. Although Barros presents a somewhat romanticized and lofty view of how the *Irmandiños* perceived attacks against women, it is clear that the rape and sexual abuse of mainly peasant women were also perceived as attacks on property, i.e. the property of husbands, fathers and the lords themselves. The outrage voiced by mostly non-noble men (peasants, middling sorts, clergymen) at the rape of their women (only one woman out of 240 witnesses testified in the Tabera-Fonseca inquisition) reflected, I think, a concern with ownership issues as much as it did a concern with the question of honour.[10]

The *Irmandiños* as guardians of legality

The wide range of victims, and the aggressive, almost desperate greed of many lords and outlaw followers, led to broad opposition – a formal brotherhood that featured representatives from *all* social orders. Leadership, as indicated earlier, came from the disaffected members of the ruling elite. And, as with most popular revolts in Spain and elsewhere in this period, the rebels claimed the mantle of legality for their actions. Here is a case that unsettles the heuristic distinction between official and unofficial violence.

Clearly, the *Irmandiños* claimed to be acting on behalf of the king and viewed their attacks against fortresses, and the slaying and exiling of noblemen, as heroic attempts to restore order and justice to the Galician realm. But behind their anger at noble abuses and their precarious economic conditions lay outrage at the upending of divine and regal order. By taking to arms, they became, to a degree, upholders of royal power and supporters of the very social structure that assigned them, their children and grandchildren a subordinate position. By rebelling, they reinserted themselves in and lay claim to what they perceived as a just and harmonious social order.

Comuneros and *Germanías*

Like the rebellion of the *Irmandiños*, the revolt of the *Germanías* had a marked popular flavour. In itself, the Valencian risings, or *Germanías*, were part of a much larger movement of resistance against the new king and soon-to-be emperor, Charles I of the Spains (Charles V of the Holy Roman Empire). Its Castilian counterpart, the revolt of the *Comuneros*, was essentially a reaction of urban elites and small nobility to the new political realities dawning in Spain. Though Spanish historiography and literature have often described the *Comunero* revolt in lyrical terms, as an attempt to protect traditional liberties and rights against the encroachments of monarchy, the reality was otherwise. Charles, born in 1500, the son of Philip the Handsome and Joanna the Mad, came into his fateful inheritance by 1517. With the death of his maternal grandfather, Ferdinand the Catholic, in 1516, and the growing incompetence of his mother, Charles added the Spanish realms and their American possessions to his already impressive legacy of Flanders, Bohemia and other northern and central European lands that had been willed to him by his paternal grandparents, Mary of Flanders and Maximilian, the Holy Roman Emperor. Born and raised in the Low Countries, he came to Spain for the first time in 1520, surrounded by a bevy of non-Spanish-speaking Flemish advisers, and issuing imperious demands of monetary subsidies and unquestioning obedience.[11]

Charles's youth, his inability to speak Castilian, and his imperial ambitions – he was by then already engaged in bidding for the elected office of Holy Roman Emperor, a frightfully expensive enterprise – made him an unpleasant new master. More important, his political programme and financial demands threatened the tight control of Castilian cities that the urban elites had thus far enjoyed. Regardless of the epic portrait painted by historians and Golden Age playwrights, the *Comunero* (from the word commune) revolt was an intra-hegemonic strife, a dispute among the ruling classes. The *Comuneros* rose up in arms to protect their substantial privileges and to challenge the king's new advisers. It was, in some respects, the last challenge to the Crown of Castile, before the Habsburg kings settled down to their peaceful rule of the realm. As such, the crushing defeat of the *Comunero* armies at Villalar on St George's Day (23 April) 1521 brought to an end the long period of internecine struggle among the elite that had lasted from the mid-thirteenth century to the reforms of the Catholic Monarchs in the late fifteenth century. The *Germanías*, however, were something completely different.

Unlike the *Comunero* revolt, the *Germanías* in Valencia and, to a lesser extent, in Mallorca pulled in a much broader swath of the population. The issues leading to the risings were distinctly local and stemmed from social and economic reversals, ethno-religious hostilities (mistrust and hatred of *Moriscos*), and the fragile relationship between city and country. Although political intrigues played a role, they were secondary to the underlying social problems. The revolt of the *Germanías*, however, has received far less historiographical attention than that of the *Comuneros*. This is partly because Spanish historians have privileged Castile in their chronicles, and partly because the rebellion and the defeat of the *Comuneros* at Villalar acquired important symbolic meaning over time; but it is also because the popular aspects of the *Germanías* did not interest historians until the last two or three decades. Histories from below, which dominated English historiography (mostly *Past & Present*) in the 1960s and 1970s, have found echoes in Spain only recently.

In Valencia, the violence erupted as a form of resistance to city officials and local nobility. It then escalated into attacks against the *Moriscos*, whose labour and taxes – as the rebels rightly perceived – nurtured aristocratic privilege, culminating in general assaults on property and overt challenges to existing institutions.[12]

The ranks of the *Germanías* were largely made up of artisans, members of Valencian guilds who had been allowed to bear arms in 1519 in the expectation of attacks from Turkish pirates. But the rebellious brotherhood also included peasants drawn to the cause because of their downtrodden position, middling sorts, clerics, and the usual flotsam of discontents often found in important maritime cities such as Valencia. For Ricardo García Cárcel, the best and most recent scholar of the *Germanías*, the roots of the revolt go back to the systemic antagonisms between Christians and Mudejars (Muslims living under Christian rule as opposed to *Moriscos*, who were nominally converted to Christianity) in the thirteenth century. Valencia weathered numerous bouts of social upheaval that were manifested as attacks against Mudejars, the dependants of feudal lords, in 1309, 1359 and 1455. On the eve of the early sixteenth-century risings, Valencia faced mounting problems: plagues, internecine fights between noble families, and what García Cárcel has described as the 'absolute disequilibrium between the city and its hinterland'. By this he meant that the city had grown rapidly at the expense of the countryside, creating volatile social and economic conditions. While an increasingly impoverished Christian peasantry competed with hard-working Moriscos, rural people flocked to the city in droves looking for work.[13] Furthermore, an expansion in the number of guild masters reduced economic opportunities for artisans. By the early sixteenth century not only was the guild system showing signs of crisis, but corn (cereal) production had declined. Famine and an unsound economy led to a riot in 1503, which broke out over the distribution of much-needed wheat that had arrived from Sicily. It was, as García Cárcel has described it, a 'general rehearsal for the *Germanías'*. And, as usual, it was harshly suppressed.[14]

The reign of a young and distant ruler (Charles I) and the complexities of Valencian politics and culture served as backdrop to the outbreak of violence in 1519. According to García Cárcel, three factors coalesced into the making of the rising. First, economic dislocation and food shortages led to unrest among the lower classes. Second, the refusal of the young emperor to come to Valencia antagonized the middling sorts and mobilized them politically. Third, the threat of North African and Turkish pirates reinforced the long-lived hatred of *Moriscos*.[15]

In many respects, the organizational entity that fomented the revolt was imposed from above. A royal decree in September 1519 encouraged guild members (*Germanías*) to arm themselves for the purpose of strengthening Valencian defences against the Turks. Thus, in a moment of crisis (the threat of the Turks), the Crown risked unleashing social antagonisms. For unlike guild organizations elsewhere in Europe, these armed *Germanías* included all social classes: guild masters, apprentices and labourers. It was not difficult for them to identify the *Moriscos* with the Turks, and to turn from defending the city to attacking bastions of privilege. Nobles did not at all like the challenge to their military status and put pressure on the Crown to rescind their charter. Charles I, or rather his advisers (since the king, a newcomer to his Iberian realms, was preoccupied with imperial ambitions), restricted the public use or display of arms by members of the *Germanías*.

In the spring of 1520, tensions erupted into violent confrontation. Armed workers and their allies stormed noble houses, the viceroy's residence, and that of royal officials. A series of royal demands for restoration of order and rebel counter-demands for recognition of their grievances, and the exile and swift return of the viceroy to Valencia, occupied most of the rest of 1520. By early 1521, however, the city remained in the rebels' hands, and the revolt had become progressively radicalized. Under the leadership of Guillem Castellón (a weaver also known as Sorolla) and Joan Llorenç, the revolt's ideological steward, the *Germanías* spread to other Valencian cities such as Castellón de la Plana, Xátiva and Alzira, to the Valencian countryside, even to the neighbouring kingdom of Aragon, and to Catalonia. The most radical elements within the *Germanías* sought to abolish royal taxes, attacked the nobility as a class, and burned titles of property. These developments paralleled similar escalations of radicalism in the English peasant risings of 1381, the Jacquerie in France (1356), and the Ciompi (1378) in Florence.[16]

Unlike the Castilian *Comuneros* or the Galician *Irmandiños*, the *Germanías* came closer to effecting a radical break with the status quo and sought to overthrow or at least to undermine the notion of a society founded on hierarchical orders. The social makeup of the *Germanías* – with its strong proletarian base

196

and ideologically committed urban core (weavers were often affiliated with radical causes) – evinces a significant amount of interaction among members of different groups, as they joined the resistance movement. In Valencia, the solidarity between social classes was parleyed into violent discourse. The rebellion's leadership introduced a programme for restructuring society which, albeit confused and vague, made no bones about urging the abolition of royal taxes, the levelling of social differences, and, at its radical best, the formation of a republican Valencia. Thus, in spite of their frequent protests of loyalty to the king, the *Germanías* repudiated royal authority. But lest we think of the leaders of the *Germanías* as enlightened revolutionaries, let us remember that most of the rebels vented their anger on the *Moriscos*.

The end came soon. The royal and noble armies regained control of the countryside in the southern parts of the Valencian kingdom, and after a siege of the city itself, the rebels surrendered, but not before attempting to convert by force the Muslims of the city. As was the case in many such uprisings – think of the German peasants' uprising of the 1520s or the English Civil War of the mid-seventeenth century – the end also marked the advent of apocalyptic dreams and hopeless millenarian expectations. In the last stages of the war, a man known as '*el encubierto*' ('the hidden one') and claiming to be the son of Don Juan and grandson of the Catholic Monarchs, rallied the final resistance to the noble onslaught. García Cárcel has speculated on the origins of this character: was he a miller, or a *Converso*? His memorable speech on 21 March 1522 in the square of the church of Xátiva echoed, as García Cárcel has suggested, Savonarolian ideals (Savonarola, an ecclesiastical reformer in late fifteenth-century Florence, attacked the excessive luxury of Florence's bourgeoisie). Resistance and radical Christian reform thus remained latent in the popular imagination and in popular uprisings.[17]

Local movements of resistance

Movements of resistance had their origins in local outbursts of violence, which, under optimal conditions, grew into wider regional or kingdom-wide up-heavals. In Valencia, as we have seen, the *Germanías* revolt began in the city proper and spread within a few months to the countryside and to other towns in the region. But the social dynamics of resistance movements that stayed within local boundaries differed greatly from those that transcended them. Within the confines of small towns or villages in late medieval and early modern Europe, almost everyone knew everyone else, and social groups functioned at various levels of interaction, familiarity and antagonism. Hatred at the local level was personal. Violence was often tied to festering kin hatreds and lineage competitions.

Spain witnessed many local risings in the fifteenth and sixteenth centuries. The causes for these risings varied greatly from location to location, ranging from spontaneous opposition prompted by abusive lordship to crises brought on by civil war and systemic noble violence. Some of these violent outbursts became enshrined in the popular imagination by theatrical re-enactment and oral tradition. This was the case of Fuente Obejuna (Fuente Ovejuna), a village in the area of Córdoba that was alienated from Córdoba and therefore from the Crown, to Don Pedro Girón (one of the greatest magnates of Castile), and eventually to the Military Order of Calatrava in 1460. Disputes over the lordship of Fuente Obejuna – between the city of Córdoba (backed by a weak John II) on one side and the Order of Calatrava and rebellious and ambitious magnates on the other – led to the town's occupation by Don Fernán Gómez of Guzmán, *comendador mayor* of the Order of Calatrava. Though the evidence is not conclusive, Fernán Gómez of Guzmán seems to have ruled Fuente Obejuna in a predatory manner. These abuses included sexual advances, kidnappings, and the rape of Fuente Obejuna's women.

Against the backdrop of the civil war that Isabella the Catholic and her followers waged against the Portuguese and their Castilian high-born allies, the citizens of Fuente Obejuna rose up in arms on 23 April 1476. Led by the officials of the municipal council, almost a thousand citizens of the town and its hinterlands stormed the house of the *comendador mayor*, brutally (ritually) killing and mutilating him. These fairly obscure events were immortalized by Lope de Vega in his play *Fuente Ovejuna* (published in 1619), which remains one of the most stirring and popular works of the Spanish theatre. Clearly, the democratic readings of this play in the last two hundred years do not always accord with the actual events – that is, with the aims of medieval peasants and small-town dwellers caught up in the snares of civil strife and abusive lordship – or with Lope de Vega's intention to privilege the justice-dispensing role of the Catholic Monarchs.[18]

Nonetheless, *Fuente Ovejuna* became an emblem of popular resistance to the abuses of the powerful, especially on the issue of sexuality (a theme informing many insurrections of the period). Over the centuries, play and embellished event alike conferred retrospective agency and honour to those on the lower rungs of society. The risings in Fuente Obejuna were, furthermore, not isolated but part of the widespread local upheavals of the 1450s, 1460s and 1470s, not all of which were concerned with sexual abuse or honour. One of these was the revolt of Alcaraz.

Most of the documentary evidence for the urban revolt of Alcaraz in 1458 has been published in a short and excellent study by Angus MacKay, one of the most insightful historians of late medieval Spain. As MacKay points out, the rebellion of Alcaraz was not caused by famine. It was not directed, as was usual in late fifteenth-century Spain, against Jews and/or *Conversos*; nor was it a result of class struggle. Rather, the rising at Alcaraz pitted town dwellers against corrupt royal agents, one urban faction confronting another. The context in Alcaraz was the endemic civil strife of John II's reign, the widespread violence in the region, the proximity of the frontier with Granada, and the threat of Granadine raids. Alcaraz thus provides us with a different instance of violence as social artefact: a case of intra-class conflict in which members of the town's oligarchical elite rose up in arms to challenge the rule of the *corregidor* (a royal official who served as head and overseer of the municipal council) and set up an alternative municipal government. But the *corregidor* and his supporters had their own vested interests in the town and represented as well other oligarchical factions in Alcaraz and its region.[19]

On 10 January 1458, a certain Fernando de Bustamante, accompanied by brothers and followers, stormed through the town, captured the towers in the centre of Alcaraz and drove the *corregidor* and his men to seek refuge in the royal castle. Their actions matched the factional urban skirmishes that were steadily breaking out in other parts of Spain (Barcelona, Valencia, Toledo, Jaén and other urban centres), in Italy, in France, and elsewhere in western Europe. In Alcaraz, this was just one episode in a long history of risings. The civil turbulence of 1439, 1444, 1456, 1460 and 1463 disclosed the deep clefts that polarized the city.

But the rebels were doomed to failure. Attacks against the *corregidor* constituted attacks against royal authority. And despite the Crown's weakened condition in the 1450s, oligarchical factions in small towns such as Alcaraz had no real chance of holding out against internal enemies supported by royal armies. Three aspects of this otherwise minor revolt should nonetheless be noted, for they were replicated in countless risings elsewhere in Spain and western Europe. First, though many local outbursts had to do with internal struggles within the oligarchy, each faction implicated its lower-class allies and servants. It could not be otherwise. Without some kind of lower-class complicity and participation, armed resistance and military success were inconceivable. In Alcaraz, depositions taken after the defeat of the rebellion mentioned servants prominently and showed them playing a significant role.[20]

Second, revolts, in Alcaraz and elsewhere, were enacted through rituals freighted with symbolic gestures and irreverent language. The rebels would seize and parade the symbols of municipal authority to promulgate the reversal of fortune that was about to take place in town. That these symbols, which lent legitimacy to their goals, were often vested in the revolt leaders' servants (*criados*) produced the gratifying effect of debasing the *corregidor* and his functionaries while impugning the competence of former municipal officials. Carnivalesque elements (status inversions, mocking representations of authority, and other forms of ribaldry), moreover, added a subversive festivity to these events. Finally, however, and as MacKay has noted, failed rebellions were followed by inquests that used the law and judicial language to reinforce the power of the ruling elite. In Alcaraz, the insurgents were branded as 'malefactors' by the victorious *corregidor* and his royal agents. The control of words proved as powerful as the control of arms. For, as we shall see below, discourse was deployed hegemonically to criminalize, and thus ban, the hostile acts of some, while licensing, and thus institutionalizing, the similarly aggressive acts of others.

Banditry, piracy and vagrancy

In the second volume of Cervantes's *Don Quixote de la Mancha*, the eponymous hero, after multiple disastrous adventures, takes the road to Barcelona, where he and his faithful servant, Sancho Panza, plan to participate in chivalrous jousts. On the road from Zaragoza to Barcelona, the main thoroughfare of the eastern kingdoms, Don Quixote and Sancho fall into the hands of a well-organized company of bandits.[21] These were not just ordinary brigands infesting the highways of Catalonia and the eastern portions of Spain; these brigands were led by the legendary Roca Guinarda (Roque Guinart). Here, as in other parts of *Don Quixote*, the boundaries between fact and fiction are obliterated, and literary artifice provides a window onto historical reality.

Cervantes's Roca Guinarda was 'a man about thirty-five years old, strong, of medium built, serious looks, dark skin. He rode a powerful horse, dressed in a mail shirt, with four pistols in his belt.'[22] A Catalan Robin Hood, Roca practised a chivalrous banditry and ruled his men with a proper mix of liberality and harshness, keeping them under strict discipline. In reality, Roque Guinart was born in the region of Vic (Old Catalonia) in 1582, the son of well-to-do peasants. In 1602, a mere twenty years old, he led a company of men against the noble adversaries of the bishop of Vic. The factional struggle between ecclesiastic and noble lords spread to other areas of Catalonia, making Roque Guinart one of the most active bandits in the region. As in many other cases, factional strife easily turned into straightforward criminal pursuit. In 1610, Roque routed the viceregal armies that had been sent to capture him, while continuing to terrorize travellers between Zaragoza and Barcelona. Unable to capture or defeat him, the Crown offered him a pardon in 1611, and Roque departed for Naples as captain of a Spanish *tercio* (a regular army unit of 3,000 men). In an extensive editorial note in his edition of *Don Quixote*, Martín de Riquer observes that in 1588 Don Luis de Queralt 'recruited a *tercio* among Catalan bandits, of which Roque became the *maestre de campo* (the leader), and which fought in Flanders in the late sixteenth-century'.[23]

Bandits turning into soldiers, and vice versa, was an old story in late medieval and early modern Europe. Recruitment was a way to diminish banditry in the countryside, and most bandits made good soldiers. Conversely, upon desertion or discharge, soldiers often turned to crime or vagrancy. But governments in Spain and elsewhere dealt with banditry in other ways as well. The number of hanged men adorning the trees on the road Don Quixote and Sancho Panza took to Barcelona tells us of the Crown's harsh measures to curtail crime.

Banditry, as Braudel once argued in a much quoted statement, 'was in the first place a revenge upon established states, the defenders of a political and even social order . . . . [It was] a form of vengeance upon the ruling class and its lopsided justice . . . [and] has been at all times, more or less everywhere, a righter of wrongs'.[24] Therefore, the record of violence, 'riots, disturbances, assassinations, reprisals and revolts in the Mediterranean', can be described as 'the story of a perpetual and multiple social tension'.[25] In the few pages dedicated to this topic in *The Mediterranean and the Mediterranean World*, Braudel paints a haunting portrait of the violent responses to the 'pauperization and oppression [of the poor and weak] by the rich and powerful'. Organized banditry and its close manifestations – vagrancy, crime, piracy – may thus be seen as stemming from, manifesting, and redistributing specific social stresses. It is thus that they have worked as sites for social exchange and negotiation.[26]

Yet Braudel's moving account somewhat obscures the implications of banditry and crime. Although I fully agree with his insistence on the social and economic roots of banditry, it is clear that not all forms of banditry (piracy, crime, vagrancy) were reactions to the state or to class disparity. In many cases, bandits sided with noble interests and fought not *against* but *for* the state. Moreover, violence allowed for a fluidity of social and political roles. That Catalan bandits – such as Guinart and Latrás, to mention the two most famous ones – could so handily shift from being criminals to being agents of the state underscores the ease with which identities could be confounded in late medieval and early modern Spain and western Europe. When it suited their purposes, pirates – North African, Turkish and Christian – also aligned themselves with the state, playing a creditable part in the struggles between nations. And, like the privateers who commanded the Atlantic in Elizabethan England, they were often faithful government agents. These caveats, however, do not mean that banditry, vagrancy and piracy were not forms of opposition to the state or symptoms of social unrest.

Like other forms of violence, banditry, vagrancy and piracy brought the social classes into close and recurrent contact. Though bandits, pirates and other criminals did not single out the upper classes as targets, they did prefer to concentrate their efforts on the wealthy. The great concern of the government, the ruling elites and the middling sorts with repressing banditry in all its variations, however, had to do with the way these activities subverted the social order and threatened the well-being of those in power. The poor, of course, suffered at least as much from criminal behaviour; as in our day, crime victims were more often than not members of the same social cohort as their aggressors. But individual (and group) transgression of the law, thievery and the kidnapping and/or killing of the upper classes by those below, became a serious menace to social peace.

The geography of crime also invites our attention. Clearly, no region in Spain suffered the scourge of banditry, vagrancy and piracy in the same way. Social conditions, topography, and a region's ability to police itself determined the level and frequency of outlaw sorties. The southeastern coast of the Mediterranean (the Levant, regions of Valencia, Murcia, Alicante and Almería) were aflutter throughout the sixteenth century with the threat of North African and Turkish pirates. Watchtowers looked over the Mediterranean; and repressive measures forbade *Moriscos* to till soil close to the sea, or to carry weapons (see Chapter 7). In *Don Quixote*, several episodes tell of contacts with pirates, escaped Christian slaves, and inhabitants of Levantine shores. The coastal Christian population was always ready for a hue-and-cry against Muslim incursions. Cervantes's fictional rendering of just such a response recreates real events of the period. When Christian captives fleeing from Argel land in the area of Vélez (Málaga), they are swiftly met by a 'coastal cavalry' positioned there to intercept supposed invaders.[27]

On large stretches of the Mediterranean coast, the rich and poor alike lived in a state of continuous alert. Here, at the same time, renegades returned to their former homes and religion; Christian slaves escaped from captivity in North Africa; Muslims were captured and enslaved; all of which provided a rich social setting, not just for fictional adventures and romance, but for broader social transactions and perspectives.

The reality of piracy and the real threat to the eastern Mediterranean coast can be measured in a brief survey of major attacks on its towns and settlements. The town of Cullera was sacked in 1503. The legendary pirate Barbarossa attacked the towns of Xilxes, Denia and Parcent between 1518 and 1529. North African pirates raided Orpesa and Borriana in 1519; Palmar suffered the same fate in 1528. Pirates landed in Oliva in 1529, and three years later sacked Piles and Cullera. For the latter, this meant being sacked twice in less than thirty years. Another landing in Parcent in 1534 (the second such attack) was followed by Barbarossa's second raid on Orpesa in 1536. To summarize: major pirate activity against Valencian coastal towns took place in 1543, 1545, 1547 (which included the sack of the monastery of the Holy Spirit in Morvedre), 1550, 1551, 1554, 1556.[28] Bear in mind that I am listing only the localities that bore the brunt of the violence.

The counterpoint to these attacks was, of course, the successful defence of the coast, the conflicts in open sea between Christians and Muslims, and the strikes against North African shores. The first of these responses required the feverish construction of towers and fortified enclaves along the coast. Strong towers were built in Orpesa and Cullera, frequent targets of pirate attacks. New batteries of artillery were added to Cullera's defences in 1547, and similar developments took place in Xàbia, Vila Joiosa, Alicante, and other locations. These activities, plus the organization of coastal mobile units along the model of the Santa Hermandad (the 'coastal cavalry' described by Cervantes), meant that a whole portion of the eastern Mediterranean remained in a permanent state of siege. Besides the financial cost – fortresses, armies, ships and naval raids of the North African coast were expensive indeed – there were also psychological and social costs. The state of siege created a context of endemic violence; it also furnished an additional excuse for hatred of and violence against *Moriscos*.[29]

But the Levantine shores were not the only region in a permanent state of unrest. As Braudel commented long ago, the road between Barcelona and Zaragoza, the main thoroughfare between Catalonia and Aragon, was extremely dangerous and almost impassable without a strong armed escort. Catalonia and parts of Aragon were lands of endemic banditry and social violence. Bandits imposed a reign of violence and disrupted the social fabric of the region, whether they worked as hired swords (and guns) in the internecine struggles of the nobility – as did Lupercio Latrás in the conflicts in Ribagorza (see Chapter 7) – or operated on their own behalf.

The same occurred in the areas around Granada, the Sierra Morena and the Sierra Nevada. They became safe havens for people fleeing from justice, the disaffected, the rebellious *Moriscos*, and the like. Don Quixote and Sancho fled to the mountains to escape the long arm of the Santa Hermandad. On the opposite border, the mountainous Basque region was, as Braudel reminds us, a magnet for vagrants. In rugged countries such as Spain, mountains easily became centres of resistance, safe havens for those fleeing the law. The landscape of crime thus paralleled the geographical contours of Iberia. The Castilian plain was better policed than were the mountainous regions in the east, north or south. This was so not only because Old and New Castile were closer to Madrid, Valladolid, and other important political centres, but because the topography allowed for extra policing.

But banditry, piracy and vagrancy were not limited to deserted shores or inhospitable mountains. Cities were nests of crime, where bandits and vagrants interacted intimately and frequently with other social groups. Seville had long enjoyed the dubious honour of being the capital of crime in late medieval and early modern Spain. A terminus of the Atlantic trade after the early sixteenth century, drawing sustenance from a rich countryside though ever susceptible to famine and severe economic recession, Seville attracted an unusual number of *pícaros*, scam artists, thieves, pickpockets, prostitutes, procuresses, and the like. Seville was also a large, heterogeneous city, the heart of a substantial floating population. In addition to its hordes of sailors, travellers to and from the New World, slaves (there were more African slaves in Seville than anywhere else in Spain), gypsies, and other marginalized people, the city drew immigrants from other parts of Castile, Spain and abroad, and grew rapidly in the fifteenth century. This was a perfect setting for criminal activities. In his short novel *Rinconete and Cortadillo*, Cervantes gives us a humorous glimpse of Seville's underworld; with its confraternity of thieves, scam artists and extortionists, the city had become a veritable 'court of miracles'.[30]

Similarly, Quevedo's *The Swindler* (written about 1608; published in 1626) shows us the demi-monde life of Salamanca, a university town that proved a fertile ground for transactions among thieves, *pícaros* and their social betters (students). Both Cervantes and Quevedo give us entry into the distinct worlds of victims and criminals. In *Rinconete and Cortadillo*, we see clerics, students, merchants, a whole range of middle-class types, coming across those below them in pickpocket and far more menacing encounters. In *Lazarillo de Tormes*, the eponymous protagonist romps through a series of crimes and liaisons with members from all walks of Spanish society, as he moves up in status from murky provenance to stained respectability.

Banditry, vagrancy and piracy were, of course, not synonymous enterprises. A bandit *qua* bandit was not a vagrant; nor was a vagrant always prone to engage in criminal behaviour. A pirate, often the agent of foreign powers, engaged in an entirely different kind of struggle. Moreover, as García Martínez and others have noted, types of banditry varied, each connoting different social linkages. Noble banditry belonged to the context of drawn-out internecine upper-class struggles that, albeit somewhat contained in Castile, still agitated certain regions of the Crown of Aragon. *Morisco* banditry was laden with religious, cultural and 'racial' overtones. Popular banditry, along the lines of Roca Guinarda's activities, came closer to the kinds of social exchange and the latent class warfare that I have been aiming to describe in this chapter. But missing from this story are the untold number of thefts, assaults, and other criminal or social forms of resistance that the poor inflicted on their peers and betters, most of them, to return to Braudel's analysis, the outcome of pauperism and brutal social conditions.

Yet these categories could be easily conflated. Bandits could at any time, or under specific circumstances, belong to all three types. In the same manner, vagrants could move from vagrancy to banditry and back again. Government crackdowns aimed to curb the vagrants' amazing ability and freedom to metamorphise into bandits and vice versa. A growing concern with controlling errant bodies was evident in the mounting efforts of those on top to escalate the policing of society, to tighten the rule of law, and to secure the protection of property. The number of treatises written by sixteenth-century Spanish theologians and scholars (a phenomenon widely parallelled elsewhere in Europe) condemning vagrancy and advocating the confinement of the poor reveal an intensifying discourse of exclusion.[31] These texts marked an unmistakable shift in the political culture and in social attitudes towards the poor. They heralded the advent of centralized power, religious uniformity and growing absolutism.

Conclusion

In the preceding pages, I have attempted to review different types of violence and resistance. My focus here has been on violence from below, that is, movements of resistance against rapacious lords, urban oligarchs, or general attacks on the social order. I have sought to provide a taxonomy of different types of violent confrontation: large regional risings, smaller local flare-ups, and isolated incidents of banditry, vagrancy and piracy.

The first category included several different movements. The *Irmandiño* revolt in Galicia at the end of the fifteenth century involved mostly peasants, a few petty-bourgeois and lower clergy taking arms against a harassing nobility. In the 1520s, the *Comunero* revolt in Castile articulated, with some exceptions, the interests of the urban political elites. At the opposite end of the spectrum, the Valencia *Germanías* (1520s), a complex social movement, drew support largely from the urban popular classes and sought, in its most radical manifestations, to overturn the established order.

Local risings, such as those of Fuente Obejuna and Alcaraz, followed different paths. The first represented a small town's resistance to harsh abuse by its lordly master. The second resulted from the internal factional struggles of well-to-do groups in Alcaraz. Both types of revolts entangled members of different social orders in increasingly violent relationships.

Finally, banditry, piracy and vagrancy provided additional outlets for violence from below. Though bandits, pirates and vagrants operated within a complex matrix of social and political inducements, their activities represented an endemic war against the rich. This type of violence stemmed, in part, from the growing gap between the social groups – the collapse of the idealized society of orders, one could say – and from the unremitting surge in poverty.

Notes

1. On the complex issues surrounding the 1391 pogroms and the 1440s anti-*Converso* riots see Yitzhak Baer, *A History of the Jews in Christian Spain*, 2 vols (Philadelphia, 1961–66), II: 166–69; Philippe Wolff, 'The 1391 Pogrom in Spain: Social Crisis or Not?' *Past & Present*, 50 (1971): 4–18; Angus MacKay, 'Popular Movements and Pogroms in Fifteenth-Century Castile', *Past & Present*, 55 (1972): 33–67.
2. For how resistance could be effectively deployed short of actual violence see the influential books by James C. Scott, *Domination and the Arts of Resistance: Hidden Transcripts* (New Haven, 1990); *Weapons of the Weak: Everyday Forms of Peasant Resistance* (New Haven, 1985).
3. See, for example, the wonderful book by Eric Hobsbawm, *Primitive Rebels: Studies in Archaic Forms of Social Movement in the Nineteenth and Twentieth Centuries* (New York, 1951).
4. On the events of 1640 see John H. Elliott, *The Revolt of the Catalans: A Study in the Decline of Spain 1598–1640* (Cambridge, 1963); and his magisterial *The Count-Duke of Olivares: The Statesman in an Age of Decline* (New Haven, 1986), 553–673.
5. See Julio Valdeón Baruque, *Los conflictos sociales en el reino de Castilla en los siglos XIV y XV* (Madrid, 1975), 189–90.
6. Carlos Barros, *Mentalidad justiciera de los irmandiños, siglo XV* (Madrid, 1990). Much of the discussion below follows Barros's research.

7. On these topics see Thomas N. Bisson's remarkable new book, *Tormented Voices: Power, Crisis, and Humanity in Rural Catalonia 1140–1200* (Cambridge, MA, 1998), and 'The "Feudal Revolution"', *Past & Present*, 142 (1994): 6–42, and the debate that followed publication, *Past & Present*, 152 (1996): 177–225; 155 (1997): 196–223.

8. Barros, *Mentalidad*, 264.

9. Ibid., 202–18; for attacks against women in other parts of Europe see Guido Ruggeiro, *Violence in Early Renaissance Venice* (New Brunswick, NJ, 1980).

10. Barros, *Mentalidad*, 209–10.

11. On Charles's ascent to the Spanish crowns, his candidacy for the Imperial throne, and the problems that ensued, see John H. Elliott, *Imperial Spain 1469–1716* (New York, 1964), 120–53.

12. Joan Reglà et al., *Història del país Valencià*, 3 vols (Barcelona, 1975), III: 7–74.

13. Ricardo García Cárcel, *La revolta de les Germanies* (Alzira, 1981), 7; see also his 'Notas sobre la población y urbanismo de la Valencia del siglo XVI', *Saitabi*, 25 (1975): 133–55.

14. García Cárcel, *La revolta*, 21. For a first-hand account of the revolt see *Les cròniques valencianes sobre les Germanies de Guillem Ramon Català i de Miguel Garcia (segle XVI)*, ed. Eulalia Durán (Valencia, 1984).

15. García Cárcel, *La revolta*, 23–37.

16. Ibid., 39–60; for rebellions in fourteenth- and fifteenth-century Europe, see Michel Mollat and Philippe Wolff, *The Popular Revolutions of the Late Middle Ages* (Winchester, MA, 1973) and Michael Mullett, *Popular Culture and Popular Protest in Late Medieval and Early Modern Europe* (London, 1987). Neither of these books addresses popular revolts in Spain.

17. García Cárcel, *La revolta*, 60ff. For English and continental messianic revolutionary movements see Norman Cohn, *The Pursuit of the Millennium: Revolutionary Millenarian and Mystical Anarchists of the Middle Ages* (New York, 1970 and many reprints thereafter); Christopher Hill, *The World Turned Upside Down: Radical Ideas during the English Revolution* (Harmondsworth, 1985).

18. There are innumerable editions, translations and critical studies of the play in Spanish, English and other languages. I have used Lope de Vega, *Fuente Ovejuna*, ed. Juan María Marín (Ediciones Cátedra: Madrid, 1995).

19. For this and what follows see Angus MacKay, *Anatomía de una revuelta urbana: Alcaraz en 1458* (Albacete, 1985).

20. The word in Spanish is *criado*, which in medieval Castilian meant something quite different from the denotation of servant that is used today. It could also refer to men of lower status who were attached to or had been raised in the household of a noble or local oligarch. Relations between *criados* and their masters were often more intimate than they are today, having a quasi-familial character.

21. Miguel de Cervantes y Saavedra, *Don Quijote de la Mancha*, ed. Martín de Riquer, 2 vols (Barcelona, 1955), II, ch. 60.

22. Ibid., II, ch. 60.

23. Ibid., II: 975, fn. 7.

24. Fernand Braudel, *The Mediterranean and the Mediterranean World in the Age of Philip II*, trans. Siân Reynolds (New York, 1975), II: 745, 746.

25. Ibid., II: 735.
26. On banditry, especially in Catalonia, an area infested with bandits and highwaymen, see the excellent book by Xavier Torres i Sans, *Els bandolers (s. XVI–XVII)* (Vic, 1991). Also Joan Reglá, *Bandolers, pirates i hugonots a la Catalunya del sigle XVII* (Barcelona, 1969). Also see below and Chapter 7.
27. *Don Quixote*, I: ch. 41.
28. Sebastià García Martínez, *Bandolers, Corsaris i Moriscos* (Valencia, 1980), 47–8.
29. Ibid., 48–55.
30. See *Rinconete and Cortadillo* in Miguel de Cervantes y Saavedra, *Obras completas* (Madrid, 1965), 834–52.
31. On these points see Linda Martz, *Poverty and Welfare in Habsburg Spain: The Example of Toledo* (Cambridge, 1983); Cristobal Pérez de Herrera, *Amparo de pobres*, intro. Michael Cavillac (Madrid, 1975). See in particular the introduction, which summarizes the debate on the poor and the vagrants, 1–clxxix.

Chapter 9

Eating and dressing: the patterns of everyday life

In fifteenth-century Valladolid, the Confraternity of All Saints (*Todos los Santos*) held ritual banquets on specific festive days. On the feast days of St Philip and St James (May Day), St Lawrence (10 August), and All Saints (1 November), the pious *cofrades* (members) enjoyed ritual meals, while hosting a number of the city's poor in the saints' honour. Composed mainly of members of the local oligarchy, merchants and other middling sorts, the Confraternity of All Saints was one of countless brotherhoods and individuals throughout Spain and the rest of the medieval and early modern West that, through wills or charitable donations, brought rich and poor together in rituals of feast or funeral.

Although these groups rarely sat at the same table or ate the same food, the highly ritualized meals served as symbols of unity, and, through charity and commensality, they forged well-regulated social bonds between the middling sorts and the poor. Conversely, what the various participants ate and how they ate it underscored the ever-widening gulf between the haves and the have-nots at the end of the Middle Ages. Not unlike festivals (of which these ceremonies were, in a sense, an extension) and mass violence, these celebratory meals articulated the power relations between social orders. And like the characteristics of diet, dress, habitat, etiquette and street life, the details of these ritual occasions were translated into taxonomies of difference.

Types and amounts of food, ceremonies of eating and dressing, and other daily activities were intimately linked to social filiation. They were, as they are today, signs of membership in privileged or marginalized groups. This chapter and the next one therefore look closely at the conventions of eating and drinking, clothing, popular religion, and spirituality in order to unveil the patterns of everyday life and the tenor and pace of social exchange in the cities and lands of late medieval and early modern Spain. These topics have not been explored in detail for Spain, and the information to illuminate these topics must be gleaned from scattered sources. The vision we obtain is thus a fragmented one. We catch glimpses, vivid ones at times, of life unfolding at a particular moment, in a particular place; but, for the most part, we are left with literary representations, chronicles, testaments, and other sources that filter events through the prejudices and ideological stances of their writers. At best, we can draw composite portraits of particular aspects of peasant life (such as diet), or we can offer averages; but seldom do we have the records to depict the real life of individual Spaniards (above all from the lower ranks in society) at the dawn of modernity.

Eating and drinking

Let us return to the tri-annual dinner of the Confraternity of All Saints. Twenty-three extant account books for the period between 1438 and 1469 supply ample information of their activities. The confraternity was a small and select group with only twenty-four members. The banquets grew to a much larger number, however, with the inclusion of servants and poor men and women. We do not know how much they ate at these ritual meals – medieval and early modern people viewed quantity, as well as quality, as significant markers of social status. Nonetheless, through Adeline Rucquoi's work, we know what they ate.

The bread and wine, the most important staples of the medieval diet, served to the confraternity members differed substantially from the ones offered to the servants and the poor. In 1447, at the banquet held on the day of All Saints, when masters, servants and the poor sat at the same table, the bread for the former cost 30 *mrs*, while the bread of the poor cost only one-third of that price. Similarly, the confraternity members insisted on being served wine of at least two years' vintage, whereas the wine brought to the servants and the poor was of the most recent vintage. The tables included in Rucquoi's article, which I am summarizing here, reveal the chasm separating the social orders. In 1439 the *cántara* (a unit of liquids, around 1.6 centilitres) of wine that was served to confraternity members cost 80 *mrs*; the same measure bought for the poor was valued less than half at 35 *mrs*. In 1442, the prices were 64 and 24 *mrs* respectively, and in 1451 they were 98.6 and 40 *mrs*. A hypothetical scenario may serve to convey the lopsided nature of these ritual protocols. Imagine that, in the name of charity, you were to invite servants and poor people to your table, but that throughout the meal, in which everyone sat side by side or across from one another, only you ate a better-quality bread – or what people in that period thought was better (usually white bread) – and drank a high-quality wine that was served from fancier flagons. This enforced difference extended beyond bread and wine to the entire feast menu.

What else was consumed at these charitable meals? Chickens, geese, capons and other poultry were reserved for the twenty-four confraternity members. Meat, usually mutton but sometimes also beef, was the traditional fare made available to the servants and the poor. If the well-to-do attending these feasts yearned for meat, it was served in the forms of veal or suckling pigs. Not surprisingly, these same foods are given a place of honour in Spain's present-day diet. Veal, suckling pigs and suckling lambs (*cordero*) – though the latter is not mentioned in the menus of the Confraternity of All Saints – remain the traditional ingredients of festive meals in Old Castile. Fish, though consumed in as great a quantity in medieval Spain as it is today, appears in the account books only when meals coincided with a fast day. Even then, distinctions were adhered to. The rich ate salmon, eel, and other tasty fishes; the poor made do with dry sardines.

This traditional fare was complemented by the usual vegetables found in late medieval and early modern diets: onions, asparagus (when in season), eggplants. Fruit, dried and fresh, and desserts completed the meal. A selection of fruit would include pears, apples, raisins, cherries, oranges, figs and lemons, of which the last three were probably brought north to Valladolid from Andalusia. Dessert was confined mainly to rice pudding, the traditional last course of medieval Spanish banquets.

Medieval and early modern food, especially that which was served to the upper and middle classes, was highly spiced. This was done to enhance the taste of the food, but also to preserve it from spoiling and to compensate for lax sanitary conditions and the lack of refrigeration. Apart from the ever-present salt and pepper, condiments included garlic, vinegar, oregano, parsley, mustard, cinnamon, saffron, clove and ginger. Most of these spices came from southern Spain, where the climate allowed for their cultivation, or from foreign trade. As shall be seen below, a large variety of spices was readily available throughout the peninsula. This availability was not limited to major cities such as Seville, Barcelona or Valladolid; spices were obtainable in small and insignificant towns and villages. Travellers could find a vast array of exotic spices just about anywhere (see below).

Finally, most of the cooking at the Confraternity of All Saints feasts was lard-based. Rucquoi calculates that 97 per cent of the frying and cooking was done with lard. Oils, olive oil above all, are barely mentioned in the account books. Valladolid was not a region of olive trees, and olive oil, which was used far more often in the south, would have been imported from those areas. What is noteworthy about lard is its function as an ethnic and religious marker. Lard (pork fat) was forbidden food to Jews and Muslims, who cooked mostly with olive oil. The peculiar smell of olive oil – ironically, the preferred and most sought-after cooking oil in Spain today – was identified with Jews and *Conversos* and could, in the troubled fifteenth century, lead to stereotyping and violence. The so-called 'smell of the Jews', which Andrés Bernáldez, a late fifteenth-century chronicler, mentions in his vitriolic attacks against Jews and *Conversos*, was just that: the smell of frying with olive oil. The food consumed at the Confraternity of All Saints thus not only reiterated the distance between the well-heeled and the poor – while simultaneously sowing solidarity through rituals of eating and religious observance – but it also reinforced the rift between Christians and religious minorities.[1]

The feasts of the Confraternity of All Saints differed little from ritual meals held elsewhere in the Spanish kingdoms, as fulfilments of testamentary legacies or as instantiations of institutional largesse. Variations had more to do with geography and climate (more fish in Galicia, the north and the Mediterranean; more oil, fruit and spices in the south) than with cultural or linguistic divides. In Barcelona, in an earlier period, the cathedral's charitable branch, the Pia Almoina, served the poor the basic food items: bread, wine, some types of beef, far more fish than in Valladolid, cheese, eggs, condiments, and other victuals.[2] What the account books do not always tell us, however, is how much was served. For the poor, this, in many respects, was what mattered most.

Eating revisited: the rich and the poor

The conspicuous consumption of high-quality food (and clothing) is to this day an emblem of class and a marker of class conflict. It was much more so in late medieval and early modern Europe, but with a twist. In the period under discussion, eating a lot was a sign of vaunted status; today, eating small portions is a sign of distinction. In Spain, where sumptuary legislation sought to preserve difference among social orders, prestige and position were asserted by copious eating. Contemporary descriptions of festivals and literary works emphasize the alimentary largesse of the powerful. They also describe how members of the elite would devote themselves to excessive and eclectic eating, always in fatuous displays that were meant to confirm rank and difference. Louis XIV made an art of gastronomic display; his binges are the best example of eating as an exercise in political power. Charles V, the great emperor and first Habsburg ruler of Spain, resigned his troubled and bankrupted rule in 1556 and then ensconced himself in the austere and isolated atmosphere of the monastery at Yuste (in Extremadura). But austerity was not what he was about. A man not yet sixty, he brought his best cooks to his Extremadurean exile and then proceeded to eat himself to death; or so the evil tongues alleged. There was hell to pay for the privilege of overeating: heart disease, gout, constipation, and other nasty consequences. Keith Thomas, in his masterful *Religion and the Decline of Magic*, paints a vivid picture of the health problems associated with the indulgent ways of early modern elites.[3]

This is, of course, very much a modern perspective, for we now know that the rough and often meatless diet of the poor was, in a perverse way, healthier than that of their masters. Today we eat the coarse breads and prefer the lean foods that were scorned half a millennium ago – because we are told they are good for us. But in late medieval and early modern Spain, neither the rich nor the poor would have listened to these lessons in nutrition. The poor would gladly have eaten what their betters ate, even if it killed them. And the rich would have considered trading their soft white bread for the peasants' grainy loaves unimaginable.

But how much did they eat? The consumption of food in medieval and early modern Europe is, of course, hard to measure, because we do not have enough records that would tell us of such things. We can reconstruct the patterns of food consumption in specific settings, but these patterns do not fully illuminate long-term practices of eating or even the average daily intake. Of one thing we can be sure, though: the rich, unless they voluntarily chose poverty and asceticism, ate in excess. And the poor, barring a few exceptions, always lived on the edge of hunger. Besides clothing, there was no greater marker of social difference in the late Middle Ages and in the early modern period than eating. What I would like to do here is to provide examples of how much the poor (and the rich) ate at particular events just before 1400 and to compare these examples with information we have from sixteenth-century documentary and literary sources.

One of the best sources for documenting patterns of feeding the poor and for tracking data on what and how much the poor ate are the charitable provisions in late medieval wills. Although few wills included such elaborate provisions as the ones I discuss here, they nonetheless give us entry into the world of elaborate funeral banquets. In 1289, Doña Elvira Alfonso, with her children, donated extensive properties in the valley of the Pisuerga river to the monastery of Santa María de Aguilar de Campóo. She did this, as was customary in testaments of this period, in exchange for a perpetual chaplaincy to pray for her soul and those of her family. In addition, she ordered that, on the feast day of the Virgin, fifty-four poor people be fed at her expense.[4] Such charitable legacies were part of a well-established pattern of feeding (and clothing) the poor; they were also a strategic step in the complex and all-important quest for spiritual salvation. We find numerous examples of testamentary donations aiming to provide food and clothing to the poor on specific feast days, or, far more often, on the anniversary of the funeral or of the donor's death. In the moral economy of salvation, these acts of charity were investments – very small investments, I should add – that sought as a return the reward of paradise. For the deceased and their families, they were also instruments of socia l glorification. As such, they were public events that established social distance between donor and recipient.[5]

Doña Elvira Alfonso's will provides us with a careful account of what and *how much* was given to the poor. To feed her fifty-four poor people, Doña Elvira allocated $1\frac{1}{2}$ *fanegas* (unit of measure for grain) of wheat, two *cántaras* of wine, and a piece of mutton for every two of the poor, dividing the sheep into sixteen pieces. Doña Elvira specified wheat bread in her will, and that is a significant departure from most testaments. Wheat bread was seldom eaten by the poor. Their fare consisted mainly of rye, barley, and other coarser (and healthier) breads. White wheat bread was practically the monopoly of the higher classes, 'the bread the angels ate'. So, for the fifty-four poor men and women sitting at the feast, Doña Elvira's largesse provided a rare opportunity to taste the bread their betters ate.

We do not know exactly what a *fanega* 'at the standard measure' of Aguilar de Campóo (that is, a *fanega* measured by the box kept in the town of Aguilar) really amounted to, but at 1.58 bushels per *fanega*, Doña Elvira's donation represented about 1.4 lb of wheat bread per person, or a loaf of bread weighing roughly 1.25 lb (a bit over 500 g). To our own dietary criteria, this may seems like a good, even excessive, amount, but it fell short of medieval standards. Little, if anything, was left to take home. Monks in monasteries throughout medieval Spain were assigned between 12 and 14 *fanegas* of bread per year, which comes out to about 2 lb (almost 1 kg) a day, or almost double what the poor were allotted at this particular meal.

Two *cántaras* of wine yielded around 0.61 litres of wine per person. We know from a travel account of 1352 and from monastic inventories of 1338 that the average wine consumption could be as much as 2 litres a day. Before the eager reader begins to experiment which such intake of wine, it is important to note that wine was often mixed with water and, with some exceptions, it did not have the potency of today's wines.

According to Fernand Braudel's great work, *The Mediterranean and the Mediterranean World in the Age of Philip II*, a sheep yielded an average of 11.96 kg of meat in the late sixteenth century.[6] In 1289, when Doña Elvira's will was drawn, more than a half-century before the wool trade took off, it is possible that the average sheep was even smaller than in the sixteenth century. One should also ask: what did Braudel mean by yield in meat? In late medieval and early modern Spain, almost every part of the animal was eaten – a method of meat consumption that was common in Western society until very recently. Viscera, lips, feet, testicles, brains – every part of the body provided sustenance to a meat-deprived population. If we assume around 25 lb of meat per sheep, each of the poor men and women received around 0.5 lb of meat at a sitting (which was probably reduced by frying or stewing). This was not much, but better than nothing; and since the meat was accompanied by greens or, most probably, served in a stew, Doña Elvira's fifty-four poor men and women should have left the table, at least once a year, without hunger.

Yet, the cost of such a feast was relatively small. Even including expenses for preparation, side dishes, and the like, the total budget to feed the poor in this particular case would not have been more than 30 *mrs*. This contrasts markedly with the 2,000 *mrs* given for daily expenses to magnates who attended the king's court in the early fourteenth century, or with the 150 *mrs* daily allowance for food given, as a sign of austerity, to both the king and queen in the mid-thirteenth century.

These figures from the thirteenth and fourteenth centuries point to the wide gulf that separated rich and poor in medieval Spain. That gulf, if anything, grew wider in succeeding centuries. And there is no evidence that it narrowed in the early modern period. On the contrary, the gap between social groups, so vivid in terms of clothing and housing (see below), became even more poignant in terms of income assigned for food.

213

Middling sorts, monks and nobles: eating and drinking

Although we know what the destitute ate only on the days they benefited from the charity of laymen and ecclesiastics and are forced to imagine how inadequate their diet must have been the rest of the year, we do have more precise information of the eating habits of other segments of society.

In sections of *Libro de buen amor* (*The Book of Good Love*, c.1337), the author Juan Ruiz describes various foods and forms of eating. Nowhere is this pre-occupation – almost an obsession – with food, a common trope in late medieval and early modern literature, more evident than in Ruiz's description of the battle between Lady Lent and Sir Carnality. The latter's armies of succulent hams, partridges, and other delectable foods are opposed, and eventually defeated, by the austere troops of Lent: dry fish, beans, and foods associated with vigils and fasting. Although Ruiz's gustatorial allegory does not bring us any closer to knowing the actual diet of specific social classes, it dramatizes the popular perception of what constituted a great meal by comparing it with the lean offerings of Lent. Notwithstanding the religious context of the opposition (Carnival versus Lent), the imaginary depictions of sumptuous banquets and abundantly available rich foods form part of a well-established peasant tradition of eating fantasies, harking back in folk memory to utopian visions of paradise and the land of Cockaigne (*jauja*, in Spanish).[7] This topos is found again and again in the late medieval literature of Spain and other European countries; it is also represented artistically, most notably in Brueghel's memorable painting of Carnival being trounced by Lent.

The Book of Good Love does finally give us a sense of the actual diet of the working poor in its description of two meals that the archpriest of Hita (Juan Ruiz) enjoyed while crisscrossing the Central Sierras. The first one is an idealized account. The female toll-keeper at the mountain pass of Malangosto takes the cold and famished archpriest to her hut. There, warmed by an oak log fire, Juan Ruiz is fed 'plenty of rabbit meat, good roasted partridges, poorly kneaded bread, good kid meat, a big measure of wine [a *quartero*], lots of cow's butter, plenty of cheese for toasting, milk, cream, and a trout'. And that is not all, for the meal is followed by the loving embraces of the sturdy toll-collector. We should not take this menu too seriously. It is obviously a fanciful account, a gastronomic (and sexual) fantasy that Ruiz indulged in, away from the constraints of ecclesiastical discipline (not that priests or monks ate badly at all!).[8] And it suggests the very opposite: that Ruiz ate very poorly on his journeys across the mountains.

At Tablada, on his way back across the mountain pass of Fuenfría, another woman lodges him, but this time the 'rye bread was sooty and dark, the wine poor, sharp, and watered'. Apart from that, he is handed only some 'salted meat, goat's cheese, and bran bread'. Here we come closer to the fare of the peasants and working poor: coarse bread, watered wine, some meat from time to time (either mutton or pork), a smattering of greens and vegetables, and cheese.[9]

Monks, on the other hand, ate much better. To eat like a monk meant eating well in the late Middle Ages, and monks and priests are often iconographically represented as fat. In 1338, the records of northern Castile's Benedictine monasteries show that allotments for feeding the monks constituted one of the most important entries in the monastic budget. Departing from the earlier strictures of St Benedict's rule, these Castilian monasteries served meat at their tables around 160 days in the year. At the monastery of San Pedro de Cardeña fish was served every day, together with a course of meat. Eggs appeared three times a week on the menu of Santo Domingo de Silos. Vegetables, fruit and of course large quantities of wine (more than 2 litres per monk per day), and 1 kg (2.2 lb) of bread per monk completed their rather Gargantuan intake.[10]

Again, at the risk of being repetitive, it is to be noted that the monks who ate so well gave a pittance of their income to charity and fed the poor food that was inferior in quality and quantity. How ubiquitously these disparities were enacted can be verified in the account of two merchants travelling in 1352 from Estella, the capital of the kingdom of Navarre, to Seville, in southern Spain. The merchants were accompanied by twenty-six employees and servants. The merchants and some of the more important employees, ten altogether, rode on mules; the rest of the company walked. On the long journey across Spain, they ate goat, fish, beef, chicken, kid, bacon, beans, cheese, lettuce, horseradishes and, as condiments, oil, garlic, vinegar, mustard, pepper, and prepared sauces, plus the omnipresent portions of wine and bread. Cherries, nuts, almonds, and other fruits made for dessert. The chickens and the kid meat were reserved for the two merchants; a stew with bacon and beans (*favas*) was prepared for the servants.[11] This was also the case of merchants travelling from Pamplona (Navarre) to the Castilian cities of Vitoria and Salvatierra in 1368. During that voyage, even the wine purchased for the bourgeois leading the company was of better quality than that which was bought for the rest of the company.[12]

So far, we have kept close to the diet of peasants, middling sorts (including monks), and the poor in the period before 1400. It may be useful to shift our attention to the eating habits of the powerful to see whether or not the diet of all groups changed over time and to ascertain how norms of eating (and dressing) articulated social difference and hierarchy in a later period. Extant sources give us several entries to the consumption frenzies of the Spanish elites. Literary works often provide evocative representations of fictional meals and/or banquets; and although they are essentially literary tropes, they reflect the eating practices of the upper classes. Far more important, they capture the moments in which eating became a site for both social interaction and segregation. Finally, sumptuary laws, accounts of expenses for naval crews

215

and prisoners, and other such sources provide us with a prescriptive sense of how much food was actually allotted to individuals according to their work and social class.

In the ordinances of the Castilian *cortes* of 1351, during the period of deep crisis that followed the Black Death, Peter I established that, when invited by either cities or the masters of the Military Orders, his hosts were to provide him and his court with a daily allotment of 45 sheep (valued at 8 *mrs* each) and, on days of vigil, 22 dozens of dry fish (12 *mrs* per dozen), and 90 *mrs* worth of fresh fish. In addition, the hosts were expected to supply a cow and a half, 20 pigs, 60 chickens, 75 *cántaras* of wine, 1,500 loaves of bread, and 60 *fanegas* of barley. The queen was to receive a similar apportionment for herself and her court.[13] Clearly, a visit from the royal court was a crushing affair; but although these abundant quantities of food were to feed the entire royal cortège, they were regarded as parsimonious by the king and his retinue. We do not know how many courtiers, servants, and other officials in the fourteenth century accompanied the kings in their peripatetic wanderings across their realms, but it is clear that the royal household consumed large amounts of a limited range of food. As always, what set the classes apart was the abundance of food and the consumption of meat and fish. In this respect, royal visits throughout the realm – very much like festivals – generated a special kind of social dynamic. On the one hand, even when it was not an elaborate royal entry, royal visits spawned a generous food supply chain that had an immediate effect on the diet of the poor. On the other hand, after the king left, the community was likely to be so depleted that hard times would prevail for a while – for the lower social groups – until the community recovered from its extravagant expenditures.

Banquets, community and difference

The king and queen, and magnates and prelates closest to the ruler, ate a far more exotic fare than the rest of their household. The evidence stems largely from exceptional occasions. The banquet for the crowning of Ferdinand of Antequera as king of the Crown of Aragon in 1412, for example, displayed a combination of very elaborate foods, such as pheasants and bird pies. This particular banquet featured sumptuous aesthetic flourishes: golden griffins, elaborate tableaux, live birds flying from within pies, and other ornate courses.[14] Ultimately, a meal's setting and adornments were, in certain circles, even more significant in establishing social distinction than the quantity or even quality of the food being served.

At the coronation feasts of Fernando de Antequera, the newly elected king of the Crown of Aragon, the displays were meant to stress the superiority of the king's position over that of his subjects. Similarly, in depicting the great festivals sponsored by the constable Don Miguel Lucas de Iranzo in Jaén in the 1460s (see above, Chapters 5 and 6), the chronicler emphasizes not only the amount of food and the constable's largesse, but also the luxurious service – plates, silverware, glasses, and serving tables – that distinguished the occasion. In reality, these descriptions in *Hechos del condestable Don Miguel Lucas de Iranzo* sought to convey to the readers of the chronicle – just as the constable's displays did to the people in Jaén – the remarkable richness of these festive displays. Although the distribution of chickens, eggs, wine and other victuals to the people of the city brought together high and low in ceremonies of commensality, the splendid service, the silver and gold of the plate settings and dinnerware, served as markers of difference.[15]

But eating together – holding banquets for festive or mournful occasions – served an important social function. Hilario Casado Alonso describes the banquets organized by small rural communities in fifteenth- and sixteenth-century Spain. Even in small villages (50 to 500 inhabitants), the villagers gathered at specific times of the year (the feast days of the town and other festive days). These banquets, from which women and single men were excluded (the latter sometimes being allowed to attend but not to speak), were held in the village church, on the church's porch, in a square, in the cemetery, or in an open meadow near the village. The cost of the banquets was paid for by the community, and the villagers were offered a set menu. At Arcos, the menu included an appetizer, roasted meat, a stew or pot-au-feu, dessert, bread and wine. At Mahamud, in 1511, the portions allotted to each villager in attendance consisted of half a quarter of mutton ragout, 2 lb of bread, and 3 *cuartillos* of wine (around 504 millilitres per *cuartillo*). The banquets, as Casado Alonso has observed, helped maintain peace and unity among the villagers.[16]

While fostering a notion of egalitarianism among the participants – who all ate the same kind and amount of food – village banquets also reaffirmed hierarchical inequalities between men and women, and between old and young. The banquets' chief role was to reinforce a sense of community among heads-of-household and property owners in the village and to unite villagers when they needed to re-negotiate terms with their lords – as was the case in Arcos, where a feast was held as the peasants met their lord's representative. Otherwise, banquets offered men a ceremonial and joyful setting for discussing the affairs of the village, without the presence of women or the young.

We have been moving slowly from small samples to larger gatherings to discern what and how much the different social classes ate. Francis Brumont's detailed study of the peasants of Old Castile during the reign of Philip II can serve as a guide to the everyday diet of peasants in late medieval and early modern Spain.[17] His is a far more realistic rendering of the actual diet of peasants than those suggested by the exceptional meals at funerals, confraternity feasts, or the charitable legacies of Spanish wills. Brumont's evidence, however, also confirms the accuracy of the sources listed above and of literary works. According to Brumont, the basic peasant diet consisted of about 500 g of bread (a bit over 1 lb) per day. This bread was mostly wheat (coarse grains, but also mixed with rye). The peasant diet in northern Castile included meat at a daily average of between 20 and 35 g. These minuscule portions reflect the sporadic eating of meat. In the Bureba, the area of northern Castile studied by Brumont, 50 per cent of the meat was pork, 35 per cent mutton, and 15 per cent beef. Other items completed the rural menu: cheeses, some poultry (for well-to-do peasants), eggs, legumes and fish. Wine consumption ranged between 1 and 2 litres.[18]

These averages come from a rather prosperous area in northern Castile; the portions and the kind of grain used to make bread changed according to topography and climatic conditions, as did the proportion of pork to mutton (more mutton in the South, less wheat in Galicia, and so on). Thus Denis Menjot's description of eating in fifteenth-century Murcia (southeast Spain) shows the same reliance on bread, meat (mostly mutton), and wine. But unlike in the North, where lard was preferred for frying and cooking, in Murcia olive oil was almost universally used for cooking, a reflection of the abundance of olive trees and the lesser importance of pigs in the region. After all, Murcia had been a Muslim stronghold into the thirteenth century.[19] These averages from the late sixteenth century cast light on the permanence and uniformity of diets – certainly the diet of lower social groups – over time, and show how basic staples and proportions were kept fairly unchanged, even in places such as the New World, where circumstances and the availability of other staples (corn, chiles, bread fruit, and other native products) dictated different eating practices. But how one eats is one of the most resilient cultural markers in human history.

Carla Phillips's genial book *Six Galleons for the King of Spain* offers a superb description of men at sea sailing in the great fleets that linked Spain to the New World and to the Philippine Islands. Diet and etiquette on board left a great deal to be desired. Sailors received about 1.5 lb of hard biscuits, for bread spoiled quickly; but biscuits, too, fermented and spoiled on long journeys. They drank about 2 pints daily, though the wine was often watered down. Phillips has rendered her findings in most useful tables, which show that, in the king's galleons, the crew (not the officers) had nineteen meat days (mostly salt pork, about 6 ounces daily), nine fish days (dried cod, 6 ounces), and three cheese days (6 ounces) every month. In addition, rice, chick peas, olive oil and vinegar complemented their monotonous and highly dangerous, spoilage-prone diet. Yet, Phillips has calculated that the daily caloric and protein intake was higher than the recommended daily allowance for a modern active male. The food may not always have been pleasant, but it was more than enough. Of course, these figures reflect the intake of the crews; ship captains and officers ate separately and better.

The high caloric content of the late medieval and early modern diet – at least for those who ate regularly – is a troubling subject indeed. I have already commented on the consequences of such types of diet, especially for the

Table 9.1 *Summary of caloric intake of Spanish sailors in the early seventeenth century*

Type of foods	Calories	Protein (grams)
Meat days (19/month)	4,130.30	77.09
Fish days (9/month)	3,743.00	209.81
Cheese days (3/month)	3,608.98	108.55
Daily average	3,967.41	118.67
Recommended daily allowance (for moderately active male, 143 lb)	3,000.00	37.00

Source: Carla Phillips, *Six Galleons for the King of Spain: Imperial Defense in the Early Seventeenth Century* (Baltimore, 1986), p. 241.

upper classes. Fat intake in the Spanish galleons amounted to about 120 g per day. It was probably worse for the upper classes. Those at the bottom of society fluctuated between the occasional feast and everyday hunger. Menjot reports intakes of about 6,500 calories per day for each of the forty magistrates of the city of Murcia attending one of their official banquets. But the prisoners in Murcia received, at least in theory, a daily intake of 4,500 calories: 1.4 kg of bread, 40 g of meat and other victuals. The figures provided by Phillips, Menjot and others stand in sharp contrast to contemporary literary representations of scarcity, to the frequent crises of subsistence and to the actual famines that, together with plagues and excessive taxation, were the scourge of Spain in this period.

Literary representations and etiquette

Norbert Elias's remarkable book *The Civilizing Process* describes the role that etiquette and manners played in constructing discourses of difference and in marking the transition from medieval 'feudal' institutions to the centralized monarchies of the sixteenth and seventeenth centuries. Baldassare Castiglioni's famous *The Courtier*, which was translated, avidly read, and imitated by the upper social groups throughout western Europe, set codes of behaviour, etiquette and dressing for the nobility and for those aspiring to the genteel life.[20] These rules of civility, to paraphrase Jacques Revel, formed part of an intense effort to control social intercourse in the sixteenth century.[21] How one moved one's hands, how one behaved, how one ate became signs of specific social filiation and established differences between the civilized and the vulgar, the elegant and the uncouth.[22]

Spain was not exempt from these developments. From the mid-thirteenth century onwards, legal codes and literary models sought to establish norms of behaviour and table manners for the king, the court and the high nobility.[23] Literary forms such as fifteenth-century chronicles also provided elaborate descriptions of eating and dressing. I will discuss the latter below; for now it suffices to say that these narratives served as models of decorous public behaviour for the dominant social groups. Romances, which flourished in the fifteenth and early sixteenth centuries, were a veritable source of conduct standards and manners. As Huizinga has shown for northern Europe in *The Autumn of the Middle Ages* and Martín de Riquer has done for Spain,[24] books of chivalry often recounted the actual feats of knights-errant. And knights-errant often imitated the fictional deeds described in books of chivalry, thus generating a circularity of tropes whereby art imitated life and vice versa.

At court, Ferdinand and Isabella commissioned a manual to regulate forms of behaviour at the household of the heir (the Infante Don Juan). It set the standard for how to serve at the table, how to dress, and how to tend to the heir at the throne. By order of Charles V, this book of etiquette, *El libro de la cámara Real del Principe Don Juan e officios de su casa e servicio ordinario*, was reissued for the use of his son and heir, the future Philip II. The prospective king grew up with codes of etiquette and court behaviour that went back to the end of the fifteenth century. Court ritual – the formal etiquette and demeanour that had become *de rigueur* in the presence of royals and their heirs – remained unchanged for over fifty years. On the other hand, the Habsburgs also brought with them a great deal of the court ceremonial they had inherited from the great dukes of Burgundy, their ancestral home.

El libro de la cámara was one of several manuals that formulated the conventions of eating and drinking among the upper classes. In books and in real practice, the ritualization of eating and serving – a widespread phenomenon throughout western Europe – was, as Allard has argued in her description of the *Libro de cámara*, an exchange between the king and the aristocracy, between the king and foreign visitors, between the king and his people.[25] It was an exchange that replicated the didactic programme of royal entries, Corpus Christi processions, and other festive displays. The rituals of eating (and dressing) and the codification of etiquette and manners made their way from the court to the upper levels of the middling sorts in clearly defined gradations. This set of behaviours became a model for all those aspiring to gentility and an emblem of social identification.

Literary representations of eating

It may not be an exaggeration to argue that a large portion of late medieval and early modern Spanish literature and art was about food, and about eating and drinking. In an earlier part of this chapter, I have referred to the descriptions of meals and foods that appear in the *Libro de buen amor*. Other fifteenth- and sixteenth-century chronicles and travel accounts describe food and banquets on numerous occasions. The *Hechos del condestable don Miguel Lucas de Iranzo*, often quoted in these pages, is one of our foremost examples of the intense concern with food and with the representation of food for political purposes.

None of these sources, however, portray the centrality of food as poignantly as the picaresque novel, a genre that advanced a dark, but humorous, and bitter critique of Spanish society. *Lazarillo de Tormes*, the pioneer and quintessential picaresque narrative, is mostly about the long struggle of its eponymous hero to feed himself. We move from the spartan and meagre fare of the avaricious cleric who methodically starves his servant Lázaro, to the kind knight, all fake elegance and manners, who partakes of the alms and food offerings that his servant Lázaro has begged for in the street. *Lazarillo de Tormes* is a narrative of scarcity, of exasperating hunger, of the difficulty of eating a square meal in Imperial Spain. In the end, Lázaro consciously becomes a cuckolded husband in return for the rewards of false respectability and daily meals.[26]

The text of *Don Quixote* similarly oscillates between hunger and excess. Although the Knight of the Sorrowful Figure, nourished by ethereal and knightly illusions, gives food little or no thought, his servant, Sancho Panza (the name Panza, belly, is significant), thinks mostly of where to get his next meal. In *Don Quixote*, Cervantes offers the reader a culinary journey through Spain. Sheep-herders and cattlemen share their humble fare with the two heroes. Inns along the roadway provide regional types of victuals. The castles and well-to-do houses, where they are welcomed as guests, offer solace from the trials of the road. Poor Sancho always gets close to the food but is seldom destined to enjoy it, for his master invariably wrenches him from the table to embark on another mad adventure. But none of Cervantes's scenes approached – in lavishness of detail – his description of Camacho's fabled feast.

The feast of Camacho, *el rico* (the rich)

In the second volume of *Don Quixote*, Cervantes tells one of the many stories within his main narrative that give the book such a rich texture. Chapters 19 to 21 describe in luxurious detail the feast given by Camacho 'the rich', a wealthy farmer (*labrador*), in honour of his impeding marriage to Quetaria 'the beautiful'. Relatives, friends, all the villagers and travellers, including Don Quixote and Sancho, are invited to partake of the feast, which takes place on an open meadow. The fantastic nature of the event, with elaborate tableaux, dances, songs, and abundant outpouring of lyrical poetry celebrating the marriage of wealth and beauty, served to spotlight the innumerable types of food that had been prepared for the delectation of the guests in gargantuan amounts.

The story has entered popular speech in Spain, and to say 'as rich as Camacho' is to imply great wealth. This was not the forbidding or distant wealth of the upper classes, but that of a farmer who, in his prosperity, lorded over his fellow villagers while remaining within the same social order. The feast of Camacho constitutes yet another rendition of the land of Cockaigne; in this version Sancho is our tour guide. The tour begins with sense of smell, with the aroma of the food, and it is followed by the visual splendour of an entire calf being slowly roasted on a spit and of immense pots in which whole lambs are stewing. Hares, hens, game birds, endless quantities of good wine, white bread, oil, honey and cheeses are 'lined up like a wall'. And over fifty cooks, 'all very clean', tend to the needs of the improvised open-air kitchen.

Sancho's first sortie produces three hens and two geese, which he sets himself to eating with relish. The fact that Quetaria ends up marrying (through cunning deception) the young, handsome and poor Basilio, leaving Camacho and all his wealth standing at the altar, does not affect the eating. Camacho, recognizing his defeat, turns his own feast into a celebration of Quetaria and Basilio's wedding. Sancho, who wisely sided with the purveyor of food, has nothing but praise for the rich Camacho on the day in which, after many frustrations, he can finally eat to his heart's (and belly's) content. Don Quixote, always partial to romance, delights in the events and tastes none of the food.[27] Cervantes ironically reminds the reader here of the difference between knight and peasant: the former dreams of heroic pursuits; the latter, thinks only of pleasing his stomach.

Clothing and difference

Like eating, dress – the fashion, above all fabrics and colours, that distinguished high and low, men and women – formed part of an important social code. Clothing was a continuous reminder to all – in the streets of towns, in court, or in the context of festivals – of differences in rank, occupation, gender and wealth. In many respects, early modern Spain was quite different from other parts of western Europe. Whereas it had shared with other European nations the medieval predilection for vivid colours and for the almost scandalous and riotous mixture of these vivid colours, by the sixteenth century, the Spanish Habsburg court, borrowing from its Burgundian ancestry, chose black (and white) as their emblematic colours of power. El Greco's portraits of aristocrats and merchants, and those of other sixteenth- and seventeenth-century artists, reflect the austerity of taste and the sharp contrast between the exuberant tastes of other parts of Europe and that of early modern Spanish elites. But that, of course, was just another form of affectation, and another discourse of difference.[28]

Sumptuary laws
Our best guide to the social distance that was inscribed in matters of clothing can be found in the sumptuary laws. Starting in the mid-thirteenth

century – when the first serious sequence of *cortes* (parliamentary) records were logged – sumptuary laws, whether in Castile or in the Crown of Aragon, sought first and foremost to limit excesses. They were restrictive measures that aimed to prevent conspicuous consumption by *all* social groups within the Spanish realms. But sumptuary laws were also clear attempts to contain social mobility and to block the perceived permeability of social orders.[29] In previous chapters, we have seen that crossing social boundaries was not impossible. Wealth, which came to merchants and masters of artisan trades in the thirteenth and fourteenth centuries, was the yeast of social change. It fostered ambitions among the middling sorts that posed a serious challenge to the hierarchical arrangement of society. Furthermore, in Spain, a land with large religious minorities, the problem of identifying a Muslim or a Jew – who often looked just like a Christian – depended entirely on differences in clothing, hair style and other ethnic and religious markers.

It is not a coincidence, therefore, that the first sumptuary laws sought to construct categories of dressing, colours and styles that would ease the job of distinguishing between noble and bourgeois, between Christian and non-Christian. Sumptuary laws did not deter the bourgeois from engaging in fatuous displays; nor did it discourage Jews or, to a lesser extent, Moors from dressing as Christians. Nonetheless, these laws, which codified a system of social segregation, purposefully attempted to keep all social orders, especially the middling sorts, in their proper places.

Certain assumptions were explicit in the sumptuary legislation of the late Middle Ages. First, there was a belief that fabrics such as scarlet cloth, silk, and certain furs (ermine, for example) were imbued with aesthetic and symbolic values that made them the domain of the upper classes. Some colours of fabrics, gold, silver and scarlet red among others, were also to be restricted to those on the higher social tiers. This was not merely because these colours were pleasing to late medieval Spanish and European sensibilities, but because – as with specific fabrics – they had become emblematic of power. In fact, these colours had become associated with royal or ecclesiastical dignity, and often, as in the case of scarlet red, with high municipal office. Second, sumptuary legislation signalled the Crown's growing power to regulate life, or at least its ambition to control particular aspects of everyday life.

Missing from most of these sumptuary laws are references to the lower social groups: the poor and the marginalized. This is not because there was no desire to control them, but because many of the relevant fabrics, colours, furs and food items were anyway unattainable by the majority of the population. About 80–85 per cent of Spain's population in the fifteenth and sixteenth centuries dressed in undyed cloth – mainly cotton, rough wool, burlap, serge, sackcloth, and other inexpensive fabrics. Most people in the Middle Ages dressed in variations of light-brown, monochrome tones, which they seldom changed over the course of the year. Sometimes, as in the wills that made provisions to feed and clothe the poor show, the testator insisted on supplying woollen clothing to the poor; but these were exceptions to the rule.

The workings of sumptuary legislation in the fifteenth century

A long tradition of active sumptuary legislation, from 1252 to the mid-fourteenth century, sought to earmark certain fabrics, colours and foods for the exclusive use of elite social groups, while barring their use by the middling sorts (the bourgeois; the lower nobility), Jews or Moors. In 1494, and almost every year afterwards until 1499, the Catholic Monarchs restricted the use of brocade, gold cloth, fabrics embroidered in gold and silver, silk, and other expensive items. They did this to decrease their subjects' lavish personal expenditures as well as to alleviate the deficit that stemmed from the import of luxury items. But legislation also sought to stop the 'disorder' that 'unregulated fashion' wreaked on the social order of the realm. The royal edict of 1499, which obviously came on the heels of previously ignored edicts, responded to the *cortes'* request for relief from the social mayhem that it attributed to the indiscriminate donning of fabrics and colours. These were to be restricted to the socially prominent, and in this particular case to the procurators of the *cortes* themselves.[30]

We should not be deceived by these restrictions, however. What was forbidden with one hand was permitted with the other. From the mid-fourteenth century onwards, royal ordinances and the *cortes'* legislation, while seeking to keep the social orders hierarchically fixed, granted exemptions that in fact circumvented official attempts to create strict codes of dressing. The greatest beneficiaries of these exemptions were the middling sorts (mainly their wives) and the Jews. The issue of fabric and colour use thus became another site of contestation, another arena in which the power of wealth sought to obliterate the privilege of birth (and did so quite successfully).[31]

The feasts of 1428 revisited

Several years ago, I examined in detail the ritual and symbolic elements of a cycle of festivities that took place in Valladolid in 1428. These events are mentioned briefly at the opening of Chapter 5; here I wish to highlight the symbolic deployment of clothing. The festivals are of particular interest because the main protagonists – the kings of Castile and Navarre and the Infante Don Enrique – though members of the same royal family, the Trastámaras, represented almost all the different political divisions of Iberia in the early fifteenth century: Castile, Navarre, and the Crown of Aragon. Their choice of symbolic colours and fabrics reveal a common culture, a broad understanding of the political and social meanings that were attached to specific items of clothing. Contemporary accounts of these and similar events also reflect the greater responsiveness of chroniclers, from the end of the fourteenth century to the end of the early modern period, to these kinds of displays.

Whether in travel accounts, chronicles, poems, or popular romances of the fifteenth century, descriptions of clothing, fabrics, and colours of the vestments leap out at us by their elaborateness. The first extensive private chronicle written in Castile in the fifteenth century, *Hechos del condestable don Miguel Lucas de Iranzo*, is nothing more than a careful depiction of festivals and of the garments and colours that the constable wore in his daily parading about the streets of Jaén. In detailing the constable's wedding, the chronicler lists a careful inventory of the garments Don Miguel Lucas de Iranzo wore for more than a week. Each item of dress, each colour, was designed for specific effect; each fabric told a particular message about power, about the relationship of the constable to his subjects in Jaén, to the Church, and to the king.[32]

In reading fashion – or feasts – as texts, it is not surprising to find that concerted efforts were taken to display certain symbols. In Valladolid in May 1428, in what was high political theatre, the king of Castile, John II, and his redoubtable foes (and cousins), the Infantes of Aragon, wore clothes of scarlet red, gold, silver and green (representing the Castilian monarch as king of May, or as king of the woods) and flew banners of red and white (the colours of the Crusade and the reconquest, which were associated with the martial role of Castilian royalty). In the long festive cycle, the king of Castile wore a diadem covered with butterflies, marched to the joust preceded by a muzzled bear and lion, and concluded the cycle of appearances dressed in white, in the guise of God the father. As indicated in Chapter 5, these were public spectacles, and most of the common people in attendance, dressed in their drab and humble clothing, understood the significance and didactic purposes of these displays.[33]

Sixteenth-century accounts

The descriptions of the royal entries and of the festivities of the powerful – including the great *autos-de-fe* and Corpus Christi processions – also included elaborate accounts of dress and colours. This was the case even in an age when the Spanish monarchs forsook the elaborate garments of their English and French counterparts. In 1560, when Philip II married Isabelle of Valois, a French princess, in Guadalajara, one of the chroniclers commented on how, in one of their visits to pay respects to the queen, the French wore no embroidered clothing; they were thus not 'worth mentioning'. He did, however, take meticulous notice of the gold chains (from Peru) sported by many of the courtiers, and above all the lavish garments worn by the king and queen. For his wedding outfit, Philip II, untypically, wore white stockings and a white jerkin with gold, a French-made garment in purple velvet with gold and precious jewels, and a black hat with white feathers. The queen came 'dressed in the French fashion', with a wide skirt of silver cloth, furs, and a cloak of black velvet with precious jewels and pearls.[34] Today, one may think this the nadir of bad taste; but then what will the twenty-fifth century think of our own fashions?

When in the same year Isabella, now fully the queen of Spain, entered Toledo – one of the realm's most important urban centres – in her first royal entry, the city held elaborate feasts in her honour. The feasts lasted several days, with the usual profusion of ceremonial arches, theatrical displays, the running of bulls, dancing, and processions by artisan crafts, civic and ecclesiastical authorities, in exhaustive demonstrations of the city's loyalty. The accounts of these events tell us how each corporate group dressed from top to bottom, and the types of garments, colours and fabrics they used. We thus learn how all the participants dressed: municipal officials, familiars of the Inquisition, Mint functionaries, members of the Santa Hermandad, and other worthies.[35] Considering that the king had just had his own official reception shortly before, the city must have been financially wrecked; but its tailors, weavers, and others engaged in the clothing trade would have profited mightily. For the people of Toledo, however, the lesson in social order would have been at least as important: as they lined up along the streets, they could see the ranking of official dignitaries and learn, through fabrics and colours, the hierarchical character of power.

This was not very different from the parade of 'honoured citizens' in Barcelona, who moved as a group along the narrow streets of the Barrio Gótico, or from the fancy knights of the Confraternity of Santiago in Burgos, who marched annually through the city in elaborate costumes and on spirited horses. Their processions were displays of power, reiterations of social difference. Imagine what it would have meant for a humble urban dweller to see, once or more times a year, a parade of knights, all dressed up in expensive fabrics and vivid colours, riding great horses, the animals themselves covered with elaborate and attractive cloths. The knights carried lances, their waists girded by swords. Their horses' vestments and their shields bore the colours and markings of their lineage. Symbols such as the coat-of-arms served to reaffirm their social status and political power within the city. And, of course, the people came out in throngs to see the parade of knights. In awe, envy and probably unconscious anger, they gazed upon their betters. It was a spectacle not unlike those described in Chapters 5 and 6; similarly, it taught lessons of distance and difference.

In truth, all social echelons were colour- and fashion-coded, starting with the florid displays of the mighty; even austere rulers such as Philip II knew that a certain type of clothing was expected of him on his wedding day. Religious orders were recognizable (and often identified) by the colours of their robes. The liturgy of the mass itself was colour-coded. The changing hues of the celebrants' cassocks and surplices taught believers about the nature of holidays and the liturgical season, indicating whether they were celebratory or mournful. Jews, until 1492, were forced to wear a yellow circle on their clothing. *Moriscos*, by choice, wore their own traditional gar-ments. Ironically, one of the charges hurled at them was that they dressed differently from Christians, and among the 1560s regulations that led to the Alpujarras revolt was an ordinance enjoining *Moriscos* to abandon their traditional clothing. The law commanded prostitutes to wear identifying colours, fabrics and headgear. The priests' mistresses (*barraganas*) were equally ordered to wear specific colours and types of clothing. And variations of folk festive colours (black, red and white) marked the important events in city and village life.

Moreover, fashion and colours – certainly among the upper classes and the middling sorts – were far from static. French, Italian and Burgundian fashions deeply influenced how people dressed. The extant documents and literary sources almost always identified the provenance of the fashion: 'dressed in the French style', 'dressed in the Spanish style', in the 'Moorish style', and so forth. The choice in colours changed rapidly; it was a society, at the top and in the middle, as conscious of style and fashion as ours.[36]

Underlying all these sumptuary codes, however, lay the fear of pollution, the fear of the too-easily-mixing social classes, and the fear of cohesive minority religious groups. These injunctions were like dams hopelessly attempting to stop up the social porosity and confusion created by wealth, conversion, geographical mobility, and the opportunities provided by imperial policies.

Conclusion

By concentrating on conventions of eating and dress, this chapter seeks to establish the social role of food and clothing. Furthermore, these categories provide additional perspectives into ways of binding different social groups, while establishing firm boundaries between them. Through commensality and offerings of food and clothing – in a complex network of gift-giving and charity rituals – those on top sought to secure the gratitude of those below. At the same time, because the food they ate and the clothes they wore were quite different, those on top reasserted their superiority in a society of orders. The same applied to etiquette (manners), which by the late fifteenth and throughout the early modern period became the true marker of class. A commoner might dress as a noble, or eat the same food, but alas! he or she would never have the breeding to use knife, fork and napkin as a noble did. Or so contemporaries thought. The kings of the diverse Spanish realms until the late fifteenth century, and of Spain afterwards, always made sure to dis-tinguish themselves in dress and in the choreography of eating from the great nobles. The great nobles expended considerable energy to distance them-selves from lesser nobles; the high bourgeoisie did the same to outrank the lower bourgeoisie; and so on down the social ladder. In the end, the social and economic changes sweeping Spain and Europe from 1500 onwards would slowly but inexorably transform many of the rules and ways of articulating power – only to be replaced by new ones, of course.

Notes

1. The information on the feasts of the Confraternity of All Saints is taken from Adeline Rucquoi, 'Alimentation des riches, alimentation des pauvres dans une ville castillane au XVe siècle', in *Manger et boire au moyen âge*, 2 vols (Nice, 1984), I: 297–312.

2. María Echániz Sans, 'La Alimentación de los pobres asistidos por la Pia Almoina de la catedral de Barcelona según el libro de cuentas de 1283–84', in *Alimentació i societat a la Catalunya medieval* (Barcelona, 1988), 173–261.

3. Keith Thomas, *Religion and the Decline of Magic* (London, 1971), ch. 1.

4. For a study of Castilian wills see my 'The Business of Salvation: Castilian Wills in the Late Middle Ages', in Donald J. Kagay and Theresa M. Vann (eds), *On the Social Origins of Medieval Institutions: Essays in Honor of Joseph F. O'Callaghan* (Leiden, 1998), 63–89. Much of the discussion that follows is drawn from this article. References and bibliography can be found there.

5. For Barcelona see Equip Broida, 'Els àpats funeraris segons els testaments vers al 1400', in *Alimentació i societat*, 263–9.

6. Fernand Braudel, *The Mediterranean and the Mediterranean World in the Age of Philip II*, trans. Siân Reynolds (New York, 1975), I: 240.

7. See G. Bullough, 'The Later History of Cockaigne', in *Festschrift Pro. Dr. Herbert Koziol* (Stuttgart, 1973), 22–35. Also Hilario Franco Jr, *Cocanha: a história de um país imaginário* (São Paulo, 1998).

8. Juan Ruiz, *Libro de buen amor*, 2nd edn (Valencia, 1960), 180–2, estrophes 959–71.

9. Ibid., 191–5, estrophes 1006–42.

10. Juan José García González, *Vida económica de los monasterios benedictinos en el siglo XIV* (Valladolid, 1972), 115–16. An edition of the 1338 accounts can be found on pp. 131ff.

11. *Desde Estella a Sevilla. Cuentas de un viaje (1352)*, ed. M. Sánchez Villar (Valencia, 1974).

12. Luis Villegas Díaz, 'Datos sobre alimentación y coste de la vida en Vitoria a mediados del siglo XIV (1369)', *Vitoria en la edad madia* (Vitoria, 1982), 779–92. For a broader view of eating in medieval and early modern Europe see B. Benassar and J. Goy, 'Contribution à l'histoire de la consommation alimentaire du XIVe au XIX siècle', *Annales, ESC*, 30 (1975): 402–30.

13. *Cortes de los antiguos reinos de León y Castilla*, 5 vols (Madrid, 1861–63), II: 16–18; sumptuary laws are discussed in José Damian González Arce, *Apariencia y poder: la legislación suntuaria castellana en los siglos XIII–XV* (Jaén, 1998), 187 et passim.

14. Angus MacKay, 'Don Fernando de Antequera y la Virgen Santa María', in *Homenaje al profesor Juan Torres Fontes* (Murcia, 1987), II: 953–54; González Arce, *Apariencia y poder*, 185.

15. This evidence is found in the *Hechos del condestable don Miguel Lucas de Iranzo. Crónica del siglo XV*, ed. J. de Mata Carriazo (Madrid, 1940) and summarized in my 'Elite and Popular Culture in Late Fifteenth-Century Castilian Festivals: The

Case of Jaén', in Barbara A. Hanawalt and Kathryn L. Reyerson (eds), *City and Spectacle in Medieval Europe* (Minneapolis, 1994), 296–318.

16. Hilario Casado Alonso, 'Le banquet de l'assemblée communale rurale en vieille Castille', *La sociabilité à la table: commensalité et convivialité à travers les âges* (Rouen, 1992), 201–8.

17. Francis Brumont, *Campo y campesinos de Castilla la Vieja en tiempos de Felipe II* (Madrid, 1984).

18. Ibid., 202–3.

19. Denis Menjot, 'Notes sur le marché de l'alimentation et la consommation alimentaire à Murcie à la fin du moyen âge', in *Manger et boire au moyen âge*, I: 199–210.

20. Norbert Elias, *The Civilizing Process*, 2 vols (New York, 1982), I: 60–88 for ritualization and ceremonial aspects of eating.

21. Jacques Revel et al., 'Forms of Privatization', in Roger Chartier (ed.), *A History of Private Life: Passions of the Renaissance*, in *A History of Private Life*, Philippe Aries and Georges Duby (general eds), 5 vols (Cambridge, MA, 1989), III: 167.

22. These distinctions had already been made, in connection with literary tropes, by Mikhail Bakhtin in his wonderful *Rabelais and His World* (Bloomington, IN, 1984).

23. See, for example, *Segunda partida*, Tit. V, ley ii ('how the king must eat and drink with measure'); Tit. VII, leyes iv–vii ('regulating the behaviour of the king's children and their eating, drinking, and clothing') in *Las siete partidas del sabio rey don Alonso el nono*, fascimile edn (Madrid, 1555), I: 11ff. Pagination is by *Partida*.

24. For Huizinga see the new edition of his *The Autumn of the Middle Ages*, trans. R.J. Payton and U. Mammitzsch (Chicago, 1996); Martín de Riquer, *Caballeros andantes españoles* (Madrid, 1967).

25. See Jeanne Allard, 'La naissance de l'etiquette: les règles de vie à la cour de Castille à la fin du Moyen Age', in Nilda Guglielmi and Adeline Rucquoi (eds), *El discurso político en la Edad Media* (Buenos Aires, 1995), 11–28. For etiquette in eating and dressing see Mark Girouard, *Life in the English Country House: A Social and Architectural History* (Harmondsworth, 1980), 22–6, 30–2, 47–52 et passim.

26. An English translation of *Lazarillo de Tormes*, together with a translation of Quevedo's picaresque novels *El buscón* (The Swindler), appears in *Two Spanish Picaresque Novels* (Harmondsworth, 1969, and in many reprints).

27. Miguel de Cervantes y Saavedra, *Don Quijote de la Mancha*, ed. Martín de Riquer, 2 vols (Barcelona, 1955), II, chs 19–21.

28. For the reading of clothing here and through the rest of the chapter, I follow Philip Hersch, Angus MacKay and Geraldine MacKendrick, 'The Semiology of Dress in Late Medieval and early Modern Spain', in *Le corps paré: ornaments et atours* (Nice, 1987).

29. See González Arce, *Apariencia y poder*, 80ff.

30. Ibid., 99–107.

31. One can think of similar developments throughout the late medieval world. Huizinga, *The Autumn of the Middle Ages*. Remember also the satirical *Letrilla* by Quevedo, quoted in an earlier chapter, bemoaning how wealth overthrows social distinctions.

32. Ruiz, 'Elite and Popular Culture', 309–10.

33. T.F. Ruiz, 'Festivités, couleurs, et symboles du pouvoir en Castille au XVe siècle. Les célébrations de mai 1428', *Annales, ESC*, 3 (1991): 521–46.

34. *Relaciones históricas de los siglos XVI y XVII*, ed. Francisco R. de Uhagón (Madrid, 1896), 'Relación VIII', 59.

35. Ibid., 'Relación 10', 65–94.

36. See the work of Carmen Bernis Madrazo, *Trajes y modas en la España de los Reyes Católicos*, 2 vols (Madrid, 1979); and her *Indumentaria medieval española* (Madrid, 1956).

Chapter 10

Religion, honour, sexuality and popular culture: the mentalities of everyday life

In the previous chapter, I focused on eating and dressing as signs of social difference. In this concluding chapter, I wish to turn to a series of interrelated topics that will illuminate the patterns of everyday life in late medieval and early modern Spain. I have chosen very deliberately to examine a few discrete topics: religion, honour (and its concomitant, shame), and sexuality. Not only are these themes grounded in the new social history, but they were of deep and abiding concern to contemporaries of the period. Literary works, religious and civic rituals (whether daily or seasonal), and governmental and Church edicts reveal a constant preoccupation with these matters. The ways in which each social stratum practised its faith, upheld its honour or failed to do so, and dealt with sexual issues served to distinguish one class from another. All these practices and beliefs formed part of a broader, overarching, and more elusive historical category: that of popular culture. In what has become a classical study, Peter Burke has depicted the popular culture of early modern Europe in broad magisterial strokes, but the same kind of analysis has yet to be done for Spain.[1] Here, I supply vignettes of everyday life, but the complex work of depicting popular culture and belief systems, what French historical anthropologists have called *mentalités*, remains to be done.

Religion and social orders

We have already seen (Chapters 5 and 6) how social orders joined in devotional services at the feasts of the Corpus Christi and in frightful but reaffirming *autos-de-fe*. Unlike most of the rest of Europe, where religion in the sixteenth century pitted Catholic against Protestant in fierce and unforgiving struggles, Spain presented, at least on the surface, a vision of unified orthodoxy. This is what James Casey has astutely described as 'the community of the faithful'.[2] Crypto-Jews and a large number of *Moriscos* were forced to practise their ancestral religion in great secret or in relative obscurity, but Spain on the whole escaped the bloody religious wars that plagued England, France, Germany and other parts of Europe throughout the early modern period. To most Spaniards, it did not matter that religious uniformity was

231

enforced by the policing of Inquisition and state; nor was the vast majority in the sixteenth century perturbed by the fact that religious concord carried a stiff price. But the regime of religious homogeneity brought not only heavy-handed censorship and state control; it was also partly responsible for Spain's being bypassed by the Scientific Revolution and the heady intellectual transformations that swept portions of western Europe in the wake of the Reformation and Copernicus's revolutionary hypothesis. Lacking the hind-sight and resources that the passing of centuries has given us, contemporary Spaniards could not have chosen to act differently. In 1530s and 1540s Iberia, the Reformation and many of the new bold theories about the physical world were thought to be enemies that had to be fought with every available ounce of energy. These cultural battles are for other histories, however; my concern here is the way in which religion in Spain served as a social bond and at the same time reinforced differences between social orders.

Late medieval and early modern men and women understood and practised their religion in ways that were quite different from our own modern under-standing and practices. In Spain and the rest of Europe, religious belief, ritual observances, and concerns about salvation and the afterlife formed an integral part of an individual's daily life. But even in this period, uniformity was hard to find. Religion in the late Middle Ages functioned, as religions always do, on two distinct planes. This sharp division occurred along social boundaries: at the top, the elites, whether ecclesiastical or secular, practised a religion that was closer to the original intentions of the Church; that is, their practice focused on theological and doctrinal truths, strict liturgical practices and ritual preciseness. Mostly in Castile, but in other parts of Spain as well, the church reforms of the Catholic Monarchs demanded a specific behaviour from the elites, a lifestyle closer to the ideal teachings of the Catholic Church in the late fifteenth century. Through these reforms (see Chapter 1), the Spanish Church dealt with many of the abuses (sexual mis-conduct, pluralism, excessive selling of indulgences) that were later denounced by Martin Luther and other reformers. In many respects, the Spanish Church was reformed *before* the Reformation.

The other religion was the religion of the people. Religious experiences among the masses consisted of complex accretions of local devotional practices, often unsanctioned by the Church hierarchy – what today we mis-guidedly might call superstition, but which for most people represented observances sanctified by time and praxis. This religion was deeply imbric-ated in the material world (the cult of images; the use of talismans; the ven-eration of saints as magicians) and borrowed from practices that predated Christianity and remained alive as local folklore. This is not to say that members of the dominant social orders did not also engage in this sort of 'popular' religion. Exceptions to this rule abound; on the whole, however, religious expression differed dramatically according to social filiation.

These two modes of experiencing and practising religion were further transformed by the Protestant Reformation and, later on, by the Catholic Reformation or Counter-Reformation. Even in Spain, where doctrinal orthodoxy was jealously defended, the Reformation had a tremendous impact. It forced the Spanish Church to reformulate its position *vis-à-vis* Protestant doctrinal claims. To the average Christian, the demands of religion and spirituality became even more challenging after the Council of Trent. In the 1560s, a series of Church councils held at Trent – the Spanish clergy played an important role in the final decisions of the Council – elaborated new theological positions, liturgical changes, and stricter forms of daily religious observances. These measures dramatically altered the life of Catholics throughout Europe, and throughout Spain and its maritime possessions. The Tridentine edicts (as the policies enacted by the Council are called) marked a turning point in the history of the Catholic Church. For our purpose, its social aspects in Spain are clear. After the 1570s, when reforms began to be implemented in Spain and elsewhere, both the Church and the state sought to eradicate popular forms of worship – the main devotional practices of the majority of the people – and to substitute them with a uniform and streamlined religion that was set and monitored from above. How, then, did religion work as a social bond? How did it work to distance those above from those below, especially after Trent?

Daily practices

On 12–14 August 1452, Johan de Ursua, a squire and master of the prince of Viana's hostel, dictated his last will and testament in Pamplona, the capital of the kingdom of Navarre – which was then ruled by a member of the Trastámara family who was at the same time king of the Crown of Aragon. There is nothing unusual about this will. It followed a tradition that, in Iberia, dated back to the twelfth century and that, through formulaic repetition, provided a set way of dealing with the impending end of one's life.

Like almost all testaments, the will began with Don Johan de Ursua commending his soul to 'Our Lord Jesus Christ, saviour and redemptor of the human lineage and to the glorious Virgin [Mary]'. Johan ordered his body to be buried at the Church of Saint Nicholas in Pamplona, in the same tomb as that of his mother-in-law, Maria Moça. Two days later, however, in an additional codicil, Johan changed his wishes and requested to be buried in the monastery of Saint Francis, in the tomb of his grandfather. He also established a chaplaincy that was to offer prayers for his soul and the souls of his relatives. Both the chaplaincy and his new burial place were provided with enough income from annuities to guarantee continuous prayers for his soul for many years to come.

These provisions comprised the formulaic introduction to his will and took up barely fifteen to twenty lines in an otherwise lengthy document. The rest of the will, more than five tightly printed pages in the published edition, is a hard-nosed settling of accounts with debtors and a shrewd attempt to convey his property to his family and friends. From the late twelfth century onwards throughout the Iberian peninsula and in the rest of the West, a dramatic shift took place in the elaboration of wills. Wills became, first and foremost, a means to control the distribution of property, to liquidate or redeem debts.[3] Deeply embedded in the materiality of the world, testaments were, above all, business transactions. At the same time, wills also serve as windows onto the transformed spirituality of the late Middle Ages and the early modern period. The clearly spelled-out contributions specified in the introductory lines of almost every will – the founding of philanthropies; the dispensing of donations to churches and monasteries – were, in essence, a bargaining for salvation or reduced time in Purgatory. That these provisions often represented a minuscule portion of the entire financial settlement – the lion's share being reserved for family and friends – did not alter the widespread, almost universal belief in the afterlife by *all* social classes, or the conviction that certain behaviour and actions were necessary to avert damnation. Especially for the middling sorts, salvation became a transaction, an opportunity to bargain for or purchase a desirable afterlife through post-humous masses, chaplaincies, candles in churches, the feeding and clothing of the poor. The latter, to be sure, could seldom afford to have a will drawn by an expensive notary; nor did they have sufficient property for it to matter whether or not they had a will. The poor negotiated for salvation in their own particular ways: by contrition, small offerings, and other such gestures. The pious manifestations in wills thus worked to mark one's standing within the community. In the centuries between 1400 and 1600, wills reflected a growing concern with the material world as well as the enduring hold of religion over all social groups. In their highly formulaic language, they ex-pressed the tangible requirements of social and religious sensibilities.[4]

Popular religion

Unlike other topics in Spanish social and cultural history, popular religion has received the attention of gifted scholars. The seminal work of William Christian, Jr. on diverse aspects of Spanish religiosity has set the standard for this area of enquiry. His influential book *Local Religion in Sixteenth-Century Spain* gives a vivid and expansive picture of peasant and city-dweller beliefs and practices in the sixteenth century, just before the Council of Trent's strong-armed edicts began to be implemented. The portrait Christian paints harkens back to the late Middle Ages. It was a world that drew on a complex religious heritage. In the world of peasants and other lower social groups, Christianity, magic and ancient non-Christian traditions merged, creating rich syncretistic traditions.[5]

In a close reading of Philip II's great survey of Spanish villages and towns (1578–80), Christian describes the religious culture and belief system of peasants in New Castile's countryside. Among the villagers of central Spain, community observances far outweighed individual practices. In crises such as plagues, droughts and frequent storms, villagers joined in vows to build shrines to saints believed to offer effective protection against agricultural catastrophes. Natural disasters drove villagers to elaborate devotions; unlike their bourgeois and noble counterparts, villagers acted communally. In some villages, peasants kept collective fasts and dispensed charity, the duty to feed a needy passer-by or village inhabitant rotating daily among households.[6] These actions by the community as a whole were then used to negotiate with patron saints or interceding holy figures for the material benefit of the village and its inhabitants. In this way, religion supplied yet another bulwark against a naturally, and politically, hostile environment.

Often, to be sure, these expiatory and placating rituals did not work. When in doubt about the efficacy of their religious practices or even as insurance, individual villagers and communities as a whole were not reluctant to turn to alternative practices. Travelling necromancers, cloud chasers, conjurers, healers, herb lore specialists and other shady characters trekked in substantial numbers throughout the peninsula and plied their trade among the urban lower social order. As such, they were no different from the palm readers, astrologers and purveyors of good luck talismans and crystals who exploit human foibles in today's developed world. In California, where I live, these vigorous and profitable activities are often intertwined with 'New Age' cults and millenarian spirituality. In late medieval and early modern Iberia, the Spanish Church often looked the other way on these competing rituals and, at least until Trent, regarded them as insignificant threats to its powerful hold on the lives of the lower social orders.

After Trent, most Spanish villages had their own churches, sacred relics, and an attending priest. As Christian has observed, the life of the village centred around the cult of 'specialized saints' (St Sebastian, St Roch), Marian cults, thaumaturgical crucifixes, and powerful relics. The annual procession in honour of the local saint, the ritual meals of the village's entire male-citizen population (see Chapter 9), and the activities of the brotherhoods – in villages large enough to have confraternities – gave a sense of security and protection.

Outside the village, peasants and labourers in towns often followed false prophets and charismatic figures of dubious orthodoxy who often wound up, together with their close followers, in front of the Inquisition. As we saw in Chapter 8, the *Encubierto* (the Hidden One) agitated the Valencian hinterland, joining the world of popular resistance with that of heterodox beliefs. The *Encubierto* was not alone. He was one among a host of visionaries treading the boundaries of heresy. Some, like Lucrecia, a character studied by Richard Kagan, could even gain a hearing at the royal court; others were ephemeral figures, barely making a dent in the popular consciousness.[7] A few of them were simply mad. The Inquisition, which was quite wise about these subtle distinctions, punished some of these prophets, ignored others, or placed them in the new places of confinement for the insane that were beginning to emerge in most of early modern Spain.[8]

Unlike in most of western Europe, there was no witch craze in Spain. The outbreaks of witch hysteria in the Basque region, or the isolated case of Magdalena de la Cruz in early sixteenth-century Córdoba, did not change the basic position of the Inquisitors: that the whole thing was sheer nonsense.[9] Thus, Spain was spared the collective and frenzied waves of violence – most of it targeting old women – that swept Europe after the late fifteenth century.

These brief descriptions, however, do not fully capture the way in which religious culture served as a seamless context to the everyday life of *all* social groups. This was a religion inherited from the central Middle Ages and deeply inscribed in popular consciousness. It revealed itself most vividly in such gestures as the making of the sign of the Cross at times of danger, when passing by a church, when witnessing a funeral. It entered everyday speech with such frequent salutations as 'if God wills', 'go with God', 'God (or the Virgin) protect you', 'let it be what God wishes'. Many of these greetings had a Muslim provenance, such as *Inshallah* (if God wills), and remain in use among the old in many parts of Spain and in Latin America, the great repository of late medieval and early modern archaic Castilian phrases and words. But the imprint of religion went beyond mere speech and gestures. Take, for example, the daily regimen of men aboard one of the King's galleons making the biannual crossing of the Atlantic. Sailors of the sixteenth and seventeenth centuries could not be accused of excessive religiosity or great spiritual sensibility. They were as rough a bunch as one could find in early modern Europe. Yet, their day began and ended with prayers. Carla Phillips has described their daily routine. It began at daybreak with the morning prayers: 'Blessed be the light, and the Holy True Cross; and the Lord of Truth, and the Holy Trinity: Blessed be the soul, and the Lord who rules it for us; Blessed be the day, and the Lord who sends it to us'. Next, the page on board who led prayers said 'a Pater Noster and an Ave Maria'; this was followed by yet another morning prayer specific to the ship and its crew. Every four-hour watch was marked by the turning of a half-hour sand clock and by a pious verse. Additional prayers came with dinner, and the evening closed with yet more prayers and a final blessing. This was the regular drill; holidays or perilous times called for a far greater output of ceremonies, prayers and rituals.[10] Among the poor and the prosperous, in the family bosom or in the public glare, life coursed within the bounds of such comforting routines. Birth, marriage and death, the great watersheds of the population's life cycle, even if not experienced as spiritual events, occurred within a weave of religious symbolism and ritual.

The religion of the middling sorts

Religious observances among merchants and patrician elites varied from individual to individual. Although participation in Corpus Christi processions, confraternity memberships, parish devotions and other forms of joint worship provided a strong communal element to the spiritual life of the middling sorts, status and education also opened a physical and mental space for private devotions. The will described at the beginning of this chapter was replicated countless times throughout late medieval and early modern Spain, often with far more pious resolutions. The mournful but formulaic declarations of piety and resignation in the face of death reveal not only a specific religious culture but also the changing attitudes of the middling sorts and the nobility toward a more heightened sense of mortality. This was evident not only in the elaborate dispositions to secure salvation that were discussed earlier, but in more fundamental attempts to conquer death by providing for the memorialization of one's life, family or lineage, and earthly deeds.

This phenomenon, which has been superbly analyzed by Philippe Ariès in two remarkable books, was widespread among the upper classes throughout western Europe in this period.[11] The dramatic shift in how the powerful thought of their own deaths, and sought to have themselves represented after death, was manifest in their exertions to have their names inscribed on tombs, and in their desire to have specific types of sculptures – including macabre representations of the dead as if still living – accompany their funerals and adorn their tombs. The emergence of new types of religiosity was deeply intertwined with the new attitudes towards death. What happened in other parts of Europe also took place in Spain. The new forms of individual spirituality, exemplified by the great popularity of Thomas à Kempis's *The Imitation of Christ*, became deeply integrated into bourgeois sensibilities. Along with the lachrymose and almost morbid types of religious observances (specific to the medieval world after the Black Death), they constituted a sea change in how the middling sorts conceived of their relationship to God, the afterlife, and the world to come.

In fifteenth-century Barcelona, the wills of rich merchants showed the same preoccupation with commending their souls to God as the Navarrese and Castilian testaments had shown. These wills also evinced the ownership of pious books, many of them dealing with the Eucharist; and they included donations aimed primarily at fostering material conditions – via the purchase of candles, lamps, vestments, and other such accoutrements – that would glorify and enhance the worship of the Host. The Eucharist was seen as the most secure and efficacious road to salvation, and frequent communion or, more likely, prayers and devotions to the Body of Christ became important spiritual practices for the well-to-do. Similarly, the cult of specific saints who were seen as personal intercessors became widespread among the elite. This was accompanied by pious readings – excerpts from the Old and New Testaments, commentaries on and exegeses of biblical texts, devotional works, the lives of Saints – which became part of the formation and lifestyle of merchants and other middling sorts in the fifteenth and sixteenth centuries.[12]

Let us remember the impact that reading the lives of the desert fathers had on Ignatius of Loyola (Chapter 3), and how romance readers, such as Catalan and Castilian merchants and even Teresa of Avila, could be turned to a pious life by reading the exemplary lives of saints. One type of reading was not incompatible with the other; together, they formed part of a rich and complex world in which religion and material culture were inextricably enmeshed. When Cervantes argued (or had his character Don Quixote argue) that 'religion was knight-errantry', he was expressing an idea that was deeply rooted in the daily life of the middling sorts and the nobility. Above all, this meant that individual lives and deeds were part of a cosmic and sacred order. The life of knight-errantry and service to others was a privilege (and burden), but it was a privilege (and burden) that illiterate peasants and poor men and women could not aspire to or have in Spain or elsewhere in Europe.

As for the rulers and the small elite at the top, the religiosity of Philip II was paradigmatic. He was a truly devout man, attentive to his spiritual obligations and the observance of rituals. This did not subordinate him to the Church or to the Pope. 'Religion', as Philip II is reputed to have said, was 'too serious a matter to be left to the Pope'.[13] And indeed religion did not prevent the king from making hard political choices. Nevertheless, those who have visited the Escorial monastery and royal palace (built by order of Philip II to celebrate a military victory against the Protestants) and have seen the austerity of his personal chambers and the small window from which he gazed on the continuous masses celebrated in the monastery's large church, know that they have entered a world very different from our own. It was a world in which religion dominated as an organic part of people's lives. But this was not so for everyone.

More than a decade ago, John Edwards, in a remarkable essay, described a group of mainly *Conversos* who were brought in front of the Inquisition and accused of 'Judaizing', and whose faith or lack thereof may have bordered on unbelief.[14] With this article, Edwards entered an old and acrimonious debate on whether there could be unbelievers or atheists in fifteenth- and sixteenth-century western Europe.[15] Lucien Febvre, discussing 'the religion of Rabelais', has argued that unbelief was not possible within the intellectual context of the age. Despite Febvre's opinions, Edwards's evidence is particularly persuasive. Unbelievers, as opposed to blasphemers and heretics, could be found in late medieval and early modern Spain, especially among those who had ceased to be Jews but did not become fully Christian. From this milieu of Jewish exiles and *Conversos* emerged such thinkers as Baruch Spinoza, whose uncompromising vision of the world lit the intellectual life of seventeenth-century Europe and challenged established orthodoxies.

Honour and sexuality

Questions of honour, and of its counterpart, shame, became cultural touchstones in late medieval and early modern Spain. Although honour and shame are two different things – there is a great deal of recent scholarship about the differences between the two[16] – the intersection of these categories with sexuality has long been a strong feature of popular culture. The honourable life was a goal to which most Spaniards aspired. The absence of honour, or the breach of honour, implied shame; in early modern Europe and in Spain in particular, there was nothing more shameful than sexual dishonour. Above all, this was brought on by women's sexual transgressions, which were thought to stain the reputation of fathers, brothers, husbands, family and the entire community. These sexual offences could be voluntary or involuntary, but the results were more or less the same. Whether women engaged in transgressive behaviour or were victims of male predatory practices – rape, seduction, kidnapping, or mere slander – they were expected to pay the price demanded by strict codes of honour. Banishment or revenge, often the killing of the seducer and the seduced, followed swiftly upon dishonour. The family's honour could not be restored until these actions had been carried out. This should not surprise us. The systematic rape of Muslim women in Bosnia and Kosovo in recent years was not only a punitive policy against a religious 'other'; it was also an attack on the masculinity and sense of honour of the enemy's leadership. Women were raped and then compelled to hide their shame from their own families; otherwise they would have been shunned by their communities, despite their innocence. In this way, they were doubly punished by the codes of honour and shame that have held western society and other societies in the world in their grip from time immemorial, particularly on both shores of the Mediterranean. The scholarly agenda for the study of this topic was set almost forty years ago in a seminal collection of essays edited by J.G. Peristiany and, above all, in the work of Pitt-Rivers. Often using an anthropological perspective that was quite novel in the 1960s, these scholars explored the ways in which honour and shame were articulated in the Mediterranean basin. I do not wish to travel along this well-trodden path; instead, I would like to focus on a series of vignettes and literary tropes that will elucidate the way in which the interlacing of honour, sexual violence and shame created social meaning.

Another category should be noted here, even if in passing. I refer to verbal abuses, curses, expletives, and similarly aggressive verbal exchanges. Many of these expressions have entered the discourse of every culture in the world. Verbal attacks served often, though not always, as a prelude to physical contestation and, like today, were highly charged with sexual innuendo. Most often they cast doubt on the honour of mothers, sisters or wives. We are all familiar with these expressions; some of them have become part of daily speech and at times are even used as a sort of shorthand for colloquial exchanges among friends. Billingsgate, references to lower bodily parts and bowel functions (what Bakhtin has described as 'the bodily lower stratum'), had its roots in the rich and open culture of the late Middle Ages. It was the language of carnival and *charivaris*,[17] but it was also the language of individual offence and dishonour. All social classes were well versed in this language of verbal abuses. But after the Reformation and the Council of Trent, roughly by the end of the sixteenth century, the upper social orders began to regard these forms of speech as vulgar and to adopt a highly formulaic code of honour, of which the duel was its ultimate physical expression.

Another type of attack on honour that was widely practised in late medieval and early modern Europe was mutilation. This was first and foremost sexual mutilation, the most extreme form of dishonour; and it was practised at all levels of society. Factional struggles in Italian communes often led to the defacement and mutilation of vanquished opponents.[18] Cutting off the enemy's genitals and stuffing them into the victim's mouth was, and in some places remains, a common and savage symbol of one man's superiority over another, and of the vanquished family's shame. Raping, dismembering and killing the enemies' wives, daughters and sisters was not uncommon either. In Chapter 7, we have seen how Lupercio Latrás's troops, in their attack on Pina, mutilated the *Moriscos*, abducting and raping their women. The *Moriscos* paid back in kind. The war of the Alpujarras was particularly vicious. Those convicted of sodomy were subsequently mutilated, usually by the severing of their genitals. These bloodthirsty scenarios were deeply rooted in fierce social antagonisms, in attitudes of intolerance toward those thought to deviate from the norm, in age-old notions of honour and shame.

The culture of honour

In Spain, the culture of honour owed much to codes of behaviour that were formulated by courtly romances throughout most of western Europe in the twelfth and later centuries. In its early stages, courtly culture (the culture of the court) was restricted to the warrior nobility. In fact, the very concept of nobility emerged out of a conflation of warriors' monopoly of arms, twelfth-century literary models, and economic benefits derived from claims to superior social status. The enduring strength of these cultural models is quite remarkable. They remain deeply resonant to the present day and have become the staple of Hollywood mega-hits, such as for example the *Star Wars* saga.[19]

Throughout the thirteenth and fourteenth centuries, a heightened notion of honour became an integral component of chronicles and literary works.

As has been seen earlier, some attacked the nobleman's lack of honour, while others, such as Jorge Manrique, sought to explain what the truly honourable life was like. Castile and the Crown of Aragon became hotbeds of fifteenth-century romance, of heroic displays and competitions for honours. Fervently produced romances created a glossy image of the chivalrous, honour-driven life; and the actual deeds of knights in joust, in combat, embellished literary accounts. Martín de Riquer, in his enchanting *Caballeros andantes españoles* (*Spanish Knights-Errant*), paints a vivid picture of the circularity between literary artifice and historical reality. He shows how closely romances imitated life, and life imitated fiction.[20] One such example is Suero de Quiñones's fantastic *pas d'armes* at a crossing over the Orbigo river near the city of León. Known as the *passo honroso*, Suero and his companions held a bridge on the pilgrimage road to Compostela against all comers from 10 July to 9 August 1434; a notary, Pedro Rodríguez de Lena, wrote a fairly faithful account of who challenged whom, how many times they fought, and what the outcomes were.[21] Suero's exploits were aimed at obtaining release from love's 'imprisonment'. Every Thursday, he wore an iron collar around his neck as a sign of his captivity to an unnamed lady. But the excesses of his *passo honroso* were, as the name indicates, an exalted expression of his own sense of honour. At the *pas d'armes* at the Orbigo river, Suero also upheld the honour and political prestige of his master, Alvaro de Luna, testing himself – not always to his advantage – against a rough and redoubtable group of Valencian knights and other passers-by. Those who refused to fight were required to relinquish a spur, a glove of their lady, or another such personal item as a token to be redeemed by combat at a future date, or as a sign of unwillingness to abide by the codes of honour and chivalry. In this culture, as is the case today, the refusal to fight in the presence of one's lady essentially meant being dishonoured.

The most revealing connection between fiction and reality, and between honour and sexual outrage, can be seen in the life of Johanot Martorell, the Valencian writer and author of the great and influential romance *Tirant lo Blanch*. Born in 1413 or 1414, Martorell lived intensely the life he described. He engaged in battles, fought duels, and based his fictional accounts on events in his own life. On 12 May 1437, he challenged his cousin, Johan de Monpalau, to a combat to death. Martorell accused his cousin of seducing his sister Damiata with offers of marriage, of dishonouring and then refusing to marry her. Monpalau denied having given his word to marry (but not the act of seduction itself), and accepted the challenge. Through a long exchange of letters – letters filled with great sarcasm and literary artifice that allow us to follow the development of this contest – the two opponents sought to establish the place, time and terms of their armed encounter. Martorell travelled to England, where, protected by the English king, Henry VI, he called on Monpalau to come and meet him. In the end, the duel did not take place, but Johan de Monpalau was forced to pay 4,000 florins (a very substantial amount) to Damiata. In 1462, years after these events, Damiata was a very rich – but still single – woman.[22]

This event from the author's life was echoed not only in Martorell's novel, but in almost all romances of the fifteenth century. The topic of the woman deceived by a false promise of marriage, the subsequent dishonour and need for revenge, makes for some of the most delightful stories in Golden Age literature. In Cervantes's *Don Quixote*, which is both the greatest of all anti-romance novels and the greatest of all medieval or early modern romances, a significant change has taken place. In the works of Cervantes, Calderón de la Barca, and other novelists and playwrights, questions of honour, reneged promises of marriage, seduction, shame and revenge bear on all members of society. Although the typical scenario is that of the noble or wealthy seducer dishonouring a rich farmer's daughter, the expectations of honour or, at least, the rules of compensation are the same across the social spectrum. One of the best tales in *Don Quixote*, the story of Dorotea, concerns two socially unequal romantic partners who are nonetheless bound together by seduction and honour. This is also the case of Rosaura in Calderón's superb play *Life is a Dream.*

Honour, one could say, was the dominant literary theme in late medieval and early modern Spain; and, in Iberian society, it could be articulated in harsh and uncompromising ways. How this affected relations between husbands and wives and shaped the terms of social exchange between men and women is not difficult to imagine. A remarkable number of plays – too numerous and popular to be dismissed as mere exercises in artistic licence – focused on marital relations and the inexorable demands of the honour code. A woman suspected of dishonouring her husband was to be put to death, even though she may have been innocent. The appearance of infidelity, even rumours of infidelity, brought the same harsh treatment. In Calderón's *El médico de su honra*, the author tells the story of a doctor who kills his beloved wife, although he knows she is innocent, because of the appearance of a liaison with a social superior. The title suggests that dishonour can be surgically 'cured' by immolating those who have, or appear to have, committed a dishonourable act. Calderón's harsh treatment of the topic disclosed the nefarious consequences of extreme jealousy and unrelenting codes of honour, but it also raised important social questions: what was a man to do when his wife was sexually compromised by a social superior? How was one to escape the dictates of socially ingrained honour codes? There were no simple answers, to be sure; but punishment often fell on the weakest link in the chain of dishonour: women. To escape the demands of the honour code was practically impossible; to do so at all levels of society meant to lose social standing, to lose face.

The counterpart to the question of honour in individual relations was the theme of national honour or its equivalents, national prestige and reputation. Sir John H. Elliott's great book *The Count-Duke of Olivares* devotes many pages to the issue of reputation and the way in which Olivares's reforms sought to restore Spain's 'reputation', or honour, among European nations. These policies were of course also driven by political necessity, but underlying his ultimately failed reforms was a dogged attempt to recover Spanish pre-eminence and honour, even at the risk of catastrophic cost. All social groups, but mostly those below, paid dearly, with their money and lives, for these endless quests for honour and glory.[23]

One ought to be a bit cautious about playwrights and novelists. Their aims were not always what they seemed to be on the surface. Clearly, most plays and novels centred on plots of honour, revenge, and the tragic (or, more rarely, the joyful) restoration of honour; but a very different concept of honour informed the literary texts of Manrique, Cervantes and other authors. Many of these writers no longer defined honour in terms of sexually correct conduct, racial filiation ('purity of blood'), or patriotism. 'True honour' emerges from these works as the outcome of individual moral integrity and right behaviour.[24] This new concept of honour now extended to all social groups.

Sexuality

Sexuality, or the history of sex, is not an easy topic.[25] On the one hand, there is the day-to-day private history of sexual relations, the history of the bedroom, that has not yet fully yielded its secrets to the historian. On the other hand, there is the public history of sex: the scandalous affairs, the public indiscretions, sex as a commodity and means of exchange. Of the former, there is little to say, except to offer the occasional vignette or anecdote that moves the private event into the public realm. Moreover, the history of the bedroom admits a multitude of variations, making it almost impossible to provide an overall synthesis. I have already touched on some of the aspects of 'public sexuality' in Chapter 4, while discussing prostitution as a form of marginality. Against the inquisitorial and ecclesiastical discourse of sexuality that sought to regulate and limit sexual relations between adults, other discourses articulated positions on sexuality that differed markedly from those advanced by the authorities.[26] A few examples will suffice.

In an anonymous work, *La carajicomedia* (written by a cleric in 1510), the author presents a long roster of prostitutes with their actual names or nicknames, describing their sexual characteristics and proclivities. Its frank and salty language walks a perilous line between pornography and satire. The text, most of it focused on female sexual organs, depicts women not only as objects of pleasure, but as insatiable pleasure seekers themselves. Unlike northern European books such as the *Malleus maleficarum* (*The Hammer of Witches*), in which women are shown to be susceptible to the devil's snares because of their sexual passion, promiscuity and weakness, in *La carajicomedia* the devil is absent and there is nothing diabolical about desire. In fact, one of the prostitutes, Mariblanca, a resident of Salamanca, is represented – in an almost blasphemous passage – as praying to the crucifix on top of her bed. After a particularly satisfying sexual encounter with one of her clients (a student), she begs of Christ 'never to deprive [her] of a man like that'. The work is a panegyric on women's – prostitutes' – sexual desires and on the naturalness of carnal relations. A male construction of female desire – for prostitution was often a brutal and cold exchange of sex for money – *La carajicomedia* is a window on male fantasies, on the fluid world of sexuality. The work gives insight into the social (and sexual) encounters among different classes; in it, the bed too becomes a site for social and economic exchange, one in which women become commodities. One prostitute has students for clients, another has merchants; and several of them serve ecclesiastics exclusively. The anonymous author writes that he visited and 'knew' (meaning, carnally) one of the prostitutes he describes in his guide, Isabel de Torres, a prostitute in Valladolid. That the author was himself a cleric points to the gulf that existed between official policy, or normative morality, and praxis.[27]

In his *La lozana andaluza* (1528), another cleric, a disaffected *Converso* named Francisco Delicado, offers a perspective on the complex world of Jews, *Conversos*, and the demi-monde of early modern Spanish neighbourhoods in Rome. *La lozana andaluza* is an important literary work (whereas *La carajicomedia* is not), but *La lozana* also includes an extensive taxonomy of prostitutes, procuresses, pimps, and other marginal and criminal types. A frank portraitist of sexual life, Delicado does not condemn any of these activities, nor does he find them abnormal. He describes them as they are.[28] In *La lozana*, as in works of the period ranging from *La Celestina* to Cervantes's *Entremeses*, desire takes a forceful stand against the rigid morality of Church and state. In many respects, two distinct worlds existed side by side. One, bound by codes of honour and shame, by theological formulations and governmental ordinances, sought to rein in sexuality. The other pushed to the extreme the official boundaries of sexual practices and human desire. The former, knowing it was impossible to interdict erotic desire, sought to regulate it (and the profit it generated) through public houses of prostitution; the latter found ways to subvert the regulatory nature of official discourse. In the end, sex proved a force as much or far more subversive than armed resistance; for it could never be fully defeated or eliminated. But, in Spain, the authorities' attitudes towards irregular passions were not puritanical. They may have condemned them; but as long as they could keep them in check, they tolerated their existence.

Following Don Quixote around Spain

In previous chapters, I have drawn repeatedly on *Don Quixote* to clarify specific aspects of Spain's social history. Novels are not like archival records; nor do they have the proximity to actual events that primary sources, the necessary tools of monographic literature, have. Fictional works nonetheless render powerful insights into the mental world of a remote past. The vignettes and sketches that move the narrative are based on a grasp of real life that can seldom be obtained from standard historical sources.[29]

I propose, in these last pages, to view late medieval and early modern Spain through the lens of fiction and to follow Don Quixote and his faithful squire, Sancho, for at least a portion of their journey through the peninsula. What *Don Quixote*'s characters say is often as important as what they do. Their dialogue is a thoughtful discussion of Spain's problems and sometimes a courageous challenge to the status quo and social inequality.

The golden age of equality

Very early in their joint adventure, Don Quixote and Sancho come upon a group of goat-herders who welcome the knight-errant and his servant and invite them to partake of their humble meal.[30] This episode, similar to many others, reveals the barrenness of New Castile's countryside and its demographic poverty. Wherever they travel, Don Quixote and Sancho do so through mostly rugged and deserted lands. Their loneliness is broken by occasional encounters with other wanderers, a stay in a solitary inn, a meeting with sheep-herders and their flocks. In this instance, the goat-herders share with them their meagre fare: a stew of salted goat meat, plenty of hazelnuts, and a very hard piece of cheese. Sitting on goat skins, around the paraphernalia of their repast, the goat-herders entreat Don Quixote to take the place of honour. In a few lines, the author unveils the diet of the poor: goat meat and little else. His description corroborates some of the evidence we encountered in the previous chapter, on the diet of poor peasants. It also contrasts vividly with the lavish feast Camacho will give later in the novel (see Chapter 9). The social differences between rich and poor farmers are extreme indeed; and the two protagonists, Don Quixote and Sancho Panza, serve as bridges between the two worlds.

Language also signals social difference. Cervantes observes the goat-herders' coarse discourse and shows how, as Don Quixote embarks on one of his typically baroque disquisitions on knighthood, the goat-herders understand nothing. In this episode, as in the rest of the book, the language spoken by the educated is barely comprehensible to the majority of the people. They speak the same Castilian, but the abstract concepts Don Quixote employs – concepts that stem from books of chivalry and other written texts – are beyond the goat-herders' grasp. A few of the characters from the lower social orders understand and even speak the same language – Dorotea, the prosperous farmers attending Camacho's feast, and others – but they are clearly literary creations. The great divide separating the haves from the have-nots applies not only to the realm of food, attire, housing and life expectations; it also touches on the fundamental area of language. Throughout the novel, the common folk do not understand what Don Quixote says or means. Sancho himself often draws a blank. Their response to the alien words of the educated is often to beat Don Quixote to a pulp. Violence, as I argued in Chapters 7 and 8, also functioned as a discourse.

The preceding scenario, then, is the setting for one of the most extraordinary statements in this extraordinary book. After forcing Sancho to sit next to him, by appealing to the egalitarian principles of the chivalric code, Don Quixote – who (in an almost Proustian moment) goes into reveries at the sight of the hazelnuts – launches into a lyrical evocation of the Golden Age: when the world was still young, food was plentiful and could be had without work, and there was no crime or fear. This was the blessed age before humans learned the words 'yours and mine'. Don Quixote's idealized description of the Golden Age resonated throughout most of the late Middle Ages and the early modern period. This vision of equality for all men – Don Quixote addresses his audience as 'my brothers' – appears, in one form or another, in Manrique's poetry, in Fernando de Rojas's bitter denunciations, and in pastoral literature. Pronouncements of this kind were also made by the *Germanías*'s most radical leaders. While poking fun at Don Quixote's lofty ideals and learned references, Cervantes pierced the Spanish constructs of race, social order, and wealth-based distinction that pulled men and women apart into separate categories. Following Plato and Thomas More, Cervantes saw property as the culprit; fittingly, in the new Arcadia conjured by Don Quixote, imaginary sheep-herders (the learned heroes of pastoral poetry) withdraw from the cities, with their bustling commercial life and money economy, and return to the simplicity of the wild, where the words 'yours and mine' are no longer uttered.[31]

Entertainment, the village and the road

David Vassberg, in a wonderful book already cited, views Spanish medieval and early modern villages not as isolated outposts of peasant life but as places that were deeply engaged in the world around them.[32] Passers-by, travelling Gypsies, recruitment officers, *Morisco* merchants, and others brought the outside world to the village; the peasants themselves travelled to nearby villages or distant towns, and in some cases to faraway worlds: to America or, often, as Spanish troops, to areas all over western Europe. In *Don Quixote*, the village, and the roads linking it to the larger world, bursts with life. In their travels, Don Quixote and Sancho meet companies of actors, a puppeteer, and other entertainers. These itinerant companies follow a circuit from village to village, providing respite from the backbreaking toil of the farm. In one adventure, Don Quixote and Sancho become acquainted with Master

Andrés, a famous puppeteer who, along with a well-trained monkey, goes from town to town enrapturing as well as deceiving his audience. At an inn, Master Andrés puts on a performance for the guests: a combination of puppet show and scam, in which he pretends that the monkey speaks to him, telling him about the past of those in the audience. The scam part, playing on the naivety of the country folk, was part and parcel of the fantasy and chicanery of the road-show. This genre, which survives to our day, walked a fine line between entertainment and crime. In this particular instance, the puppeteer re-enacts the romance of Don Gaiferos and Lady Melisandra.[33] Close to the end of the sixteenth century, fifteenth-century romances still supplied the bulk of entertainment in the Spanish countryside. Travelling shows brought the urban world to the countryside and education to the illiterate. Cervantes tells us that Sancho barely knew how to sign his name – a mark of accomplishment among a vast rural population incapable of reading and writing. But this does not mean at all that villagers were uneducated. The commerce between high and low culture, between city and countryside, depended largely on these companies of actors. They served as intermediaries between one world and another, between different social orders and cultures. In the course of its transmission, however, the romance culture of the elite was inevitably transformed. Watching the performance, Don Quixote becomes so incensed at the liberties the puppeteer has taken with the story and the prurient slant he has given it that he wrecks the performance. But the peasants do not know or care what the fuss is about. Thus, the elite culture was continually remade and adapted to suit peasant tastes and needs.

Theatrical companies also brought serious plays to the hinterland. On the road, Don Quixote and Sancho meet a group of actors who rush from one village to another to put on yet another performance, probably of one of Lope de Vega's religious plays, *Las cortes de la muerte* (*The Courts of Death*).[34] The actors have so little time between performances that they take to the road still dressed in their costumes. How much of the play's sophisticated language or moral teachings – as opposed to the puppet-show's mostly visual representations – the peasants understood is hard to tell. The depictions of death, redemption and punishment were after all re-enactments of the sermons peasants heard in the village church, the rhetoric of itinerant friars (another powerful source of entertainment), and of the engravings they saw in books owned by the village *hidalgo*, priest, or well-to-do farmer who could afford and, more important, read such literature. Forms of speech may have widened the abyss between the social orders, but in Don Quixote's and Sancho's fictional village, the barber, the priest, and the university-trained son of a rich villager are able to engage in a sophisticated literary discussion and actually own quite a number of books.

Books and plays, alas, were not the only forms of entertainment in the village. Gambling houses, many of them noble-owned and a vital source of income for the village lord, proliferated in the Spanish countryside.[35] Like the church and the theatre, they constituted venues for popular amusement. To these, one must add the houses of prostitution in large villages, and the itinerant or unregulated prostitutes in small ones. Theatre, gambling, prostitution, and the rough ball games that fostered great rivalry between neighbouring villages were, in many respects, as much a part of village life as the church.

Villages and roads were, perhaps for this reason, highly policed. As we follow Don Quixote and Sancho to the village of the Toboso, Dulcinea's home, we learn that the priest keeps a list of all of the town's citizens.[36] Throughout Castile, this was an important form of control over the community's fiscal and religious life. In one of their earlier escapades, our heroes rested at an inn where the innkeeper was a member of the Santa Hermandad, a 'police' force organized by the Catholic Monarchs and in charge of fighting crime in the countryside.[37] Ready to take arms at the first sign of disturbance or crime, the Santa Hermandad hovers over the novel's first volume as a menacing presence. When Don Quixote frees a convoy of prisoners destined for the royal galleys, fear of the Santa Hermandad sends him and Sancho fleeing to the safety of nearby mountains.

Conclusion

Through the telling of a series of vignettes, I have sought to introduce the reader to the mental world of Spain's social orders. Religion, which played a significant role in the life of all Spaniards, served both as social bond and as marker of social difference. The peasant's practice and understanding of his or her faith differed considerably from the observances and beliefs of a merchant or nobleman. Gender also affected religious practices. Women related to God and observed the rituals of religion in ways that differed greatly from those of men. But religion does not admit broad generalizations; nor was religion stagnant in early modern Spain. Two important watersheds brought about significant changes in observance and liturgy: the Catholic Monarchs' religious reforms in the late fifteenth century, and the Council of Trent in the 1560s. Both movements, however, took time to filter down to the population at large, especially to the lower orders. Reform met with the usual resistance and inertia that mark traditional practices and long-held beliefs.

From religion we turned to considerations of honour and sexuality. In Spain, questions of honour and sexuality, categories that are often intertwined, pertained to all levels of society. Although each social class had different ways of dealing with dishonour, retribution was always expected. Sexuality, or what early modern people regarded as irregular sex, worked as a counter-discourse to the ecclesiastical and secular policing of sexual behaviour. On the other side of strict religious observance and pious dictums were the explicit texts on pleasure and carnality's enduring power. Finally, using Cervantes's *Don Quixote* as our guide, we briefly explored the mental and physical world of Spain's countryside at the end of the sixteenth century. Filled with contradictions, village and city were worlds far more complex and elusive than the formulation of social orders, with which this book began, would lead us to believe.

Notes

1. See Peter Burke, *Popular Culture in Early Modern Europe* (Aldershot, 1988).
2. James Casey, *Early Modern Spain: A Social History* (London, 1999), ch. 10.
3. See Teofilo F. Ruiz, *From Heaven to Earth: The Reordering of Late Medieval Castilian Society* (forthcoming).
4. See Carlos Eire, *From Madrid to Purgatory: The Art and Craft of Dying in Sixteenth-Century Spain* (New York, 1995); also María del Carmen Carlé, *Una sociedad del siglo XV: los castellanos en sus testamentos* (Buenos Aires, 1993).
5. See William A. Christian, Jr., *Local Religion in Sixteenth-Century Spain* (Princeton, 1981); also his *Apparitions in Late Medieval and Renaissance Spain* (Princeton, 1981). For late medieval syncretism see Carlo Ginzburg, *The Night Battles: Witchcraft and Agrarian Cults in the Sixteenth and Seventeenth Centuries* (Baltimore, 1992).
6. See Ruth Behar, *Santa María del Monte: The Presence of the Past in a Spanish Village* (Princeton, 1986).
7. Richard L. Kagan, *Lucrecia's Dreams: Politics and Prophecy in Sixteenth-Century Spain* (Berkeley, 1990). Sara Nalle has been at work on a study of an obscure visionary in southern Castile. In her forthcoming case study, the subject treads a very fine line between religious fervour and madness.
8. Jeronimus Munzer, who travelled in Spain in the late fifteenth century, reported seeing an insane asylum in Valencia. In Zaragoza, during Philip II's visit to the city, the *mentecatos* (the mentally impaired), who marched in one of the processions in honour of the king, lived in a house supported by public funds. See *Viajes de extranjeros por España y Portugal*, ed. José García Mercadal, 3 vols (Madrid, 1952), I: 343. See also Chapter 6. Munzer wrote of having seen a *Converso* held in a cage, completely naked.
9. See Julio Caro Baroja, *The World of the Witches*, trans. O.N.V. Glendinning (Chicago, 1965), 143–98. For Magdalena de la Cruz, a nun who confessed voluntarily to dealings with the Devil, a contemporary account of her case is found in *Relaciones históricas de los siglos XVI y XVII*, ed. F.R. de Uhagón (Madrid, 1896), 'Relación III', 28–33.
10. Carla R. Phillips, *Six Galleons for the King of Spain: Imperial Defense in the Early Seventeenth Century* (Baltimore, 1986), 159–60.
11. Philippe Ariès, *Western Attitudes Towards Death from the Middle Ages to the Present*, trans. Patricia M. Ranum (Baltimore, 1974), 1–54; and his *The Hour of Our Death*, trans. H. Weaver (New York, 1982).
12. The spiritual life and concerns of Barcelona's mercantile elite have been studied by Jaume Aurell and Alfons Puigarnau, *La cultura del mercader en la Barcelona del*

siglo XV (Barcelona, 1998), 195–326. See also Jaume Aurell, *Els mercaders catalans al Quatre-cents: mutació de valors i procés d'aristocratitzció a Barcelona (1370–1470)* (Lleida, 1996).

13. Two new studies of Philip II discuss his religion and practical attitude towards politics. See Geoffrey Parker, *The Grand Strategy of Philip II* (New Haven, 1998); Henry Kamen, *Philip of Spain* (New Haven, 1997). For this idea see Sir John H. Elliott, *Imperial Spain, 1469–1716* (New York, 1964), 223.

14. John Edwards, 'Religious Faith and Doubt in Late Medieval Spain: Soria *circa* 1450–1500', *Past & Present*, 120 (1988): 3–25.

15. Lucien Febvre, *The Problem of Unbelief in the Sixteenth Century: The Religion of Rabelais*, trans. B. Gottlieb (Cambridge, MA, 1982), 243–353.

16. The literature on the subject of honour and shame is extensive indeed. The classical formulations of these two concepts in the Mediterranean basin appeared in J.G. Peristiany (ed.), *Honour and Shame: The Values of Mediterranean Society* (Chicago, 1966), and, above all, in Julian Pitt-Rivers, *The Fate of Shechem, or the Politics of Sex: Essays in the Anthropology of the Mediterranean* (Cambridge, 1977). Several recent works have questioned the uniformity of concepts of honour and shame throughout the Mediterranean world. See Michael Herzfeld, 'Honour and Shame: Problems in Comparative Anthropology', *Man*, 15 (1980): 339–51; David D. Gilmore (ed.), *Honour and Shame and the Unity of the Mediterranean* (Washington, 1987).

17. See Mikhail Bakhtin, *Rabelais and His World*, trans. Hélène Iswolsky (Bloomington, IN, 1984), 368–436.

18. See Richard Trexler, *Public Life in Renaissance Florence* (New York, 1980); Edward Muir, *Civic Ritual in Renaissance Venice* (Princeton, 1981).

19. See the survival of these ideas in nineteenth-century England in Mark Girouard, *The Return of Camelot: Chivalry and the English Gentleman* (New Haven, 1981).

20. Martín de Riquer, *Caballeros andantes españoles* (Madrid, 1967), 9–14 and 168–70 et passim.

21. Ibid., 52–8. The entire episode is described in detail by an eyewitness, the notary, Pedro (Pero) Rodríguez de Lena, *El passo honroso de Suero de Quiñones* (Madrid, 1977).

22. De Riquer, *Caballeros*, 41–4. *Tirant lo Blanch* was one of Don Quixote's favourite books in Cervantes's fantastic tale. The book was printed late in the fifteenth century, carried to America by the conquistadors, and translated into many languages soon afterwards.

23. John H. Elliott, *The Count-Duke of Olivares: The Statesman in an Age of Decline* (New Haven, 1986), 131–320, 499–673.

24. Diego Marín and Angel del Río, *Breve historia de la literatura española* (New York, 1966), 126.

25. The most profound reflection on the history of sexuality is Michel Foucault, *The History of Sexuality*, trans. Robert Hurley, 3 vols (New York, 1988).

26. Most of this discussion is informed by Abigail Dyer's unpublished doctoral dissertation, 'Heresy and Dishonor: Sexual Crimes before the Courts of Early Modern Spain', Columbia University, 2000. See also Alain Saint-Saens (ed.), *Sex and Love in Early Modern Spain* (New York, 1995).

27. A partial text of *La carajicomedia* can be found in Francisco Núñez Roldán, *Mujeres públicas: historia de la prostitución en España* (Madrid, 1995), 99–100, and glossed by Angel Luis Molina Molina, *Mujeres públicas, mujeres secretas: la prostitución y su mundo: siglos XIII–XVII* (Murcia, 1998), 168–9.
28. Francisco Delicado, *La lozana andaluza*, ed. Bruno Daminiani (Madrid, 1984).
29. See, for example, Natalie Z. Davis, *Fiction in the Archives: Pardon Tales and Their Tellers* (Oxford, 1987).
30. Miguel de Cervantes y Saavedra, *Don Quijote de la Mancha*, ed. Martín de Riquer, 2 vols (Barcelona, 1955), I, ch. 11.
31. In *Don Quixote* there are several pastoral stories, and the protagonist entertains the idea of abandoning the life of a knight to live in the woods as a sheep herder. The great opening to the Golden Age of Spanish Literature was, itself, Garcilaso de la Vega's pastoral poem, *La galatea.*
32. David Vassberg, *The Village and the Outside World in Golden Age Castile: Mobility and Migration in Everyday Rural Life* (Cambridge, 1996), 1–11.
33. *Don Quixote*, II, chs 25 and 26.
34. Ibid., II, ch. 11.
35. Ibid., II, ch. 49.
36. Ibid., II, ch. 9.
37. Ibid., I, ch. 45.

Conclusion

Ambrose Paré, a sixteenth-century French physician, author, and reputed magician, told a story about Charles I (Charles V of Germany), king of Spain and emperor of the Holy Roman Empire. At the siege of Metz in 1552, Paré quotes Charles I as having asked whether the Spanish troops, dying in appalling numbers outside the walls of the besieged city, were noble or not. When told by his courtiers that they were poor men, that is, men of low social standing, the emperor is reported to have answered that their loss was then of no interest; for if they had been 'good' men (meaning here: men of good sense and good breeding), they would not have served him for a salary of six pounds.[1]

In time, the siege of Metz became a frightful economic and social burden on the Spanish monarchy. Just a few years afterwards, Charles had to declare bankruptcy, signalling the financial collapse of Spain and his imperial dreams. Most of the soldiers who died at Metz – far away from their homes and families – were Castilian peasants. They were the same men who had fought in the wars of Granada, Italy, Germany, the Low Countries, North Africa, the Valley of Mexico, Peru, and in other imperial military ventures. Some of them had volunteered, seeking to escape the confines of their villages; others had sought adventure and profit. It must be said that many indeed found such opportunities in the New World. Yet the vast majority were unwilling recruits in an army that demanded endless sacrifices, as Spain's fortunes ebbed in Europe and abroad.

Discourses of difference

Charles I's words, whether apocryphal or not, unveil a harsh view from above and echo one of the two main themes of this book: the social distance between those above and those below; the disdain of the former for the latter. In late medieval and early modern Spain, the gap between social groups stemmed in part from economic inequality. The wealthy, whether noble or not, enjoyed rights and privileges denied to the majority of the population. But wealth was not the only marker of social difference. Social filiation, with its inherent rights and obligations; lineage or lack of distinguished blood lines; manners; dress; diet; education; mode of employment; place of residence;

252

gender; ancestry (an important category for those of Jewish or Muslim origin); Christian orthodoxy (or its counterparts, heterodoxy and heresy) – all worked, in myriad combinations, to identify individual Spaniards and to secure their ranking within specific orders.

As I have sought to demonstrate, festivals, violence, debates over dress, diet and honour codes, and other cultural artefacts served as sites for social inter- action. They provided fluid contexts within which social groups mingled, jostled, came into close contact. At the same time, these events continually reinforced the distinctions between different levels of society. Festivals, which marshalled the social orders in tame and entertaining fashion, were carefully scripted by those on top. Violence, though far more open-ended and unpre- dictable, was also highly choreographed. We have enough evidence to know that, although violence did from time to time get out of hand and turn on those on top, in most cases it reflected the struggles of an elite competing for power in the fifteenth century and resisting a centralizing Crown in the six- teenth. Middling sorts and the poor were often caught in the middle or drawn into one camp or another. Ritual violence – often inscribed in festive cycles, *autos-de-fe*, public executions, and ritualized mutilations of the enemy or of those found guilty of sodomy – also served a pedagogical purpose and taught lessons, brutal ones, about hierarchy and difference to the masses.

In general, the distance between social orders increased during the trans- ition from the late Middle Ages to the early modern period. Moreover, ways of signalling social distance also changed. The shift began at the top, with the incremental removal of the powerful from the public gaze and the deployment of highly ornate codes of conduct, dress and diet that were inaccessible to the majority of the population. The middling sorts often aped their betters and sought in turn to carve out a space that would set them apart from the despicable poor. In many respects, these codes of difference were replicated in a descending order, each social cohort attempting to emu- late the lifestyle of the one immediately above it. Not only were the various orders increasingly segregated, but interpersonal barriers within groups were introduced as well. As a result, the social gulf grew steadily between the high noble and the *hidalgo*, the rich merchant and the petty-bourgeois, the pros- perous farmer, as we have seen with the rich Camacho, and the lowly peasant.

The making of a community

Under no circumstances, however, do I wish to leave the reader with an impression of a society rigidly stratified into tiers. Many of these cultural phenomena (festivals, violence, conventions of honour and shame) reinforced hierarchy, but they also bonded people across social boundaries into a broader community: a community of subjects loyal to the king; a community of Christians; and, eventually, a community of Castilians and Spaniards. This

253

is in fact the second point I have sought to make through ample use of historical and literary vignettes. Although the king was more removed from his people in the late sixteenth century than he had been in the early fifteenth, royal authority and regal representations were far more universally recognized, far more familiar to the people, in the latter period than they had been in the Middle Ages. This was a consequence not only of more efficient methods of governance – that is, a greater ability to wield power through the army, the bureaucracy and the Church – but also of the fashioning, certainly in Castile, of a venerated royal image. The new representation of the king and his power and its ability to command such loyalty was intimately linked to the emergence of national identities.

Promoted by plays, festivals, religious ceremonies, and certain types of violence (especially against religious minorities), royal representation and the construction of national identities – and, for Spain, one must always make clear that an undivided national identity was never a real possibility, then or now – paralleled the divisive construction of difference discussed earlier. The latter process sought to maintain distance between social orders; the former linked all social orders into one community.

In a country as geographically, linguistically and culturally fragmented as Spain, the building of community and the making of national identity required endless toil. The barrage of royal propaganda, the pageantry of secular and religious symbols, sought to encourage the popular support of imperial ambitions and strict observance of Catholic orthodoxy. As we have seen in earlier chapters, this often meant the wholesale persecution or exile of those deemed unfit to participate in this centralizing project. It meant the marginalization of certain people within society. But this should not surprise us. It was, after all, a common procedure throughout most of early modern Europe, an inevitable concomitant of the construction of the nation-state.

Social mobility

And yet, the story is still too neat, too clear-cut. The nation-state and national identities did not emerge as clear entities or concepts simply because festivals were deployed or the 'other' was persecuted. The genesis of the state was complex, requiring nuanced explanations. The same applies to social relations. Throughout the book, another of my main concerns has been to point out the fluidity of social categories. The need to create discourses of difference, to draw sharper distinctions between social groups, was prompted by the growing subversion of social boundaries. From the late Middle Ages onwards, the evidence points to a considerable erasure of barriers between social groups, most of all between the middling classes and the nobility. But this upending of an imaginary tripartite society of orders was not limited to small social circles. It affected all classes, putting in jeopardy the carefully laid fences that divided one group from another. The codes of etiquette that regulated the growing abyss between orders, and the legislation that sought to keep those below in their God-ordered place, reveal, especially among the upper classes, an escalating fear of social transgression. It was a well-founded fear. The zeal with which late fifteenth-century sumptuary laws sought to impose statutes of cleanliness or purity (*pureza*) of blood and other such measures shows a society hell-bent on keeping taxonomies of blood, class and religion fixed in place. Reality, however, worked otherwise.

There were ways of circumventing these barriers, of crossing over the imaginary walls that kept middling sorts from entering the ranks of the nobility; in time and with good lawyers, New Christians became respectable Old Christians. In previous chapters, while showing how social differences were articulated and enforced, I have also depicted how these differences were undermined. The mechanisms for subverting difference were often the very ones that served to create difference: education, wealth, lineage. Groups did not change their status as a whole; individuals did. Each case was *sui generis*. In previous chapters, the examples of the Chirino and Bernuy families, of St Teresa of Avila and St John of the Cross, point to the assorted paths that could lead an individual from suspicious *Converso* origins to respectable noble ranks and erase all traces of Jewish descent. In some cases, the successful elision of ancestry brought heightened social prestige (the Bernuys) and even sainthood (St Teresa de Avila).

More commonly, crossing over entailed moving across the city, marrying one's daughter into a better family, dressing as one's betters did – and getting away with it – or sending one's son to university, as Sansón Carrasco did in *Don Quixote*. What I have sought to describe and explain in previous chapters is the dialectic between nominally rigid social norms and the complex ambiguities of everyday life. Clearly, the period between the end of the Middle Ages and the onset of modernity – an age fraught with political, economic, cultural and social transformations – witnessed deep alterations in the fabric and structure of Spanish society. As I have indicated throughout the book, these transformations unleashed a multitude of what, for lack of a better term, must be described as anxieties: the anxieties of upper social groups, trying to defend their privileges; the anxieties of *Conversos*, middling sorts, and others, trying to create a space within the ranks of the privileged; the anxieties of those below, trying merely to survive.

Though many factors contributed to the unsettling of social categories, I think that money played a significant role. I began this book with some verses from Jorge Manrique and Quevedo. For the former, death underscored the equality of all men, of all Christians; for the latter, wealth was a reprobate slayer of difference and distinction. In Don Quixote's famous speech on the Golden Age (see Chapter 10), Cervantes mounted a serious critique of property, not because it erases social boundaries but because it creates them. For Cervantes, distinctions had to be based on chivalric notions and the idealized tripartite order, whereas property and money ushered in distinctions based on other values: wealth, purchasing power, materialistic priorities. If we explore *Don Quixote* in even further detail, we see that the book is, among many other things, an extended disquisition on wealth: on the perceived need to get it, on its insidious effects, on its hastening the demise of chivalric ideals.

The influx of gold and especially silver from the New World, the development of economies of scale – all the constituents that we associate with the birth of capitalism – had a dramatic impact not only on Spain's economy but on the mentality of its inhabitants. Wealth subverted the best laid plans of a society of orders. But wealth did not abolish differences; it created new ones, often far less forgiving and more oppressive than the ones that existed before. In the literary works and the documentary evidence of the period, one detects a frantic activity, a hope for accelerated social mobility, and a yearning for new bonds between social groups. One also perceives a sense of loss, a nostalgia for a bygone era, when the chimera of social orders – each individual neatly ensconced in his or her ordained place – still defined social relations.

I have sought throughout to portray the tensions that existed between different social agendas: that of creating discourses of difference and that of binding all Spaniards into a community. These tensions were not resolved in this period or in any subsequent period for that matter. The tensions themselves are part of a continuous unfolding of history, of a continuous shifting of social categories. This account is one of successes and failures, often more of the latter than of the former. What it does not fully capture, however, is the utter complexity of individual lives, the yearnings, desires and frustrations. What it does not depict is the small but painful failings, the uncertainty and arbitrariness of everyday life. But individuals and society in general ought not to be judged solely by their glorious deeds or failures, but also by their unfulfilled aspirations and ideals. I think it is fitting here to conclude with Cervantes's articulation of these ideas in *Don Quixote*. After all, this eponymous hero has guided us throughout most of our long journey.

In one of the most thoughtful sections of the novel's second volume, the protagonist gives Sancho advice on how to govern his newly acquired *insula*. Don Quixote counsels his squire never to deny his humble peasant origins, and always to be a 'virtuous humble man [rather] than a sinful proud one . . . for people of low birth have risen to the highest ecclesiastical and secular dignities'. Then Don Quixote adds, 'Look, Sancho, take virtue as your goal and be proud of doing virtuous deeds, [for] there is no need to envy those who have [possessions, glory, prestige], even if they are princes and lords; because blood is inherited, and virtue is acquired, and virtue is worth by itself that which blood is not'.[2] In the end, then and now, against the straitjacket of social difference, virtue, right conduct, and the reflected life were, and are, of far more value than the highest title or the 'purest' blood.

Notes

1. Paré is cited in Jaume Vicens Vives (ed.), *Historia de España y América: social y económica* (Barcelona, 1972), III: 101.
2. Miguel de Cervantes y Saavedra, *Don Quijote de la Mancha*, ed. Martín Riquer, 2 vols (Barcelona, 1955), II, ch. 57, 840–1: 'Mira Sancho; si tomas por medio la virtud, y te precias de hacer hechos virtuosos, no hay para que tener envidia a los que tienen principes y señores, porque la sangre se hereda, y la virtud se aquista, y la virtud vale por si sola lo que la sangre no vale'. I was guided to this quote by an uncited quotation in Ángel Luis Molina Molina, *Mujeres públicas, mujeres secretas: la prostitución y su mundo: siglos XIII–XVIII* (Murcia, 1998), 184.

Appendix I: Chronology of events, 1390–1600

1390–1406	Henry III, king of Castile
1390	Shlomoh Ha-Levi, the great rabbi of Burgos, converts to Christianity
1391	Anti-Jewish pogroms throughout the peninsula, most notably in Seville, Córdoba, Baeza, Jaén, Burgos and Toledo in Castile, and Valencia, Barcelona, Lérida and Gerona in the Crown of Aragon
1395–1410	Martin the Humane, king of the Crown of Aragon
1398–1458	Iñigo López de Mendoza, marquis of Santillana, poet and book collector
1406–54	John II, king of Castile
1411–56	Juan de Mena, poet and author of the *Laberinto de fortuna*
1412	Compromise of Caspe: the regent of Castile, Fernando de Antequera, becomes king of the Crown of Aragon, 1412–16
1412–13	Disputation of Tortosa leads to further Jewish conversions
1415	Ceuta is taken by the Portuguese
1416–58	Alfonso V, king of the Crown of Aragon
1438	Writing of *El Corbacho* by the archpriest of Talavera (Alfonso Martínez de Toledo)
1440?–79	Jorge Manrique, poet
1442–43	Alfonso V of Aragon gains control of Naples
1449	Anti-*Converso* riots in Toledo
1453	Execution of Alvaro de Luna, favourite of John II of Castile
1453–1515	Gonzalo Fernández de Córdoba, the 'Great Captain', reformer of the Castilian army
1454–74	Henry IV, king of Castile
1458–79	John II (Aragon), king of the Crown of Aragon and Navarre
1459–64	Attacks against *Conversos* in Burgos
1461	Attacks against Jews and French merchants in Medina del Campo (Castile)
1462–72	Civil and *remença* wars in Catalonia
c.1465	Writing of *Cárcel de amor* by Diego de San Pedro (printed in 1492)
1469	The marriage of Ferdinand and Isabella
1469–1529	Juan de Encina, playwright, first Castilian plays

1473	Massacre of *Conversos* throughout the peninsula
1474	First book, a collection of Catalan poems to the Virgin, printed in Spain (Valencia)
1474–1566	Bartolomé de las Casas, protector of the Indians
1474–1504	Isabella I, the Catholic, queen of Castile
1476–1541	Francisco Pizarro, conqueror of Peru
1476	The *Santa Hermandad* is organized in Castile
1478	Setting up of the Inquisition
1479–1516	Ferdinand the Catholic, king of the Crown of Aragon
1479	Dynastic union of Castile and Aragon
1480	*Cortes* legislation reorganizes the governance of Castile
1480?–1546	Francisco de Vitoria, theologian and philosopher
1483	Creation of the Supreme Council of the Inquisition
1485–1547	Hernán Cortés, conqueror of Mexico
1491–1556	Ignatius of Loyola, founder of the Jesuits
1492–1540	Juan Luis Vives, noted humanist and philosopher
1492	Conquest of Granada (1–2 January)
1492	31 March, Edict of Expulsion of the Jews
1492	Antonio de Nebrija publishes *Arte de la lengua castellana*, first grammar in a modern European language
1492	August, Columbus sails into the Atlantic Ocean on his way to the 'Indies'
1492	12 October, Columbus's landfall in the New World
1492	*Amadís of Gaula*, the most popular chivalrous novel in Spain, is compiled by Garcí Rodríguez de Montalvo in Valladolid
1493	Columbus's second voyage; first permanent European settlement in the New World; beginning of the colonization of the Caribbean
1494	Treaty of Tordesillas dividing the New World between Spain and Portugal
1495–97	Spanish Intervention and War in Italy
1499	First Alpujarras rebellion
1499	First publication of Fernando de Rojas's *La Celestina*
1501–04	War in Italy
1501?–1536	Garcilaso de la Vega, poet; beginnings of the Golden Age with the publication of his poetry by Juan Boscán's widow in 1543
1502	Muslims in Granada forced to choose between baptism and expulsion
1504–55	Juana, the Mad, queen of Castile
1506	Death of Philip the Handsome, consort of Juana the Mad
1506	Francisco Jiménez de Cisneros, regent in Castile

259

1508	Cisneros founds the university of Alcalá de Henares; preparation of the *Polyglot Bible*
1512	Occupation and integration of Navarre into the Spanish Crown
1516–56	Charles I, king of Castile and the Crown of Aragon; emperor (1519–56) as Charles V
1515–82	St Teresa of Avila, reformer and mystic
1519–40	Conquest of Mexico and Peru
1520–21	Revolt of the *Comuneros* in Castile
1520–21	Revolt of the *Germanías* in Valencia
1530?–97	Juan de Herrera, one of the architects of El Escorial
1535–1624	Juan de Mariana, Jesuit historian
1540–1611	Antonio Pérez, secretary to Philip II
1541–1614	El Greco, painter
1542	*Leyes Nuevas*, a new legal compilation of Castilian law
1542–91	John of the Cross, poet and mystic
1545	First Spanish Index of forbidden books
1547–1614?	Mateo Alemán, author of *La vida de Guzmán de Alfarache*, a picaresque novel published in two parts (1599 and 1604)
1547–1616	Miguel de Cervantes y Saavedra, author of *Don Quixote* and many other works
1550	Debate between Las Casas and Sepúlveda at Valladolid on whether it was lawful to wage war on the natives of the New World and to enslave them
1554	Publication of *El Lazarillo de Tormes*, first picaresque novel
1556–98	Philip II, king of Spain
1557	Philip II suspends payment to bankers; Spain's bankruptcy
1558 or 1559	Publication of Jorge de Montemayor's *La Diana*
1559	Peace treaty of Câteau-Cambrésis between Spain and France
1561–1627	Luis de Góngora, poet
1562–1635	Félix Lope de Vega y Carpio, playwright
1568–70	Second Revolt of the Alpujarras
1571	Defeat of the Turkish fleet at Lepanto
1580	Annexation of Portugal
1580–1645	Francisco de Quevedo y Villegas, writer
1588	Sailing of the Invincible Armada against England
1591	Revolt in Aragon
1596	Second Armada sails against England
1598–1621	Philip III, king of Spain
1605	Publication of *El Ingenioso hidalgo Don Quixote de la Mancha*, Part I

Appendix II: Glossary of terms

arrendatarios	Renters holding the usufruct (use) of the land and paying a *censo*, a fixed rent, usually established by custom.
auto-de-fe	The great trials held by the Inquisition. Differing in size, duration, theatricality and number of victims, *autos-de-fe* were performances enacted by the Holy Office, bonding the spectators in powerful spectacles of punishment of heretics.
caballero	A rank of nobility above that of *hidalgo*.
cañada	The roads used by the Mesta livestock (see *Mesta*).
caserío	A type of household and farming organization typical of the Basque region (see Chapter 2).
censo, census	A fixed rent paid for the use of a property, usually land under cultivation.
Converso	Literally, anyone who converted from one religion to another. In Spain, it usually meant conversion from Judaism to Christianity. The term 'New Christians' was also used to describe Jewish converts.
Corona de Aragón, *Crown of Aragon*	The union of three distinctive political units – Aragon, Catalonia and Valencia – into a political entity ruled by one king. Each of the constituents retained its parliament, political institutions, culture and language.
cortes, corts	Parliament; assemblies of representatives of the nobility, the clergy, and a selected number of cities. *Cortes* in Castile and *corts* in Catalonia and Valencia – in the latter two regions there were four branches, with lower nobility and ennobled bourgeois constituting a separate branch.
Don, Doña	Titles denoting social and economic standing. Often associated with noble rank, but also used as an appellative among rich farmers, well-to-do artisans and merchants.
fidalgo, hidalgo	Literally, the son of someone who owned something. The term was used to describe the lowest rank of the nobility.

261

Infante(a)	The title of the heir to the throne and immediate members of the royal family.
Inquisition	The Holy Office or Supreme Council of the Inquisition. Introduced in Spain in the 1480s, the Spanish Inquisition was different from the papal or diocesan inquisitions. In Spain, the Inquisition was under the direct control of the Crown. Though its main purpose was to ferret out heretics, bring them to trial, and punish them, the Inquisition in Spain came to play a significant political, social and economic role.
jornaleros	Daily workers, journeymen; often used to describe agricultural workers who were paid a daily salary.
labradores	Literally, those who worked the land. In the late Middle Ages and early modern period, the word meant those who held their land outright or worked it under long-term leases.
latifundia	Large holding of lands, often owned by a great lord, the Military Orders, or great religious establishments. The *latifundia* originated in Roman times and were found mainly in southern Spain and in the New World.
mal usos	Arbitrary and abusive customs imposed on the Catalan servile peasantry.
manumission	The setting free of serfs or slaves. The practice was common in early modern Spain and in the Iberian New World.
maravedí	A type of coin or monetary unit that fluctuated widely in the fifteenth and sixteenth centuries.
mas	A form of organizing the land in late medieval Catalonia (see Chapter 2).
Mesta	The sheep-herder's guild which controlled the transhumance: the movement of livestock from summer to winter pastures.
minifundio	Small, fragmented holdings, often not sufficient to support a peasant and his family.
montes	Wooded areas. In the fifteenth and sixteenth centuries, these areas were also used for grazing.
Moriscos	The name given to Muslims who converted to Christianity, but who were perceived to practise their ancestral religion (and they often did). The *Moriscos* kept their forms of dress, diet, and the use of the Arabic language.
Mudejares	Mudejars, Muslims living under Christian rule and still practising Islam.

pícaros   Tricksters, scam artists, con men who plied their trades in early modern Spain. Their adventures provided the plot for the first picaresque novel in western Europe, *Lazarillo de Tormes*.

propietarios   Owners. The term was used to indicate those who held or owned the land or other property outright.

pureza de sangre,   A series of statutes enacted in late fifteenth- and
(purity/cleanliness   sixteenth-century Spain restricting or denying those of
of blood)   Jewish or Moorish descent access to endowed colleges, Military Orders, and other privileges.

Reconquista   The name given to the process of recovering most of Iberia from the Muslims. The 'reconquest' came to underpin most of the political ideology of medieval Spain and shaped subsequent historiography. The meaning, origins and use of the term have provoked endless controversies.

remença   A redemption fee paid by servile peasants to secure their freedom in late medieval Catalonia.

Remenças, war of   The successful late fifteenth-century war waged by
the   Catalan serfs to gain their freedom.

sumptuary laws   Legislation aimed at restricting excessive eating, use of fashionable clothing, types of fabrics, and colours. The main goal of these ordinances was to keep the middling sorts in place.

villano   A villain, rustic, or villager. The term acquired pejorative connotations in the late Middle Ages and early modern period. The social and economic rank of the *villano* varied greatly: from rich *villanos* (prosperous and influential farmers) to poor ones.

yuguero   A ploughman; also someone who, owning a plough and a team of oxen, hired himself out at harvest time in return for a percentage of the crop.

Bibliography

This is a short select bibliography, noting the most salient (and accessible) titles in the field. Emphasis has been placed on titles in English, although most of the historical literature on these subjects is in either Spanish or French.

Published sources

There are few primary sources translated into English, except for literary works. They are cited throughout the book. One notable exception is the collection of short excerpts of Christian, Jewish and Muslim medieval sources edited by Olivia R. Constable, *Medieval Iberia: Readings from Christian, Muslim, and Jewish Sources* (Philadelphia, 1997).

Chapter 1: Spain in the making

General works

In English
Bisson, Thomas N. 1986. *The Medieval Crown of Aragon: A Short History*. Oxford.
Braudel, Fernand. 1972. *The Mediterranean and the Mediterranean World in the Age of Philip II*, trans. S. Reynolds, 2 vols. London.
Domínguez Ortiz, Antonio. 1971. *The Golden Age of Spain, 1516–1659*. London.
Elliott, John H. 1963. *Imperial Spain, 1469–1716*. London.
—— 1989. *Spain and Its World*. New Haven.
Hillgarth, Jocelyn N. 1976–78. *The Spanish Kingdoms, 1250–1516*, 2 vols. Oxford.
Kamen, Henry. 1983. *Spain 1469–1714: A Society in Conflict*. London.
—— 1993. *Crisis and Change in Early Modern Spain*. London.
Lynch, John. 1984. *Spain under the Habsburgs*, 2nd edn, 2 vols. New York.
MacKay, Angus. 1977. *Spain in the Middle Ages: From Frontier to Empire 1000–1500*. London.
O'Callaghan, Joseph F. 1975. *A History of Medieval Spain*. Ithaca.
Vicens Vives, Jaume. 1969. *An Economic History of Spain*, trans. F.M. López-Morillas, Princeton.
Way, Ruth. 1962. *A Geography of Spain and Portugal*. London.

In Spanish
Fernández Alvarez, M. and A. Díaz Medina. 1987. *Historia de España: Los Austrias mayores y la culminación del imperio (1516–1598)*, vol. VIII of *Historia de España*, ed. Angel Montenegro Duque. Madrid.

García de Cortázar, José Angel. 1973. *La época medieval*, vol. II of *Historia de España Alfaguara*. Madrid.

Tuñon de Lara, M. (ed.). 1984. *Historia de España*, vol. XI: *Textos y documentos de historia antigua, media y moderna*. Barcelona.

Social history

Casey, James. 1999. *Early Modern Spain: A Social History*. London.

Dufourcq, Charles E. and J. Gautier-Dalché. 1976. *Histoire économique et sociale de l'Espagne Chrétienne au Moyen Âge*. Paris.

Fernández Alvarez, Manuel. 1989. *La sociedad española en el Siglo de Oro*, 2nd edn, 2 vols. Madrid.

Vicens Vives, Jaume (ed.). 1972. *Historia de España y América: social y económica*, 5 vols. Barcelona.

Chapter 2: Peasants and town dwellers

Peasants

In English

Behar, Ruth. 1986. *Santa María del Monte: The Presence of the Past in a Spanish Village*. Princeton.

Freedman, Paul H. 1988. 'Cowardice, Heroism and the Legendary Origins of Catalonia', *Past & Present*, 121, 3–28.

—— 1991. *The Origins of Peasant Servitude in Medieval Catalonia*. Cambridge.

Hamilton, Earl. 1969. *War and Prices in Spain, 1615–1800*, 2nd edn. New York.

Heer, Richard. 1989. *Rural Change and Royal Finances in Spain*. Berkeley.

Klein, Julius. 1920. *The Mesta: A Study in Spanish Economic History, 1273–1836*. Cambridge.

Ringrose, David R. 1983. *Madrid and the Spanish Economy (1560–1860)*. Berkeley.

Ruiz, Teofilo F. 1994. *Crisis and Continuity: Land and Town in Late Medieval Castile*. Philadelphia.

—— 1998. 'The Peasantries of Iberia, 1400–1800', in Tom Scott (ed.), *The Peasantries of Europe: From the Fourteenth to the Eighteenth Centuries*. London. 48–73.

Vassberg, David E. 1984. *Land and Society in Golden Age Castile*. Cambridge.

—— 1991. *The Village and the Outside World in Golden Age Castile: Mobility and Migration in Everyday Rural Life*. Cambridge.

Weisser, Michael R. 1976. *The Peasants of the Montes: The Roots of Rural Rebellion in Spain*. Chicago.

In other languages

Anes Alvarez, Gonzalo. 1970. *Las crisis agrarias en la España moderna*. Madrid.

Artola, Miguel, et al. 1978. *El latifundio: propiedad y explotación, ss. XVIII–XX*. Madrid.

Brumont, Francis. 1984. *Campo y campesinos de Castilla la Vieja en tiempos de Felipe II*. Madrid.

—— 1993. *Paysans de Vielle-Castille aux XVIe et XVIIe siècles*. Madrid.

García de Cortázar, José Angel. 1988. *La sociedad rural en la España medieval*. Madrid.

García Sanz, Angel. 1986. *Desarrollo y crisis del antiguo régimen en Castilla la Vieja*. Madrid.

Huetz de Lemps, Alain. 1967. *Vignobles et vins du nord-ouest de l'Espagne*, 2 vols. Bordeaux.

Solomon, Noël. 1964. *La campagne de Nouvelle Castille à la fin du XVIe siècle d'après les 'Relaciones Topográficas'*. Paris.

Viñas y Mey, Carmelo. 1941. *El problema de la tierra en España de los siglos XVI–XVII*. Madrid.

Yun Casillas, Bartolomé. 1980. *Crisis de subsistencias y conflictividad social en Córdoba a principios del siglo XVI*. Córdoba.

—— 1987. *Sobre la transición al capitalismo en Castilla: economía y sociedad en Tierra de Campos (1500–1830)*. Valladolid.

Town dwellers

In English

Amelang, James S. 1986. *Honored Citizens of Barcelona: Patrician Culture and Class Relations 1490–1714*. Princeton.

Bensch, Stephen P. 1995. *Barcelona and Its Rulers*. Cambridge.

Casey, James. 1979. *The Kingdom of Valencia in the Seventeenth Century*. Cambridge.

Kagan, Richard L. (ed.). 1989. *Spanish Cities of the Golden Age: The Views of Anton van den Wyngarde*. Berkeley.

Nader, Helen. 1990. *Liberty in Absolutist Spain: The Habsburg Sale of Towns, 1516–1700*. Baltimore.

Phillips, Carla Rahn. 1979. *Ciudad Real, 1500–1750: Growth, Crisis and Readjustment in the Spanish Economy*. Cambridge, MA.

Pike, Ruth. 1972. *Aristocrats and Traders: Seville in the Sixteenth Century*. Ithaca.

Reher, David. 1990. *Town and Country in Pre-Industrial Spain: Cuenca, 1550–1870*. Cambridge.

Ringrose, David. 1983. *Madrid and the Spanish Economy, 1560–1850*. Berkeley.

Ruiz, Teofilo F. 1994. *Crisis and Continuity: Land and Town in Late Medieval Castile*. Philadelphia.

Smith, R.S. 1972. *The Spanish Guild Merchant: A History of the Consulado, 1250–1700*. New York.

Weisser, Michael. 1973. 'The Decline of Castile Revisited: The Case of Toledo', *Journal of European Economic History*, 2, 614–40.

In other languages

Asenjo González, María. 1986. *Segovia: la ciudad y su tierra a fines del medievo*. Segovia.

—— 1999. *Espacio y sociedad en la Soria medieval, siglos XIII–XV*. Soria.

Barrios García, Angel. 1983–84. *Estructuras agrarias y de poder en Castilla: el ejemplo de Avila (1085–1320)*, 2 vols. Salamanca.

Battle y Gallart, Carmen. 1973. *La crisis social y económica de Barcelona a mediados del siglo XV*, 2 vols. Barcelona.

Benassar, Bartolomé. 1967. *Valladolid au siècle d'or: une ville de Castille et sa campagne au XVIe siècle*. Paris.

Casado Alonso, Hilario. 1987. *Señores, mercaderes y campesinos: la comarca de Burgos a fines de la Edad Media*. Valladolid.

Collantes de Terán, Antonio. 1977. *Sevilla en la baja Edad Media: la ciudad y sus hombres*. Sevilla.

Estepa, Carlos, et al. 1984. *Burgos en la Edad Media*. Valladolid.

Reglà, Joan, et al. 1975. *Historia del país Valencià*, 3 vols. Barcelona.

Rucquoi, Adeline. 1983. *Valladolid en la Edad Media*, 2 vols. Valladolid.

Chapter 3: Nobility and clergy

Nobles

In English

Barton, Simon. 1997. *The Aristocracy in Twelfth-Century León and Castile*. Cambridge.

Bush, M.L. 1988. *Rich Noble, Poor Noble*. New York.

Dewald, Jonathan. 1996. *The European Nobility, 1400–1800*. Cambridge.

Díaz de Gámez, Gutierre. 1928. *The Unconquered Knight: A Chronicle of the Deeds of Don Pero Niño, Count of Buelna*, trans. J. Evans. London.

Evans, P.G. 1993. 'A Spanish Knight in Flesh and Blood. A Study of the Chivalric Spirit of Suero de Quiñones', *Hispania* (NY), 15, 141–52.

Jago, Charles. 1979. 'The "Crisis of the Aristocracy" in Seventeeth-Century Castile', *Past & Present*, 84, 60–90.

Maltby, William S. 1983. *Alba: A Biography of Fernando de Toledo, Third Duke of Alba 1507–1582*. Berkeley.

Nader, Helen. 1977. 'Noble Income in Sixteenth Century Castile: The Case of the Marquises of Mondéjar, 1480–1580', *Economic History Review*, 2nd ser., 30, 412–28.

—— 1979. *The Mendoza Family in the Spanish Renaissance 1350 to 1550*. New Brunswick.

Pierson, Peter. 1989. *Commander of the Armada: The Seventh Duke of Medina Sidonia*. New Haven.

Powers, James F. 1988. *A Society Organized for War: The Iberian Municipal Militias in the Central Middle Ages, 1000–1284*. Berkeley.

Russell, Peter E. 1967. 'Arms versus Letters: Towards a Definition of Spanish Fifteenth-Century Humanism', in Archibald R. Lewis (ed.), *Aspects of the Renaissance: A Symposium*. Austin. 47–58.

In other languages

de Riquer, Martín. 1967. *Caballeros andantes españoles*. Madrid.

Gerbert, Marie-Claude. 1979. *La noblesse dans le Royaume de Castile: Etudes sur ses structures sociales en Extremadure 1454–1516*. Paris.

—— 1997. *Las noblezas españolas en la Edad Media, siglos XI–XV*. Madrid. French original published in 1994.

Gil Pujol, Xavier. 1997. 'Una cultura cortesana provincial. Patria, comunicación y lenguaje en la monarquía hispánica de los Austrias', in P. Fernández Albadalejo (ed.), *Monarquía, imperio y pueblos en la España moderna*. Alicante. 225–57.

Martín de Marco, José A. 1990. *La institución de caballeros hijosdalgo de los doce linajes de la ciudad de Soria*. Soria.

Rodríguez Velasco, Jesús D. 1996. *El debate sobre la caballería en el siglo XV: la tratadística caballeresca castellana en su marco europeo*. Salamanca.

The clergy

In English

Alcalá, Angel (ed.). 1987. *The Spanish Inquisition and the Inquistorial Mind*. Highland Lake, NJ.

Avila, St Teresa of. 1957. *The Life of Saint Teresa of Ávila by Herself*. London.

Bilinkoff, Jodi. 1989. *The Ávila of Saint Teresa: Religious Reform in a Sixteenth-Century City*. Ithaca.

Christian, Jr., William A. 1981. *Local Religion in Sixteenth Century Spain*. Princeton.

Cruz, Anne and Mary E. Perry (eds). 1992. *Culture and Control in Counter-Reformation Spain*. Minneapolis.

Eire, Carlos M. 1995. *From Madrid to Purgatory: The Art and Craft of Dying in Sixteenth-Century Spain*. New York.

Haliczer, Stephen. 1990. *Inquisition and Society in the Kingdom of Valencia 1478–1834*. Berkeley.

Hamilton, Alistair. 1992. *Heresy and Mysticism in Sixteenth-Century Spain: The Alumbrados*. Cambridge.

Kamen, Henry. 1985. *Inquisition and Society in Spain in the Sixteenth and Seventeenth Centuries*. Bloomington, IN.

Lea, Henry C. 1966. *A History of the Inquisition of Spain*, 4 vols. New York. Originally published in 1905.

Linehan, Peter. 1971. *The Spanish Church and the Papacy in the Thirteenth Century*. Cambridge.

Monter, William. 1990. *Frontiers of Heresy: The Spanish Inquisition from the Basque Lands to Sicily*. Cambridge.

Nalle, Sara T. 1992. *God in La Mancha: Religion, Reform and the People of Cuenca 1500–1650*. Baltimore.

Netanyahu, Benzion. 1995. *The Origins of the Inquisition in Fifteenth-Century Spain*. New York.

Peers, E. Allison. 1954. *Handbook to the Life and Times of St Teresa and St John of the Cross*. London.

In other languages

Astrain, A. 1912–25. *Historia de la compañía de Jesus*, 7 vols. Madrid.

Aurell, Jaueme and A. Puigarnau. 1998. *La cultura del mercader en la Barcelona del siglo XV*. Barcelona.

Bataillon, Marcel. 1966. *Erasmus y España: estudios sobre la historia espiritual del siglo XVI*. Mexico.

Bennasar, Bartolomé. 1979. *L'inquisition espagnole*. Paris.

Caro Baroja, Julio. 1978. *Las formas complejas de la vida religiosa: religión, sociedad y carácter en la España de los siglos XVI y XVII*. Madrid.

Dedieu, Jean-Pierre. 1989. *L'Administration de la foi: l'inquisition de Tolède XVIe–XVIIIe siècles*. Madrid.

García Cárcel, Ricardo. 1980. *Herejía y sociedad en el siglo XVI: la inquisición en Valencia 1530–1609*. Barcelona.
Pou i Martí, J.M. 1930. *Visionarios, beguinos y fraticelos catalanes (siglos XIII–XV)*. Vic.

Chapter 4: On the margins of society

In English

Baer, Yitzhak. 1966. *A History of the Jews in Christian Spain*, 2 vols. Philadelphia.
Blackmore J. and G.S. Hutchenson (eds). 1999. *Queer Iberia: Sexualities, Cultures, and Crossings from the Middle Ages to the Renaissance*. Durham, NC.
Freund, S. and T.F. Ruiz. 1994. 'Jews, *Conversos*, and the Inquisition in Spain, 1391–1492: The Ambiguities of History', in J.M. Perry and F.M. Schweitzer (eds), *Jewish-Christian Encounters over the Centuries: Symbiosis, Prejudice, Holocaust, Dialogue*. New York. 169–95.
Geremek, Bronislaw. 1987. *The Margins of Society in Late Medieval Paris*. Cambridge.
Kamen, Henry. 1988. 'The Mediterranean and the Expulsion of Spanish Jews in 1492', *Past & Present*, 119, 30–55.
Meyerson, Mark D. 1991. *The Muslims of Valencia in the Age of Fernando and Isabel*. Berkeley.
Mollatt, Michel. 1986. *The Poor in the Middle Ages*. Chicago.
Nirenberg, David. 1996. *Communities of Violence: Persecution of Minorities in the Middle Ages*. Princeton.
Perry, Mary E. 1990. *Gender and Disorder in Early Modern Seville*. Princeton.
Phillips, Carla and W.D. Phillips (eds). 1989. *Marginated Groups in Spanish and Portuguese History*. Minneapolis.
Phillips, William D., Jr. 1985. *Slavery from Roman Times to the Early Transatlantic Trade*. Minneapolis.
—— (forthcoming). *Slavery and Freedom in Spain and the Spanish World*.
Wolff, Phillipe. 1971. 'The 1391 Pogrom in Spain: Social Crisis or Not?' *Past & Present*, 50, 4–18.

In other languages

Cardillac, Louis. 1977. *Morisques et chrétiens: un affrontement pólemique (1492–1640)*. Paris.
Domínguez Ortiz, Antonio and B. Vincent. 1978. *Historia de los moriscos: vida y tragedia de una minoría*. Madrid.
Lapeyre, Henri. 1986. *Geografía de la España morisca*. Valencia.
Leblon, Bernard. 1985. *Les gitans d'Espagne: le prix de la difference*. Paris.
López Alonso, Carmen. 1986. *La pobreza en la España medieval: estudio histórico-social*. Madrid.
Monsalvo Antón, José M. 1985. *Teoría y evolución de un conflicto social: el antisemitismo en la corona de Castilla en la Baja Edad Media*. Madrid.
Vincent, Bernard. 1970. 'L'expulsion des Morisques du royaume de Grenade et leur répartition en Castille (1570–1571)', *Mélanges de la Casa de Velázquez*, 6, 211–46.
—— 1987. *Minorías y marginados en la España di siglo XVI*. Granada.

Chapters 5 and 6: Festivals

In English

Avilés, Miguel. 1985. 'The Auto de Fe and the Social Model of Counter-Reformation Spain', in Angel Alcalá (ed.), *The Spanish Inquisition and the Inquisitorial Mind*. Highland Lakes, NJ. 249–64.

Bakhtin, Mikhail. 1984. *Rabelais and his World*. Bloomington, IN.

Barber, R. and J. Barker. 1989. *Tournaments, Jousts, Chivalry and Pageants in the Middle Ages*. Woodbridge.

Brown, Jonathan and J.H. Elliott. 1980. *A Palace for a King: The Buen Retiro and the Court of Philip IV*. New Haven.

Bryant, Larry. 1990. 'The Medieval Entry Ceremony at Paris', in Janos M. Bak (ed.), *Coronations: Medieval and Early Modern Monarchic Ritual*. Berkeley. 88–118.

Elias, Norbert. 1982. *The Civilizing Process*, 2 vols. New York.

Hanawalt, B. and K. Reyerson (eds). 1994. *City and Spectacle in Medieval Europe*. Minneapolis.

Keen, Maurice. 1984. *Chivalry*. New Haven.

Lea, Henry C. 1906–07. *A History of the Inquistion in Spain*, 4 vols. New York.

Orgel, Stephen. 1975. *The Illusion of Power: Political Theater in the English Renaissance*. Berkeley.

Rubin, Miri. 1990. *Corpus Christi: The Eucharist in Late Medieval Culture*. Cambridge.

Ruiz, T.F. 1994. 'Elite and Popular Culture in Late Fifteenth-Century Castilian Festivals: The Case of Jaén', in B.A. Hanawalt and K.L. Reyerson (eds), *City and Spectacle in Medieval Europe*. Minneapolis. 296–318.

Strong, Roy. 1984. *Art and Power: Renaissance Festivals, 1450–1650*. Woodbridge.

Turner, Victor. 1982. *Celebrations: Studies in Festivities and Ritual*. Washington.

—— 1992. *From Ritual to Theatre: The Human Seriousness of Play*. New York.

In other languages

Ariño, Antoni. 1988. *Festes, rituals i creences, temes d'etnografia Valenciana*. Valencia.

Caro Baroja, Julio. 1965. *El carnaval (análisis histórico-cultural)*. Madrid.

—— 1984. *El estío festivo (Fiestas populares del verano)*. Madrid.

de Andrés Díaz, Rosana. 1984. 'Las entradas reales castellanas en los siglos XIV y XV, según las crónicas de la época', *En la España medieval*, IV. Madrid. 46–62.

de Riquer, Martín. 1967. *Caballeros andantes españoles*. Madrid.

Díaz, José S. (ed.). 1982. *Relaciones breves de actos públicos en Madrid de 1541 a 1650*. Madrid.

—— 1999. *Fiestas, juegos y espectáculos en la España medieval*. Madrid.

Heers, Jacques. 1983. *Fête des fous et carnivals*. Paris.

Jacquot, Jean (ed.). 1984. *Les fêtes de la Renaissance*. Paris.

Muñoz Fernández, Angela. 1990. 'Fiestas laicas y fiestas profanas en el Madrid medieval', in J.C. de Miguel Rodríguez (ed.), *El Madrid medieval. Sus tierras y sus hombres*. Madrid. 151–76.

Núñez Rodríguez, Manuel (ed.). 1994. *El rostro y el discurso de la fiesta*. Santiago de Compostela.

Portús Pérez, Javier. 1993. *La antigua procesión del Corpus Christi en Madrid*. Madrid.

Ruiz, T.F. 1991. 'Festivités, couleurs et symboles du pouvoir en Castille au XVᵉ siècle: les celebrations de mai 1428', *Annales ESC*, 3, 521–46.

Chapters 7 and 8: Violence

In English

Armstrong, Nancy and L. Tennenhouse. 1989. *The Violence of Representation*. London.

Bisson, Thomas N. 1994. 'The Feudal Revolution', *Past & Present*, 142, 6–42.

—— 1998. *Tormented Voices: Power, Crisis, and Humanity in Rural Catalonia 1140–1200*. Cambridge, MA.

Davis, Natalie Z. 1973. 'The Rites of Violence: Religious Riots in Sixteenth-Century France', *Past & Present*, 59, 51–91.

Elliott, John H. 1963. *The Revolt of the Catalans: A Study in the Decline of Spain*. Cambridge.

Foucault, Michel. 1979. *Discipline and Punish: The Birth of the Prison*. Harmondsworth.

Fourquin, Guy. 1978. *The Anatomy of Popular Rebellion in the Middle Ages*. New York.

Freedman, Paul H. 1993. *The Origins of Peasant Servitude in Medieval Catalonia*. Cambridge.

Haliczer, Stephen. 1981. *The Comuneros of Castile: The Forging of a Revolution 1475–1521*. Madison, WI.

MacKay, Angus. 1972. 'Popular Movements and Pogroms in Fifteenth-Century Castile', *Past & Present*, 55, 33–67.

Mollat, Michel and P. Wolff. 1973. *The Popular Revolutions of the Late Middle Ages*. Winchester, MA.

Mullett, Michael. 1987. *Popular Culture and Popular Protest in Late Medieval and Early Modern Europe*. London.

Nirenberg, David. 1996. *Communities of Violence: Persecution of Minorities in the Middle Ages*. Princeton, NJ.

Ruggeiro, Guido. 1980. *Violence in Early Renaissance Venice*. New Brunswick, NJ.

Ruiz, T.F. 1995. 'Violence in Late Medieval Castile: The Case of the Rioja', *Revista de História*, 133, 15–36.

Scott, James C. 1985. *Weapons of the Weak: Everyday Forms of Peasant Resistance*. New Haven.

—— 1990. *Domination and the Arts of Resistance: Hidden Transcripts*. New Haven.

Wolff, Philippe. 1971. 'The 1391 Pogrom in Spain: Social Crisis or Not?', *Past & Present*, 50, 4–18.

In other languages

Barros, Carlos. 1990. *Mentalidad justiciera de los Irmandiños, siglo XV*. Madrid.

Enciso, L.M. et al. (ed.). 1992. *Revueltas y alzamientos en la España de Felipe II*. Valladolid.

García Cárcel, Ricardo. 1981. *La revolta de les Germanías*. Alzira.

Gutiérrez Nieto, Juan I. 1973. *Las comunidades como movimiento antiseñorial*. Barcelona.

MacKay, Angus. 1985. *Anatomía de una revuelta urbana: Alcaraz en 1458*. Albacete.

Reglá, Joan. 1969. *Bandolers, pirates i hugonots a la Catalunya del segle XVII*. Barcelona.

Sobrequés i Vidal, Santiago and J. Sobrequés i Callicó. 1973. *La guerra civil catalana del segle XV. Estudio sobre la crisi social i econòmica de la Baixa Edat Mitjana*, 2 vols. Barcelona.

Torres i sans, Xavier. 1991. *Els bandolers* (*s. XVI–XVII*). Vic.

Valdeón Baruque, Julio. 1975. *Los conflictos sociales en el reino de Castilla en los siglos XIV y XV*. Madrid.

Chapters 9 and 10: The patterns of everyday life

In English

Aries, Philippe. 1974. *Western Attitudes Towards Death from the Middle Ages to the Present*, trans. P. Ranum. Baltimore.

Aries, Philippe and Georges Duby (eds). 1989. *A History of Private Life*, 5 vols. Cambridge, MA. Above all see vol. III, *Passions of the Renaissance*, ed. Roger Chartier.

Burke, Peter. 1988. *Popular Culture in Early Modern Europe*. Aldershot.

Christian Jr., William A. 1981. *Local Religion in Sixteenth-Century Spain*. Princeton.

—— 1981. *Apparitions in Late Medieval and Renaissance Spain*. Princeton.

Defourneaux, Marcelin. 1970. *Daily Life in Spain in the Golden Age*. London.

Edwards, John. 1988. 'Religious Faith and Doubts in Late Medieval Spain: Soria *circa* 1450–1500', *Past & Present*, 120, 3–25.

Eire, Carlos M. 1995. *From Madrid to Purgatory: The Art and Craft of Dying in Sixteenth-Century Spain*. New York.

Elias, Norbert. 1982. *The Civilizing Process*, 2 vols. New York.

Gilmore, David D. (ed.). 1987. *Honor and Shame and the Unity of the Mediterranean*. Washington.

Girouard, Mark. 1980. *Life in the English Country House: A Social and Architectural History*. Harmondsworth.

Hersch, Philip, A. MacKay and G. MacKendrick. 1987. 'The Semiology of Dress in Late Medieval and Early Modern Spain', in *Le corps paré: ornaments et atours*. Nice.

Kagan, Richard L. 1974. *Students and Society in Early Modern Spain*. Baltimore.

—— 1990. *Lucrecia's Dreams: Politics and Prophecy in Sixteenth-Century Spain*. Berkeley.

McKendrick, Melveena. 1974. *Woman and Society in the Spanish Drama of the Golden Age*. New York.

Peristiany, J.G. (ed.). 1966. *Honour and Shame: The Values of Mediterranean Society*. Chicago.

Perry, Mary E. 1990. *Gender and Disorder in Early Modern Seville*. Princeton.

—— 1991. *Crime and Society in Early Modern Seville*. Berkeley.

Phillips, Carla R. 1986. *Six Galleons for the King of Spain: Imperial Defense in the Early Seventeenth Century*. Baltimore.

Pike, Ruth. 1975. 'Crime and Criminals in Sixteenth Century Seville', *Journal of Sixteenth Century Studies*, 6, 3–18.

—— 1983. *Penal Servitude in Early Modern Spain*. Madison, WI.

Ruiz, T.F. 1998. 'The Business of Salvation: Castilian Wills in the Late Middle Ages', in D.J. Kagay and T.M. Vann (eds), *On the Social Origins of Medieval Institutions: Essays in Honor of Joseph F. O'Callaghan*. Leiden. 63–89.

Saint-Saens, Alain (ed.). 1995. *Sex and Love in Early Modern Spain*. New York.

Thomas, Keith. 1971. *Religion and the Decline of Magic*. London.

In other languages

1988. *Alimentació i societat a la Catalunya medieval.* Barcelona.

Allard, Jeanne. 1995. 'La naissance de l'etiquette: les règles de vie à la cour de Castille à la fin du Moyen Âge', in Nilda Guglielmi and A. Rucquoi (eds), *El discurso político en la Edad Media.* Buenos Aires. 11–28.

Benassar, B. and J. Goy. 1975. 'Contribution à l'histoire de la consommation alimentaire du XIVe au XIXe siècle', *Annales ESC,* 30, 402–30.

Bernis Madrazo, Carmen. 1956. *Indumentaria medieval española.* Madrid.

—— 1979. *Trajes y modas en la España de los Reyes Católicos,* 2 vols. Madrid.

Casado Alonso, Hilario. 1992. 'Le banquet de l'assemblée communale rurale en vielle Castille', in *La sociabilité à la table. Commensalité et convivialité à travers les âges.* Rouen.

de Riquer, Martín. 1967. *Caballeros andantes españoles.* Madrid.

García Mercadal, José (ed.). 1952. *Viajes de extranjeros por España y Portugal,* 3 vols. Madrid.

González Arce, José D. 1998. *Apariencia y poder: la legislación suntuaria castellana en los siglos XIII–XV.* Jaén.

MacKay, Angus. 1987. 'Don Fernando de Antequera y la Virgen Santa María', in *Homenaje al profesor Juan Torres Fontes.* Murcia.

—— 1984. *Manger et boire au moyen âge.* Nice. (See articles by Adeline Rucquoi and Denis Menjot.)

Maravall, José A. 1984. *Poder, honor y élites en el siglo XVII.* Madrid.

Molina Molina, Angel L. 1998. *Mujeres públicas, mujeres secretas: la prostitución y su mundo, siglos XIII–XVII.* Murcia.

Núñez Roldán, Francisco. 1995. *Mujeres públicas: historia de la prostitución en España.* Madrid.

Index